THINKING BIG, LEARNING BIG
CONNECTING SCIENCE, MATH, LITERACY, AND LANGUAGE IN EARLY CHILDHOOD

by Marie Faust Evitt,
with Tim Dobbins and Bobbi Weesen-Baer

ABOUT THE COLLABORATORS

Tim Dobbins has more than 20 years experience as a preschool teacher. Trained originally as an actor, Tim has a flair for the dramatic plus an ability to demonstrate and explore science principles in easy-to-understand activities.

Bobbi Weesen-Baer, a children's librarian for 30 years, teaches library reading readiness programs for 3- and 4-year-olds. She especially enjoys incorporating art, science, and math into literacy activities.

ACKNOWLEDGMENTS
Thanks to

■ The staff of the Mountain View Parent Nursery School in Mountain View, CA, for teaching me how to think BIG. Betsy Nikolchev and Claire Koukoutsakis demonstrated how to build on children's interests and knowledge in developmentally appropriate ways. Tim Dobbins could always figure out how to carry through any idea, using stuff we already had at school. Theresa Lo and Wilma Chu added important perspectives.

■ The Mountain View Parent Nursery School families for their enthusiasm and permission to photograph their children. Children in my classes gave instant feedback on the activities. Parents tried out the directions and offered suggestions on how to improve them. Special thanks to Jenny Robertson, who read all the chapters in draft form, and to Rahul Parekh and Margaret Poor, who read sections of the manuscript. Jim Lobdell reviewed the book proposal.

■ Mountain View Parent Nursery School parents Michelle Kokel, Loretta Cazanjian, and Lisa Gefken for taking great photos of cute kids.

■ The staff of the city of Mountain View Public Library for helping me find just the right books for my classes. Children's librarian Bobbi Weesen-Baer made this entire book more possible. Not only did she compile the wonderfully annotated book lists, she enthusiastically brainstormed curriculum ideas, edited numerous chapter drafts and provided moral support.

■ Fellow writers for their encouragement and advice, especially MaryAnn Kohl, Peggy Ashbrook, and Ellen Parlapiano; also my writing group: Colleen Anderson, Phyllis Argent Castren, Trisha Clifford, Shirley Climo, Karen Jessen, Alison Kibrick, Ann Reh, Diana Reynolds Roome, Lora R. Smith, and Robin Worthington.

■ Gwen E. Cox, an interpreter for the deaf who is the international director of Sign2Me® Educational Network, for generously advising me on the best way to present vocabulary in American Sign Language.

■ Scientists for their tutoring, especially Thomas Baer, Ph.D., who advised me on the optics of rainbows and the physics of ramps and road surfaces. Don Richey, Content Specialist at the NASA Ames Exploration Center, advised me on space rocks.

■ Teachers for critiquing chapters. Anita Carter and Devin Reese contributed important ideas to the inventions chapter. Laura Goodman, Debbie Clark, Lori Anderson, Kerry Moore, and Sandi Snider read early drafts.

■ Gryphon House Editor-in-Chief Kathy Charner for stepping in many times during the long publishing process to give Thinking BIG, Learning BIG her personal attention.

■ My family for their unfailing support and help. My son Mark was the copy editor on many initial versions and my son David checked the science. My parents, Mary and Phil Faust, my in-laws, Gisela and Bill Evitt, my siblings, Gin and John, and my extended family were extremely patient listening to me talk about the book all these years.

■ My husband, Eric, for teaching me science, fixing computer snafus, managing the photo database, backing up files, and a million billion jillion other things in this BIG project.

Connecting Science, Math, Literacy,
and Language in Early Childhood

THINKING BIG, LEARNING BIG

Marie Faust Evitt

with Tim Dobbins and Bobbi Weesen-Baer

Photographs by Marie Faust Evitt, Michelle Kokel, Loretta Cazanjian, and Lisa Gefken

Illustrations by Deborah Johnson

Gryphon House, Inc. ■ **Beltsville, Maryland, USA**

THINKING BIG, LEARNING BIG
by Marie Faust Evitt, with Tim Dobbins and Bobbi Weesen-Baer

© 2009 Marie Faust Evitt
Published by Gryphon House, Inc.
PO Box 207, Beltsville, MD 20704
800.638.0928; 301.595.9500; 301.595.0051 (fax)

Visit us on the web at www.gryphonhouse.com

Illustrations: Deborah Johnson
Photographs: Marie Faust Evitt, Michelle Kokel, Loretta Cazanjian, and Lisa Gefken
Cover Art: Straight Shots Photography, Ellicott City, Maryland.

Library of Congress Cataloging-in-Publication Information:
Evitt, Marie Faust.
  Thinking big, learning big / by Marie Faust Evitt, with Tim Dobbins and Bobbi Weesen-Baer ; photographs by Marie Faust Evitt ... [et al.] ; illustrations by Deborah Johnson.
    p. cm.
  ISBN 978-0-87659-067-6
  1. Science--Study and teaching (Elementary)--United States. 2. Education, Elementary--Standards--United States. I. Dobbins, Tim, 1947- II. Weesen-Baer, Bobbi. III. Title.
  LB1585.3.E96 2009
  372.3'5--dc22
                    2008050673

TABLE OF CONTENTS

PREFACE 9
   Learning to Think BIG 9
   The Power of BIG 11

INTRODUCTION 13
   Why Focus on Science, Math, Literacy, and
      Language? 13
   The Benefits of an Inquiry-Based Curriculum..........13
   Science Themes in Thinking BIG, Learning BIG......14
   Math Benefits 15
   BIG Math..15
   Literacy Benefits 16
   BIG Literacy 16
   Language Benefits 17
   Words for BIG Thinking 17
   What About the Rest of the Curriculum? 18
   Philosophy 19
   BIG Outcomes 19
   References 20

HOW TO USE THIS BOOK 23
   BIG Beginnings 23
   BIG Questions for Growing Minds......................23
   Words for BIG Thinking 24
   BIG Activities 24
   BIG Outcomes 24
   BIG Connections: More Activities Across the
      Curriculum 24
   Good Books for Facts and Fun.........................24
   BIG News: The School-Home Connection 25
   Tips 25
   Appendix..25
   A Note About Age Spans..............................25

**CHAPTER 1—THINKING BIG ABOUT
LITTLE CREATURES: WORMS** 27
Objectives 27
Standards...27
   National Science Education Standards...................27
   National Council of Teachers of Mathematics
      Standards 27
   Standards for the English Language Arts................27
The BIG Picture 27
BIG Beginning: Introducing Worms by Doing the Hokey
   Pokey 28
Who Has Touched a Worm? Introducing Graphing 30
Making a Graph..31
Go on a Worm Hunt and Create a Worm Habitat 32
Maintaining the Habitat: What Do Worms
   Need to Live? 34

Look Closely: Worms on the Move 36
Build a Giant Worm......................................38
The Scientific Method: What Is an Experiment? Do
   Worms Prefer Light or Dark? 40
BIG Drama: Five Little Earthworms 42
Over, Under, Around and Through: Children face a BIG
   Obstacle Course 44
BIG Connections: More Activities Across the
   Curriculum 45
BIG Outcomes 47
   Group Assessment 47
   Individual Assessment 47
Good Books for Facts and Fun 47
   Information About Worms 47
   Stories about Worms..................................48
BIG News from School: A Note to Families
   About Worms 49

**CHAPTER 2—THINKING BIG ABOUT
LITTLE CREATURES: SPIDERS** 51
Objectives 51
Standards...51
   National Science Education Standards...................51
   National Council of Teachers of Mathematics
      Standards 15
   Standards for the English Language Arts................51
The BIG Picture 51
BIG Beginning: Introducing Spiders........................52
Itsy Bitsy or Eency Weency: A Little Spider Who Thinks
   BIG 54
Hunting for Spiders and Webs 56
Make a Giant Spider.....................................58
Make a Giant Spider Web 60
Spider or Fly? Arachnid or Insect? 62
BIG Drama: Little Miss Muffet............................64
The Sticky Web Game 65
BIG Connections: More Activities Across the
   Curriculum 66
BIG Outcomes 67
   Group Assessment 67
   Individual Assessment 67
Good Books for Facts and Fun 67
   Information About Spiders 67
   Folktales About Spiders 68
   Stories with Facts About Spiders 68
   Stories About Spiders 69
BIG News from School: A Note to Families About
   Spiders 70

CHAPTER 3—THINKING BIG ABOUT GROWING BIG: SEEDS 71

Objectives 71
Standards 71
   National Science Education Standards..................71
   National Council of Teachers of Mathematics Standards 71
   Standards for the English Language Arts 71
The BIG Picture 71
BIG Beginning: Introducing Seeds 72
How Do Seeds Germinate? 74
Making a Giant Number Line Calendar to Record Seed Growth 76
Seed Experiment: How Much Water Do Seeds Need to Germinate? 78
Seed Tasting and Graphing: Raw and Roasted 80
How Far Will Popcorn Fly? 81
BIG Drama: The Little Red Hen Does a BIG Job All By Herself 83
The Real Work of The Little Red Hen: Planting Wheat ...84
The Real Work of The Little Red Hen: Grinding Flour ...85
Traveling Seeds Game 86
BIG Connections: More Activities Across the Curriculum ..88
BIG Outcomes 91
   Group Assessment 91
   Individual Assessment 91
Good Books for Facts and Fun 91
   Information About Seeds............................91
   Stories About Seeds 92
   The Little Red Hen Stories 93
BIG News from School: A Note to Families About Seeds ..94

CHAPTER 4—THINKING BIG ABOUT RAIN: DRIP, DROP, DOWNPOUR........95

Objectives 95
Standards 95
   National Science Education Standards..................95
   National Council of Teachers of Mathematics Standards 95
   Standards for the English Language Arts..................95
The BIG Picture 95
BIG Beginning: Introducing Rain 96
Is it Waterproof? 98
Go for a Rain Walk 100
Water Table Explorations................................102
Exploring Drops in a BIG Way.........................103
Making Rain 104
Experiment: How Long Does It Take for Water to Evaporate Outside? 106
Rainfall in the Sandbox 108
We Are Meteorologists..................................109
Measure the Rain with Rain Gauges 111
BIG Drama: Here Comes the Rain 113
Puddle Game 115

BIG Connections: More Activities Across the Curriculum 117
BIG Outcomes 119
   Group Assessment 119
   Individual Assessment 119
Good Books for Facts and Fun 119
   Information About Rain............................119
   Stories About Rain 120
BIG News from School: A Note to Families About Rain ..122

CHAPTER 5—THINKING BIG ABOUT LIGHT, COLORS, AND RAINBOWS .123

Objectives 123
Standards 123
   National Science Education Standards..................123
   National Council of Teachers of Mathematics Standards 123
   Standards for the English Language Arts..................123
The BIG Picture 123
BIG Beginning: Introducing Rainbow Colors............124
BIG Beginning II: Mixing Rainbow Colors.............126
Make a Giant Rainbow 128
Make a Giant Rainbow, Part Two.....................129
Hunt for Rainbow Colors 130
What Is Your Favorite Rainbow Color?.................132
BIG Rhythm: Rainbow Rap 133
Make a Living Rainbow 134
Giant Rainbow Bubbles 135
Experiment: Are Rainbow Colors Always in the Same Order? 137
Rainbow Color Toss Game 138
Create a Giant Mural of Rainbow Colors 139
Rainbow Dance 140
BIG Connections: More Activities Across the Curriculum 141
BIG Outcomes 142
   Group Assessment 142
   Individual Assessment 142
Good Books for Facts and Fun 142
   Information About Rainbows............................142
   Stories and Poetry About Colors 142
   Stories About Rainbows 143
BIG News from School: A Note to Families About Rainbows 144

CHAPTER 6—THINKING BIG ABOUT WIND: HUFFING AND PUFFING AND BLOWING 145

Objectives 145
Standards 145
   National Science Education Standards..................145
   National Council of Teachers of Mathematics Standards 145

Standards for the English Language Arts 145
The BIG Picture 145
BIG Beginning: Introducing Air and Wind 146
Experiment: Wind Power 148
How Does the Wind Blow? 150
Air Soccer 151
BIG Drama: "The Three Little Pigs" 152
Hear the Wind Blow: Wind Chimes 154
Hear the Wind Blow: Small Wind Chimes 155
It's a Great BIG Flag 156
Take Flight 157
Run Like the Wind 158
BIG Connections: More Activities Across the
    Curriculum 159
BIG Outcomes 161
    Group Assessment 161
    Individual Assessment 161
Good Books for Facts and Fun 161
    Information About the Wind 161
    Stories About Wind 162
    Stories of "The Three Little Pigs" 163
BIG News from School: A Note to Families About
    Air and Wind 164

CHAPTER 7—THINKING BIG ABOUT ICE: BRRR, IT'S COLD!

Objectives 165
Standards 165
    National Science Education Standards 165
    National Council of Teachers of Mathematics
        Standards 165
    Standards for the English Language Arts 165
The BIG Picture 165
BIG Beginning: Introducing Ice 166
Make Icees 168
BIG Thermometer 170
Learning About Temperature and Thermometers 171
What Is Your Cold Count? 173
Ice Experiment: Where Will Ice Cubes Melt the Slowest
    and Fastest? 175
BIG Building: Make an Ice Castle 177
Ice Races 179
Making Ice Crystals 181
Ice Cube Hockey 182
BIG Drama: "Goldilocks and The Three Bears" 184
BIG Connections: More Activities Across the
    Curriculum 185
BIG Outcomes 187
    Group Assessment 187
    Individual Assessment 187
Good Books for Facts and Fun 187
    Information About Ice and Snowy Weather 187
    Stories and Poetry About Ice and Snow 188
    Goldilocks and the Three Bears 189
BIG News from School: A Note to Families About Ice 190

CHAPTER 8—THINKING BIG ABOUT OUTER SPACE: ASTRONAUTS AND THE MOON 191

Objectives 191
Standards 191
    National Science Education Standards 191
    National Council of Teachers of Mathematics
        Standards 191
    Standards for the English Language Arts 191
The BIG Picture 191
BIG Beginning: Introducing the Moon and Space
    Travel 192
What Do Astronauts Need to Breathe in Outer Space?
    Make Jet Packs 194
Make a Space Helmet 195
Blasting Off to the Moon: Make a Giant Spaceship ...196
Building Mission Control 198
Build Your Own Spaceship 200
A Really BIG Idea: Gravity 202
Astronauts Jump High 203
Astronauts Jump Far 205
Make Pretend Moon Dust 206
Crater Experiment: How Do Craters Form? 208
Turn the Sandbox into the Moon 210
Make a Giant Lunar Rover 212
Gravity Painting 214
Astronaut Drawing 215
Astronaut Food 216
Moon Bounce Adventure Game 218
BIG Connections: More Activities Across the
    Curriculum 220
BIG Outcomes 222
    Group Assessment 222
    Individual Assessment 222
Good Books for Facts and Fun 222
    Information About Gravity 222
    Information About the Moon 223
    Information About the Moon and Space
        Exploration 223
    Stories About the Moon 224
BIG News from School: A Note to Families About
    Astronauts and the Moon 225

CHAPTER 9—THINKING BIG ABOUT BUILDING: HOW BIG CAN WE BUILD? 227

Objectives 227
Standards 227
    National Science Education Standards 227
    National Council of Teachers of Mathematics
        Standards 227
    Standards for the English Language Arts 227
The BIG Picture 227
BIG Beginning: Introducing Construction 228

Go on a Building Hunt 230
Architects Draw Building Plans......................232
BIG Building......................234
How High Can We Build Egg Carton Skyscrapers?.....236
Sandbox Construction: Sandcastles to Skyscrapers 238
BIG Drama: We've Been Building Up a Building.......239
Tool Time: What Tool Is This?......................240
Create a BIG City......................242
Knock Down the Building Game......................243
BIG Connections: More Activities Across the
    Curriculum 244
BIG Outcomes 245
    Group Assessment 245
    Individual Assessment 245
Good Books for Facts and Fun 245
    Information About Construction......................245
    Information About Skyscrapers......................246
    Stories About Construction......................246
BIG News from School: A Note to Families About
    Construction 247

CHAPTER 10—THINKING BIG ABOUT TRAVELING: ROADS, RAMPS, BRIDGES, AND TUNNELS 249

Objectives 249
Standards......................249
National Science Education Standards......................249
National Council of Teachers of Mathematics
    Standards......................249
Standards for the English Language Arts......................249
The BIG Picture 249
BIG Beginning: Introducing Roads 250
Studying Our Road 252
Over, Under, Across, Around, and Through: Ramps,
    Curves, Bridges, and Tunnels......................253
Steep or Level? Gravity at Work 255
Bumpy or Smooth? Road Surface Testing......................257
Where Do These Roads Go? BIG 3-D Maps......................259
Roads, Ramps, Bridges, and Tunnels in the Sandbox 260
The Road Builders' Song......................262
BIG Drama: The Three Billy Goats Gruff 263
Red Light/Green Light BIG Style......................264
BIG Connections: More Activities Across the
    Curriculum 265
BIG Outcomes......................267
    Group Assessment 267
    Individual Assessment 267
Good Books for Facts and Fun 267
Information About Bridges, Ramps, Roads, and
    Tunnels 267
Stories About Roads......................268
The Three Billy Goats Gruff Stories......................269
BIG News from School: A Note to Families About
    Roads 270

CHAPTER 11—THINKING ABOUT BIG IDEAS: INVENTIONS.........................271

Objectives 271
Standards......................271
National Science Education Standards......................271
National Council of Teachers of Mathematics
    Standards......................271
Standards for the English Language Arts......................271
The BIG Picture 271
BIG Beginning: Introducing Inventions......................272
Let's Make Band-Aids 274
Look What's Inside: Taking Apart Machines 275
What Did We Find Inside? Sorting, Counting, and
    Graphing 277
BIG Ideas: Invention Workshop 279
Making an Assembly Line: BIG Production...............281
Be a Cleaning Machine 284
Make a GIANT Robot 285
Circuit Boards......................286
BIG Drama: The Power of Imagination Brings the
    Robot to Life 287
BIG Connections: More Activities Across the
    Curriculum 289
BIG Outcomes......................291
    Group Assessment 291
    Individual Assessment 291
Good Books for Facts and Fun 291
    Information About Inventions 291
Stories About Imagination, Inventions, and Problem
    Solving......................292
Stories About Boxes......................293
BIG News from School: A Note to Families About
    Inventions......................294

APPENDIX 295

We're Going BIG: Letter to Families.........................296
Gathering BIG Stuff.........................297
Adding a Librarian to Your BIG Team: How to Get the
    Most Out of Your Public Library 298
BIG Materials.........................300
    Giant Die.........................300
    Giant Graph.........................301
    Huge Funnel/Super Scoop.........................302

INDEXES 303

Index of Children's Books 303
Index 305

Author's Note: I would love to hear about your experiences with BIG thinking and learning. You can reach me at thinkingbig@rocketmail.com or through Gryphon House.

PREFACE

LEARNING TO THINK BIG

Joe raced across the play yard yelling, "Teacher Tim, Teacher Marie, there's a spider on the ladder! We need to get it!"

"What do you think we need to catch it?" Tim asked.

"A cup or something, so we can look at it. It's huge!" Joe shouted.

"OK, I have something we can use." Tim reached for a magnifying insect container and said, "Show me where it is." Joe, Teacher Tim, and a line of children made their way to the ladder. Tim put the bottom of the container underneath the spider and slowly lowered the clear plastic top. "Caught it!" The spider was huge. Now six kids were clamoring, "I want to see!" "Eeeeuw." "Gross." "Smash it." "Don't smash it." "I want a turn." "I can't see."

I knew we needed to move into BIG mode. Kids naturally want to see and touch and be part of the action, but that's often difficult in a group. Expanding the activity lets more kids be involved.

"Let's go on a spider hunt and see if we can find more spiders," I suggested. "Where do you think we can find some more?"

"In the bushes," and "under the sink," the children said.

They raced off in little groups.

"I see a web. And there's a spider!" Nikhil yelled.

"Does it look the same as the one Joe found?" I asked.

"No, it's much littler," Nikhil replied.

"I'll get a BIG sheet of paper and we can keep track of where we find spiders," I said. We created a large graph listing the locations of the spiders written across the bottom. Children drew spiders on the graph when they found one. Some kids kept looking for spiders through the whole outdoor time.

After school I asked Tim, "What can we do for a spider encore?" Teacher Tim, the longtime assistant teacher at our preschool, is the master of BIG. His projects are more than hands-on. They're arms- and legs-on, too.

"How about making a really BIG spider web?" he said. "But not like those Halloween decorations. A giant web made with packing tape so stuff will stick to it."

"But where will we put it?" I asked, looking around our tiny classroom.

"Oh, we can make it outside at the end of the overhang," Tim said. "It won't be hard."

Now, I'm hardly an expert on spiders, but fortunately we have good children's books at school, so I read up on web-making. Then, I stopped by the public library on my way home to get more books. My librarian friend Bobbi said, "I know just the book you need."

The next day at Circle Time I asked the children if they'd ever seen a spider web. "There was a huge one in my garage," JaneAnn said. "My mom knocked it down with a broom."

"Let's see how a spider spins a web," I told the children. Following the illustrations from the activity, Make a Giant Spider Web, I drew a very lopsided web, drawing the non-sticky anchoring lines in green and the sticky spiral in red.

"That doesn't look like the pictures, Teacher Marie," Daniel pointed out.

"No it doesn't. It's hard to draw pictures, isn't it?" I said. "Maybe it would be easier to make a BIG one of our own. I bet you can make one with Teacher Tim."

During activity time, Teacher Tim brainstormed about web-building with the kids. "What could we use to make the threads that aren't sticky?" Tim asked.

"String," Maria said.

"Rope," said Alex.

"And what about the sticky threads?"

"Glue," "gum," and "tape," came the answers.

Meanwhile, a project I had set up—making yarn spiders—was not nearly so popular. Yes, the children wanted to have a completed spider, but they had a hard time wrapping the yarn and attaching the pipe cleaner legs. They quickly ran back to help build the giant web.

Tim helped the children tape the yarn to the posts, while asking the children how long they thought the pieces needed to be. "This web is going to catch really BIG stuff," Maria said.

"Yeah, it can even catch bad guys," Nikhil said.

Before they'd even strung two long pieces of tape, kids began testing how sticky the web was by adding bits of grass and leaves. Very sticky. The web grew.

"Where's the spider that made the web?" Zachary asked.

"Yeah, we need a BIG spider. A really gigantic spider," said Joe, standing on his tiptoes, stretching out his arms as far as he could.

THE POWER OF BIG

Kids love BIG. They want to be BIG. They want to do BIG things. They love ENORMOUS numbers like a hundred million billion and LONG words like "tyrannosaurus rex." They love HUMONGOUS rockets that can blast to the moon. They love to spread their arms wide and run as fast as they can across a HUGE field.

BIG can be daunting for grownups, particularly when we have small spaces and even smaller budgets and limited time. We wonder where are we going to get the supplies for BIG activities and where can we keep them. We worry that BIG activities might get out of control or be too messy.

Bigger doesn't have to be harder. In many ways, it is easier because kids love BIG projects. They are totally engaged when they can use their whole bodies, rather than just their hands.

BIG activities build community. Kids learn to share and negotiate when they are working together. They learn to take turns and to help each other out. They learn to problem-solve. When we help kids think BIG, it helps them become BIG by expanding their sense of what's possible.

Kids love telling their families about their BIG projects at school. The day after building the huge spider web, Joli's mom asked me, "Where is the giant web? Joli told us all about it last night. She said some parts aren't sticky and some are and that's how the spiders don't get caught in their own webs. I didn't know that."

"Yes, that information really stuck with her," I joked.

Children learn best by seeing, feeling, and doing. Making things on a grand scale helps them see better and understand more. When they build a giant spider with eight legs and eight eyes and a giant fly with six legs, two eyes, and two wings, children can see the creatures are quite different, not just generic "bugs." Supersizing experiences makes them more fun, more memorable, and, therefore, more educational.

I wasn't always an advocate of BIG. When I started teaching preschool, I was more comfortable with easel painting, blocks, and books. I learned the value of BIG from the experienced teachers I joined who love planning projects on a grand scale. When our preschool kids explore outer space, they don't just build paper towel roll rockets, they set up mission-control stations and create giant rocket ships BIG enough for a crew of six.

You don't need to have a BIG space, a BIG staff, or a BIG budget to think BIG. Our small staff shares one classroom. We clean up and reorganize materials between each morning and afternoon class, every day. We use many recycled materials, and have learned to have children help us take apart our creations so we can use the space and materials again.

Nor do you need a Teacher Tim to think BIG. We have included directions for activities that virtually any teacher can do, even if you are not mechanically inclined.

Here's the beginning of a thousand million billion jillion BIG, fun ways to bring science, math, and language to life.

Marie Faust Evitt

INTRODUCTION

WHY FOCUS ON SCIENCE, MATH, LITERACY, AND LANGUAGE?

Early childhood education programs have long recognized the need to develop children's social and emotional skills as well as the sense that they can learn. But it hasn't always been clear what young children *specifically* need to learn to succeed in school and the world as they get older. Researchers and professional organizations are now identifying key content areas and have found several that need greater emphasis—vocabulary and language skills along with literacy, mathematics concepts, and scientific inquiry (Copple & Bredekamp 2006; Bowman, Donovan, & Burns 2000). *Thinking BIG, Learning BIG* presents a curriculum that integrates those key content areas, making it easy for children to learn how to observe their environment, pose questions, try out ideas, quantify their observations, and share investigations, all while having fun. While exploring wind, for example, children experience scientific discovery by observing how a paper cup moves when they blow it with a straw compared to fanning it with a large piece of cardboard. They learn how to measure distance in that same paper cup experiment and learn the vocabulary of "gust of wind." They build literacy by hearing stories and facts about wind in a variety of books and acting out "The Three Little Pigs."

Connected curriculum is more effective than content taught in unrelated bits and pieces. Young children learn best when teachers introduce concepts, vocabulary, and skills in a related, meaningful way (Copple & Bredekamp 2006).

THE BENEFITS OF AN INQUIRY-BASED CURRICULUM

Children are natural scientists. They constantly want to know *how* and *why*. Science is dynamic and, therefore, exciting. Water pours. Ice melts. Toy cars roll. Wind blows.

As children observe these events, they ask questions: "What will happen if I pour water into the bucket of sand?" "What will happen if I roll my toy car over this bumpy cardboard?" Questions like these are the basis of science as inquiry, a fundamental standard of the National Science Education Content Standards developed by the National Academy of Sciences.

I saw the benefits of nurturing scientific inquiry with my own children. As an English major, I avoided science. I fulfilled my college science requirement by taking a geology course known as "Rocks for Jocks." Later, I loved seeing my chemist husband, Eric, encourage our two boys to question, explore, and experiment in their environment. One day when my son David, then about four, kicked his wooden blocks because his tower kept tumbling down, Eric didn't reprimand him or say, "David, you need to make a BIG base to balance the blocks." Instead, Eric asked David questions: "What isn't working?" "What do you think might happen if you tried using a different size of blocks?"

When my son Mark wanted to make the garden hose squirt farther, Eric did not tell him to turn up the faucet and partially cover the end of the hose. Instead, Eric asked Mark, "What do you think you can do to change how much water comes out of the hose?"

Many years later, Mark is a journalist who is comfortable discussing motion and force. David is a mechanical engineer who loves designing and building car engines.

I did not really start learning the science until I became a preschool teacher. It's clear you don't need a formal science background to teach scientific inquiry. The beauty of an early childhood curriculum is that with just a little advance preparation, you can learn along with the children about how to predict how far toy cars will roll over different surfaces. You do not need to know the answers to children's questions. You can model the scientific method and explore together. All you need is the same attitude that you'll be fostering among your students: an openness to wonder and a willingness to say, "Let's try to find out."

The formal process of scientific inquiry is readily adaptable to early childhood programs. Children can conduct the five-step process of **observe, hypothesize, predict, experiment, and record** with just a little modification and coaching. Take our spider experience:

Children see a spider in the play yard. **Observe**
You say, "I wonder where we can find more spiders?" **Ask**
"In the bushes," the children say. **Guess (hypothesize and predict)**
They look for more spiders. **Try their idea (experiment)**
They find another spider. It is smaller than the first. **Measure and compare**
They mark where they find spiders on a graph. **Record and communicate**
Return to steps 1, 2, or 3 to continue their investigations.

There's your scientific method, preschool scale.

Another reason to use science themes in an integrated curriculum is the enthusiasm that children have for the subject matter. Exuberant children are eager to share their experiences and new knowledge. Families are excited to learn along with their children. Over the years, many families have told me, "I'm glad you're doing so much science. I never learned this stuff myself."

SCIENCE THEMES IN THINKING BIG, LEARNING BIG

I chose the themes in *Thinking BIG, Learning BIG* because I wanted them to be relevant and meaningful to children and aligned with the National Science Education Content Standards (1996) that were developed for grades K–12. We have excerpted and adapted the standards to make them useful and relevant for early childhood educators. Topics covered relate to these standards: science as inquiry, life science, physical science, Earth and space science, and science and technology. The standards are presented in detail at the website for the National Academies Press at www.nap.edu/openbook.php?record_id=4962.

Hands-on, real activities are crucial to learning science, but imagination is also a key element of scientific discovery. Imagination is what led scientists to figure out a better way to keep shoes on feet (Velcro) or mark their pages in a book (Post-it Notes).

Identifying problems and experimenting with solutions are two of the key elements in the science and technology standard. Therefore, *Thinking BIG, Learning BIG* includes chapters on inventions and astronauts exploring the moon. No, children can't really go to the moon, but they can pretend their sandbox is the moon and imagine what it might be like to live in a place without rain or wind, flowers or trees. Children can also imagine new inventions that look for monsters under water, using pieces of discarded appliances. This early foundation might eventually lead to a real discovery of how to keep markers from drying out when someone leaves the caps off.

You do not need to use the themes in the order presented here. The book has timing tips, but you can choose what works best for your group.

MATH BENEFITS
Because math gives children the tools to quantify and describe their observations, science and math go hand in hand with BIG activities. When children say, "Worms go down the ramp faster than snails," that's math. When they guess there are "a million thousand" screws in the broken coffee maker, that's math. Math is more than counting. It's measuring, comparing, sorting, estimating, and recognizing patterns.

The challenge is helping children develop a math sense and confidence—a basic comfort with mathematical skills much deeper than knowing that eight comes after seven.

It's easy to weave math activities into the curriculum using science themes. You do not have to be a science expert to guide scientific inquiry, and you do not need to be a math whiz to make math doable and fun. The key is combining appropriate math concepts with experiences guided by open-ended questions and statements such as:
- How many will we need?
- How can we check your guess?
- What else can we try?

BIG MATH
Most of the math activities in *Thinking BIG, Learning BIG* work on a BIG scale. When children do math with their whole bodies they literally get a feel for numbers. Gross motor games have dual benefits of building physical and mathematical skills. For example, you can quickly create a spider game where children roll a huge die and move *themselves* around a giant web, hopping from vertical strand to vertical strand drawn with chalk on the ground. They can feel that six is more than two when they hop six times toward the center of the web.

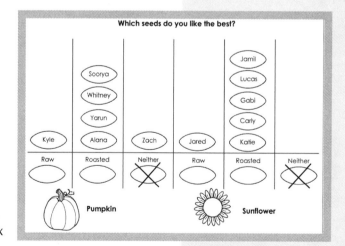

You can help children create BIG graphs to highlight what they are discovering and thinking by sorting their data, counting, and making comparisons.

In *Thinking BIG, Learning BIG,* we point out how activities relate to national standards developed in 2000 by the National Council of Teachers of Mathematics and the Curriculum Focal Points announced in 2006. Excerpts from the standards are highlighted in each chapter. The complete standards for pre-kindergarten through Grade 2 are described on the NCTM Web site at http://standards.nctm.org/document/chapter4/index.htm. The focal points for pre-kindergarten are described at www.nctm. org/standards/focalpoints.aspx?id=300.

LITERACY BENEFITS

Learning to read and write provides the foundation for a child to succeed in school and later in life. Children need a wealth of experiences to motivate them to master the necessary skills (Neuman, Copple, & Bredekamp 2000). Hearing stories read aloud and studying books of information can boost print awareness and inspire children to want to learn to read and write themselves. Playing with rhyming words helps children distinguish the individual sounds that make up a word. Children see the power of writing things down when they dictate stories for an adult to record. Literacy instruction runs throughout all content areas in a planned curriculum (Bowman, Donovan, & Burns 2000).

BIG LITERACY

Literacy is built into the entire *Thinking BIG, Learning BIG* curriculum. The first step in each unit is asking children what they know about the topic, recording these responses, and then asking the children what they want to find out. These questions give focus to future activities. You can add questions as they come up during the inquiry process. Graphs, charts, and activities are labeled. A giant spider web looks official when it has a BIG sign telling everyone "Giant Spider Web." Photographing activities and recording children's observations heightens their interest and documents learning. At the end of the unit, refer back to the children's initial ideas and questions and lead a discussion about what the children have learned. Recording the results and the new knowledge acquired reinforces the importance of the children's achievements and allows you to share them with families and visitors.

Children also see the power of literacy as they learn poems and songs and act out classic stories related to different topics. "Goldilocks and the Three Bears," for example, provides a fun way to learn about the science of temperature, while developing such literacy skills as predicting what happens next in the story and creating new endings to the tale.

In *Thinking BIG, Learning BIG*, we point out how activities relate to the 1996 *Standards for the English Language Arts* developed by the International Reading Association and the National Council of Teachers of English. We have excerpted and adapted the standards to make them useful and relevant for early childhood educators. The complete standards can be found at www.reading.org/resources/issues/reports/learning_standards.html.

Additionally, we present a comprehensive list of books in each chapter that describes the best stories, folktales, poetry, and books of pictures and facts to bring the topic to life, along with suggestions on how to use the books during each unit. Children's librarian Bobbi Weesen-Baer developed this list.

LANGUAGE BENEFITS

When children know the words—the vocabulary—related to an experience or activity, they can communicate their observations. New words are a challenge to the ear, the mouth, and the mind. Numerous studies have shown that vocabulary is essential to building reading comprehension (Boote 2006). Children can learn the words *spider, mosquito, arachnid,* and *insect,* in addition to the vague term *bug* just as they learn the words *pineapple, cucumber, fruit,* and *vegetable* in addition to the general term *food.* Adults often shy away from using specific BIG words with children, but think how easily children rattle off *brontosaurus* and *locomotive* when they hear the correct terms. Specific words empower children to speak, read, and write precisely.

Not knowing the correct word leads to misunderstandings. I remember a time when my son Mark, then about four years old, said, "My neck hurts."

"What happened, honey?" I asked. "Did you twist it?"

"No, it just hurts." After much back and forth I said, "Oh, you mean your throat hurts, the part inside your neck."

WORDS FOR BIG THINKING

BIG words are just plain fun. When they are introduced and used repeatedly with enthusiasm, children rise to the challenge and take them home to amaze family and friends.

One afternoon when the class was studying seeds, I said, "I wonder how long it will take our seeds to germinate." Seth thought that was a very funny word. "It sounds like germ. Do the seeds have germs?" he asked. "No, they don't have germs, but the words do begin the same way," I said. "They are in the same family of words. *Germinate* is a BIG word that means to begin growing. Let's clap out the syllables so we can learn the word." The children loved saying *germinate* and then pretending they were little seeds starting to grow. Two days later when the seeds did germinate and the children could see the start of a root, Seth shouted, "The seeds are germinating but they aren't sick."

Studies have shown that children learn words quickly when they are specifically taught in context (Boote 2006). It isn't necessary to drill children on new words. If you introduce the words as you talk and read to children and help them practice saying the words, their vocabulary will grow. This is the four-step process I use when the children learn a new word, what we call the SCAD system: Say, Clap, Act out, and Do again.

1. Say the word slowly, in context. "Your seeds are starting to germinate. Can you see the roots?"
2. Clap the word with the children, one clap for each syllable as they say it out loud: *ger-mi-nate,* with the emphasis on the "ger" syllable. Use loud and soft claps that mimic the natural rhythm of the word.
3. Act out the word, using American Sign Language (ASL) where possible. Because there is not an ASL sign for germinate, I invited the children to crouch down in little balls and then stick out a leg as if a root were starting to grow.
4. Do it again. Use the word frequently in conversation. "I wonder if any more seeds will germinate today."

I first learned the benefits of acting out words from a gifted nature educator in the San Francisco Bay Area, Keith Gutierrez. As the children stood by a rushing creek, Keith introduced them to the word *evaporate*. "Pretend you are a drop of water," Keith said. "Crouch down, get real small, and say 'eeee.' Now slowly stand up, raise your arms up high, and jump while you say 'vap-o-rate.' EEEE-vap-o-rate!" Weeks later the children still remembered *evaporate*.

Then I discovered the power of using American Sign Language to introduce vocabulary to hearing children. In her book *Dancing with Words: Signing for Hearing Children's Literacy,* Marilyn Daniels, associate professor of speech communication at Pennsylvania State University, describes research showing that hearing children who used sign language in their pre-kindergarten and kindergarten classes scored better on vocabulary tests and attained higher reading levels than their non-signing peers. It is important to use real ASL signs where possible. Making up signs can lead to confusion and mistakes, points out Gwen E. Cox, an interpreter for the deaf who is the international director of Sign2Me® Educational Network. Recognize, however, that not all words have signs. Often there are signs for related words that work well. There are a number of excellent resources for ASL signs. I used the Michigan State University ASL browser located at www.commtechlab.msu.edu/sites/aslweb, *The Gallaudet Dictionary of American Sign Language,* and *Talking with Your Hands, Listening with Your Eyes* by Gabriel Grayson.

The text and illustrations describing ASL in *Thinking BIG, Learning BIG* portray the right hand as the dominant hand. If you are not comfortable signing with your right hand, use your left hand.

You can reinforce the BIG words the children are learning by creating a word wall. While few children will actually be able to read the words, just seeing the words will increase familiarity, especially if you illustrate the word with a picture. Children can also incorporate the expanded vocabulary when they draw and dictate stories. Be sure to use the words on your word wall in conversation with the children.

Another way to reinforce the new vocabulary is to tell families the words the children are learning through a note or newsletter. To help you do this, *Thinking BIG, Learning BIG* includes a sample note for each theme. Several studies have shown that children's vocabularies reflect their families' vocabularies (Hart & Risley 1995). When you tell families the new words they can use them and help their children use them also.

In some cases, the highlighted vocabulary words aren't long or difficult but they are important. It's fun to introduce *roots* and *shoots* in the midst of learning *germinate*. In addition, key words such as *scientist, experiment,* and *prediction* are repeated in many chapters to reinforce them.

WHAT ABOUT THE REST OF THE CURRICULUM?

The BIG Connections section presents activities for integrating the theme throughout the curriculum—in sensory experiences, art, music, dramatic play, and fine and gross motor skills. The interplay between BIG and small and individual and group allows children to explore and create on many different levels. Children learn different skills when they construct a paper towel roll spaceship *and* a giant spaceship out of appliance boxes.

PHILOSOPHY

Thinking BIG, Learning BIG embodies the educational philosophy of developmentally appropriate practice as outlined by the National Association for the Education of Young Children (NAEYC). Grounded in the research of Jean Piaget and Lev Vygotsky, it meets children where they are and helps each child reach challenging and achievable goals by building on each discovery. Using children's interests and observations to launch explorations makes learning exciting. At the same time it's important to make sure activities help develop key skills (Copple & Bredekamp 2006).

Learning something new is easier when it's meaningful and when it builds on something we already know (Copple & Bredekamp 2006; Bowman, Donovan, & Burns 2000). Likewise, depth is important. Children become more engaged when they have time to wonder, explore, and experiment over time. The themes and activities in *Thinking BIG, Learning BIG* can be used to plan curriculum over several weeks, as long as children are interested. While the individual activities stand on their own, they easily link to one another to provide a coherent curriculum.

BIG OUTCOMES

Assessment is a key part of early childhood education programs. Although assessment can mean testing, it has a much broader scope. It is the process of observing children systematically, asking questions, and studying children's work (McAfee, Leon, & Bodrova 2004). *Thinking BIG, Learning BIG* will help you gather the information you need to assess children's progress and document the learning taking place.

Thinking BIG, Learning BIG follows the NAEYC recommendation that assessments take place in many different forms, on many occasions, as part of the everyday classroom life (McAfee, Leon, & Bodrova 2004). We present suggestions on how to use different types of assessments in each chapter.

First, each chapter invites you to explore with children what they know about a topic, what they want to find out, and finally what they did learn by recording their comments on chart paper. This group assessment helps you establish the curriculum based on children's knowledge, interests, and needs.

Second, suggestions for documenting group and individual learning through photos and children's quotes are highlighted in each chapter in a Photo Tip. Creating photo boards is an effective way to record explorations and experiences in the classroom. To create a photo board, take close-up shots of individual children and group shots that show children interacting. During the activity times, jot down quotes from children. Mount the photos on a freestanding three-panel poster board that you can put on a classroom table at children's eye level, or if you have low bulletin boards, mount them on flat poster paper directly on the bulletin board. Label the photos and include vocabulary words and quotes from the children. Children love looking at the photos and so do families. At the end of the unit, you can use the boards as part of a group assessment. Make additional copies of the photos to keep in children's portfolios.

For example, in the worm unit you might create a photo board about children hunting for worms in your play yard. You might have photos of children digging in the dirt, placing worms and dirt in your worm habitat, and making a graph of where they found worms. You might include quotes such as, "Look, I found a worm under this bush. It's wiggling," Gabriela said. Also include vocabulary words on the poster board such as *fertilizer* and *tunnel*.

Third, many activities highlight skills and questions for individual assessment. While studying spiders, for example, you can assess children's grasp of one-to-one correspondence as they count the legs of real spiders, build giant models of spiders, and construct graphs of where they discover spiders in the classroom. This type of assessment, during regular classroom activities, leads to an accurate picture of what children can do and understand (Copple & Bredekamp 2006).

Fourth, throughout the book are activities that will produce examples of children's work for their portfolios. Drawings and dictated stories, for example, provide a snapshot of what children understand. Additionally, anecdotal observations you make about individual children's work rounds out their portfolios.

When using *Thinking BIG, Learning BIG,* assessment is not an additional chore; it becomes a valuable part of the curriculum.

REFERENCES

Boote, C. 2006. Reading comprehension requires word meaning knowledge: A classroom model for teaching word meanings in primary grades. A paper presented at a symposium on Literacy Research at the annual conference of the International Reading Association, May 1, 2006.

Bowman, B.T., Donovan, M.S, & Burns, M.S. eds. 2000. *Eager to learn: Educating our preschoolers.* Washington, DC: National Academies Press.

Copple, C. & Bredekamp, S. 2006. *Basics of developmentally appropriate practice: An introduction for teachers of children 3 to 6.* Washington, DC: National Association for the Education of Young Children.

Copley, J. V. 2000. *The young child and mathematics.* Washington, DC: National Association for the Education of Young Children, National Council of Teachers of Mathematics.

Daniels, M. 2001. *Dancing with words: Signing for hearing children's literacy.* Westport, CT: Bergin & Garvey.

Epstein, A. S., Schweinhart, L. J., DeBruin-Parecki, & A. & Robin, K. B. 2004. *Preschool assessment: A guide to developing a balanced approach.* New Brunswick, NJ: National Institute for Early Education Research.

Grayson, G. 2003. *Talking with your hands, listening with your eyes: A complete photographic guide to American sign language.* Garden City, NY: Square One Publishers.

Hart, B. & Risley, T. R. 1995. "The early catastrophe: The 30 million word gap by age 3" excerpted from *Meaningful differences in the everyday experiences of young American children.* Baltimore, MD: Brookes.

International Reading Association, National Council of Teachers of English. 1996. *Standards for the English language arts.* Washington, DC: International Reading Association, National Council of Teachers of English.

McAfee, O. Leon, D. J., & Bodrova, E. 2004. *Basics of assessment: A primer for early childhood educators.* Washington, DC: National Association for the Education of Young Children.

Michigan State University Communication Technology Laboratory. 2000. *American sign language browser.* East Lansing, MI: Michigan State University.

National Council of Teachers of Mathematics. 2000. *Principles and standards for school mathematics.* Reston, VA: National Council of Teachers of Mathematics.

National Research Council, 1996. *National science education standards.* Washington, DC: National Academy Press.

Neuman, S.B, Copple, C. & Bredekamp, S. 2000. *Learning to read and write: Developmentally appropriate practices for young children.* Washington, DC: National Association for the Education of Young Children.

Valli, C., ed. 2006. *The Gallaudet dictionary of American sign language.* Washington, DC: Gallaudet University Press.

Worth, K. & Grollman, S. 2003. *Worms, shadows, and whirlpools: Science in the early childhood classroom.* Washington, DC: Heinemann and National Association for Education of Young Children.

HOW TO USE THIS BOOK

Thinking BIG, Learning BIG is designed to provide everything you need for an integrated, inquiry-based curriculum organized by science topics. The 11 topics in this book provide more than a full year's worth of curriculum, or you can choose topics based on the children's interests and your own curiosity.

Each topic includes these sections:
- Objectives—including related science, math, and language arts standards
- BIG Beginnings—ideas to launch the topic in Circle or Group Time
- BIG Questions for Growing Minds—questions to pose to individual children or to the group
- Words for BIG Thinking—key vocabulary words
- BIG Activities (including science explorations, math activities, songs, drama, games, and gross motor activities, each listing: Materials, What to Do, Discussion Starters, Skills Assessment, and Teacher-to-Teacher Tips)
- BIG Outcomes—assessment suggestions
- BIG Connections—more activities across the curriculum
- Good Books for Facts and Fun—annotated lists of both fiction and non-fiction
- BIG News from School—notes home to families

The activities include notes if they require advance preparation for the activities, such as asking families to save egg cartons or make BIG blocks of ice.

BIG BEGINNINGS

Because a dynamic Circle or Group Time sets the tone and interest level for activities each chapter opens with a suggestion for introducing the theme. With simple props and a dose of drama, you can build excitement during group times. Tim, one of my fellow teachers, who is a trained actor, loves any excuse to raid the school's dress-up supply. He wears a construction hard hat when we are learning about machines. He brings out an American flag when we are about to land on the moon.

Another key part of launching each unit is asking children what they know about the topic and what they want to find out. By writing their responses on chart paper you reinforce literacy and nurture the ability to formulate questions. At the end of the day or the unit, you can refer back to "What We Know About Spiders" and "What We Want to Learn About Spiders" and record "What We Learned About Spiders."

BIG QUESTIONS FOR GROWING MINDS

In addition to questions the children have, be sure to ask your own questions to stimulate thinking. When introducing children to science topics, it's easy to focus on questions with a specific answer, such as, "How many legs does a spider have?" It takes practice to generate open-ended, exploratory questions to foster children's independent thinking, such as, "What do think it would feel like to have as many legs as a spider?" When at a loss as to how to pose an open-ended question, you can always try, "Why do you suppose…?" "What do you think would happen if…?" "What can you tell me about…?" and the ultimate all-purpose question, "I wonder why…."

Note: Be careful not to label original ideas "right" or "wrong." Instead, highlight how observations let you improve on what you first thought. As Laura Ristrom Goodman, an Arizona early elementary school teacher, says, "Some kids equate being 'right' as being 'good' and 'wrong' as 'bad.' We don't want to cross out an incorrect thought, but fix it up to be true." Also, we want children to take risks with their thinking and to pose questions so they can figure out answers, which is hard to do if they are worried they might be "wrong." Peggy Ashbrook, author of *Science Is Simple*, encourages discussion by saying, "Some of us thought…and some of us thought…" and then relating those different ideas to the work of scientists who don't always agree.

WORDS FOR BIG THINKING

Each unit highlights key vocabulary words and directions for introducing the words using the SCAD system: Say, Clap, Act out, and Do again. The words are listed and defined under the heading and then woven into the activities. It is not necessary to drill children on the words. Use them in conversation as appropriate.

BIG ACTIVITIES

Most activities and experiments are designed to be set up for an entire activity period with children taking turns participating. Some children may want to stick with the experience the whole period; others will stay a few minutes and move on. For example, when children build ramps to see how far toy cars will travel, there are children who become race car testers for days on end.

The activities build on each other but it is not necessary to do them all. Choose those you think are most appropriate for your group. Most chapters include drama, games, and gross motor activities as well as science explorations, math activities, and art activities.

The BIG activities are designed to work even if you don't have much space or time. *Thinking BIG, Learning BIG* includes tips for working in limited space and tips for supersizing the projects if you are fortunate enough to have lots of room.

Because the process is just as important as the product, taking down BIG projects is often part of the activity.

BIG OUTCOMES

This section reviews activities that will help you assess your group and the individual children.

BIG CONNECTIONS: MORE ACTIVITIES ACROSS THE CURRICULUM

This is where you will find suggestions for activities that include writing, art, cooking, dramatic play, and gross motor fun. We have also included ideas for fine motor activities, small-scale projects and sensory table activities.

GOOD BOOKS FOR FACTS AND FUN

Thanks to the skills and knowledge of children's librarian Bobbi Weesen-Baer, each chapter of *Thinking BIG, Learning BIG* includes a list of books that describes the best stories, folktales, poetry, and books of pictures and facts to bring each topic to life. Based on her many years of experience presenting story times and book talks for children, she adds comments about the suitability of these materials for certain ages or group size. She evaluates the facts, the photos, and the presentation in non-fiction books for accuracy and accessibility. She recommends classics that are widely available and recently published titles that are the most useful and engaging. Although some of the books may be out of print they are worth looking for at the library or Internet sites that sell used books.

BIG NEWS: THE SCHOOL-HOME CONNECTION

Because families can help reinforce children's learning by following up at home with what their children are doing at school, each chapter includes a note you can use to tell families what has been happening at school and suggest conversation starters that families can use. Families know the frustration of asking, "What did you do today?" and getting the answer, "Nothing." or "I don't know." If families know that children have been making rainbows with prisms and creating a graph about the children's favorite colors, they can say, "What did you choose for your favorite color at school?" "What were other children's favorite colors?" These questions can cue the children's memories of their school day activities and allow them to share the excitement and the fun.

The notes also highlight vocabulary words children are learning so families can learn and use the words themselves in conversation.

TIPS

The teacher-to-teacher, timing, planning, and photo tips are based on real-life, hard-earned experiences.

APPENDIX

You will find notes about supplies, resources, and directions for curriculum items here.

A NOTE ABOUT AGE SPANS

The activities in *Thinking BIG, Learning BIG* are suitable or adaptable for children between the ages of three and eight. Many activities include suggestions for ways to simplify an activity or make it more challenging; this allows you to use your own judgment about what will work best for your group.

THINKING **BIG**, LEARNING **BIG**

THINKING BIG ABOUT LITTLE CREATURES: WORMS

THE BIG PICTURE

At first, many children are squeamish about worms, which are little creatures with a BIG job to do. By studying worms, children learn about the important role of these animals. Worms loosen the soil as they tunnel underground, helping plants and trees.

Worms eat dead leaves and parts of food that people usually don't eat such as carrot peels. Worm waste, called *castings,* fertilizes soil. Children learn how worms are different from people: for example, worms don't have teeth, so instead of chewing their food they use dirt and a gizzard to grind it up.

Children also learn about habitats—what worms need to live—and children learn how to handle worms gently. This unit also introduces children to the process of inquiry—how to form questions and try to find out answers, such as whether worms prefer light or dark locations.

OBJECTIVES

- Learn about a common animal, its characteristics and habitat
- Practice handling creatures gently
- Become familiar with the scientific method

STANDARDS

National Science Education Content Standards

- Science as inquiry—ask questions; plan and conduct a simple investigation; communicate investigations and explanations
- Life science—study characteristics of organisms; learn about the life cycles of organisms; explore organisms and their environments

National Council of Teachers of Mathematics Standards

- Number and operations—count with understanding
- Algebra—sort, classify, and order objects
- Measurement—understand how to measure using nonstandard and standard tools
- Data analysis and probability—represent data using pictures and graphs
- Communication—organize, analyze, and evaluate mathematical thinking; use the language of mathematics

Standards for the English Language Arts

- Experience a wide range of print and non-print texts, including fiction and non-fiction to build an understanding of the world and acquire new information
- Use spoken, written, and visual language to communicate and learn
- Generate ideas and questions and pose problems
- Build vocabulary

TIMING TIP

Studying worms is a good way to introduce the scientific method in the beginning of the school year because the creatures are easy to study. This theme also works well when a child has discovered a worm after a rainstorm or while digging in a class garden. Worms are most plentiful near the soil surface during warm weather. Worm study could be part of an extended exploration of life science including spiders and seeds. If you don't have easy access to places where you can dig, you can buy red worms online or at a bait store.

BIG BEGINNING:

Introducing Worms by Doing the Hokey Pokey

FOCUS AREAS

Science: studying characteristics of organisms

Gross Motor: wriggling and squirming like a worm

MATERIALS

Diary of a Worm by Doreen Cronin (optional)

Cardboard boxes large enough for children to wiggle through or a large sheet and low table or chairs to construct a tunnel

2 clear containers

2 real worms, each in a clear container

2 sheets of chart paper

Marker

2 hand stamps any shape

2 ink pads

PREPARATION

● Before group time, set up a tunnel of boxes in front of the area where you hold your gathering or make a tunnel by covering a low table and chairs with a sheet.

● Label one sheet of chart paper "What We Know About Worms" and the other sheet "What We Want to Learn About Worms."

WHAT TO DO

1. When you call the children for group time, invite them to pretend they are worms by wiggling through the tunnel. When all the children have squirmed and wiggled their way into the group area, tell them they are going to learn about worms.

2. Show the children the real worm in a clear plastic container. (If you and another adult each go around the circle in opposite directions, the children's waiting time is cut in half.)

3. Ask the children what they know about worms. Record the children's responses including the name of child after his response on the chart paper labeled "What We Know About Worms." Ask what they would like to find out about worms. Record their responses and names on the chart paper labeled "What We Want to Learn About Worms."

4. Tell the children they are going to compare being a person with being a worm. Stamp every child's right hand with a stamp. (Two adults going around the circle in opposite directions will cut waiting time.)

5. Do "The Hokey Pokey" slowly, taking time to make sure the children are using their right hand. Start by saying, "Show me your right hand, the one with the stamp." When it's time to put your left hand in say, "Do you know which hand is your left? It's the one that doesn't have a stamp, the one that's left."

6. Do the right and left foot slowly, reviewing how the right foot is on the same side as the right hand, the left foot is the one that's left. Continue with head and whole self.

7. Now talk about worms. "Do worms have a right hand or a left hand? Right foot or left foot?" Do "The Worm Hokey Pokey," an activity inspired by Doreen Cronin's book *Diary of a Worm*. Ask what worms can use to dance "The Hokey Pokey" (head, tail, whole self). Invite the children to pretend they are worms, placing their arms tight by their sides and their legs close together. If you like, you can all get down on the ground and put your heads together.

8. Remember not to clap after the last line of the song. If someone forgets, smile and ask, "Would worms be able to clap?"

9. Tell the children, "Now it's time to crawl out through the tunnel so we can learn more about worms."

A Note from the Author: The activities in this chapter are designed to build on each other. However, please feel free to choose those that meet the interests and abilities of your class. If parts of an activity seem like too much to do on a particular day, save them for a later time. Every class is different, even from day to day, and the activities are adaptable to meet the needs of your class.

BIG QUESTIONS FOR GROWING MINDS

Use the following questions to engage the children in a discussion about worms during group time or with an individual child during activity time:

- What does a worm look like?
- What would it be like to have a body without arms and legs?
- What would it be like to live in the ground?
- How do you think worms eat?

WORDS FOR BIG THINKING

Look for these words highlighted in italics throughout the activities in this chapter. Write the words out in large letters and introduce them a few at a time with the "**S**ay, **C**lap, **A**ct out, **D**o again" (SCAD) system. Using the words during activities and discussions will reinforce their meaning.

- Castings—worm waste
- Clitellum—the thick park of a worm's body that creates the egg sacks
- Experiment—test to find out something
- Fertilizer—something that improves the soil to help plants grow better
- Prediction—like a guess, what you think might happen based on what you already know
- Scientist—person who studies the natural world
- Segment—part of a body
- Tunnel—long passageway dug underground
- Wormlet—tiny worm

PHOTO TIP

You can record the children's explorations of worms by creating photo boards about hunting for worms, observing worms move, and making a giant worm. Look for close-ups of individual children and group shots that show children interacting. Also note vocabulary words and quotes from children to document the learning. Review the photo boards with the children as part of your assessment process.

Who Has Touched a Worm?
Introducing Graphing

FOCUS AREAS

Math: counting, comparing

Language Arts: identifying YES and NO

MATERIALS

Green sheet of paper
Red sheet of paper
Black marker
2 clipboards
Red yarn and green yarn
Scissors (adult-only)
Ruler
2 containers to hold yarn worms

PREPARATION

- Write the word YES in large letters across the top of the green sheet of paper. Write the word NO in large letters across the top of the red sheet of paper. Attach each sheet to a separate clipboard.
- Cut the red and green yarn into 4" pieces and place in two different containers. Make enough for each child to choose either color.

WHAT TO DO

1. At group time, tell the children they are going to find out how many people have touched a worm. Ask the children, "Who has touched a worm?" Tell the children who have touched a worm to put a finger on their nose. Offer them the container of green yarn pieces and invite them to choose one.

2. Ask, "Who has not touched a worm?" Tell those children to put a finger on their chin. Offer those children the container of red yarn pieces and invite them to choose one.

3. Tell the children they are going to make two long lines—one line of children who have held a worm and one line of children who haven't held a worm.

4. Hold up your YES and NO signs and then prop them on chairs. The children who have held a worm (and are now holding a green yarn worm) will make a line starting at the YES sign. The children who have not held a worm will make a line starting at the NO sign. If you have a small group and lots of space, the children could lie down head to toe and create two long worms on the floor. For young children, cut long lengths of green yarn and red yarn and place them on the floor for children to line up on.

5. Invite the children to count with you as you touch each child's hand (worm held out) in the two lines. Then go through the lines again and quickly write the children's names from each line on the corresponding sign as you invite each child to say his name.

6. After group time, do a small-group activity with the children to turn the results of the human graph into a graph on paper. See the following activity, Making a Graph.

7. The children can keep the yarn worms in their pockets or place them in their cubbies. They will use them in the following graphing activity.

8. After the children have had a chance to dig for worms or do other worm activities, make another human graph to see how many children have now held a worm. The children will be excited to see the difference. Then you can create a second graph on paper to show the change.

DISCUSSION STARTERS

Use these questions to spark children's thinking during and after the activity:
- Which line is longer—the one of people who have touched a worm or the one of people who have not touched a worm?
- Why do you think there are more people in the "have not touched a worm" line?
- If you have touched a worm, what did it feel like?

SKILLS ASSESSMENT

Use these questions to determine a child's abilities and understanding:
- Can the child count the number of children in each line?
- Does the child observe the difference in numbers between the two lines?

Making a Graph

PREPARATION

- Label one sheet of chart paper "Have You Touched a Worm?" and below that write "Before We Studied Worms." On the other sheet write, "Have You Touched a Worm?" and below that write "After We Studied Worms." Create two columns on each sheet of chart paper, one column labeled "YES" and the other labeled "NO." See page 301 in the Appendix for directions on constructing graphs.
- Cut the red and green construction paper into strips, about 3" long and 1" wide, one strip of each color per child.

WHAT TO DO

1. Use the graph labeled "Have You Touched a Worm? Before We Studied Worms" at activity time. Working with a small group of children, invite each child to match the color of his yarn worm to the color of a paper strip. The child then writes his name (or an adult writes it for him) on that paper strip.
2. The child glues the strip in the correct column, green = YES or red = NO, starting from the bottom of the poster sheet building the strips like a stack of bricks.
3. Show the children the YES and NO tally sheets with the children's names listed to compare with the graph you are constructing. Count the names and count the paper strips. How do they compare? (By the end of activity time the number of names on the YES and NO sheets should match the paper graph.)
4. Show the children the second graph "Have You Touched a Worm? After We Studied Worms" and tell them you will count again and make the second graph at the end of your worm study to see if the numbers have changed.

DISCUSSION STARTERS

Use these questions to spark children's thinking during and after the activity:
- How many strips are in the YES column? How many in the NO column?
- Which column has more?
- After the second graph is complete, ask how are the two graphs different? Have more people touched a worm now than when we started our worm study?

SKILLS ASSESSMENT

Use these questions to determine a child's abilities and understanding:
- Can the child print his name on the strip?
- Can the child accurately count the red and green strips?
- Can the child compare amounts?
- Does the child speculate about the reasons children may or may not have touched a worm?

FOCUS AREAS

Math: counting, exploring relationships among numbers, graphing, analyzing data, comparing, communicating results

Language Arts: labeling

MATERIALS

Tallies and names of the children from the human graphs showing who has or has not held a worm

Yarn worms from the previous activity

2 sheets of chart paper

Red and green construction paper

Scissors (adult-only)

Crayons or markers

Glue sticks

Go on a Worm Hunt and Create a Worm Habitat

FOCUS AREAS

Science: studying organisms and their environments, using data to construct a reasonable explanation, communicating investigations and explanations

Math: counting, graphing, analyzing data, comparing, communicating results

Language Arts: labeling, experiencing a wide range of literature—songs

MATERIALS

2 pieces of chart paper
Markers or crayons
BIG shovel
Trowels
Tongue depressors
Magnifying lenses
Aquarium, terrarium or large plastic containers
Dirt and leaves

PREPARATION

- Go on a quick worm hunt yourself. You may need a BIG shovel to loosen the soil. You'll probably have the most luck in a compost pile or garden.
  Safety Note: Be sure to check the area for any hazards such as broken glass or poison ivy.

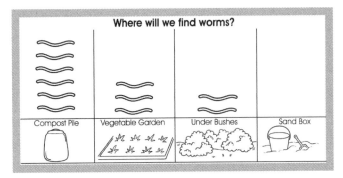

- Label one sheet of chart paper "Where We Found Worms." See page 301 in the Appendix for directions on constructing graphs.
- Label the other sheet of chart paper "What Worms Need in Their Home."

WHAT TO DO

1. During activity time, invite the children to go on a worm hunt. Ask them where they think they will find worms. If you are fortunate to have multiple possibilities to hunt for worms outdoors, encourage the children to name all the locations—in the compost pile, the vegetable garden, under bushes, and any other locations. Record each location along the bottom of the chart paper to create a graph. Include all suggested locations, even if they seem unlikely, such as the sandbox or the sidewalk.

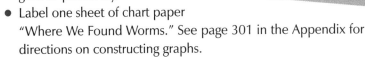

Where will we find worms?

Compost Pile | Vegetable Garden | Under Bushes | Sand Box

2. Ask the children what they will need to make a home for the worms so the class can study them. If no one suggests the dirt where they find the worms, add that to the list and tell the children when they find a worm, they should dig up some of the dirt and leaves to place with the worm in the container.

3. Demonstrate how to gently dig and pick up a worm with a tongue depressor in case some children are reluctant to handle worms.

4. Using the tune of "Here We Go 'Round the Mulberry Bush," make up a song, "Here We Go to Find Some Worms…," which includes the locations the children suggested. "This is the way we'll dig in the dirt…looking for our worms." "This is the way we'll check the garden…where we might find worms." "This is the way we'll pick them up…when we find our worms."

5. Go outside. Give each child a trowel or tongue depressor to dig for worms. When the children find a worm, they can observe it with a magnifying lens before putting it and some of the surrounding dirt and leaves into the aquarium or plastic container. **Safety Note:** It is important to follow appropriate safety guidelines such as washing hands before and after handling worms. The National Science Teachers Association guidelines about using live animals in the classroom are listed at www.nsta.org/positionstatement&psid=44. Stress that worms are living creatures that are harmless to people, so we must be gentle with them.

6. After they put the worm in the container, they can record where they found it by drawing a squiggly line above the location on the graph.

7. At the end of the activity make sure the children wash their hands.

8. Review the graph with the class using the Discussion Starters listed below.
   Note: Keep the habitats for several weeks to allow children to observe the worms and do *experiments* with them. Worms in a terrarium do best in temperatures ranging from 55°–77°. Temperatures below freezing and above 80° can harm the worms. Worms like moist but not soggy soil. You can also add damp newspaper torn into strips for bedding. Don't use glossy magazine paper. Feed the worms fruit and vegetable scraps such as carrot and apple peels and lettuce leaves.

SUPERSIZE IT!

To cultivate worms in a BIG way, set up a worm composting bin. You can find directions online by entering the search term "worm bin."

TEACHER-TO-TEACHER TIPS

- If you have a child who is extremely opposed to touching a worm, you can offer him a pair of thin plastic gloves to wear.
- When hunting outside for worms, the children may find other little animals like beetles and sow bugs.
- Encourage the children to examine the creatures they find and compare them to worms. You can add columns on your graph for the other discoveries and add them to your habitat.

DISCUSSION STARTERS

Use these questions to spark children's thinking during and after the activity:

- How many worms did we find?
- Where did we find the most worms?
- Why do you suppose we found more worms there?
- Where do worms like to live?
- What do worms feel like?
- What do worms look like?

SKILLS ASSESSMENT

Use these questions to determine a child's abilities and understanding:

- Can the child count how many worms were found in different locations?
- Does the child make observations about where worms like to live?
- What words does the child use to describe the look or feel of worms?

Maintaining the Habitat: What Do Worms Need to Live?

FOCUS AREAS

Science: studying characteristics of organisms, studying organisms and their environments

Language Arts: learning vocabulary, recording observations

MATERIALS

Worm habitats created during the Worm Hunt activity

A variety of fresh and old leaves such as maple, dandelion, and celery leaves

Compost material such as carrot and apple peels

Paper plates or plastic trays

Magnifying lenses

Paper and markers or crayons for children to draw observations

WHAT TO DO

1. Give the children plenty of opportunities to observe the worms over several weeks. Keep paper by the terrarium so an adult can record the children's observations.

2. Allow the children to carefully and gently remove a worm and study it on a paper plate or plastic tray. Provide magnifying lenses.

3. Invite the children to draw pictures of the worms.

4. Worms like to eat leaves. Place a variety of leaves on top of the dirt. Ask the children which leaves they think the worms will prefer. Record each child's answer. Over the next days, observe whether the worms have pulled any leaves underground to eat.

5. Add apple peels and carrot peels or other compost waste to see if worms will eat them. Talk about how worms help the soil. They eat parts of food we don't need and then make *castings*, which fertilize the soil.

6. Introduce the word *castings*, another word for worm waste. Say and clap out the syllables, **cast**-ings, with the emphasis on the "cast" syllable. Say *castings* as you make the ASL sign for *bowel movement*—make a thumbs-up gesture with your right hand. Place your left hand around your thumb, and then pull your thumb out and down.

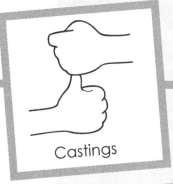

Castings

7. Introduce the word *fertilizer*, something that improves the soil to help plants grow better. Say and clap out the syllables, **fer**-til-**iz**-er, with the emphasis on the "fer" and "iz" syllables. Say *fertilizer* as you make the ASL signs for *help* and *plant*. For *help*, your left hand is flat, palm up. Your right hand makes a fist and rests on the left hand. Lift both hands together. Then make the ASL sign for *plant*. Your left hand grasps your right as the right slowly rises up and the fingers spread apart as if the plant were growing.

Note: Be sure children wash their hands before and after touching the worms.

Help

DISCUSSION STARTERS

Use these questions to spark children's thinking during and after the activity:

- Are the worms on top of the dirt? Where are they?
- What do worms look like?
- Does the head look different from the tail?
- How does the worm move?

SKILLS ASSESSMENT

Use these questions to determine a child's abilities and understanding:

- Does the child have the ability to observe closely?
- What does the child notice?
- Does the child use a variety of language to describe the worms?

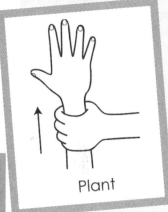

Plant

Look Closely: Worms on the Move

FOCUS AREAS

Science: studying characteristics of organisms

Math: estimating, measuring—time and distance using standard and non-standard tools, communicating results

MATERIALS

Plastic rain gutters, 2'–4' long, or long strips of rigid cardboard and plastic wrap or cardboard tubes from gift wrap rolls and white or clear contact paper

Spray bottle filled with water

Worms

Snails or other compost creatures (optional)

Sand timers, stopwatches, or clock with second hand

Rulers and Unifix cubes

Paper and markers to record *predictions*

Pencils

Post-it notes

PREPARATION

- Set up two parallel tracks using the plastic rain gutters or rigid cardboard or cardboard tubes. Prepare the rigid cardboard by cutting strips about 6" wide and 2' long, then covering them in plastic wrap or contact paper. Prepare the cardboard tubes from gift wrap rolls by cutting the rolls in half lengthwise, and then covering them with clear or white contact paper.

WHAT TO DO

1. Work with a small group of children. Make sure that the children wash their hands before and after handling the worms. Have the children spray the track lightly with water from a spray bottle. The children take turns gently placing a worm at one end of a track. Start two worms at approximately the same time. Ask the children to predict how far the worms will go in one minute. Start a one-minute sand timer or stop watch.

2. Observe the worms. How do the worms move? Note how they scrunch up the rear part of their body then scoot forward.

THINKING BIG, LEARNING BIG

3. Measure how far the worms traveled in one minute using a ruler and a non-standard tool such as Unifix cubes. Did both worms travel the same amount?

4. The children can name the worms if they want and then mark the length traveled with a Post-it strip including the worm's name. Corresponding results could be noted on paper: "Wonder Worm" traveled four inches in one minute.

5. If you have snails or other compost creatures, the children can observe how those animals move compared to the worms. Invite the children to predict which type of animal will travel the most distance in one minute. Record their comments on a sheet of paper.

6. Try varying the length of time the children watch the worms move. How far can a worm move in 10 seconds, 20 seconds? How far can it move in two minutes? Does it go twice as far in two minutes as it went in one minute?

TEACHER-TO-TEACHER TIP
Make sure the children treat the worms carefully. Don't allow the children to handle worms too much. Return the worms to their habitat after a few minutes.

DISCUSSION STARTERS
Use these questions to spark children's thinking during and after the activity:
- How are the worms moving?
- Why do you suppose one worm is moving faster than another?
- Do bigger worms move differently than small worms?
- How are other animals moving?

SKILLS ASSESSMENT
Use these questions to determine a child's abilities and understanding:
- Can the child make a *prediction*?
- Do the child's *predictions* become more realistic with experience?

Build a Giant Worm

FOCUS AREAS

Science: studying characteristics of organisms, identifying body parts

Math: counting, sequencing, studying three-dimensional shapes, problem solving

Language Arts: learning vocabulary, labeling, experiencing a wide range of literature— non-fiction

MATERIALS

Books with large photographs of worms (see Good Books for Facts and Fun on pages 47–48)

Brown lunch bags, several for each child

Old newspapers

2 sheets of brown construction paper 8½" x 11"

Clear packing tape

Roll of plastic wrap

Paper and marker to label parts of model

WHAT TO DO

1. Study a clear illustration or photo of a worm. Ask, "What are the parts of a worm? Which parts look the same and which look different?"

2. Introduce the word *clitellum*, the slightly wider part of the worm where the egg sacks are made. One way to tell the head from the tail of a worm is that the *clitellum* is located closer to the head. Say and clap cli-**tel**-lum, with the emphasis on the "tel" syllable. Say *clitellum* as you point to that part of the worm in the photo.

3. Introduce the word *segment*, part of a body. Say and clap **seg**-ment, with the emphasis on the "seg" syllable. Say *segment* as you make the ASL sign for *segment*, the pinkie side of the right hand cuts across the palm of the left hand.

4. Invite the children to crumple sheets of newspaper and stuff them into lunch bags. Each bag will represent a worm *segment*. After the bags are about half full, help the children twist the end shut. The children keep stuffing bags until there are enough *segments* to construct at least one giant worm. (You will need at least 11 bags.) Tape two of the stuffed lunch bags together with clear packing tape and then wrap them in brown construction paper to represent the *clitellum*.

5. Invite the children to lay out their *segments* and count them. They can decide if they want to make one really long worm or have enough to make several BIG worms, or a BIG worm and a "baby" worm. Will they need to make more *segments*?

Segment

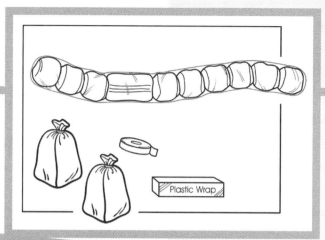

6. Starting with the *clitellum*, tape the other lunch bags together on either end with packing tape, making sure the *clitellum* is about one fourth of the way from the head. For example, if you add two *segments* to the head end, adding nine *segments* after the *clitellum* would keep your worm in the right proportion. Shape the first and last *segments* to be pointed to represent the head and the tail.
Note: To make a sturdier worm, wrap the whole model in a single layer of plastic wrap, circling the worm from head to tail, as if you were creating a mummy. This will also help represent the worm's moist skin

7. Help the children label the head, tail, *clitellum*, and *segments*.
Note: Larger-than-life models help children see all the parts of the worm.

8. Mount the worm on a classroom wall or find it a habitat in your dramatic play corner.

MORE IDEAS

- Create a giant worm using 2" sections the teacher has cut from paper towel rolls. The children thread the tubes on a long length of yarn. Near the top, the children add a long section to represent the *clitellum*. Tape the ends of the yarn to the first and last *segment*.

- After you've built your giant worm, play Hap Palmer's song "Walter the Waltzing Worm" from the CD of the same name. You can dance with the giant worm while the children dance with yarn worms. Then the children can take turns dancing with the giant worm.

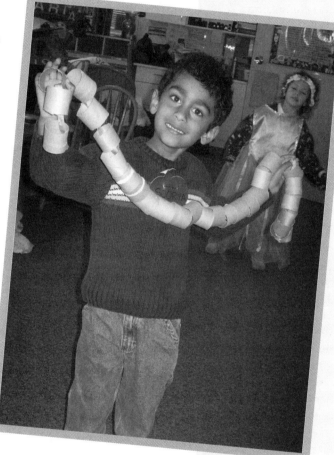

DISCUSSION STARTERS

Use these questions to spark children's thinking during and after the activity:
- How does this worm look compared to a real worm?
- What words can you use to describe this worm?

SKILLS ASSESSMENT

Use these questions to determine a child's abilities and understanding:
- Can the child describe similarities and differences between a real worm and the class model?
- Does the child enjoy working in a group?
- Can the child count the number of segments?

The Scientific Method: What Is an Experiment? Do Worms Prefer Light or Dark?

FOCUS AREAS

Science: formulating questions, planning and conducting a simple investigation, using data to construct a reasonable explanation, communicating investigations and explanations

Math: graphing, analyzing data, communicating results

Language Arts: labeling, learning vocabulary

MATERIALS

Shallow tray or pan about 11" x 14"

Damp paper towels

Several worms

Shoebox or black construction paper to cover half the tray

Paper to record *predictions*

Marker

White lab coat or long-sleeved white shirt (optional)

PREPARATION

● At the top of a piece of paper write "Do Worms Prefer Light or Dark?" Draw a line down the middle and label one side "Light" and the other side "Dark."

● Cut a thin wide notch in each shoebox so worms can get in and out.

WHAT TO DO

1. At group time, put on a white long-sleeved shirt if you have one. Tell the children they are going to become *scientists*. Introduce the word *scientist*, a person who studies the natural world. Say and clap out the syllables, **sci**-en-tist, with the emphasis on the "sci" syllable. Say *scientist* as you hold your closed hands in front of your body, thumbs sticking out. Move your hands in alternate circles, pointing the thumbs down as if they were test tubes being poured out. This is the sign for science. Then add the sign that indicates a person's occupation: flat palms face each other in front of the chest, then move down to indicate the sides of the body.

2. Say, "*Scientists* study questions people have about nature, such as if you gave worms a choice between a light place or a dark place, which would they choose?" With younger children you might want to personalize the concepts of *light* and *dark* by asking the children, "Do you like to be in the light or the dark? Do you think worms are the same?"

3. Using the ASL sign for *scientist*, ask, "*Scientist* Maria, what do you think the worms will choose, light or dark?" Record the children's responses.

4. Say, "*Scientists*, let's see whether worms will choose to be in the light or the dark." Place wet paper towels on the bottom of a tray or shallow container. Cover one side of the container by inverting the shoebox, notch down so worms can get in. Have several children gently place a few worms in the middle of the container.

5. It will take several minutes for the worms to move to one side or the other so use the time to read a book to the children, practice making the ASL sign, sing to

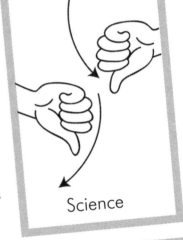

Science

Person Marker

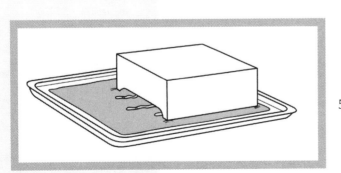

the worms, or talk about the activities you'll do next. After at least 10 minutes, check on whether the worms have moved under the box.

6. Record the result on the chart. Ask the children why they think that happened.
7. Provide materials so the children can do the *experiment* again in a small group. For added interest, give the children flashlights to make the bright side brighter.
   Note: Sometimes the worms explore their environment before they settle on one side or the other. Leave the *experiment* set up for the whole activity time, at least an hour, then check on the worms to see if they have moved.

TEACHER-TO-TEACHER TIP
Use your knowledge of the interests and abilities of the children in your class to determine whether to present this activity about light and dark on the same day as the one on vocabulary, or to present it at a later day or time.

MORE IDEAS
- If the children are ready, introduce more vocabulary words. Say, "*Scientists* make *predictions*—another word for guesses—based on what they think might happen and on what they already know. Say and clap out the syllables, pre-**dic**-tion, with the emphasis on the "dic" syllable. Say *prediction* as you make the ASL sign for guess—an open hand passes by your forehead and grabs the air.
- Say, "*Scientists* test their *predictions* by doing *experiments*, tests to see what will happen. Say and clap out the syllables, ex-**per**-i-ment, with the emphasis on the "per" syllable. Say *experiment* as you make the sign for *science*, (hands moving in alternate circles using the E handshape, fingers curled, resting on the thumb.

DISCUSSION STARTERS
Use these questions to spark children's thinking during and after the activity:
- Why do you suppose worms prefer the dark?
- What would it be like to live in the dark?

SKILLS ASSESSMENT
Use these questions to determine a child's abilities and understanding:
- Does the child clap the syllables to the vocabulary words?
- Does the child attempt to make the ASL signs?

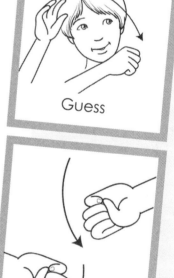

Guess

Experiment

BIG DRAMA:
Five Little Earthworms

FOCUS AREAS

Science: studying characteristics of organisms

Math: counting, sequencing

Language Arts: experiencing a wide range of literature— poem, retelling a story, learning vocabulary

MATERIALS

Books with large photographs of worms (see Good Books for Facts and Fun on pages 47–48) or photos downloaded from the Internet. Search term: earthworm images

Flannel board

5 felt or yarn earthworms, about 4" long

5 tiny yarn worms

5 giant felt worms or BIG, fat yarn worms, about 8" long

Felt dirt and leaves
Felt bird

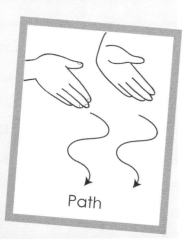

Path

Tiny

Worm

WHAT TO DO

1. Show the children photos or drawings of worms, giant night crawlers and tiny worms, called *wormlets*. Tell the children that night crawlers are BIG worms that come to the surface at night. Fishermen use night crawlers as bait to catch fish.

2. Introduce the word *wormlet*, a tiny worm. Say and clap out the syllables, **worm**-let, with the emphasis on the "worm" syllable. Say *wormlet* as you make the ASL signs for *tiny* and *worm*: for *tiny*, your two open hands face each other and move together in several short movements as if something were getting smaller. For *worm*, your right index finger wiggles up and down as it travels across the left palm held vertically, as if a worm is *tunneling* in the dirt.

3. Introduce the word *tunnel*. Say and clap **tun**-nel, with the emphasis on the "tun" syllable. Say *tunnel* as you make the ASL signs for *worm* and *path*. Your right index finger wiggles up and down across the left palm and then for path, the two hands face each other and outline a curvy path.

4. Recite the following fingerplay with the children as you move the felt worms in the same rhythm as "Five Little Pumpkins."

Five Little Earthworms by Marie Faust Evitt and Bobbi Weesen-Baer

Five little earthworms tunneling to the light (right open hand up, palm out, fingers and thumb spread out)

The first one said, "Let's stop, it's much too bright." (right index finger extended, other fingers closed)

The second one said, "No, this is fun." (index and middle fingers extended, other fingers closed)

The third one said, "I see the sun." (thumb, index, and middle fingers extended)

The fourth one said, "There are scary things up here." (four fingers extended, thumb tucked in)

The fifth one said, "Don't worry. I'll stay near." (right open hand up, facing palm out, fingers and thumb spread out)

Then along hopped a bird (extended thumb and index fingers face out in front of your mouth and open and shut, as if a bird were opening and shutting its mouth)

And, "Look out!" yelled the worms.

And the five little earthworms tunneled safely home. (index finger make a squiggling worm along your vertical open palm)

(Additional verses)

Five giant night crawlers, using a BIG, deep voice...

Five tiny wormlets, using a high, tiny voice...

5. After reciting the fingerplay several times, have five children play the roles of the earthworms and one child play the bird. You and the rest of the children are the narrators. Each of the five children in turn wiggles from a crouching position to standing and says his line. (The children will need coaching on their lines.) The bird hops by and the five earthworms crouch back down.

DISCUSSION STARTERS

Use these questions to spark children's thinking during and after the activity:

● What kind of animals eat worms?

● How does it feel when you pretend to be a BIG worm, a little worm, or the bird?

● How can the worms help each other?

SKILLS ASSESSMENT

Use these questions to determine a child's abilities and understanding:

● Does the child change his voice when reciting the verses about night crawlers and *wormlets*?

● Does the child enjoy performing in front of the group?

● Can the child remember his line when it is his turn?

Over, Under, Around, and Through: Children Face a BIG Obstacle Course

FOCUS AREAS

Math: measuring—distance and time

Language Arts: learning vocabulary, parts of speech

Gross Motor: wriggling, crawling

MATERIALS

Chairs, low tables, boxes, step stools, saw horses (optional)

Boxes and old sheets to create *tunnels*

Pillows, small rugs (rolled up), napping mats or other soft obstacles

Felt bird or bird puppet attached to a piece of string or yarn

Large tarp, if you are setting up the obstacle course outside

Climbing structure, if you are setting up the obstacle course outside

Stopwatch (optional)

WHAT TO DO

1. Working with a small group of children, set up an obstacle course either indoors or outdoors so the children can pretend to be worms. Focus on making *tunnels* and obstacles for the children to squirm over and through.

2. The children love this activity so much you can do it on multiple days, varying the obstacles and building it both inside the classroom and outdoors. (When you set up an obstacle course outdoors place a giant tarp on the ground to make it easier for the children to wiggle.)

3. Invite one child to hold the bird on a string in between elements of the obstacle course so it will surprise the "worms" (the rest of the children) when they pop up their heads.

4. Suggest that the children mimic the way worms move by keeping their arms on the ground, then scrunching up their legs and scooting forward. Children quickly discover that it is really hard to move like a worm and will usually start crawling on their hands and knees. That's fine. They have learned how handy it is to have arms and legs.

5. Using a stop watch—or simply counting out loud—makes it possible for the children to measure how long it takes them to get through the obstacle course.

DISCUSSION STARTERS

Use these questions to spark children's thinking during and after the activity:

● How does it feel to move like a worm?

● What part of the worm *tunnel* was the hardest to wiggle through? What was hard about it?

SKILLS ASSESSMENT

Use these questions to determine a child's abilities and understanding:

● Can the child move through the obstacle course?

● Does the child enjoy the challenge of moving differently?

More Activities Across the Curriculum

LANGUAGE ARTS

- Children draw pictures of worms and dictate stories about worms. Include books about worms and vocabulary words at the table for inspiration. Possible topics for different days:
  - Where did you find worms when you hunted for them outside?
  - What are the worms doing in the classroom habitat?
  - What would it be like to be a worm without arms and legs?

  For added interest, give the children the choice of drawing on long narrow pieces of paper (11" x 14" sheets of paper cut in fourths lengthwise). Mount the stories on brown butcher paper "soil" on a bulletin board. You can create a 3-D effect by making the "worms" stick out from the wall in a soft accordion. When you take down the display, place the drawings in each child's portfolio.

ART/MATH

- Children create worms out of clay or playdough. Have rulers available so children can measure how long their worms are. Ask the children if it's easier to make a thick worm or a thin worm. Challenge the children to work together to make a BIG worm.

SCIENCE/MATH/FINE MOTOR

- Children sort a collection of plastic worms, insects, and spiders with tweezers and tongs. They compare sizes and colors and count how many of each type.
- Children estimate how many plastic worms fit without squishing in a variety of small containers. They put a felt-backed number card (dots = number guessed) or felt numeral on a felt board behind each container to record the estimate and then count the actual number.
- Children measure with worms. Using 1' yarn worms, they measure tables, floor tiles, the distance between objects, the length of a child lying on the floor, the side of a sandbox, the length of a fence—anything and everything. Help the children create a chart of the items measured. Also, the children can measure small items with plastic worms.

ART

- Children create a large mural of "worm" wiggles, wriggles, squiggles, and squirms by dipping a 1' section of thick yarn or clothesline rope in tempera paint. Then attach the 1' section to a long string (at least 4'). Set the rope worm at the far end of a long strip of paper and give the string to a child lined up on one side of the paper. Have the first child wiggle the paint-worm until it nearly reaches him, and then hand the string to another child on the other side of the paper who wiggles it back down the

other side. Re-dip the worm as needed and continue with trails moving the length of the paper. Let the mural dry. Add different-colored trails at another time or set out multiple trays of paint at the same time and let the children create colored trails that cross, blend, and smear as desired. Mount on a classroom wall or cut in *segments* for the children to take home.

- Children can make a smaller version of this mural to take home with string art. They dip the string into tempera paint in a small tray, hold the dry end of the string with a clothespin, and then make the "worm" wiggle across the paper.

- Children create a giant mural of underground life. The children cut worms from brown construction paper (3"–4" wide strips for younger cutters, full 8½" x 11" sheets for older, experienced cutters) in wiggling, zigzag designs you have drawn ahead of time. The children then glue the worms on brown butcher paper to form a large worm trail system. The children can also glue or tape yarn worms to the mural. Then the children make leaf litter from scrunched up pieces of tissue and other paper scraps and attach it to the top of the mural, or glue on real dried leaves.

ART/MATH/ SCIENCE

- Children make worms to take home by cutting long strips of construction paper and then folding the paper accordion style. They can then show how a worm moves by scrunching up their paper worms and having them scoot forward. They can count the number of *segments* they folded. Younger children will need adult help with folding.

SENSORY TABLE

- Fill the table with dirt or potting soil. Put plastic worms in the dirt and add sandbox shovels. The children practice digging gently for worms.

BIG Outcomes

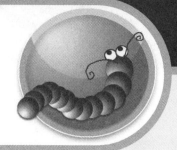

Group assessment: During group time, review the photo boards about hunting for worms, observing worms move, and making a giant worm. Review chart paper sheets from the beginning of the exploration of what the children know about worms and what they want to learn. On a third sheet of chart paper titled "What We Learned About Worms," record the children's comments about what they learned, including the name of the child who made the comment. Be sure to note answers to their original questions, or note what they still want to learn and explore.

Individual assessment: Review your notes and quotes from individual observations during activities such as the light and dark *experiment*, worms-on-the-move observation, and obstacle course. Review the children's work and save it in their portfolios. Note areas in which the children need further practice and those in which they excel.

GOOD BOOKS FOR FACTS AND FUN

Stories about worms are harder to find than recently published, accurate, well illustrated books of facts. Most of the non-fiction titles listed below explain everything you need or want to share, but if you are asked, or are really curious, only *Lowdown on Earthworms* gets into detail about how worms create *wormlets*.

INFORMATION ABOUT WORMS

An Earthworm's Life by John Himmelman
An earthworm burrows up under a bare foot in the first of the precise, full-page
    watercolor illustrations. Simple text, one to two sentences per picture, and a word
    list clearly explain an earthworm's life cycle through the seasons. Ages 3–6

Garden Wigglers: Earthworms in Your Backyard by Nancy Loewen
Facts and functions of earthworms presented in a casual, kid-conversational tone—a
    casting is "worm waste"—include worm farm directions, a glossary, anatomical
    diagram, and websites. Bright, flat paintings accent a longer text. Ages 5–6

Lowdown on Earthworms by Norma Dixon
With solid, detailed information on Darwin's sound, light, and earthworm feeding
    experiments, the photos and drawings in this book take the curious beyond worm
    basics to really BIG words such as *prostomium*, the worm's lip that finds its food.
    Ages 6 and up

Tunneling Earthworms by Suzanne Paul Dell'Oro
Questions focus the presentation of simple facts about life and habitats in a photo-
   filled, small format book suitable for younger earthworm scientists. A glossary, map,
   and a clearly drawn diagram of an earthworm's body are included. Ages 3–6

Wiggling Worms at Work by Wendy Pfeffer
Colorful collages combine with short sentences to convey many interesting facts about
   earthworm life and behavior in this longer, story-like text for young listeners that
   includes hints for worm hunting and a soil test experiment. Ages 5–6

STORIES ABOUT WORMS

Diary of a Worm by Doreen Cronin
Clever and creative, Cronin captures the world's perils and pleasures from a school-age
   worm's point of view. Wearing a red baseball cap, the mostly sweet little worm
   recounts his spring and summer adventures with dry humor. Ages 5 and up

Inch by Inch by Leo Lionni
Colorful Caldecott Honor-winning collages illustrate this classic story of an inchworm
   who outsmarts the nightingale by figuring out how to cleverly measure the bird's
   song. Not an earthworm, but worth sharing. Ages 4–6

Wake Up, It's Spring by Lisa Campbell Ernst
Soft, morning pastel colors glow as the sun wakes the earthworm who passes on the
   message of spring's arrival. Dancing with the family in their pajamas, the worm plays
   a limited but important link in spreading the seasonal news. Ages 3–5

A Note to Families About Worms

Dear Families,

Worms might seem yucky at first to some children. When we began learning about worms, only a few children had held a worm. Now almost all of the children have felt one of those wiggling creatures on their hands.

Worms give us a chance to practice learning how to handle animals. The children have learned how to pick them up gently and carefully place them in a container. We have learned about worms by doing experiments. You can ask your child whether worms like light or dark locations better.

We also have been learning about how useful worms are for our Earth. Worms are wonderful recyclers. They help break down garbage and dead plants. Their tunnels help loosen the soil so plants and trees can grow, and their waste (called castings) fertilizes the dirt.

Have fun with your child as you learn about worms—our wiggly, helpful friends in the Earth.

THINKING ABOUT LITTLE CREATURES: SPIDERS

THE BIG PICTURE

Many children are afraid of spiders. Their first reaction is often to scream or to try to kill them. In this unit, children have opportunities to express their fears and learn how spiders help people by eating flies and mosquitoes. By observing real spiders and making oversized models of a spider and web, children learn interesting details such as spiders have eight legs and eight eyes. They also learn that spiders spin two kinds of silk—one type that isn't sticky for building the frame of a web, and another kind of silk that is sticky to catch insects.

This topic also introduces children to the idea that creatures have specific names. Many children and adults use the word "bug" to describe all small crawling and flying creatures. Children can start to appreciate the richness of language and the variety in the natural world when they learn that spiders are a special type of animal with eight legs called an arachnid, and that arachnids are different from insects such as butterflies, mosquitoes, and bees, which have six legs.

OBJECTIVES

- Become familiar with a common animal children frequently fear
- Observe similarities and differences among spiders, insects, and people
- Explore the value of all living things
- Learn that there are specific words for creatures

STANDARDS

National Science Education Content Standards

- Science as inquiry—ask questions; plan and conduct a simple investigation; use simple equipment and tools; communicate investigations and explanations
- Life science—study characteristics of organisms; become familiar with life cycles of organisms; study organisms and their environments

National Council of Teachers of Mathematics Standards

- Number and operations—count with understanding
- Algebra—sort, classify, and order objects
- Measurement—understand how to measure using nonstandard and standard tools
- Data analysis and probability—represent data using pictures and graphs
- Communication—organize, analyze, and evaluate mathematical thinking; use the language of mathematics

Standards for the English Language Arts

- Experience a wide range of print and non-print texts, including fiction and non-fiction, to build an understanding of the world and acquire new information
- Use spoken, written, and visual language to communicate and learn
- Generate ideas and questions and pose problems
- Build vocabulary

TIMING TIP

It is fun to explore spiders after a child finds one at school, or before Halloween when homes are decked out with giant spider webs. Consider the best season for indoor or outdoor spider hunting in your area.

Introducing Spiders

FOCUS AREAS

Science: studying characteristics of organisms, studying organisms and their environments

Music: singing

MATERIALS

Spider puppet or large plastic spider

2 sheets of chart paper

Marker

Tape or CD including Raffi's song "Spider on the Floor" on *Singable Songs for the Very Young,* (optional)

PREPARATION

● Label one sheet of chart paper "What We Know About Spiders" and the other sheet "What We Want to Learn About Spiders."

WHAT TO DO

1. Before group time, place a spider puppet or large plastic spider in your pocket or behind your back. When the children are gathered, tell them you have a friend who is feeling nervous about being at school. Talk to the spider while it is still hidden from view. Say, "Don't be afraid. The children are here to meet you. I know they look really BIG and scary, but they won't hurt you." Ask the children if they have any ideas about who your friend could be. Give clues such as, "My friend has lots of legs." Gradually bring out your spider, talking softly and petting it. Introduce the children to your friend, Spider. Bring Spider around to show each of them, making sure not to get too close to children who appear apprehensive or frightened.

2. Set Spider down close to you, and ask the children, "What do you know about spiders?"

3. Record the children's responses, including each child's name, on the first sheet of chart paper.

4. Ask, "What do you want to find out about spiders?" Record their responses on the second sheet of chart paper.

5. Ask the children questions, such as:
    ● Is my spider friend alive?
    ● How do you know?
    ● If this is not a real live spider, what is it?

6. Tell the children that they will have a chance to play with Spider and do various spider activities.

A Note from the Author: The activities in this chapter are designed to build on each other. However, please feel free to choose those that meet the interests and abilities of your class. If parts of an activity seem like too much to do on a particular day, save them for a later time. Every class is different, even from day to day, and the activities are adaptable to meet the needs of your children.

MORE IDEAS

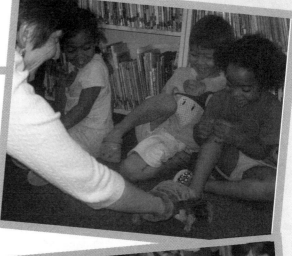

- Tell the children you have a special song about someone who is afraid of spiders. Say, "You can meet my friend, Spider, while the song plays, if you want, but you don't have to meet Spider today." Play Spider on the Floor" on *Singable Songs for the Very Young*. Move your spider to the words in the song, around the circle of children. Gently touch the leg of an adult assistant or brave child, in keeping with the words of the song. Watch each child carefully. If he or she acts afraid, move the spider back to the floor or over to the next child in a friendly way. The intent is to make the spider seem fun.

BIG QUESTIONS FOR GROWING MINDS

Use the following questions to engage the children in a discussion about spiders during group time or with an individual child during activity time:

- What animals have more legs than you do? (dog, cat, octopus, centipede)
- If you had eight legs, what would you look like? How would you walk?
- Does a chair need eight legs?

WORDS FOR BIG THINKING

Look for these words highlighted in italics through the activities in this chapter. Write the words out in large letters and introduce them a few at a time with the "**S**ay, **C**lap, **A**ct out, **D**o again" (SCAD) system. Using the words during activities and discussions will reinforce their meaning.

- Abdomen—middle part of the body in people; end part of *insects* and spiders
- Arachnid—type of creature with eight legs. Spiders are arachnids, as are ticks and scorpions.
- Insect—small creature with six legs such as ladybug and fly
- Spiderling—baby spider
- Spider—small creature with eight legs
- Spinneret—part of a spider that creates the silk for a web
- Tiny—very small
- Web—spun creation of a spider

PHOTO TIP

You can record children's explorations of spiders by creating photo boards about hunting for spiders and webs, and building the giant *spider* and *web*. Look for close-ups of individual children and groups of children interacting. Also include vocabulary words and quotes from children on the photo boards to document the learning. Review the photo boards with the children as part of your assessment.

Itsy Bitsy or Eensy Weensy: A Little Spider Who Thinks BIG

FOCUS AREAS

Math: exploring size, seriation, and patterns

Language Arts: learning vocabulary and rhyme

Music: singing, learning about rhythm

MATERIALS

2 sheets of chart paper

Marker

Picture of a tarantula (See Good Books for Facts and Fun on pages 67–69) or an image downloaded from the Internet

Drain pipe or illustration of a drain pipe (optional)

PREPARATION

- Write out the words to "Itsy Bitsy Spider" or "Eensy Weensy Spider" on a sheet of chart paper.

Big

WHAT TO DO

1. Say the words to the song and then sing this classic song with the children. Introduce the word *spider*. Say and clap out the syllables, **spi**-der, with the emphasis on the "spi" syllable. Say *spider* as you make the American Sign Language (ASL) sign for *spider*. Cross your wrists and spread out and wiggle your fingers, keeping your thumbs still on your arms.

2. Ask the children what *itsy bitsy* means. Ask what other words mean the same as *itsy bitsy*. As the children suggest words say them slowly and clap them out with small, quiet finger claps: *tiny, teeny, little, very small*. Write the words on chart paper or a white board. Make the ASL sign for *tiny*, two hands facing each other, a short distance apart, then bring your hands toward each other in several short movements.

3. Review what a *waterspout* is—a drain pipe for gutters. (Show a drain pipe or a picture of drain pipe if you have one.)

4. Make the ASL sign for *tiny* again and ask, "What is the opposite of itsy bitsy?" As the children suggest words, say them slowly and clap out each syllable with BIG claps: *big, huge, enormous, gigantic, humongous*. Write each word and the name of the child who suggested it on the chart paper or white board.

   Note: Children sometimes make up words like "gigundo." Write those down, too. Playing around with language and sounds is a great way to learn vocabulary. Show the children the ASL sign for *big*—right and left hands facing each other, thumb up, index finger bent, and other fingers tucked in. Then spread your hands apart past your shoulders, showing something small getting bigger.

5. Tell the children you are going to make up some more verses to the song. First you are going to sing about a really huge *spider*—the tarantula. Show a photo if possible. Use some of the children's words for BIG, such as *enormous* or *huge*, to make up a verse about a BIG tarantula, such as the following example. Sing the verse using a BIG, deep voice.

Spider

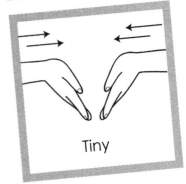

Tiny

The great BIG tarantula went up the waterspout
Down came the rain and washed the tarantula out.
Out came the sun and dried up the rain,
And the great BIG tarantula went up the spout again.

6. Introduce the word *spiderling*, a baby *spider*. Say and clap **spi**-der-ling, with the emphasis on the "spi" syllable. Say *spiderling* as you make the ASL signs for *baby* and *spider*. For baby, put your arms in the natural position for rocking a baby and then make the *spider* sign, crossing your wrists and wiggling all eight fingers.

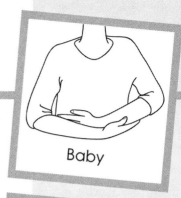

Baby

7. Create another verse with *spiderling*, using some of the synonyms for itsy bitsy that you generated with the children. Sing it all the way through in a high *tiny* voice:

The teeny tiny spiderling went up the waterspout….

Spider

DISCUSSION STARTERS

Use these questions to spark children's thinking during and after the activity:

- Why do you think the *spiders* keep climbing back up the waterspout?
- Where do you suppose *spiders* go when it rains?

SKILLS ASSESSMENT

Use these questions to determine a child's abilities and understanding:

- Did the child participate in the group time?
- Did the child suggest synonyms for *itsy bitsy* and *huge*?

TEACHER-TO-TEACHER TIPS

- Playing around with the classic song "The Itsy Bitsy Spider" is a fun, engaging way for children to learn a variety of vocabulary words and concepts such as *size*.
- Children often connect spiders with Spider-Man. Read Gerald McDermott's *Anansi* story (see Good Books for Facts and Fun on page 68) that ties in superhero powers, African folklore, and the *spider* theme.
- One of the easiest and fun ways to demonstrate *spiders'* good qualities is by reading the picture book classic *Be Nice to Spiders* by Margaret Bloy Graham. Use the story as a way to spark discussion about appreciating, not killing, *spiders*.

Hunting for Spiders and Webs

FOCUS AREAS

Science: studying organisms and their environments, using data to construct a reasonable explanation, communicating investigations and explanations

Math: counting, graphing, comparing, analyzing data

Language Arts: labeling

MATERIALS

1 sheet of chart paper
Markers
Insect collector magnifying containers (available online; search term bug magnifiers) or clear plastic containers with lids (such as mayonnaise jars) to keep *spiders* for brief observation
Drawn or precut paper *spiders* and *webs* (optional)
Post-it notes or construction paper squares about 3" x 3"
Glue sticks

TEACHER-TO-TEACHER TIPS

- Hunting for spiders often relieves children's anxieties about the little creatures. Instead of being frightened when they see a spider, they are thrilled that they found one. They are more in control.
- While most spiders are absolutely harmless to people there are a few that can bite. You are unlikely to see these spiders in your classroom or play yard. Consult books and websites (search term: spiders) for further information. Just to be safe, advise children to look with their eyes and not put their hand into an area they cannot see so they do not get bitten or squish any *tiny* creatures.
- To collect a spider, place a clear plastic container over it, and then slide a thin piece of cardboard under the spider. Turn the container over, remove the cardboard and screw on the lid.

PREPARATION

- Make a giant graph on chart paper. Label it "Where We Found Spiders and *Webs*." See page 301 in the Appendix for directions on constructing graphs.
- Go on a quick *spider* and *web* hunt before doing this activity with the children. Even if you have a very small outdoor area or inside space you may find *spiders* in a quiet stairwell or window corner or under radiators.
- Draw or cut paper *spiders* and *webs* for young children to use on the graph.

WHAT TO DO

1. Work with a small group of children. Tell them that they are going to hunt for real *spiders* and their *webs*. Ask, "Where do you think you will find *spiders*?" Record their responses along the bottom of the chart paper to construct a graph
2. Ask the children, "How can we show *spiders* and *webs* on our graph?" For older children, demonstrate how to draw a *spider* picture. On a Post-it note or construction paper square, draw a circle (head). Draw four legs on each side. Draw a circle for the *abdomen*. For a *web*, the children can draw three concentric circles with an X through the circles. Or you can give the children *spiders* and *webs* you have drawn or cut.

3. Talk about how most *spiders* do not bother people, but tell the children to look with their eyes and not put their hand into an area they cannot see so they do not get bitten or squish any *tiny* creatures. Tell them to come get you or an adult assistant rather than try to capture a *spider* themselves.

4. Go on a *spider* and *web* hunt. Be sure to check all the places the children think they will find *spiders* and places where you found *spiders*. When a child finds a *spider* or *web*, have her draw a picture and add it to the graph in the correct column or attach a precut *spider* or *web* to the graph. If it's safe, carefully collect one or two *spiders* in *insect* holders or plastic containers so all the children can look at them closely.

5. Allow the children time to examine each *spider*. Remind the children to handle the containers gently.

6. Search for *spiders* and *webs* for as long as you and the children are interested. At the end, review your graph and tally. (See Discussion Starters below.) You can do this activity multiple times and keep adding to your graph.
    Note: Be sure to release *spiders* at the end of the activity back into their own spaces and tell children the *spiders* need to return to their homes to live.

MORE IDEAS

● Sing a song about hunting for *spiders* to the tune of "Here We Go 'Round the Mulberry Bush." Make up verses about looking for *spiders*. "This is the way we search for *spiders*…," or "This is the way we search our classroom…."

DISCUSSION STARTERS (READING THE GRAPH)

Use these questions to spark children's thinking during and after the activity:

● How many *spiders* did the class find all together?
● Where did you find the most *spiders*? What about spider webs?
● Why do you suppose more *spiders* were located there?
● Where did you think you would find *spiders* but didn't?
● Did you find *spider webs* where you found *spiders*?
● Did you see any *insects* caught in the *webs*?

SKILLS ASSESSMENT

Use these questions to determine a child's abilities and understanding:

● Can the child count accurately?
● Does the child understand one-to-one correspondence?
● Can the child interpret results? For example, "There were lots of *spiders* in the closet because it's quiet or dark there."

Make a Giant Spider

FOCUS AREAS

Science: studying characteristics of organisms, learning that different structures serve different functions, identifying body parts

Math: counting, sequencing, exploring three-dimensional shapes

Fine Motor: cutting, using tape

MATERIALS

Books with large photographs of *spiders* (see Good Books for Facts and Fun on pages 67–69)

Large, black plastic garbage bag

Large paper grocery bag

Old newspapers

Clear packing tape

16 black, gray, or brown pipe cleaners

Several sheets of construction paper in a variety of colors or 14 plastic milk jug caps

Markers

Sturdy string

Large safety pin

Child-safe scissors

WHAT TO DO

1. Study a clear illustration or photo of a spider with a small group of children. Ask, "Where are the *spider*'s legs? Note the surprising fact that the legs attach near the base of the first body part. Note the four pairs of legs. Note how the legs are long and thin. (Some toys and non-scientific drawings incorrectly show the *spider* legs on the *abdomen*.)

2. Say, "You and I are going to work together to make a **giant** *spider*. We can make our *spider*'s legs out of pipe cleaners. How can we make really long legs?" Show the children how they can join two pipe cleaners together by making two hooks and twisting them together to make a really long leg.

3. Now tell the children, "We are ready to make the head." Turn the large grocery bag inside out to hide the letters. Help the children poke the pipe cleaners through the bag, about midway on each side, bend them and then tape them securely inside the bag.

4. After the legs are taped have the children crumple old newspaper one sheet at a time to fill the grocery bag about half full. Twist the bag shut, creating a neck that you will later attach to the *abdomen*.

5. Study the *spider* illustration again to observe the placement of the eight eyes. (**Note**: a brown recluse is one of the few *spiders* that has six eyes.) Invite the children to trace and cut out eight construction paper eyes or use milk jug caps. Have them tape the eyes to the head. Ask the children what else the *spider* head needs. Some children may suggest a mouth or fangs. Encourage them to decorate the head as they wish with markers.

6. Study the *spider* illustration to notice the large *abdomen*, the bottom part of a *spider*'s body. In people it's the part where the stomach is located. Help the children create the *spider*'s *abdomen* by crumpling newspaper one sheet at a time

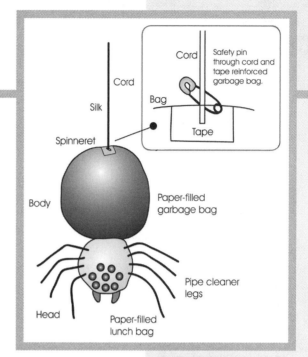

to fill the garbage bag about three-fourths full, leaving part of the bag to attach to the head. Notice the *spinnerets* on the rear of the *spider*. *Spiders* have either four or six spinnerets, the part of the body that produces the *spider's* silk for *webs* and traveling. Invite the children to trace and cut out four small circles for spinnerets. Tape them to the bottom of the garbage bag. Or they could attach milk jug caps with packing tape. Attach the head to the *abdomen*, placing the twisted end of the paper bag into the open end of the garbage bag. Use lots of tape so it will be sturdy.

7. Place several pieces of packing tape on the bottom of the garbage bag (see illustration). Insert a large safety pin through the tape and a long length of sturdy string. The string represents silk coming out of the *spider's* spinnerets and allows you to hang up and raise and lower the *spider*.

8. Let the children take turns gently raising or lowering the *spider* by looping the string over a tree branch or an open door. (Use a door stop so the door holds still.) You could also hang the *spider* over the edge of a loft in your classroom or on a climbing structure. Or, you could tape the string to your classroom wall and let the *spider* hang against the wall. Invite the children to find good *spider* locations. **Note:** Seeing the *spider* suspended from a rope may make the children think of a piñata, and they may want to swat it. Emphasize that they need to be gentle with their creation that they worked so hard to make.

MORE IDEAS

- Review the BIG spider vocabulary. Say and clap out the syllables, **ab**-do-men, with the emphasis on the "ab" syllable. Say *abdomen* as you point to your stomach. Say and clap out the syllables spin-ner-**et**, with the emphasis on the "et" syllable. Say *spinneret* as you demonstrate the ASL sign for *spin*. Hold your two index fingers facing each other. One finger spins around the other.

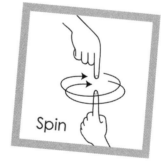

- Write the words for key parts of the *spider* (head, eyes, *abdomen*, *spinnerets*) and invite the children to tape them to the model.
- Use the giant *spider* to act out "Little Miss Muffet," the "Itsy Bitsy Spider," or an Anansi story.

SUPERSIZE IT!

If you are fortunate to be in a classroom where you can attach a screw eye to an overhead beam you can make the *spider* move more smoothly. Hang an S-hook from the screw eye and then hang a small awning pulley from the hook and thread the string through. A properly placed knot in the rope on the *spider* side of the pulley will ensure that the *spider* does not go too high and get caught in the pulley. Another knot on the "puller" side of the pulley will make sure your *spider* does not crash to the ground.

DISCUSSION STARTERS

Use these questions to spark children's thinking during and after the activity:

- How does this *spider* look compared to a real *spider*?
- Do you think this *spider* looks scary or friendly? What makes it look that way?

SKILLS ASSESSMENT

Use these questions to determine a child's abilities and understanding:

- Can the child describe similarities and differences between the photo or illustration of a real *spider* and the class model?
- Does the child enjoy working in a group?
- Does the child offer suggestions for adding to the *spider*?

Make a Giant Spider Web

FOCUS AREAS

Science: studying characteristics of organisms, studying organisms and their environments

Math: measuring— length, estimating, sequencing

Language Arts: labeling

Fine Motor: using tape, tying

MATERIALS

Books describing web construction such as *A Spider's Web* by Christine Back and Barrie Watts, Eric Carle's *The Very Busy Spider,* or *Be Nice to Spiders* by Margaret Bloy Graham (see Good Books for Facts and Fun on pages 67–69)

Chart paper

1 green marker

1 red marker

Yarn or string, about 25'–50'

Clear tape

One binder or key ring, shower curtain ring, teething ring, or any other hollow circle

Construction paper for children to make insects

child-safe scissors

WHAT TO DO

1. At group time, read a book about *spider webs*.
2. Review vocabulary of *spiders* spinning *webs*. Make the ASL sign for *spider*. Introduce the word *web*. Clap out **web**, which has just one syllable. Say *web* as you first spin your fingers as you did for spinneret and then outline the *web* in the air.
3. Say, "I'm going to try to draw a *web*, following the pictures in the book. What do I need to do first?" Use a green marker for the non-sticky strands and red for the sticky strands. Discuss the sequence of *web* building: the first green horizontal line, then the rest of the frame, then the radiating diagonal lines, and finally the red sticky spiral.
4. Ask the children, "What could we use to build a BIG *web*?" Brainstorm possible materials. Ask, "Where could we build it?" Choose a location where you have room to work—outdoors is ideal—at one end of a patio or on a chain-link fence or the base of a climbing structure. You can also construct a *web* on a classroom wall or corner.
5. Make the *web* as large as your space permits. Help the children cut the non-sticky perimeter strands of yarn or string. Ask, "How long should the pieces be?" Talk in terms they can understand—as tall as the doorway, as long as their arm. Help the children attach the ends of the yarn with packing tape or tie them to posts or the fence.
6. Ask, "What part do we add next?" The *web* will look most *web*-like if you place a hollow circle in the middle by attaching yarn to two sides of the circle and anchoring it to the sides. Have the children cut lengths of yarn and attach them from the center circle to the edges. Children often underestimate how long a strand needs to be so they will have lots of loose ends. That's okay. You can tell the

Spider

children, "It looks like an *insect* broke some of the strands and got free."

7. Help the children attach tape between the non-sticky strands. It doesn't matter how many pieces of tape the children attach or how far apart they space the pieces of tape. The children will just enjoy filling in the *web*.

8. Suggest that the children draw and cut out flies or other *insects* to attach to the sticky *web* strands. If you made a giant *spider*, the children can raise and lower the *spider* to check on "*insects*" caught in its *web*.

TEACHER-TO-TEACHER TIPS

- If you have a tree in your school yard with a low branch you can build a *web* under the tree. Use the branch for the top, tie multiple strings to the branch and anchor them to the ground with tent stakes.
- It is okay if the children's creation does not look like a real *spider web*. The key concepts are the non-sticky and sticky threads, and the hard work a *spider* does to build a *web*.

MORE IDEAS
- Ask the children, "How should we label our *web*?" Record their ideas and decide on a label. Create and post a sign with the children such as "Room 4's Giant *Web*."

DISCUSSION STARTERS
Use these questions to spark children's thinking during and after the activity:
- What do you think we can catch in our *web*?
- How do you think *spiders* choose a place to build a *web*?
- Where do you think we could find real *webs*?

SKILLS ASSESSMENT
Use these questions to determine a child's abilities and understanding:
- Can the child work as part of a team?
- Can the child estimate the length of yarn and tape needed?

Spider or Fly? Arachnid or Insect?

FOCUS AREAS

Science: studying characteristics of organisms

Math: counting, sorting

Language Arts: learning vocabulary

MATERIALS

BIG vocabulary words written out in BIG letters: *ARACHNID, INSECT*

2 flannel boards or felt squares

Flannel pieces of parts of a *spider* and *insect* (see preparation below)

Trays or plastic bags to hold the flannel pieces

Spider puppet, *spider* photos, or plastic *spider* (Be sure it is scientifically correct with the legs attached on the head, not *abdomen*.)

Insect puppet such as ant or bumblebee or plastic *insect* (Be sure it is scientifically correct with a pair of legs in each of the three sections, head, thorax, and *abdomen*.)

Assortment of small plastic *spiders* and *insects*

Tongs or tweezers to pick up plastic creatures

Sorting trays

Spider

Insect

PREPARATION

- Cut flannel pieces for a large spider and insect. For the spider, provide one circle for the head (technically a cephalothorax, which is the head and thorax combined) and one larger oval for the abdomen, eight legs, eight small circles for eyes, and four triangles for spinnerets.
- For the insect, provide one small circle for the head, and two ovals for the thorax and abdomen, six legs, two small circles for eyes, two antennae, and two wings (optional).
- Set out the flannel pieces on small trays or in plastic bags.

WHAT TO DO

1. Show a small group of children the *spider* puppet, plastic *spider*, or photo or illustration of a *spider*. Ask a child to point out the eight legs and two body parts. Review the word and ASL sign for *spider*.

2. Invite the children to take turns building a felt spider, adding pieces one at a time and naming the part: the head and abdomen, eight legs attached to the head (four on each side) near the base, and eight eyes. To make it like a game, put the felt pieces in a bag and have children reach in the bag and pull out a piece.

3. Introduce the word *arachnid*. A *spider* is an *arachnid*, a type of creature with eight legs. Ticks and scorpions are also *arachnids*. Say and clap out the syllables, a-**rach**-nid, with the emphasis on the "rach" syllable. Say *arachnid* as you once again make the ASL sign for *spider* by crossing your wrists, holding your thumbs still and wiggling your eight fingers.

4. Show the children a plastic *insect*, such as a fly or ant, or a photo or illustration of an *insect*. Ask a child to point out the six legs and three body parts. *Insects* also have two eyes and two antennae.

5. Introduce the word *insect*. Say and clap **in**-sect, with the emphasis on the "in" syllable. Say *insect* as you make the ASL sign for *insect* and bug by placing the tip of your right thumb on the tip of your nose, pinkie and ring fingers tucked in. Then bend and straighten the index and middle fingers as if the fingers are an *insect's* antennae.

6. Invite the children to take turns building an *insect* from felt pieces.

7. Add a challenge to the activity by suggesting that children build a creature and then have you guess what it is.

DISCUSSION STARTERS

Use these questions to spark children's thinking during and after the activity:
- How are *insects* and *arachnids* different?
- How are they the same?

SKILLS ASSESSMENT

Use these questions to determine a child's abilities and understanding:
- Does the child use the vocabulary words?
- Can the child accurately count legs and eyes?

BIG Drama: Little Miss Muffet

FOCUS AREAS

Math: sequencing
Language Arts: learning vocabulary, experiencing different types of literature, retelling a story

MATERIALS

Spider puppet or plastic spider ring
Low stool or chair for the tuffet
Plastic bowls and spoons
Variety of hats and costumes so children can choose to be Miss Muffet, Mr. Muffet, or a different character such as a firefighter (optional)
Variety of different puppets (optional)

WHAT TO DO

1. Recite the following nursery rhyme with the children:

   Little Miss Muffet sat on her tuffet   *Along came a spider and sat down beside her*
   Eating her curds and whey.   *And frightened Miss Muffet away.*

2. Review the vocabulary in the rhyme. A *tuffet* is a low stool. *Curds* and *whey* are the lumps and liquid of cottage cheese. *Beside* means *next to*.
3. Ask the children how they could act out what is happening.
4. Have the children take turns being Miss (or Mr.) Muffet. The child using the *spider* puppet or wearing the *spider* ring creeps up and surprises Miss Muffet.
   Note: Initially, children often hesitate to be Miss Muffet so you may need to volunteer to be the frightened one at first.
5. Have the other children recite the rhyme along with you until everyone has a turn to be frightened or to be the *spider*. It often works for you to supply the beginning of the line and have the children supply the end: "Little Miss _____ sat on her _____"

TEACHER-TO-TEACHER TIP

When you have many children who want to participate, encourage those waiting to say the poem with you. Emphasize that everyone will get a turn. Remind the children that real *spiders* are quiet and small. The children can become *spiders* by crawling on their hands and knees, or by doing a crab walk on their hands and feet with their back in the air. This slows them down, allowing the *spiders* to take turns surprising the Muffets. The children love doing the poem again and again, varying the animal that does the scaring and the character who is frightened.

DISCUSSION STARTERS

Use these questions to spark children's thinking during and after the activity:
- Why do you think people are afraid of *spiders*?
- How is the *spider* different from Miss or Mr. Muffet?
- Has a real *spider* ever surprised you? What did you do?
- Do you think *spiders* can be afraid of people?
- What are some of the good things *spiders* do?

SKILLS ASSESSMENT

Use these questions to determine a child's abilities and understanding:
- Does the child enjoy acting out the story?
- Can the child recite some of the poem?

The Sticky Web Game

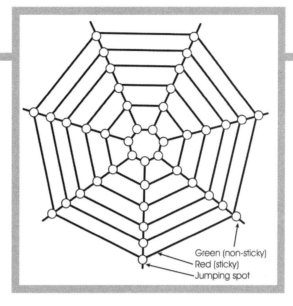

Green (non-sticky)
Red (sticky)
Jumping spot

PREPARATION

- Decide if you want to play the game indoors or outdoors. Outdoors, draw a giant *spider web* with two different colors of chalk—green for the outside edges and lines radiating out from the center (not-sticky silk) and red concentric rings (sticky silk). Draw a BIG green dot at each place a red and green line intersect. Indoors, use colored tape to make the *web* and tape a colored paper circle in the places where the red and green lines intersect. **Note:** If you have a small indoor space, use fewer lines.

WHAT TO DO

1. Ask a small group of children if they want to be a spider, a fly, or some other insect. It doesn't matter what they choose. It's just fun to imagine they are a *spider* trying to catch an *insect*, or an *insect* trying to avoid getting caught in the sticky *web*.

2. One child rolls the die and steps onto a green dot at any place on the outer edge of the *web* and continues to jump from green dot to green dot corresponding to the number of the throw. The next child rolls, gets on the *web* at any green dot, and makes the corresponding number of jumps.

3. As the children continue to roll the die (an adult or a child hands it to them) and jump, they can jump across the *web* or around the edge, whatever they like. Some hop to the center and say, "I made it." Some hop to the center and out the other side and say, "I made it." This is a free-form game that can be played with any number of children as long as there's room for them to hop without bumping into each other. There isn't an object to the game. Children just enjoy rolling the die, counting, and jumping.

DISCUSSION STARTERS

Use these questions to spark children's thinking during and after the activity:

- Is it more fun to be a *spider* or a fly?
- What would it feel like to be a real *spider* in a *web* when an *insect* lands there?

SKILLS ASSESSMENT

Use these questions to determine a child's abilities and understanding:

- Can the child count the dots on the die accurately?
- Does the child hop the correct number of dots?

FOCUS AREAS

Science: studying characteristics of organisms, studying organisms and their environments—web construction

Math: counting, learning one-to-one correspondence

Gross Motor: jumping, hopping, stepping backwards

MATERIALS

Books describing web construction such as *A Spider's Web* by Christine Back and Barrie Watts, Eric Carle's *The Very Busy Spider,* or *Be Nice to Spiders* by Margaret Bloy Graham (see Good Books for Facts and Fun on pages 67–69)

Chalk, red and green, or tape in two contrasting colors

Giant die (directions on page 300 in appendix)

More Activities Across the Curriculum

LANGUAGE ARTS

- Have the children draw pictures of *spiders* and *webs* and then dictate stories for an adult to write on their drawings. Possible topics:
  - Where would you like to live if you were a *spider*?
  - Why do *spiders* seem scary at first?
  - What would happen if a *tiny spider* built a really BIG, sticky *web*?
    Include books about *spiders* and vocabulary words at the table for inspiration.
- Create a giant *web* mural with the children's drawing and stories.

SCIENCE/MATH

- Provide small and BIG plastic spiders. Challenge the children to estimate how many small plastic *spiders* fit easily in a variety of containers. Children put a felt-backed number card (dots = number guessed) or felt numeral on a felt square behind each container to record the estimate and then count to check their estimates. After the children have estimated the number of small spiders that fit into each container, ask them to estimate how many BIG plastic spiders fit into each container.

FINE MOTOR

- Children use yarn and double-sided tape on black paper to make a model to take home of the BIG *web* they made at school with yarn.

SENSORY TABLE

- Line the table with contact paper, sticky side up. Include small manipulatives such as plastic *insects* so children can experiment with stickiness. Vary the experience by adding strips of masking tape, duct tape, and packing tape, each sticky side up. Make it BIG with a large piece of cardboard that the children can turn upside down and shake to see if any *insects* fall off.

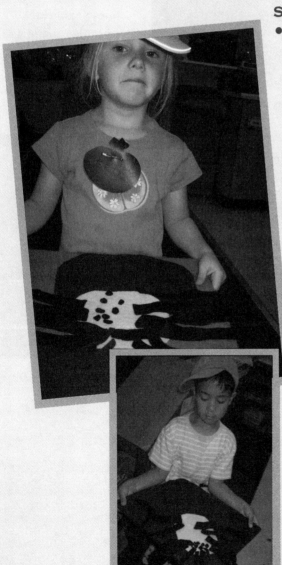

BIG Outcomes

Group assessment: During group time, review the photo boards about hunting for spiders and webs, and building the giant *spider* and *web*. Review the graph of the *spider* hunt. Review chart sheets from the beginning of the exploration of what the children know about *spiders* and what they want to learn. On a third sheet of chart paper titled "What We Learned About Spiders," record the children's comments about what they learned, including the name of the child who made the comment. Be sure to note answers to their original questions, or note if you still have more to learn and explore.

Individual assessment: Review your notes and quotes from individual observations during activities such as the *spider* hunt and sticky *web* game. Review the children's drawings and story dictation and save in individual portfolios. Note areas in which the children need further practice and those in which they excel.

GOOD BOOKS FOR FACTS AND FUN

Many excellent books contain lots of photos for true *spider* fans, but some children may be afraid of spiders, even pictures of spiders, at first. Previewing all books before you use them with your class allows you to gently introduce the wonder of spiders to the most sensitive children a little at a time.

INFORMATION ABOUT SPIDERS

Life Cycle of a Spider by Jill Bailey
Large, detailed illustrations and simple text follow the life of a garden spider as it spins, catches, and eats a fly, mates, and produces spiderlings. Ages 4–6

Spider (Bug Books) by Karen Hartley
Clear color photos show spiders close-up while simple sentences answer *how*, *where*, and *what* questions with spider facts. A body diagram, and a glossary, with additional questions encourage curious young spider scientists to think for themselves. Ages 3–6

A Spiderling Grows Up by Pam Zollman
Follow the birth and growth of a baby spider in color photographs and learn spiderling facts from this direct text with a strong emphasis on vocabulary. Ages 3–6

Spiders by Gail Gibbons
Carefully acknowledging spiders as possibly scary, this book combines bright drawings with a fact-filled text, perfect to dip into for pronunciations, a bit of mythology, spider types, and samples of different web styles. Ages 3–6

A Spider's Web by Christine Back and Barrie Watts
Black and white line drawings pair with color photos of a garden spider spinning a web, thread by thread, throughout the book. Questions invite closer investigation of the spider, web structure, and trapped insect. Ages 3–6

Spinning Spiders by Melvin Berger
All sorts of web facts, locations, types, and web builders are portrayed in realistic illustrations with a focus on the spider's position in the food chain. Clear pictures of a brown recluse and a black widow accompany a note which puts spider fears in perspective. Ages 3–6

FOLKTALES ABOUT SPIDERS

Anansi and the Moss-Covered Rock by Eric A. Kimmel
Little Bush Deer outwits lazy Anansi, turning the moss-covered rock trick against the sneaky spider in this West African tale. Best suited for older children who will enjoy the verbal trap as they add the sound effects to this story! Ages 5–6

Anansi the Spider: A Tale from the Ashanti by Gerald McDermott
This rhythmic retelling of an Ashanti tale highlights Anansi's rescue from danger by his six sons through the cooperative combination of their individual super powers. Bold, geometric illustrations work well for a larger group. Ages 3–6

STORIES WITH FACTS ABOUT SPIDERS

Be Nice to Spiders by Margaret Bloy Graham
Zookeepers discover the importance of spiders when Helen and her web keep the flies from annoying the animals. This easy ecology lesson includes step-by-step illustrations of web-building. Ages 3–6

The Lady and the Spider by Faith McNulty
The lady gardener disrupts and endangers the spider's life before her close observation reveals the beauty of the delicate creature after which she returns the spider to her garden. The small format and muted colors suit quiet sharing times. Ages 4–6

The Very Busy Spider by Eric Carle
It takes focus, concentration, and persistence on the part of this motivated arachnid to create her beautiful web in Eric Carle's collage-illustrated classic, a treat to see and touch. Ages 3–6

STORIES ABOUT SPIDERS

Aaaarrgghh! Spider! by Lydia Monks

Spider's attempts to join a family as a pet all backfire until she dazzles them with her sparkly webs. This simple story, exaggerated with bright colors, imaginative perspectives, and visual jokes, demonstrates many common reactions to spiders. Ages 3–6

Diary of a Spider by Doreen Cronin

Wry humor and the clever illustrations in this book delight older children, who can appreciate the events, dangers (vacuum cleaners), and the plea for understanding in Spider's journal. Ages 5–6

Eensy-Weensy Spider Mary Ann Hoberman

A cute, pink spider in a blue hat washes out at first, but carries on with adventures in further verses that take her through the day and back home again. Ages 3–6

Itsy Bitsy, the Smart Spider by Charise Mericle Harper

Determined not to let the rain get her down again, this savvy spider goes to work to earn the solution to her problem. New verses add to this classic fingerplay. Ages 3–6

BIG NEWS FROM SCHOOL:

A Note to Families About Spiders

Dear Families,

In our classroom, we are learning that spiders might seem scary at first but they are really helpful animals because they eat pesky insects like flies and mosquitoes. We are building a giant spider so we can see all eight of its legs, and we're building a giant web so we can see how spiders don't get caught in their own webs. Ask your child what we used to make the spider and web, or talk with your child about whether spiders still seem scary to him or her.

Songs are a fun way to learn new words. We are singing the old song "The Itsy Bitsy Spider," which you may have learned as "The Eensy Weensy Spider."

The itsy bitsy spider went up the waterspout
Down came the rain and washed the spider out.
Out came the sun and dried up all the rain
And the itsy bitsy spider went up the spout again.

We're adding verses about a big tarantula, a kind of spider that lives in warm climates, and about a baby spider, which is called a spiderling. You can talk with your child about other animals that have different names for their babies besides spiders, including cats, which have kittens, and dogs, which have puppies.

The song gives us a chance to talk about lots of words that mean the same thing as itsy bitsy, such as little, teeny, and tiny. And we're learning words that mean the same as big such as huge, enormous, and gigantic.

Here are some of the words your children are learning about spiders:
- Arachnid is the scientific name for tiny animals like spiders that have eight legs.
- A spinneret is the part of a spider that spins the spider silk for a web.

Enjoy learning about spiders from your budding scientist!

3 THINKING BIG ABOUT GROWING BIG: SEEDS

THE BIG PICTURE

Children are fascinated by how people and animals grow but it's hard to see day-to-day changes. Seeds give children an opportunity to observe growth relatively quickly. Sprouting seeds give children a chance for careful observation and an opportunity to take responsibility for nurturing living things. When children sprout many seeds, they can see the process again and again. Planting the sprouted seeds in containers or an outdoor garden plot extends the experience. Learning about seeds also helps children see the connection between their familiar world of food from a grocery store and the natural world.

OBJECTIVES
- Learn about life cycles
- Experience the wonder of new life
- Begin learning the necessary requirements for plant life
- Practice doing experiments
- Learn how most plants start from seeds
- Explore the connection between seeds and food we eat

STANDARDS
National Science Education Content Standards
- Science as inquiry—ask questions; plan and conduct a simple investigation; use simple equipment and tools; communicate investigations and explanations
- Life science—study characteristics of organisms; become familiar with life cycles of organisms; study organisms and their environments

National Council of Teachers of Mathematics Standards
- Number and operations—count with understanding; make reasonable estimates
- Algebra—sort, classify, and order objects
- Measurement—understand how to measure using nonstandard and standard tools
- Data analysis and probability—represent data using pictures and graphs
- Communication—organize, analyze, and evaluate mathematical thinking; use the language of mathematics

Standards for the English Language Arts
- Experience a wide range of print and non-print texts, including fiction and non-fiction, to build an understanding of the world and acquire new information
- Use spoken, written, and visual language to communicate and learn
- Generate ideas and questions and pose problems
- Build vocabulary

TIMING TIP
Seed exploration works well in the fall when children discover seeds in flowers and fruit such as sunflowers, pumpkins, and apples. Spring is also a natural time to explore seeds because you can plant outdoors.

BIG BEGINNING:
Introducing Seeds

FOCUS AREAS

Science: studying characteristics of organisms, learning about the life cycle of organisms

Language Arts: learning vocabulary, discussing

MATERIALS

Book about seeds such as *The Tiny Seed* by Eric Carle (See Good Books for Facts and Fun on pages 91–93.)

Bean seeds such as lima beans from seed packets, at least one per child

Container with a wide top for the beans

Empty flower pot

Dandelion seed head (optional)

2 sheets of chart paper

Marker

Tray

PREPARATION

- Label one sheet of chart paper "What We Know About Seeds" and the other sheet "What We Want to Learn About Seeds."
- Place bean seeds in a container next to an empty flower pot.

WHAT TO DO

1. When the children enter the group area, have them choose a seed from the container and put it into the flower pot.
2. When everyone has gathered in the group area, take the seeds that the children placed in the flower pot and spread them out on a tray. Ask the children if they know what the seeds are. Introduce the word *seed*. A *seed* is a part of a plant that can grow into a new plant. Say and clap **seed**. Say *seed* as you invite the children to crouch down in little balls as if they were *seeds*.
3. Put the seeds back in the empty flower pot.
4. Read *The Tiny Seed* by Eric Carle. Review the story with the children. Blow on the dandelion seed head if you have one. Watch where the little seeds fly. Ask, "Where did the little seed in the book travel? Where did it sprout?"
5. Show the children the seeds in the empty flower pot. Ask, "Will these seeds grow into plants if we leave them in the flower pot just like this?" Ask, "What will help the seeds grow?" Record their answers on the sheet labeled, "What We Know About Seeds."
6. Ask the children what else they know about seeds. Can they name any fruit or vegetables or flowers that have seeds? Have they ever eaten any seeds? Record their responses on the sheet, including each child's name.
7. Ask what they want to find out about seeds. Record those responses on the second poster sheet labeled, "What We Want to Learn About Seeds." Use the children's interest to guide your activities. Some children may be interested in planting a garden. Others might want to see what's inside a seed.
8. Tell the children they are going to do some experiments to find out what seeds need to grow.

A Note from the Author: The activities in this chapter are designed to build on each other. However, please feel free to choose those that meet the interests and abilities of your children. If parts of an activity seem like too much to do on a particular day, save them for a later time. Every class is different, even from day to day, and the activities are adaptable to meet the needs of the children in your class.

TEACHER-TO-TEACHER TIPS

- While the children are learning about seeds, it is fun to try sprouting a BIG avocado seed. Avocado seeds are not as reliable as bean seeds and take longer to germinate but the roots and shoots are easier to see. Hold the seed with the pointy end up and the rounded end down and stick three or four toothpicks around the middle. Place the seed in a jar or glass filled with water, held by the toothpicks (see illustration). Place the glass on a windowsill where it is warm and bright but not in direct sunlight. Change the water every other day. In a few weeks a root may sprout. The stem will shoot next. Transfer the sprouted seed to a large pot filled with potting soil and grow it indoors. The plant will not produce fruit but it has attractive dark green leaves. Many avocado seeds do not sprout so it is good to try more than one.
- Invite the children to bring in a seed from home early in your exploration of seeds. Looking for seeds at home will help reinforce the concept that there are seeds in almost all the fruits and vegetables they eat.

BIG QUESTIONS FOR GROWING MINDS

Use the following questions to engage the children in a discussion about *seeds* during group time or with an individual child during activity time:

- Where do seeds come from?
- Have you ever planted any seeds? What happened?
- What do you think seeds need to grow?

WORDS FOR BIG THINKING (LARGE GROUP)

Look for these words highlighted in italic throughout the activities in this chapter. Write the words out in large letters and introduce them a few at a time with the "**S**ay, **C**lap, **A**ct out, **D**o again" (SCAD) system. Using the words during activities and discussions will reinforce their meaning.

- Experiment—a test to see what will happen
- Germinate—sprout, start growing
- Prediction—like a guess—what you think might happen based on what you already know
- Root—part of a plant that grows down into the ground and takes in water
- Scientist—someone who studies the natural world
- Seed—part of a plant which can grow into a new plant
- Shoot—first stem and leaves of a new plant

PHOTO TIP

You can record children's explorations of seeds by creating photo boards about growing seeds, about the children acting out "The Little Red Hen," and of the children grinding wheat. Look for close-up shots of individual children and groups of children interacting. Also include vocabulary words and quotes from children on the photo boards to document the learning. Review the photo boards with the children as part of your assessment.

How Do Seeds Germinate?

FOCUS AREAS

Science: studying the life cycle of organisms

Math: measuring—time and calendars

Language Arts: learning vocabulary

Fine Motor: peeling off bean *seed* skin and gently handling newly sprouted plants, using a pencil grip to draw *seeds* and *roots*

MATERIALS

Books with photos or illustrations showing seeds sprouting (see *Good Books for Facts and Fun* on pages 91–93)

Bean seeds, 4 per child (Lima bean seeds work well because they are BIG and germinate quickly. If you can plant the sprouted seeds later in a school garden or BIG container, use Scarlet Runner beans or Blue Lake beans.)

Magnifying lenses, 1 per child in the group

Clear plastic cups, 1 per child

Permanent marker

Paper towels

Tray of water

Spray bottle of water or plant mister

Plastic wrap or a cookie sheet

Pencils or markers

Paper

TEACHER-TO-TEACHER TIP

When bean *seeds* are presoaked overnight they usually germinate quickly and changes are obvious in many *seeds* from day to day. Some *seeds*, however, never sprout. That's why the children should try germinating at least three *seeds*. It's also good for you to germinate additional *seeds*.

PREPARATION

- Soak the bean *seeds* overnight. (Just one night, as they may rot if you leave them submerged longer.)
- Use the permanent marker to write each child's name on one of the clear plastic cups.

WHAT TO DO

1. At activity time, work with a small group of children. Tell them they are going to become *scientists*, people who study the natural world. Say and clap out the syllables, **sci**-en-tist, with the emphasis on the "sci" syllable. Say *scientist* as you hold your closed hands in front of your body, thumbs sticking out. Move your hands in alternate circles, pointing the thumbs down as if they were test tubes being poured out. This is the sign for *science*. Then add the *person* sign, which is two palms facing each other, then moving downward.

2. Each child chooses one soaked bean *seed* to study. Encourage the children to look at their *seed* with a magnifying lens. Help them gently take the cover off the bean *seed*. Ask what they think this cover does. (It protects the *seed*.)

3. Help the children gently separate the two halves of the *seed*. Invite them to study the inside of the *seed* with the magnifying lens. Can they see the tiny baby plant? What is the rest of the *seed*? (It is food for the baby plant.)

4. The children fold a paper towel in half so it will fit inside the cup, put the folded towel in a tray of water to wet it, and then place it snugly against the inside of the plastic cup. Then the children scrunch up one or two additional dry paper towels and place the towels in the center of the cup to hold the wet towel in place.

5. Help the children place three of the pre-soaked bean *seeds* between the paper towel and the side of the cup, about halfway down. Once the *seeds* are in place,

the children use the spray bottle or plant mister to dampen the paper towels in the center of the cup.

6. Place the cups in a warm, bright place, but not on a heater or in the sun because the *seeds* will dry out. Cover the cups with plastic wrap or a cookie sheet so the paper towels stay moist. Remove the plastic wrap or cookie sheet for a time each day so the children can observe the *seeds*. They can lightly spray inside the cup to keep the paper towels moist.

7. At group time each day, note the progress of the *seeds* on the number line calendar you create (see following activity).

MORE IDEAS

- The children draw pictures of what their *seeds* look like each day. (You can make a little book, a *seed* journal, for each child with 8 ½" x 11" paper folded in half and stapled. Save drawings or journals for their portfolios.)
- Younger children may have a hard time drawing their beans. Give them precut bean *seed* shapes to trace or to glue on the paper. Then they can add lines for *roots* and *shoots*. See the Teacher-to-Teacher Tip for suggestions on how to teach drawing.
- When leaves appear on the sprouted *seeds*, the children plant the seedlings carefully in dirt so they can keep growing. The children can plant them in pots or a garden plot at school or they can plant them in plastic cups to take home.

TEACHER-TO-TEACHER TIP

Use "BIG arm drawing" first when showing the children how to draw their seeds. Draw a large bean shape on a white board or chart paper as the children watch. Trace around it with your finger. Ask if the line is straight (draw an example of a straight line, if necessary) or curved. Ask if the shape is more like a circle, square, or oval. Tell the children to do the following: Put their "drawing arm" into the air up high and outline the bean shape: "Here we go up in a curve, over the top, down the side, now head back to where we started with a little hill in the middle. Repeat 2–3 times, as needed. Then say, "Let's make the same shape only smaller." Using this technique, many children can transfer this movement to paper.

DISCUSSION STARTERS

Use these questions to spark children's thinking during and after the activity:
- What helped the *seeds* sprout?
- How long did it take for leaves to grow?
- Have you ever eaten beans? What kind of beans have you eaten? How do they taste? How do they feel when you bite into them? Are they soft, smooth (refried), crisp, or crunchy?

SKILLS ASSESSMENT

Use these questions to determine a child's abilities and understanding:
- What kind of pencil grip does the child use?
- Can the child draw the *seed* and the growing plant?
- Can the child use the *seed* vocabulary, such as *root* and *shoot*

Making a Giant Number Line Calendar to Record Seed Growth

FOCUS AREAS

Science: communicating investigations

Math: counting, learning numerals, measuring—time

Language Arts: learning vocabulary

MATERIALS

Books about seed growth such as *From Bean to Bean Plant* (see Good Books for Facts and Fun on pages 91–93)

Photocopied illustrations of seed germination and growth (optional) from books or downloaded images from the Internet

Sign for number line "How Our Seeds Germinate and Grow"

4 sheets of 8½" x 11" paper

Marker

PREPARATION

- Tape the four sheets of paper together lengthwise to make one long sheet. Draw vertical lines to divide each sheet into three sections to create a BIG number line with 12 sections. This will cover two weeks of school plus the weekend in between.

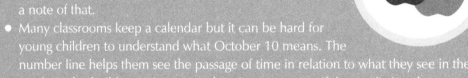

How Our Seeds Germinate and Grow

1. Mon	2. Tues	3. Wed	4. Thur	5. Fri	6. Sat	7. Sun	8. Mon	9. Tues	10. Wed	11. Thur	12. Fri
Put seeds in cup.	Seeds look the same.	We see a root.	The root gets longer.	We see root hairs and shoots starting.	?	?	The shoot is taller.	The shoot is even taller.	Leaves are growing.	Leaves grow bigger.	Plant our seeds.

WHAT TO DO

1. With the children, review book illustrations or downloaded images of *seed* germination.

2. Introduce vocabulary at each stage. Introduce the word *germinate*. *Seeds germinate* when the baby plant inside starts to grow. (Children find *germinate* a funny word and sometimes ask, "Do *seeds* have germs?" Say, "No, but the words sound similar don't they? They come from the same family of words.") Say and clap the syllables **ger**-mi-nate, with an emphasis on the "ger" syllable. Say and act out *germinate* by inviting the children to crouch in a little ball as if they were *seeds* and then stick out a leg as if a *root* were starting to grow. **Note**: This is not American Sign Language.

3. Show an illustration of the *root* sprouting and introduce the word *roots*. The *root* is the part of the plant which grows down into the ground. *Roots* take in water.

4. Say, "We are going to make a kind of calendar so we can keep track of how long it takes for our *seeds* to *germinate* and grow. It is called a number line, and it will

have spaces for 12 days." Mark the day the children put the bean *seeds* in their cups as Day 1. Invite the children to count slowly to 12 as you write the numbers 1–12 in each section.

5. Tell the children they can make *predictions* about the different stages of growth, based on information you have found in books or from the Internet.

6. Review the vocabulary of *prediction*, which is like a guess, something you think might happen based on what you already know. Based on a book or photos downloaded from the Internet they can predict that the *seed* will *germinate* about Day 2 or 3. On the number 3 square write, "We predict the *roots* will sprout today." Draw a little picture of a *root* or paste in a photocopied illustration.

7. Fill in other *predictions* based on a book or downloaded illustrations: *Root* hairs will appear about Day 5. The *shoot* starts growing up about Day 6.
   Note: To help the children keep track of time you can also add events from your school calendar to your plant growth number line. Write in the days of the week, noting which ones are school days and which are not.

8. Every day invite the children to check on their *seeds* and note their progress. Record the actual growth on your number line. Does it meet their *prediction*? (On weekends and days your class doesn't meet you won't have any growth noted.) Continue making observations for 12 days or longer.

MORE IDEAS
- Introduce the signs for the BIG vocabulary. Say and clap **roots**. Say *roots* as you make the ASL sign. Place your left harm horizontally in front of your body. The right hand goes under the left hand and the right fingers spread out and down as if the roots were growing.

Root

- Say and clap the syllables, pre-**dic**-tion, with the emphasis on the "dic" syllable. Say *prediction* as you make the ASL sign for guess. Your open hand passes by your forehead and grabs the air.

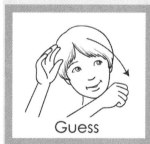

Guess

- Introduce the word *shoot*. A *shoot* is the first stem and leaves of a new plant. Say and clap *shoot*. Say *shoot* as you make the ASL sign for plant. Your left hand grasps your right as the right slowly rises up and the fingers spread apart as if the plant were growing.

DISCUSSION STARTERS
Use these questions to spark children's thinking during and after the activity:
- Did our *seed* changes match our *predictions*?
- How many more days is it until we think we will see leaves?
- What part of the new plant took the longest to grow?

SKILLS ASSESSMENT
Use these questions to determine a child's abilities and understanding:
- Can the child count the number of days on the number line until the class expects to see *root* growth?
- Can the child see difference between the *prediction* and what actually happened?

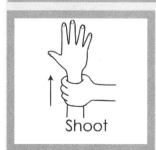

Shoot

Seed Experiment: How Much Water Do Seeds Need to Germinate?

FOCUS AREAS

Science: planning and conducting a simple investigation, studying organisms and their environments

Math: measuring— volume

Language Arts: labeling

MATERIALS

Clear plastic cups, at least 3 for each small group
Paper towels
Pea seeds or bean seeds, at least 9 seeds for each small group
Spray bottle or mister full of water
Pitcher of water
Paper and permanent markers
Large sheets of paper
Marker

PREPARATION

- Label a large sheet of paper "What Will Happen to Seeds in a…" and label three columns: *Dry paper towel, Wet paper towel* and *Full cup of water.*
- Use the permanent marker to label the cups.

WHAT TO DO

1. Ask a small group of children, "How can we find out how much water seeds need to *germinate?*" Record their ideas. Three-year-olds may need a more specific question such as, "Do you think *seeds* need to be covered in water to sprout?"

2. Introduce the word *experiment.* An *experiment* is a test to discover something. Say and clap the syllables, ex-**per**-i-ment, with an emphasis on the "per" syllable. Say *experiment* as you make the sign for science, (hands moving in alternate circles) but using the E handshape, fingers curled, resting on the thumb.

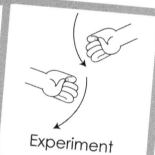

Experiment

3. Review the vocabulary of *prediction*, which is a guess, something you think might happen, based on what you already know. Ask the children, "What do you predict will happen if we put three *seeds* in this cup with a dry paper towel and don't put in any water?" Record their responses, including the name of the child for each response, on a sheet of paper for the group (see illustration). Say, "Let's try it." Have a child put three *seeds* in the empty cup with a dry paper towel.

What will happen to seeds in a...		
Dry paper towel	**Wet paper towel**	**Full cup of water**
Nothing - Jessie They won't grow - Jasmine	They will sprout - Sara They will get green - Josh	Grow best - Kylan Drown - Anna

4. Ask, "What do you think will happen if we put a little water in a different cup with a wet paper towel like we did with our *seed* germinating activity?" Record their responses. Say, "Let's try it." Invite a child to wet a paper towel, place it against the inside of the cup and place three *seeds* between the paper towel and the side of the cup as they did in the first germinating activity on page 74. The children add two dry paper towels to the center and spray them with a mister so there is a little water in the bottom of the cup.

5. Ask, "What do you think will happen if we put three *seeds* in a different cup with a lot of water?" Record their responses. Say, "Let's try it." Repeat the steps from above but instead of spraying water, invite a child to fill the cup so the paper towels and *seeds* are totally submerged.

    Note: Also carry out the children's ideas, if feasible. Perhaps a child suggests putting a *seed* in a cup in the refrigerator. Try it, although you should point out that *scientists* try to make their *experiments* as simple as possible, and only test one type of *prediction* at a time. (The refrigerator is a different temperature from the classroom. Explain that the amount of water and temperature are different things that can be tested.)

6. Cover the cups with plastic wrap or a cookie sheet so the wet paper towels stay damp as you did with the first germination test. The children mist the damp paper towels every day and check on the *seed* progress. Note what happens. (The *seeds* submerged in water soon start rotting and the water gets really yucky. The damp *seeds* will sprout. The dry *seeds* will stay the same.)

TEACHER-TO-TEACHER TIP
Repeating the seed germination activity with the damp paper towel helps children see a familiar pattern and reinforces the sequence and events.

DISCUSSION STARTERS
Use these questions to spark children's thinking during and after the activity:
- What did you learn about how much water seeds need to germinate?
- Do have any other ideas for experiments we could do with seeds?

SKILLS ASSESSMENT
Use these questions to determine a child's abilities and understanding:
- Can the child identify which column on the chart describes which cup—the dry cup, a little water, and a lot of water?
- Does the child use vocabulary words—*germinate*, *roots*, and *shoots*?
- Can the child make a *prediction*?
- Does the child explain his *prediction*, such as, "I think *seeds* need lots of water so the *seeds* in the cup with the most water will grow the best."

Seed Tasting and Graphing: Raw and Roasted

FOCUS AREAS

Science: studying characteristics of seeds

Math: counting, adding, subtracting, graphing, communicating results

Language Arts: labeling

MATERIALS

Four types of seeds, enough for each child to be able to taste several of each kind:

Dried sunflower seeds in the shell, not roasted or salted

Roasted sunflower seeds, out of the shell, no salt added is preferred

Dried pumpkin seeds (saved from cutting jack-o-lanterns, if possible)

Roasted pumpkin seeds (you can roast your own if available, see curriculum note)

Precut construction paper seeds, large enough for children's names

Markers

Glue stick

Sheet of chart paper

Four containers to hold seeds

PREPARATION

- Label a sheet of chart paper "Raw and Roasted—What We Like Best." Create a giant graph with six columns along the bottom labeled "pumpkin *seeds* raw, roasted, neither" (draw an X through the *seed*) and "sunflower *seeds* raw, roasted, neither." See page 301 in the Appendix for directions on constructing graphs.

WHAT TO DO

1. Have a small group of children wash their hands. Then invite them to taste both kinds of sunflower *seeds*. Ask which they prefer. They may not like the sunflower *seed* shells. Demonstrate how to crack them open and take out the kernel.

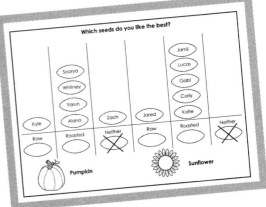

2. The children print their names on paper *seeds* (or an adult prints the names) and glue them in the correct column (starting from the bottom) based on their choices. Some may not like either kind. Their paper *seeds* go in the "neither" column.

3. Repeat the process with the pumpkin *seeds*.

4. As the children taste and create the graph, guide them to interpret the information by asking them questions: "Which kind of *seeds* do most children prefer?" "How many children like that kind?" "How many more prefer roasted to raw?" "How do the sunflower *seed* results compare with the pumpkin *seed* results?"

Note: Some children will enjoy snacking on the seeds. If you have enough seeds you may let children eat more than one seed during the experiment or you may serve the different types of seed at snack or lunch time.

DISCUSSION STARTERS

Use these questions to spark children's thinking during and after the activity:

- Have you ever eaten sunflower or pumpkin *seeds* before? How were they the same or different to these *seeds*?
- What other kinds of *seeds* have you eaten?
- How is the roasted *seed* different from the raw *seed*?

SKILLS ASSESSMENT

Use these questions to determine a child's abilities and understanding:

- Can the child count the number of paper *seeds* in a column?
- Does the child understand one-to-one correspondence: one number for each *seed*?
- Can the child read the graph and determine which *seed* most people like the best?

How Far Will Popcorn Fly?

FOCUS AREAS
Science: observing, planning and conducting a simple investigation
Math: counting, estimating, measuring—distance and time

MATERIALS
Hot air popcorn popper
Plain popcorn seeds (not a microwave bag)
Large tray or clean shallow box
Large bowl to hold popped popcorn
Small paper cups to serve popcorn
Several paper napkins
Paper to record comments and predictions
Marker
1-minute sand timer

PREPARATION
● Cover the bottom of a large tray or clean shallow box with paper napkins unfolded. Number the squares of the napkin to create a grid.

WHAT TO DO
Note: Before this activity, have the children wash their hands because they will be eating the popcorn for a snack later.

1. Show a small group of children the popcorn kernels and ask if they know what the kernels are. Many children have never seen uncooked popcorn because they buy popcorn ready-made or microwave it in a bag. Invite the children to hold the kernels and squeeze them. Do they look and feel like popcorn? Ask, "What would these seeds be like to eat before they are popped?" Record the children's observations. Say, "These are not ready to eat yet."

2. Set a shallow box or tray on a table near an electrical outlet for the popper. Place the popper in front of the box and place the numbered napkin squares in the box to catch the popped corn. Ask the children on which numbers they think most popcorn kernels will land. Record their *predictions*, including each child's name, on a sheet of paper. (Most popcorn will land in front of the popper.)

3. Ask the children how long they think it will take for the popcorn to pop. Record their *predictions*.

4. Make half a batch or less of popcorn following the directions on the popper. Invite a child to start the sand timer. The children take turns flipping it and counting the flips until the popcorn finishes popping. While you are waiting, ask the children if they know what makes popcorn pop. (*Seeds* contain a little moisture. When heated, the water becomes steam, which puffs up the starchy interior. Eventually the outer *seed* coat bursts, sending the kernels flying.)

5. Record how long it takes for the first *seed* to pop and how long it takes for the rest of the batch to pop. Where do most kernels land? How many are on each square? Compare the results with the children's *predictions*.

6. Empty napkins of popped popcorn into the bowl to share. You can either serve it immediately or wait until lunch or snack time.

7. Make multiple small batches; ask for new *predictions* each time.

DISCUSSION STARTERS

Use these questions to spark children's thinking during and after the activity:
- How does this popcorn taste compared to popcorn you've eaten before?
- Did the popcorn land where you thought it would?

SKILLS ASSESSMENT

Use these questions to determine a child's abilities and understanding:
- Can the child make a *prediction* about where most of the popcorn will land after seeing the initial trial?
- Can the child make a *prediction* about how long it will take for the popcorn to pop after seeing the first batch pop?
- Does the child change his *prediction* based on experience?

The Little Red Hen Does a BIG Job All By Herself

PREPARATION

- Cut construction paper into strips about 2" x 8½" to make headbands. Each child will need two strips per headband. Cut paper squares so the children can draw and cut ears or feathers to represent the characters: the little red hen, the cat, dog, duck, or other characters. For younger children, precut a variety of ears and feathers.

WHAT TO DO

1. Read one of the books about "The Little Red Hen." Review what happens in the story. Review the characters: the hen, cat, dog, and duck or other characters, depending on which version of the story you read. Review the message of the story—helpfulness is rewarded.
2. Ask the children what props they need to act out the story. You will be the narrator and line prompter as the children act out the story. The children won't actually grind wheat or make bread, but they can use a shovel for pretend planting, a rock for pretend grinding, and a mixing bowl for pretend mixing.
3. Invite the children to make headbands for the different characters.
4. Perform the play multiple times and encourage the children to try different roles. The children look at the story differently when they are the hen or one of the other animals.
5. Invite the children to suggest other endings to the play. Should the Little Red Hen give the other animals another chance? Should she share anyway even if they didn't help? When different children play the Little Red Hen they can make up their own endings.

DISCUSSION STARTERS

Use these questions to spark children's thinking during and after the activity:

- Why do you think the cat, dog, and duck didn't want to help?
- Has someone ever asked you to help? Did you want to help? What did you do?
- Can you tell about a time when you wanted someone to help you do some work?
- How does it change the work when everyone helps?
- Do you think the cat, dog, and duck will help next time?

SKILLS ASSESSMENT

Use these questions to determine a child's abilities and understanding:

- Can the child remember the different characters and retell the story?
- Does the child enjoy acting out the story?
- Can the child remember the sequence of the story?

FOCUS AREAS

Math: counting, sequencing

Language Arts: experiencing a wide range of texts, retelling the story

Fine Motor: drawing, cutting

MATERIALS

Story of "The Little Red Hen" to read (see Good Books for Facts and Fun on pages 91–93)

Optional props for the play:

Sand shovel

Smooth stone

2 sacks, one to carry the wheat and one to carry the flour

Apron

Large mixing bowl, unbreakable

Wooden spoon

Baking pan for bread

2 hot pads

Construction paper

Pencils

Scissors (adult-only)

Staplers

The Real Work of The Little Red Hen: Planting Wheat

FOCUS AREAS

Science: studying *seed* germination

Math: counting, estimating, measuring—time

Language Arts: learning vocabulary

Fine Motor: transferring potting soil and filling the cups, drawing on the cups

MATERIALS

Wheat seeds (available from grocery stores that sell grains in bulk—¼ pound would be plenty for a class of 20 children)

Bowl to soak seeds

Plastic cups, 1 per child, or a large shallow plastic tub

Permanent markers, if giving children individual cups

Spoons

Potting soil

Stalk of wheat (optional) available at crafts stores or flower shops

Chart paper

Marker

PREPARATION

- Soak some wheat *seeds* overnight—several teaspoons for each child. Reserve the remaining wheat for the children to grind in the following activity.

WHAT TO DO

1. Invite a small group of children to compare the soaked *seed* with the dry *seed*. What's the same? What's different? Record their comments, including each child's name.

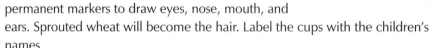

2. If you are giving the children individual cups to grow their own wheat, have them decorate their cups using permanent markers to draw eyes, nose, mouth, and ears. Sprouted wheat will become the hair. Label the cups with the children's names.

3. The children then spoon potting soil into the cup with a spoon, until the cup is about ⅔ full. Older children can estimate how many spoonfuls that will take.

4. The children spread a few spoonfuls of the soaked wheat *seeds* on top of the dirt. They cover the *seeds* lightly with a couple more spoonfuls of potting soil. If you are making a few BIG plastic tubs of wheat, then the children can each spoon some potting soil into the container. When everyone has had a turn, they can then spoon in the soaked kernels and cover lightly with potting soil.

5. Review vocabulary words by asking the children to *predict* how long it will take for the wheat *seeds* to *germinate*. Record their *predictions*. (Soaked *seeds germinate* in a few days. The children will have luxuriant wheat grass in a week.) The children check on the wheat every day and mist with spray bottles to keep the soil moist.

DISCUSSION STARTERS

Use these questions to spark children's thinking during and after the activity:

- Does this look like the wheat in The Little Red Hen book we read? How is it the same or different?
- How does the growing wheat look different from the stalk of wheat?
- How do the wheat *seeds* look compared with other *seeds* such as beans or pumpkins?
- How does the growing wheat look compared with the sprouting beans?

SKILLS ASSESSMENT

Use these questions to determine a child's abilities and understanding:

- Can the child control the spoon while loading the cup with soil?
- Can the child estimate how many spoonfuls will fill the cup to the planting level?
- Does the child make a connection between the *seeds* planted and the sprouts?
- Does the child use the vocabulary words of *germinate* and *shoot*?

The Real Work of The Little Red Hen: Grinding Flour

WHAT TO DO
1. The children, wearing safety goggles, pick up a few grains of wheat and place them on a brick in a cardboard box or outdoors in a paper bag tray (see the Teacher-to-Teacher Tip).
2. Give each child a smooth rock (preferred) or a small metal hammer. The children carefully grind or tap the wheat *seeds* with their rocks or hammers.
   Safety Note: Instruct children in the proper use of the hammers or rocks and supervise closely.
3. The children gently pour the flour they create in the box or tray into a small container.
4. After the children have worked a while to make flour, have them compare their flour to commercial flour.

DISCUSSION STARTERS
Use these questions to spark children's thinking during and after the activity:
- How did it feel to grind the flour? Is it a BIG job?
- How is the flour that you made the same as the kind you can buy?
- How is it different?

SKILLS ASSESSMENT
Use these questions to determine a child's abilities and understanding:
- Is the child able to grind the wheat?
- Does the child see the connection between the wheat *seeds* and flour?

FOCUS AREAS
Science: understanding science and technology—grinding
Math: counting, measuring—time
Language Arts: learning vocabulary
Gross Motor: pounding, grinding

MATERIALS
Wheat seeds from the original ¼ pound used for the wheat planting activity
Smooth hand-size stones or small metal hammers
Safety goggles
Bricks or cement sidewalk
Shallow cardboard boxes or plastic tubs to contain the flour if using a brick
Paper grocery bags if grinding the wheat outdoors on cement
¼ cup of commercial whole wheat or white flour to compare to the flour the children grind
Two small plastic containers with covers to hold the children's flour and the commercial flour

Traveling Seeds Game

FOCUS AREAS

Science: studying *seeds* and their environment, the characteristics of *seeds*, and how *seeds* travel

Math: counting, learning one-to-one correspondence, representing numbers

Gross Motor: jumping, twirling, hopping

Language Arts: learning vocabulary

MATERIALS

A story about traveling *seeds* (optional) (see Good Books for Facts and Fun on pages 91–93)

About 15 carpet squares or masking tape squares on the floor inside or squares drawn in chalk outdoors

Picture cards (see end of chapter for drawings to copy)

Bean *seeds* or another type of *seed*, so each child can hold one while playing the game (optional)

Picture of a plant (optional)

1 sheet brown construction paper to represent good soil

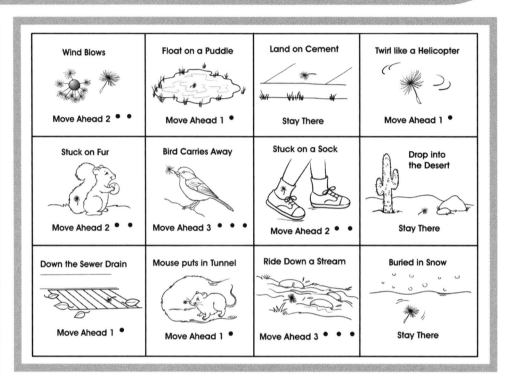

Wind Blows Move Ahead 2 • •	**Float on a Puddle** Move Ahead 1 •	**Land on Cement** Stay There	**Twirl like a Helicopter** Move Ahead 1 •
Stuck on Fur Move Ahead 2 • •	**Bird Carries Away** Move Ahead 3 • • •	**Stuck on a Sock** Move Ahead 2 • •	**Drop into the Desert** Stay There
Down the Sewer Drain Move Ahead 1 •	**Mouse puts in Tunnel** Move Ahead 1 •	**Ride Down a Stream** Move Ahead 3 • • •	**Buried in Snow** Stay There

PREPARATION

● Copy and laminate two sets of game cards (above).

WHAT TO DO

1. Help a small group of children design the playing area by laying out carpet squares or drawing chalk squares, or making squares with masking tape on the floor inside. Arrange the 15 squares to be within hopping distance of each other. It is fun to play this game outdoors, but you can set up in a large area indoors.

2. The beginning of the path is the plant where the *seed* starts. Place the plant picture, if you have one, at the start. The other end of the path is the good soil. Place a sheet of brown construction paper at the end.

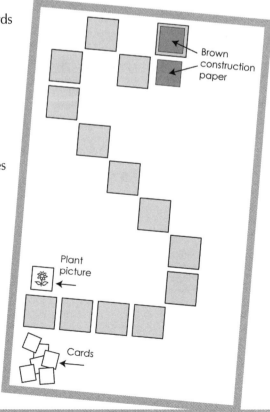

Brown construction paper

Plant picture

Cards

3. The children begin one at a time at the starting square. The first child chooses a picture card and follows the directions. An adult can help the child interpret the picture and move the correct number of spaces. For example, the child may choose a picture of a squirrel. The squirrel picked up the *seed* in its fur so the child hops two squares forward.

4. The children take turns choosing a card and following the directions. Some cards are bad news and the child doesn't move forward, such as the card that says the *seed* lands on the sidewalk. It's okay if two children land on the same square.

5. Any number of children can play. When the children finish they can immediately start again at the beginning.

MORE IDEAS

- For younger children who have trouble taking turns, add and arrange squares so everyone can start and move together and reach good ground in various locations. The children take turns choosing a card, but all the children move when the card is chosen.
- The children use different movements—hopping on one foot, jumping, or twirling.
- If the square that a child lands on is a good place for a seed to grow, the child sends down *roots* by pointing one arm down and sends up a *shoot* by raising one arm up.

DISCUSSION STARTERS

Use these questions to spark children's thinking during and after the activity:

- What was your *seed* path like? Fast, slow? Did you stop anywhere?
- Do you like cards with lots of jumps or just one jump? Which card did you like best?
- What are some of the ways *seeds* travel?
- Which ways are fast and take *seeds* far away?

SKILLS ASSESSMENT

Use these questions to determine a child's abilities and understanding:

- Can the child count correctly the number of dots on the card?
- Can the child move the correct number of squares?
- Does the child understand one-to-one correspondence?
- How does the child respond to a "bad news" card? Taking turns?

BIG CONNECTIONS:

More Activities Across the Curriculum

LANGUAGE ARTS

- Invite the children to draw *seeds* and plants and dictate *seed* adventure stories. Include *seed* books and vocabulary words at the table for inspiration. Topics for different days:
  - What kind of *seed* would you like to grow?
  - What kind of *seed* would you like to be?
  - If you were a *seed* where would you like to travel?
  - Do you think the Little Red Hen should share her bread with the other animals?

  Mount the stories on the bulletin board in the shape of a giant plant. Variation: Cut paper in the shape of a seed. "Plant" the seeds in a BIG mural of dirt. When you take down the display keep the drawings in each child's portfolio.

SCIENCE/MATH

- Invite the children to bring in *seeds* from home—either from food they have eaten or plants in their yards or neighborhoods. Add to the BIG *seed* collection yourself so you have an assortment of *seeds* in a wide range of sizes—from tiny poppy and sesame *seeds* to BIG mango and avocado *seeds*. Children are really impressed to learn a coconut is a *seed*. The children study the *seeds* with magnifying lenses; count and organize the *seeds* from smallest to largest.

- Children sort different types of *seeds*. The children roll a die and pick the corresponding number of *seeds* out of a general container. Then they sort them into different colored bottle caps. Several small caps fit into larger lids (use lids from mayonnaise and other jars) so the children can have their own assortment. The children can pretend they are running a bird or squirrel restaurant and take orders for different numbers and types of *seeds* on segmented plates.

- Children make *seed*-row patterns with different types of *seeds*: bean, corn, bean, corn; or pea, bean, pumpkin, pea, bean, pumpkin. Challenge them to make a really long line of *seeds* in pieces of rain gutter or lengths of gift-wrap paper tubes cut in half lengthwise.

- Children use a variety of *seeds* to make weight comparisons on a balance scale. How many bean *seeds* does it take to equal one avocado *seed*? How many pumpkin *seeds* equal one peach pit?

ART/MATH/LANGUAGE ARTS

- Children sift birdseed using different size strainers then layer different types of *seeds* in baby food jars to make patterns or stripes. They can compare the different sizes and types of *seed*.
- Children create collage pictures with birdseed. Invite the children to count the different kinds of *seeds*.
- Children invent and draw a giant new *seed* for a giant's garden using a full 8½ x 11" sheet of paper. They cut out their *seed* and place it in "dirt" on the classroom wall. On the same day or future days, the children add construction paper *roots*, *shoots*, leaves, and flowers to their *seed*, creating a giant mural. They dictate stories about their plant for an adult to record and post by their plant. What is the name of their *seed*? How long does it take to grow? Does it make flowers or vegetables or something unusual like ice cream? How many new *seeds* will it make?

COOKING/MATH

- Help the children make bread like The Little Red Hen. Their bread might contain cracked wheat or mixed grains with other *seeds* such as poppy or sunflower.
- Help the children make granola and include a variety of *seeds*: sunflower, pumpkin, and sesame. If there are no nut or peanut allergies in your class you can include nuts, another type of *seed* people can eat. Add dried fruit if you want. The children can make up their own recipes for granola, such as 1 teaspoon sunflower *seeds*, 1 teaspoon pumpkin *seeds*, and so on, etc. and put it in a paper cup. Invite each child to dictate a recipe for you to record. Save the recipes in each child's portfolio. The children can enjoy their creations at lunch or snack time.
- Prepare and eat edamame (soybeans, available fresh and frozen.) The children guess how many beans will be in each pod before they eat them.
- Help the children prepare and eat three-bean salad. This is a child-friendly recipe without onion:

> ½ pound fresh green beans, if available, or a 15-ounce can green beans,
>   drained and rinsed
> 1 15-ounce can kidney beans, rinsed and drained
> 1 15-ounce can waxed beans, rinsed and drained
> 3 stalks celery, sliced thinly
> ½ cup fresh parsley, sliced
> ⅓ cup apple cider vinegar
> ⅓ cup granulated sugar
> ¼ cup olive oil
> ½ teaspoon salt

1. Rinse the fresh green beans if you have them and give them to the children to slice with plastic knives or pumpkin carving knives.
2. When the beans are sliced, steam them in a pot safely away from the children.
3. While the beans steam, mix the dressing in a large bowl: vinegar, sugar, olive oil, and salt.

4. An adult opens the cans of beans. The children take turns emptying cans into a strainer, rinsing beans, and adding them to the bowl with dressing.
5. When the fresh beans are steamed, drain them and add to the bowl.
6. The children take turns stirring. The salad tastes best if the beans can soak in the dressing several hours, but this step is not necessary. Serve and enjoy.

DRAMA/MUSIC

- Children act out *The Carrot Seed* by Ruth Krauss.
- Children act out Charlotte Diamond's song "The Garden Song" on her CD, *10 Carrot Diamond*.
- Children act out *seeds* sprouting. The children start in "criss-cross applesauce position" with head tucked down and hands wrapped up over their head. One foot wiggles out, then the leg slowly wiggles out to become a *root*. Sit up and stretch one arm up with fingers together to be the *shoot*. Stand up and spread legs wide for BIG *roots* and extend arms wide for stems or branches. Wiggle fingers to become leaves. The children pretend their head is the flower and give a BIG smile. Play quiet music in the background. Wind shakes out their nuts/fruit/*seeds* and they curl up again as a new *seed*.
- Children make shakers from empty plastic water bottles and birdseed, or staple two rigid paper plates together with birdseed in the center. The children can decorate the shakers. *Experiment* with different tones in the shakers. Shakers with just a few *seeds* sound different from those which are half full of *seed*. Tape lids on bottles securely.

SENSORY TABLE

- Fill the table with birdseed. Add measuring cups, plastic trowels, funnels, and magnifying lenses for the children to explore the *seed*.

BIG Outcomes

Group assessment: During group time, review the giant number line calendar and the photo boards about growing seeds, acting out "The Little Red Hen," and grinding wheat. Review sheets from the beginning of the exploration of what the children know about *seeds* and what they want to learn. On a third sheet of chart paper titled "What We Learned About Seeds," record the children's comments about what they learned, including the name of the child who made the comment. Be sure to note answers to their original questions, or note if you still have more to learn and explore.

Individual assessment: Review your notes and quotes from individual observations during activities, such as the *seed* germination *experiments* and *seed* traveling game. Review the children's work and save in portfolios. Note areas in which children need further practice and those in which they excel.

GOOD BOOKS FOR FACTS AND FUN
A bountiful harvest of books about pumpkins, apples, dandelions, beans, and sunflowers, from seeds to plants, is available in your library, at bookstores, or online. Focus on one variety or select your own favorite mix. Enrich the cooperation theme in "The Little Red Hen" stories by exploring the problem of harvesting giant vegetables.

INFORMATION ABOUT SEEDS
From Acorn to Oak Tree, From Seed to Dandelion and *From Seed to Pumpkin* by Jan Kottke
Each of these three titles in the *How Things Grow* series pairs simple sentences, usually two per page, with an exceptionally clear color photograph illustrating each stage of growth for the particular type of seed and plant. Ages 3–5

From Bean to Bean Plant, From Seed to Apple, and *From Seed to Sunflower* by Anita Ganeri
Excellent color photos offer close-up views of seeds germinating, of *roots* and *shoots*, and of bees pollinating. A life-cycle diagram and plants with clearly labeled parts follow the easy-to-read text. A glossary defines highlighted vocabulary words. Ages 3–6

Plant Packages: A Book About Seeds by Susan Blackaby
Watercolor paintings illustrate basic information about seeds, how seeds travel from place to place, the sizes and shapes of seeds, and a pumpkin planting lesson. Ages 4–6

Seeds by Vijaya Khirsty Bodach

An excellent introduction, this easy-to-read text explains how seeds grow, how seeds scatter, and how seeds are used as food. All the information about seeds is clearly illustrated with large color photographs. It includes a glossary, booklist, and websites for more information. Ages 3–5

STORIES ABOUT SEEDS

The Carrot Seed by Ruth Krauss

In print since 1945, this small, spare story models a little boy's determination to believe that his carrot seed will grow in spite of his family's unanimous doubt. His patience and tender care are rewarded with a huge carrot. Ages 3–6

Dandelion Adventures by Patricia Kite

Seven seeds blow away; one by one their stories are told. Some flourish, one is eaten by a bird, and one travels far away. Through these adventures, children will follow the perils and possibilities of seeds, painted in pastel watercolors. Ages 4–6

The Empty Pot by Demi

Only little Ping, with a natural green thumb, has the honesty to admit to the emperor that his flower seed did not grow. This classic tale of dedicated care, fear, courage, and wisdom will inspire discussion of values and actions. Ages 4–6

The Giant Carrot by Jan Peck

Sweet Little Isabelle's singing and dancing encourages her carrot to grow and helps when it comes to pulling it out at last. Warm, exuberant pictures accent a longer story making this "turnip" variation best for older students. Ages 5–6

Grandma Lena's Big Ol' Turnip by Denia Hester

The Russian classic retold with a focus on a feisty gardener and soul-food cook who needs help to harvest her humongous turnip but no help turning it into a delicious meal. Ages 4–6

One Little Seed by Elaine Greenstein

Using just two to five words per page, this small gem of a book reduces the explanation of the seed-to-sunflower process with an elegant simplicity, which is complimented by a full-page painting and a spotlighted detail under the brief text. Ages 3–5

A Promise Is a Promise by Eve Tharlet

Bruno, a little marmot, befriends a dandelion who promises all will be fine after she goes to seed. Bruno worries, but his patience and trust are rewarded. A large format and sweet illustrations support this story. Good for sharing and discussion. Ages 4–6

Pumpkin Town! or, Nothing Is Better and Worse Than Pumpkins by Katie McKy
All's well for José and his brothers, master pumpkin growers, until a gusty wind blows
the best and biggest pumpkin seeds down into the nearby town. Wild, rowdy
collage illustrations capture the extravagant fun in this cyclical story. Ages 4–6

Rolli by Koji Takihara
Follow the dramatic adventure of Rolli, a round red seed, as he searches for his place
and purpose in the world. Bold, child-like watercolor and crayon-resist pictures set
off the action in this tale of kindness, friendship, and a seed's cycle of life. Ages 4–6

A Seed Is Sleepy by Dianna Hutts Aston
Each page features beautiful, life-size watercolor paintings of common and exotic
seeds and a short, fact-filled paragraph expanding upon the single poetic phrase
characterizing such aspects as seed size, texture, and means of travel. Ages 4–6

Seeds, Seeds, Seeds by Nancy Elizabeth Wallace
One day in March, "five days of fun" arrive in a box for Buddy. His clever Gramps has
packaged a lesson about seeds that engages his grandson with help from Mom.
Bright collage pictures compliment the detailed text and activities. Ages 4–6

Sunflower House by Eve Bunting
In this gentle, joyful story, as the seasons move from spring to summer to fall, a young
boy's awareness of the natural cycle of life, death, and rebirth grows through
observing and sharing a circle of sunflower plants with his friends. Ages 4–6

The Tiny Seed by Eric Carle
A vibrantly-colored giant flower eventually grows from one tiny seed that survives dire
and dramatic perils. Carle's bold illustrations carry this story of hope and
perseverance to larger groups. Ages 4–6

THE LITTLE RED HEN STORIES
The Little Red Hen by Paul Galdone
This classic version of the popular tale emphasizing the value of hard work and
cooperation follows the process that takes home-grown wheat from seed to bread
in a simple text with charming illustrations. Ages 3–6

The Little Red Hen by Jerry Pinkney
This master illustrator adds characters and details that vary the well-known tale. His
realistic watercolors include a rat, goat, pig, Little Red Hen's chicks growing up as
the story progresses and Pinkney, himself, pictured as the miller. Ages 4–6

Out of the Egg by Tina Matthews
Even the Red Hen learns a lesson about sharing from her wise little red chick in a fun
twist on the classic tale that begins when Red Hen finds a little green seed. Fat Cat,
Dirty Rat, and Greedy Pig add to the story's modern, urban setting. Ages 3–6

A Note to Families About Seeds

Dear Families,

Isn't it amazing to think there is a baby plant inside every seed! When seeds sprout it seems like magic, but at school your children are learning the science of seeds and what it takes for those baby plants to start growing into something much bigger. Ask your child to tell you about how a seed first starts to grow, sending down a root and then sending up a shoot.

Learning about seeds also helps children see the connection between their familiar world of grocery stores and food they eat with the natural world. Point out seeds as you see them or as you eat them, such as sunflower seeds or popcorn. Help your child notice the size, color, and pattern of seeds when you cut open an orange or apple or watermelon.

Here are some of the words we've been learning about seeds:
- Germinate means to start growing.
- Roots grow down into the ground. Roots help plants take in water.
- A shoot is the part of the plant that contains the first stem and leaves. Shoots grow up towards the sky.

Have fun noticing and learning about the wonder of seeds with your child!

4

THINKING BIG ABOUT RAIN: DRIP, DROP, DOWNPOUR

THE BIG PICTURE

Water is endlessly fascinating for children—whether they are jumping in puddles, playing in the bathtub, or simply washing their hands. This unit helps children see the connection between rain and water from a faucet. Children will explore the basic concepts of wet and dry and the larger concept of weather. Observing the weather is an opportunity to start learning about the daily news through something that is directly observable. Children will also explore positive and negative feelings about rain—how rain helps plants grow but how BIG storms can be scary. It's hard for children to understand all the parts of the water cycle because children usually cannot see the water vapor in the air around us, but through activities that explore evaporation and condensation, they can start building a foundation for later understanding.

TIMING TIP
Rain exploration works well during an extended rainy period when children can go out in the rain. This might be winter in the western part of the United States or spring elsewhere.

OBJECTIVES
- Begin understanding weather
- Explore water
- Practice doing experiments
- Explore the connection between *rain* that falls from the sky and water that comes out of the faucet

STANDARDS
National Science Education Content Standards
- Science as inquiry—ask questions; plan and conduct a simple investigation; use simple equipment and tools; communicate investigations and explanations
- Physical science—study properties of objects and materials; understand that materials can exist in different states: solid, liquid, and gas; learn that some common materials, such as water, can be changed from one state to another by heating and cooling
- Earth and space science—study properties of earth materials; observe changes in the Earth and sky; understand that weather can be described by measurable quantities such as precipitation
- Science and Technology—explore the abilities of technological design

National Council of Teachers of Mathematics Standards
- Number and operations—count with understanding; make reasonable estimates
- Algebra—sort, classify, and order objects
- Measurement—understand how to measure using nonstandard and standard tools
- Data analysis and probability—represent data using pictures and graphs
- Communication—organize, analyze, and evaluate mathematical thinking; use the language of mathematics

Standards for the English Language Arts
- Experience a wide range of print and non-print texts, including fiction and non-fiction, to build an understanding of the world and acquire new information
- Use spoken, written, and visual language to communicate and learn
- Generate ideas and questions and pose problems
- Build vocabulary
- Communicate results

BIG BEGINNING:
Introducing Rain

FOCUS AREAS

Science: studying weather, learning about water-resistant fabric

Language Arts: learning vocabulary, using spoken language to communicate, generating ideas and questions

MATERIALS

Paper towels, ¼ per child
Adult or child's raincoat or jacket
Adult or child's boots
2 eyedroppers or pipettes
2 small containers of water
2 sheets of chart paper
Marker

PREPARATION

- Label one sheet of chart paper "What We Know About Rain" and the other "What We Want to Learn About Rain."
- Cut paper towels in quarters.

WHAT TO DO

1. As the children gather for group time, give each child a piece of paper towel.
2. Say, "I think it's going to rain. I wonder if these paper towels can keep us dry. What do you think?" After the children respond, say, "Hold your paper towel over your hand and we will test it."
3. Go around the circle, dripping water on each child's paper towel. (If an adult assistant goes around the circle in the opposite direction, it will cut waiting time in half.) Ask the children, "What happens when I drip water on the paper towel? How does your hand feel?"
   Note: Collect the paper towels and save for a future activity.
4. Ask the children if they have ever been outside in the rain. Ask if they know what *rain* is made of. Introduce the word *rain*. Rain is water that falls from the sky. Say and clap **rain**. Say *rain* as you hold both hands with fingers gently curved, palms facing down, and then move them up and down several times while wiggling your fingers as if rain were falling.
5. Ask, "What do you wear when you are outside in the rain? Do you get wet?" Say, "What could you wear to keep dry?"
6. Put on a rain jacket or have a child put on a rain jacket. Ask, "Do you think the rain jacket will help keep me dry?" Have a child drip water on your rain jacket sleeve. What happens? Take your arm out of the sleeve to show that it's dry. Repeat with boots.
7. Tell the children they will have a chance during activity time to test several materials to find out which would help keep things dry.
8. Ask the children what they know about rain. Record their responses, including the children's names on the chart paper labeled, "What We Know About Rain."
9. Ask what they want to find out about rain. Record these responses including the names of the children who said each response on the second chart paper. Use the children's interests to guide your activities.

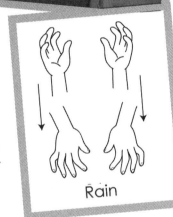

Rain

A Note from the Author: The activities in this chapter are designed to build on each other. However, please feel free to choose those that meet the interests and abilities of your class. If parts of an activity seem like too much to do on a particular day, save

them for a later time. Every class is different, even from day to day, and the activities are adaptable to meet the needs of your class.

BIG QUESTIONS FOR GROWING MINDS

Use the following questions to engage children in a discussion about *rain* during group time or with an individual child during activity time:

- What does rain feel like?
- What does rain sound like?
- Where do you think the rain goes?

BACKGROUND

Where does rain come from? The sun warms water on the surface of oceans, rivers, lakes, and puddles. As the water warms, tiny bits rise into the air as water vapor. Water vapor surrounds us but we can't always see it. (Steam and fog are water vapor that we can see.) Eventually, warm air carries the water vapor high up into the sky where it cools down and starts forming tiny water droplets. The droplets join with other droplets to make clouds. As more droplets join together, the clouds get darker and it begins to rain. The heavy raindrops fall to the ground, starting the whole water cycle over again.

WORDS FOR BIG THINKING

Look for these words highlighted in italics throughout the activities in this chapter. Write the words out in large letters and introduce them a few at a time with the "**S**ay, **C**lap, **A**ct out, **D**o again" (SCAD) system. Using the words during activities and discussions will reinforce them.

- Absorbent—the ability of a material to soak up a liquid
- Drop—a small amount of water or any liquid
- Evaporate—to change from a liquid (like water) into vapor, which is part of the air around us (When water evaporates, it is hard to see it)
- Experiment—a test to see what will happen
- Meteorologist—a person who studies the weather
- Prediction—like a guess—what you think might happen based on what you already know
- Rain gauge—an instrument used to measure how much rain has fallen
- Rain—water that falls from the sky
- Waterproof—material that keeps out water

PHOTO TIP

You can record children's explorations of rain by creating photo boards about walking in the rain, testing to find out what is waterproof, and experimenting with water in the water table. Look for close-ups of individual children and groups of children interacting. Also include vocabulary words and quotes from children on the photo boards to document their learning.

Is it Waterproof?

FOCUS AREAS

Science: conducting simple investigations, communicating results

Language Arts: learning vocabulary

Fine Motor: practicing a pincer grasp

MATERIALS

Recording sheets for each child (see PREPARATION)

Small trays, 1 per child in the group

Eyedroppers or pipettes, 1 per child in the group

Small containers of water for children to fill eyedroppers

Plastic spoons, 1 per child

Magnifying lenses, 1 per child

Absorbent fabric—pieces of fabric such as cotton T-shirt or sheets, enough for each child to have dry samples at least 3" square

Absorbent paper—pieces of absorbent paper, such as paper towels, construction paper, or newspaper, at least 3" square

Small plastic bags

Waterproof materials— umbrella, rain jacket, boots, either adult or child-size

The vocabulary words WATERPROOF and ABSORBENT written in large letters

PREPARATION

● Prepare a recording sheet for each child, labeled, "What is *waterproof*?" Make a copy for each child in the class. On the sheet, alternate *waterproof* and *absorbent* materials.

WHAT TO DO

1. Work with a small group of children at the activity table, demonstrate how to use an eyedropper or pipette and introduce the word *drop*, a small amount of water or another liquid. Say and clap **drop**. Show the children a *drop* of water. Invite the children to practice using the eyedroppers to make water *drops* by sucking up water and dripping it on their tray. Allow plenty of time for practice. (See Teacher-to-Teacher Tips on the following page.) **Note**: If some children get frustrated with the eyedroppers, suggest that they use a plastic spoon to pick up the water.

2. Invite the children to look at the *drops* with a magnifying lens.

3. Give each child a recording sheet and show them the different items you will be testing. Tell the children they will be scientists doing an *experiment* to see what material will keep water out and which will soak up the water. Introduce the word *waterproof*. When something is *waterproof,* it keeps water out. Say and clap the syllables, **wat**-er-proof, with an emphasis on the "wat" syllable. Say *waterproof* as you make the ASL signs for *water* and *protect*. To make the sign for *water*, extend your three middle fingers and tuck back your pinkie and thumb (the W handshape), and tap your chin. *Protect* is arms crossed at the wrist, closed fists, moving out as if you were protecting yourself.

4. Say, "Some materials will not keep water out. Water goes into the material and the material becomes wet." Introduce the word *absorbent*. When something is *absorbent*, water soaks in. Show the children how a piece of cotton fabric absorbs the water. Say and clap the syllables, ab-**sorb**-ent, with the emphasis on the "sorb"

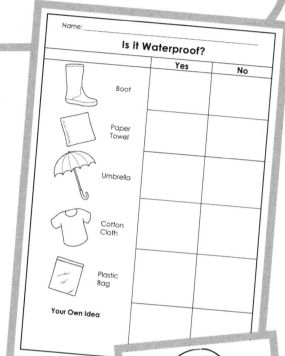

Is it Waterproof?		
Name:		
	Yes	No
Boot		
Paper Towel		
Umbrella		
Cotton Cloth		
Plastic Bag		
Your Own Idea		

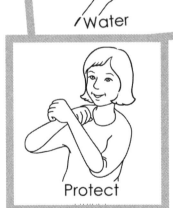

/Water

Protect

syllable. Say *absorbent* as you make the ASL signs for *water* plus *enter*. To make the sign for *water*, extend your three middle fingers and tuck back your pinkie and thumb (the W handshape), and tap your chin. *Enter* is your left hand held horizontally in front of your body while your right hand goes down and under your left hand.

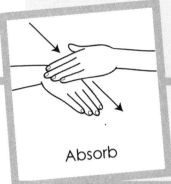

Absorb

5. Encourage the children to make a *prediction* about which materials will be *waterproof* and which will absorb water. Review the word *prediction*—a guess, something you think might happen, based on what you already know. Say and clap the syllables, pre-**dic**-tion, with the emphasis on the "dic" syllable. Say *prediction* as you make the sign for *guess* by moving your open right hand across your forehead and grabbing the air.

6. Before the children put *drops* of water on an item, have them predict whether it will absorb the water or not. Then have them try it. Was their *prediction* correct? Ask the children to mark whether the item was *waterproof* or *absorbent*.

7. Repeat with each item. Save the recording sheets in each child's portfolio.

Water

MORE IDEAS
- Encourage the children to explore the different materials. If they put a dry piece of cloth or paper in the plastic bag or *rain* jacket sleeve and then drip water on it, does the item stay dry?
- Invite the children to test additional items to see what might be *waterproof* such as the back of their hand, green leaves, a plastic tablecloth, a plastic chair.

Guess

TEACHER-TO-TEACHER TIPS
- Using an eyedropper can be tricky for some children. To teach them how to use an eyedropper say, "Dip in, squeeze, unsqueeze, hold gently—no squeezing, now get ready for a *drop*, squeeze slowly."
- It is fun to test if umbrellas are *waterproof*; just be aware that some people are superstitious about opening umbrellas indoors. Consider doing this test outside.
- Use your knowledge of the children's interests and abilities to determine whether to introduce all of the BIG vocabulary words at the same time, or to introduce them over the span of a few days.

DISCUSSION STARTERS
Use these questions to spark children's thinking during and after the activity:
- What would be good to wear out in the rain?
- What items would help clean up spilled water?

SKILLS ASSESSMENT
Use these questions to determine a child's abilities and understanding:
- What kind of pencil grip does the child use?
- Can the child mark the appropriate box on the recording sheet?
- Can the child use the vocabulary—*waterproof*, *absorbent*, and *drop*?

Go for a Rain Walk

FOCUS AREAS

Science: studying weather

Math: counting, measuring—size

Language Arts: learning vocabulary, experiencing a wide range of print and non-print texts—song

MATERIALS

Rain gear for you and the children

Sheet of chart paper

Marker

TEACHER-TO-TEACHER TIPS

- It's a wondrous experience for children to be out in the *rain* but it is important to be sensitive to families' concerns. Some may worry that their children will get wet or cold. Before taking a *rain* walk with your class, send a note to families about your exploration of *rain* and your plan to go for a walk during a gentle rain. (See BIG News from School: A Note to Families About Rain on page 122.) Assure families that you will choose a time during a gentle rain, or just after a storm. Ask parents to send their children with *rain* gear or a change of clothes and a towel on all days when there is a chance of rain. Ask the children's families if they have any extra *rain* gear they can lend other children. You can look for *rain* gear at garage sales and thrift shops so you'll have some extras. Dollar stores sometimes sell ponchos.
- You can stay on the walk for as long as the children are engaged. It is a treat for most children to be out in the rain. If you want to take a longer walk outside the school grounds, make sure you have permission slips.
- When children go outside in the *rain,* they are often eager to run and splash. To encourage them to observe carefully explain ahead of time how they are going to use their senses to notice what is different about the rain. Invite them to "tiptoe like raindrops" outside so they can hear and smell the rain. Save splashing for the very end of the walk.

WHAT TO DO

1. On a day of a gentle *rain* or just after a rainstorm, tell the children they are going to go for a *rain* walk. Ask what they think they will see and hear. Note their responses on chart paper, including the name of each child.
2. While you are still inside, ask the children to close their eyes and listen for sounds. What do they hear inside? Help the children put on their *rain* gear. Talk about what's *waterproof.*
3. When you get outside, ask the children to close their eyes again. What sounds do they hear outside? Tell the children to open their eyes and look for the source of new noises such as gutters dripping.
4. Observe raindrops on *rain* gear. What do the *drops* look like? Observe *drops* on boots and on the sidewalk. Do they look different? Observe *rain* on trees and plants and grass. How do the plants look in the *rain*? Are they bent over? Are the colors brighter? Ask the children, "How does the *rain* feel?" and "What do you smell?"
5. Do the children see any animals? Worms often get flooded out of their tunnels. The children can carefully "rescue" them from puddles and put the worms on the grass.

6. Walk to your outside play space. Notice *rain* on the slide. Is the slide absorbing water? Is the *rain* running off the roof? Follow the *rain* trail. Where does it go next? Is it coming out of a downspout, running down gutters, or going down drains?

7. Do the children see any puddles? Invite the children to count the number of puddles. Ask, "Can you measure how BIG a puddle is with a stick?" Can the children see reflections in the puddles? Can the children see raindrops splashing in the puddles? What happens when a *drop* splashes? What happens if they drop a pebble in the puddle? Count how long it takes the ripples to get to the edge.

   Note: Tell the children to drop only one small item in the puddle at a time and be careful not to splash anyone. Take turns dropping (discourage throwing), and counting the number of little waves as they reach the edge of the puddle. When the waves stop it is the next child's turn to drop something small.

8. When you return to the classroom, make sure the children are dry. Change clothes as necessary. Have the children wash their hands, especially if they handled worms or sticks or touched oily puddles.

9. Talk about what the children saw, heard, smelled, and felt. Record their observations, noting each child's name.

DISCUSSION STARTERS
Use these questions to spark children's thinking during and after the activity:
- What was something surprising that you saw or heard outside in the *rain*?
- Did any part of you get wet when you were outside?

SKILLS ASSESSMENT
Use these questions to determine a child's abilities and understanding:
- Does the child make observations?
- Can the child distinguish different senses such as seeing compared with listening?
- Does the child use vocabulary words such as *waterproof* and *absorbent*?

Water Table Explorations

FOCUS AREAS

Science: studying properties of water

Math: measuring—volume

Language Arts: learning vocabulary

Fine Motor: pouring

MATERIALS

Water table

Additional large containers of water such as plastic tubs or dishpans

Assortment of containers such as measuring cups, ice cube trays, plastic cups, small pitchers, clear plastic bottles, liquid laundry detergent jug caps. Safety note: Be sure recycled containers did not contain a toxic product. Clean all containers thoroughly.

Funnels

Plastic eyedroppers, turkey basters, plastic bottles with squirt tops or pumps

Clear plastic tubing

Variety of items that will sink such as pebbles, keys, and marbles

Variety of items that will float such as corks, Styrofoam packing noodles, Popsicle sticks, plastic lids

Food coloring or liquid water color (optional)

TEACHER-TO-TEACHER TIPS

- The water table will be an essential part of your *rain* exploration every day so that over time the children can experience many different actions of water—flowing, dripping, spilling, and splashing, as well as objects sinking or floating. (See *Exploring Water with Young Children* by Ingrid Chalufour and Karen Worth for an in-depth look at water table science explorations.) Introduce different materials over a period of days and weeks to give the children time to explore and investigate how water works. Color the water periodically to add a different element to the water table.
- The water table is always popular with children. They will be particularly interested in it while you explore *rain*. Set out multiple tubs of water so the children have space to try their own investigations without crowding.

WHAT TO DO

1. Introduce a small group of children to different supplies to the water table or water tubs on different days and allow plenty of time for free exploration. It is easiest to start with an assortment of containers for pouring. Funnels add a new element to pouring.
2. After a period of time, introduce items that squirt and make *drops*.
3. Add clear plastic tubing to introduce the idea of carrying water like pipes do.

DISCUSSION STARTERS

Use these questions to spark children's thinking during and after the activity:

- How do you think the eyedropper works?
- What does a funnel do?
- What happens when you pour that BIG container of water into the little measuring cup?
- How many little cups does it take to fill that BIG container?

SKILLS ASSESSMENT

Use these questions to determine a child's abilities and understanding:

- Is the child trying different types of containers and tools?
- Is the child using imaginative play as she works such as, "I'm making lemonade."
- Is the child interacting with other children at the table?
- Is the child making *predictions* about the outcome of actions?
- Are the child's *predictions* becoming more accurate or realistic over time?

Exploring Drops in a BIG Way

PREPARATION

- Fill ice cube trays or egg cartons half full with water. Add a few *drops* of red, blue, and yellow to three of the sections.
  Safety note: Egg cartons must be washed thoroughly to eliminate any trace of egg.
- Place a sheet of waxed paper in a tray for each child.

WHAT TO DO

1. Encourage a small group of children to *experiment* using the eyedroppers to see if they can get just one *drop* at a time to come out. This will be very challenging for young children. Allow lots of time for free exploration. The children may prefer mixing the colors in the ice cube trays or egg cartons to making *drops* with them. That is fine.
2. Invite the children to *experiment* with the *drops*. What happens if they place two *drops* right next to each other on a piece of waxed paper? What happens if the *drops* are different colors? What happens if they put a *drop* right on top of another *drop*? What happens if they hold the eyedropper up higher when they squeeze? What happens if they tilt the tray?
3. After the children have had time to *experiment* with water *drops*, invite them to make a print of their *drops* by quickly pressing a paper towel on the waxed paper. Write the children's names on the paper towels and invite them to hang the paper towels up. If a paper towel gets really saturated, it works better to lay it flat on a tray so it does not drip on the floor. See the following activity, Making Rain, to introduce the concept of *evaporation*.
4. Encourage the children to make many different prints of their explorations. Save at least one print for each child's portfolio including their comments about the shapes and colors.

DISCUSSION STARTERS

Use these questions to spark children's thinking during and after the activity:

- Is the waxed paper *waterproof* or *absorbent*? How can you tell?
- Is the paper towel *waterproof* or *absorbent*? How can you tell?
- How do the *drops* move on the waxed paper?
- What shapes do your *drop* puddles form?

SKILLS ASSESSMENT

Use these questions to determine a child's abilities and understanding:

- Can the child make just one *drop* come out at a time?
- Does the child keep trying to make *drops* if she has trouble at first?
- Can the child predict what will happen when the *drops* combine?
- Does the child use her imagination when describing her print?

FOCUS AREAS

Science: studying properties of water
Math: counting
Language Arts: learning vocabulary
Fine Motor: practicing a pincer grasp

MATERIALS

Eyedroppers, 1 per child
Ice cube trays or Styrofoam egg cartons filled with water.
Liquid water color or food coloring in red, blue, and yellow
Waxed paper cut in sheets
Trays to hold the waxed paper sheets
Magnifying lenses, 1 per child
Paper towels
Permanent marker to write children's names

Making Rain

FOCUS AREAS

Science: studying liquids and gas; learning about changes in the Earth and sky

Language Arts: learning vocabulary

MATERIALS

Steaming teakettle or thermos of boiling water

Hot pad to rest the kettle on

Large clear jar with a wide mouth

Plate to cover the jar

Metal pie pan filled with ice

PREPARATION

- Boil water in a teakettle or pan. Set the kettle on a hot pad on the floor in your group area before the children are gathered or pour it into a thermos. **Safety note:** Be sure the children are seated a safe distance from the hot kettle.
- Place a tray of ice cubes in a metal pie pan immediately before group time and set it on the floor along with a large clear jar with a wide mouth.

WHAT TO DO

1. At group time say, "I wonder if we can make it *rain* inside our classroom today. What do you think?"
2. Pour several inches of hot water from the kettle into the glass jar. You will probably be able to see steam. Cover the jar with a plate. Ask the children, "Do you think the water in the jar is hot or cold?"
3. Show the children the metal pie pan of ice. Go around the group, letting them briefly feel the underside of the pan. Ask, "How does it feel?" Ask, "What do you think will happen if hot steam from the tea kettle touches the cold pie pan?" Listen to their responses and say, "Let's find out." Take the plate off the jar, pour in a little more hot water from the kettle and then place the pie pan of ice over the jar. *Drops* of water should condense and run down the inside of the jar. Ask, "What do you see?" Ask, "Where did the water come from?"
4. Say, "This isn't *exactly* what happens when it *rains*, but it is similar. Water from puddles and rivers and lakes and the ocean gets warm from the sun's heat, just like we warmed water in our kettle. Little bits of the water *evaporate* and go into the air, just like the steam from this hot water."
5. Introduce the word **evaporate**. Say and clap the syllables e-**vap**-o-rate, with the emphasis on the "vap" syllable. Say and act out *evaporate*. Invite the children to crouch down like they are little *drops* of water. They slowly rise as they say "eee" and then spread their arms to make a giant V and jump up into the air as they say "evaporate!"(This is not American Sign Language.) **Safety note:** Be sure the kettle is away from the children when they start to move around.
6. Have the children sit down and continue with your discussion of the *rain* demonstration. "The warm water that has *evaporated* and is now in the air rises up into the sky. It is cool high in the sky, like the bottom of our pie tin is cool. When the water in the air cools down, tiny water droplets join together and make clouds. When there is a lot of water in the clouds they turn gray and heavy *drops* of water fall to the ground as rain, like the water running down the sides of the jar."

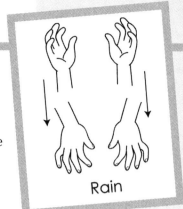

Rain

7. Make the American Sign Language sign for *rain* as you hold both hands gently curved, palms facing down, and then move them up and down several times while wiggling your fingers as if *rain* were falling.
8. Take the pie pan off the jar and let the children touch the wet underside.
9. Tell the children they will be able to try evaporation activities later, outside. (See the evaporation activity on page 106.)

MORE IDEAS
● Sing "Rain Falls Down" to the tune of "Row, Row, Row Your Boat."

Rain Falls Down *by Tim Dobbins*
Rain, rain, rain falls down (curved hands, fingers wiggle while moving down)
To the earth below.
The water cycle is at work.
This is how it goes.

Sun, sun, sun dries up (index finger points to the sky and circles around)
The water in the sea.
Invisible, it hides in air.
Watch and you will see.

Clouds, clouds, clouds of white (right and left hands are curved in front of the face,
    palms facing each other; gently move hands across the face while making
    small circular motions)
Drifting in the sky.
There's our water once again,
Floating way up high.

Rain, rain, rain falls down (curved hands, fingers wiggle while moving down)
To the earth below.
The water cycle starts again.
'Round and 'round it goes.

DISCUSSION STARTERS
Use these questions to spark children's thinking during and after the activity:
● Have you ever felt the outside of a milk jug when it comes out the refrigerator or a glass filled with a cold drink? What does it feel like? Does it feel like the pie pan with ice?
● What do clouds look like before it *rains*?

SKILLS ASSESSMENT
Use these questions to determine a child's abilities and understanding:
● Does the child pay attention during group time?
● Does the child try to make the ASL signs?
● Does the child join in with the singing?

Experiment: How Long Does It Take for Water to Evaporate Outside?

FOCUS AREAS

Science: planning and conducting a simple investigation, studying properties of water—water can exist in different states—liquid and gas

Math: counting, measuring—time

Language Arts: learning vocabulary

MATERIALS

Large paintbrushes (ask families to lend clean brushes for painting with water)

Sand pails or buckets of water

Chalk

Cardboard for fanning

Small chalkboards and easel paintbrushes (optional)

TEACHER-TO-TEACHER TIPS

- This activity works best on a warm sunny day, but you can repeat it numerous times in different types of weather (cloudy, windy) and compare the results. Children **love** to paint with BIG paintbrushes and don't mind at all that the water *evaporates*. That's the perfect excuse for another coat of "paint." Good, clean fun!

- Use the word *evaporate* rather than *disappear* when doing this activity. Disappear suggests that the water is gone, when really it has just changed states to become part of the air. This is a hard concept to grasp, but just using the BIG word *evaporate* will introduce children to the idea.

WHAT TO DO

1. Work with a small group of children. Invite each child to fill a sand pail or bucket with water and choose a paintbrush.

2. The children can "paint" with water whatever they want—the sidewalk, the school building, a playhouse.

3. Ask, "Will the water stay on the sidewalk?"

4. Introduce the word *evaporate*. Water *evaporates* when it becomes part of the air. Say and clap the syllables e-**vap**-o-rate, with the emphasis on the "vap" syllable. Say and act out *evaporate*. Invite the children to crouch down like they are little *drops* of water. They slowly rise as they say "eee" and then spread their arms to make a giant V and jump up into the air arms as they say *"evaporate!"* **Note**: This is not American Sign Language.

5. On a hot day, water on a sunny sidewalk, will *evaporate* right before their eyes. As soon as they swipe the sidewalk with a wet brush have them or a classmate outline the wet spot with chalk. They can draw multiple circles as the wet spot shrinks. Have the children count how long it takes the water to *evaporate*. They can also time the evaporation with sand timers.

6. Ask, "How can you make the water *evaporate* faster?" The children can team up to fan the wet spots.

7. Ask, "Where will it take longer for the water to *evaporate*?" Repeat the *experiment* in the shade. The children can paint in the sun and shade at the same time and compare.

MORE IDEAS

- Children paint their names or pictures with water on the sidewalk and watch it *evaporate*. Can they outline the letters in their name before the water dries up?

- Children paint with water on small chalkboards in the sun. Water will *evaporate* quicker on the chalkboard than it will on the sidewalk.

- Children "write" with water using an inverted water bottle or dish detergent bottle with a squirt top and time how long it takes to *evaporate*.
- Children spray water with spray bottles and compare evaporation times with water spread with a paintbrush. (Tell them they must aim the spray on the ground or a wall, not at a person.)
- Children dump a small bucket of water on the sidewalk and outline it in chalk. Does it take longer for a lot of water to *evaporate* than just a little bit of water?
- Children draw circles with chalk around puddles after the *rain* and observe how long they take to dry. They can draw multiple circles as the puddles *evaporate*. They measure puddle depths and compare evaporation times.

- Children compare evaporation times when they wash doll clothes and hang them up to dry. Set up a water table with doll clothes and a small scrub brush. Hang up two clothes lines—one in the shade and one in the sun or one in a windy place and one in a place out of the wind.
- Hang a BIG wet sheet on a clothesline (half sun and half shade would be ideal). Check on it every 10 minutes. Where does it start drying first—top or bottom, in the sun or shade?
- Give children large cotton scarves or squares of material cut from old sheets. Invite them to dunk the scarf in the water, squeeze it out, and then run with it. Does running help it dry?
- Fill two identical clear jars with about 2" of water. Cover one jar tightly with a lid. Leave the other uncovered. Mark the water level on both jars with permanent marker. Place the jars in a warm location indoors. Check every day to see what happens. How long does it take the air in the open jar to *evaporate*?

DISCUSSION STARTERS

Use these questions to spark children's thinking during and after the activity:

- Where is the water going?
- Can you see any steam rising from the evaporating puddles?
- Why do you think water *evaporates* more quickly on the chalkboards than the sidewalk?

SKILLS ASSESSMENT

Use these questions to determine a child's abilities and understanding:

- Can the child make a *prediction* about where the water will *evaporate* the fastest?
- Can the child use the vocabulary word *evaporate*?
- Is the child able to outline shapes such as letters with chalk before the water dries up?

Rainfall in the Sandbox

FOCUS AREAS

Science: studying changes in the Earth and sky, technological design

Math: counting, exploring three-dimensional shapes, estimating

MATERIALS

Plastic gutters

Large assortment of containers to mold sand—sand pails, thoroughly washed plastic containers, plastic cups

Sand shovels or homemade scoopers from laundry detergent containers (see page 302 in the Appendix for directions)

Garden hose or buckets of water

Saw horses or step stools to elevate one end of the gutter

WHAT TO DO

1. Help the children arrange gutters and hoses so they can explore how water flows downhill in gutters.

2. This activity is fun to do when it's *raining* as long as the children are dressed for the weather. It's also fun to do on a warm day when it doesn't matter if they get wet. If you can attach a garden hose to a gutter with a C-clamp, the children will explore for hours how water runs down gutters and creates pools. **Note**: Be sensitive to water use if your area is experiencing a drought. Catch the water at the end of the gutter to reuse.

3. One variation is to put a sprinkler head at the end of the hose to create *rain*.

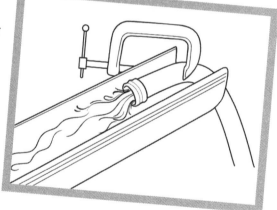

DISCUSSION STARTERS

Use these questions to spark children's thinking during and after the activity:

● Where is the water going?

● What happens to the sand when the water pours down the gutter?

● How does the water change the way sand feels?

● Is it easier to build with sand that is wet or dry?

SKILLS ASSESSMENT

Use these questions to determine a child's abilities and understanding:

● Can the child problem-solve when water doesn't flow where she wanted it?

● Can the child work as part of a team?

We Are Meteorologists

PREPARATION

- Prepare a graph labeled "Our Weather Record" to record the weather. It should have three columns: sun, clouds, and *rain*. Fill in the days you have school so you can record the weather.

- Make a red NO sign and green YES sign by folding each sheet of paper in half like a tent and writing the words in large letters on one side. Display the signs in back of two trays on a low table or the floor. If possible, prop or hang a *rain* photo or drawing above the green YES tray.

WHAT TO DO

1. When the children are gathered ask, "What is the weather today? Is it sunny? Is it cloudy? Is it *raining*? Ask the children how they can find out what the weather is. (Look out the window. Go outside).

2. Say, "People who study the weather are called *meteorologists*. Say and clap the syllables, me-te-or-**ol**-o-gist, with an emphasis on the "ol" syllable. Ask. "Have you seen a *meteorologist* on TV? Say *meteorologist* as you make the ASL sign for weather and a person who studies the weather. To sign *weather* make the sign for the letter W (three middle fingers sticking up, thumb and pinkie tucked in) with both hands. Make this sign by twisting both hands back and forth. Then add the sign that indicates a person's occupation: hold both palms facing each other in front of the chest, then move them down to indicate the sides of the body.

3. Say, "*Meteorologists* keep records about the weather for a long time. We are going to keep track of the weather like *meteorologists*. We'll check every day by looking out the window to see if we have a sunny day, a cloudy day, or a *rainy* day. Then we can count how many of each kind we have at the end of the week."

4. Show the children the weather recording graph. Say, "Here is our place to record our weather for each day. Because we agreed it is sunny now, I'm going to draw a sun in the sun column. Every day we are in school, we will record whether it is sunny, cloudy, or *rainy*."

FOCUS AREAS

Science: using data, studying weather

Math: counting, compiling data, graphing

Language Arts: learning vocabulary

MATERIALS

2 containers of square unit blocks, one per child

Photos or drawings of rain

Red sheet of construction paper

Green sheet of construction paper

2 trays

Chart paper and marker

Markers to draw sun, clouds, rain

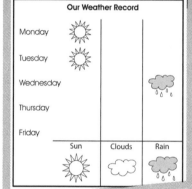

Our Weather Record

	Sun	Clouds	Rain
Monday	☀		
Tuesday	☀		
Wednesday			🌧
Thursday			
Friday			

Weather

Person Marker

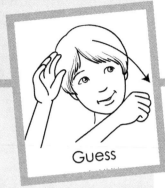

Guess

5. Say, "*Meteorologists* also make *predictions* about what the weather will be like later. Do you think it will *rain* by the end of school today?" (If it's already *raining* ask, "Do you think it will still be *raining* at the end of school today?")

6. Review the word *prediction*, something that you think might happen based on what you already know. Say and clap the syllables, pre-**dic**-tion, with the emphasis on the "dic" syllable. Say *prediction* as you make the sign for guess by moving your open right hand across your forehead and grabbing the air.

7. Ask, "How can you predict if it will *rain* or not? (Look out the window. Look for clouds. Watch the weather news on TV. Listen to weather reports on the radio.) Say, "Because you are all *meteorologists* you can each make a *prediction*. We'll keep track of your *predictions* with blocks."

8. You and an assistant pass around bins of blocks. Each child selects one block. Show the children the red NO and Green YES. Ask them what they think the signs say. Invite the children one at a time to put their block on the NO tray if they think it will not *rain*, or put their block on the YES tray if they think it will *rain*, to create two stacks. Count both stacks. Which stack has more?

9. Say, "At the end of school, we will check the weather again to see if it is *raining* or not."

TEACHER-TO-TEACHER TIPS
- Be careful not to make children feel they are "wrong" if they predict incorrectly. You or another adult can put a block in the least likely column so the children will feel comfortable making a *prediction*. If your *prediction* is wrong say, "It didn't *rain* after all. I'll try again tomorrow." Or say, "Weather is not always easy to predict, even grown-up *meteorologists* don't always know exactly when it will *rain* or snow or be windy or sunny." The children may forget what they predicted or insist they were right regardless. That's okay.
- You can keep track of the weather for as long as you and the children are interested. Depending on the time of year or your climate, you can later add columns for snow, wind, or any other kind of weather.

DISCUSSION STARTERS
Use these questions to spark children's thinking during and after the activity:
- Do you think it will rain tomorrow?
- Do you wear different clothes when it is raining outside?

SKILLS ASSESSMENT
Use these questions to determine a child's abilities and understanding:
- Can the child explain why she made the prediction: "I think it will rain because it is very cloudy."
- Can the child clap the syllables for *meteorologist*?

Measure the Rain with Rain Gauges

FOCUS AREAS

Science: using simple equipment, studying weather

Math: counting, measuring—length, using standard and nonstandard measuring tools

Language Arts: learning vocabulary

MATERIALS

Clear plastic containers with straight sides, such as deli containers (Containers don't need to be the same size—they just need to have straight sides. **Safety note:** Make sure recycled containers did not contain toxic materials and that they are cleaned well.)

Tongue depressors, 1 for each child

Masking tape

Permanent markers

Duplicated copies of a ruler, one per child

Clear wide packing tape or clear contact paper

Yarn, enough for each child to have several inches

Commercial rain gauge (optional)

PREPARATION

- Draw a model of a *rain gauge* at least 2' tall, or as tall as you like, depending on the usual rainfall in your area. Label this drawing "How Much Rain Falls at Our School?"
- Make copies of a ruler about 3" tall, one for each child. You can either copy about 3" of a ruler directly on a copying machine if you have one with clear, BIG numbers but it may be easier to draw one yourself and then make copies.
- Cut clear tape or contact paper into strips 3" long to cover the paper rulers

WHAT TO DO

1. Ask the children if they have ideas how they can measure how much *rain* falls. Show the children a commercial *rain gauge* if you have one and explain how it catches the *rain*.

2. Say, "We can make our own *rain gauges*. Introduce the word *rain gauge*, an instrument for measuring *rain*. Say and clap the syllables, *rain gauge*. Say *rain gauge* as you make the ASL signs for *rain* and *measure*. For *rain*, hold both hands with fingers gently curved, palms facing down, and then move them up and down several times while moving your fingers as if *rain* were falling. For measure, hold right and left Y hands (thumb and pinkie extended middle three fingers tucked in) palm down and touch the thumbs together several times.

3. Ask, "Do you have any ideas how we could measure how much *rain* falls?" Give each child a plastic container. Invite them to write their name using a

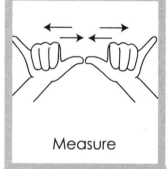

How Much Rain Falls at Our School?

Measure

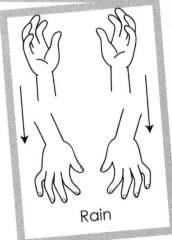

Rain

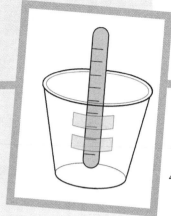

permanent marker on a piece of masking tape, or an adult can write it for them, and place it on the container. Older children can write "rain gauge" on another piece of tape or an adult can write it for them and then place the tape on the container.

4. The children cut out a paper ruler, and then lay the ruler face down in the center of the packing tape or contact paper strip, sticky side up. The children place the tongue depressor or Popsicle stick on the paper ruler and then wrap the edges of the tape around the tongue depressor. (Some children may need help to make sure the packing tape covers and protects the paper numbers.) Then the children tape the tongue depressor to the plastic container, numbers facing out.

5. If you make the *rain gauges* on a *rainy* day, the children place their containers outside, away from trees or buildings.

6. Ask the children to predict how much *rain* will be in their container by snack time or the end of the day, whenever you are going to bring them in. Record their *prediction*.

7. At the end of the day, the children can check how much water is in their containers. They will need help to read the amount. Help them cut a piece of yarn or paper the height of the water and compare it to something they are familiar with such as the length of their thumb or from the floor to the top of their shoe.

8. Keep either a commercial *rain gauge* or a homemade one at school and record the rainfall on your giant paper chart after each storm. Note the date and the amount of water and color it in with blue marker.

MORE IDEAS

- Invite children to draw a picture of the *rain* and dictate a story about how much *rain* fell in their gauge. "It was *raining* so hard that the *rain* was as high as two blocks stacked on top of each other."
- The children can take their *rain gauges* home; just let them know that the paper numbers might not last in the *rain*. They can still measure how high the water gets with a plastic ruler.

DISCUSSION STARTERS

Use these questions to spark children's thinking during and after the activity:

- How does *rain* get into our *rain* gauges?
- Did you collect as much *rain* as you thought you would?

SKILLS ASSESSMENT

Use these questions to determine a child's abilities and understanding:

- Can the child compare the *rain* measurement with the height of a familiar item?
- How did the child's estimate compare with the result?

Here Comes the Rain

TEACHER-TO-TEACHER TIPS

- The sound of a gentle *rain* can be soothing, but fierce thunder and lightening storms are scary. Acting out a storm can help children feel more in control.
- You can teach children that they can tell how far away a BIG storm is by counting the time between a lightning flash and the thunder. It's about one mile for every five seconds. So if they count to 10, (one one thousand, two one thousand, and so on) the storm is about two miles away.

FOCUS AREAS

Science: studying weather

Math: counting how far away a storm is

Language Arts: experiencing different types of texts, retelling a story

Music: learning different sounds

MATERIALS

Story of a rainstorm such as *Listen to the Rain* by Bill Martin Jr. (See Good Books for Facts and Fun on pages 119–121.)
Rainstick (optional)
Drum (optional)
Strips of aluminum foil or silver Mylar about 6" long, 1 per child
Sheet of chart paper
Marker
Words to the poem (see left) written out in large letters

WHAT TO DO

1. Read a story about a thunderstorm. Ask the children what sounds they heard in the story. Ask what sounds they hear when it *rains*. Write their responses on chart paper, noting each child's name.
2. Say, "Let's make our own storm and we can decide when to make it loud and soft."
3. Introduce the elements of the storm. Demonstrate your *rain*stick if you have one. Ask, "How could we make a noise that sounds like soft gentle *rain*?" Demonstrate soft tapping on your legs. Invite the children to do what you do.
4. Move through the sounds of a storm with louder and louder pats on your legs and the floor.
   - Say, "Get ready for lightning." Pick up your aluminum foil and wave it in the air.
   - Say, "Get ready for thunder. How should we make a loud boom?" Clap your hands.
   - Say, "Get ready for wind." Make a whooshing sound.
5. Reverse the actions from loud to quiet.
6. Introduce the following *rain* poem and create the sounds and actions with the children.

Rainstorm *by Tim Dobbins*
It's calm before the storm.
I hear no sound at all.
It's hush, hush, hush.
Now something's happening.
I hear the breeze rustle, rustle, rustle.
The leaves flutter, flutter, flutter.
The chime goes tinkle, tinkle, tink.
Do I hear the rain going pitter, pitter pat?
Yes, I hear it drop, drop, drop.
I hear it plop, plop, plop.
The wind goes whoosh, whoosh, whoosh.

The flag goes flap, flap, flap.
The rain pounds the roof.
I see the lightning flash.
I hear the thunder crash.
I see the people dash,
Until they're safe inside.
Now the storm is passing.
I hear it pitter, pitter, pat.
I see the sun peek out.
I see a puddle!
Let's go splash, splash, splash!

7. At another time, go around the circle having each child take a turn deciding whether to act out loud or soft *rain;* lightning, thunder, or wind; or puddle splashing.

SUPERSIZE IT!

- After you have done a few rainstorms, you can add more elements. Tell the class you are going to make the room a little darker like it's a BIG storm. Either turn off some lights or close some blinds. (Don't make it totally dark; that's too scary.) Invite a child to take a turn turning on the lights when it's time for lightning. The rest of the group can wave their aluminum foil.
- Ask the children what's a bigger noise you could make for thunder (a drum). Be sensitive to children who don't like loud noises. Don't make the noise too loud and tell these children when the thunder is coming so they can cover their ears.

DISCUSSION STARTERS

Use these questions to spark children's thinking during and after the activity:
- What did you think when we made lightning?
- What did you think when we made thunder?
- Do you like loud *rain* or quiet *rain* better?

SKILLS ASSESSMENT

Use these questions to determine a child's abilities and understanding:
- Can the child follow directions?
- Can the child vary the sounds from soft to loud to match the poem?

Puddle Game

FOCUS AREAS
Math: counting, learning one-to-one correspondence
Language Arts: learning vocabulary
Gross Motor: jumping, hopping

MATERIALS
Chalk for outdoors
String or yarn indoors
Tape for indoors
Giant die (see page 300 in the Appendix for directions to make)
Game cards (see below)

Rescue Worm — Jump Ahead 2 • •

Get Stuck in Mud — Stay Where You Are

Car Splashes You — Jump Back 3 • • •

Get Water in Boots — Jump Back 2 • •

Frog Jumps in Your Puddle — Jump Ahead 3 • • •

Splash Your Teacher — Stay Where You Are

Wind Blows — Jump Ahead 4 • • • •

Rain Jacket Leaks — Jump Back 3 • • •

PREPARATION
- Copy and laminate two sets of game cards (see illustration).

WHAT TO DO
1. Work with a small group of children. Decide whether you want to play indoors or outdoors. If playing outdoors, invite the children to draw about 15 BIG chalk puddles a comfortable jumping distance from each other in an open area. Tell the children the puddles have to be BIG enough to stand in. They can make them in a long line or a circle. The advantage of placing them in a circle is that there is no beginning or end, so no one "wins" and the children go around the circle as long as they like. If playing indoors, make "puddles" out of string, as many as you have room for. Help keep the string puddles in place with a few pieces of masking tape.
2. The children begin one at a time at any puddle of their choosing. The first child chooses a picture card and follows the directions. An adult

can help the child interpret the picture and move the correct number of spaces. For example, the child may choose a picture of rescuing a worm. The child jumps ahead two puddles.

3. The children take turns choosing a card and following the directions. Some cards are bad news so the child jumps back. It's okay if two children land on the same puddle.

4. The children pick cards and jump as long as they like. The fun is in counting and jumping.

MORE IDEAS

- Give the children a choice of picking a card or rolling a giant die and jumping the number shown on the die.
- Challenge the children to change the types of jumps, "three giant splashing jumps, four little jumps so you barely make a ripple." (Model using descriptive vocabulary: "I see you are making gigantic jumps in those huge puddles. Are you getting all wet?")
- Change the movement: hop on one foot, giant steps.
- Make the game formal by creating a path with a beginning puddle and a picture of a dry home at the end. The children begin at the beginning puddle and draw cards or roll the die to eventually reach "home."
- If the die lands in the puddle when a player rolls it, everyone gets to hop into as many puddles as the die says. If the die lands outside a puddle then they move back that many.

TEACHER-TO-TEACHER TIP

When children draw puddles for the game and are themselves the game pieces, they "own" the game and often create their own variations. In our class, one child decided to draw a bridge across the circle as a shortcut. Another decided to walk around the puddles on her turn.

DISCUSSION STARTERS

Use these questions to spark children's thinking during and after the activity:
- Do you prefer BIG jumps or little jumps?
- What happens when you jump in real puddles?

SKILLS ASSESSMENT

Use these questions to determine a child's abilities and understanding:
- Can the child count correctly the number of dots on the card or the die?
- Can the child move the correct number of puddles?

More Activities Across the Curriculum

LANGUAGE ARTS

- Invite the children to draw pictures of *rain* and dictate stories. Include *rain* books and vocabulary words at the table for inspiration. Topics for different days:
  - What do you like do on a *rainy* day?
  - If you were a raindrop, where would you like to travel?
  - How does a quiet *rain* or BIG noisy *rain*storm sound and feel?
  - Which type of storm do you like best?

  To heighten interest, cut paper in the shape of a raindrop for the children to draw on. Mount the stories under the shape of a giant umbrella or raincloud. When you take down the display, keep the drawings in each child's portfolio.
- The children can explore their feelings about *rain* by making up new verses to the chant:

  Rain, rain, go away,
  Come again another day.

  Suggestions:
  Rain, rain, come today,
  We want to splash and play.

  Rain, rain, come today,
  Plants need water right away.

ART/SCIENCE

- Children *experiment* drawing with washable markers compared with permanent (*waterproof*) markers. The children drip water on their drawings using eyedroppers or pipettes. What happens? (Children often decide they don't want their drawing to wash away and use only the permanent markers. Suggest they make "scribble drawings" to test the washable markers.) Make sure the child's name is written in permanent marker. **Variations**: Children make multiple drawings or a group one in both washable and permanent markers and choose one to place outside in a light *rain* to see what happens. Children make group drawings on giant butcher paper and then place them outside in a light *rain*. Ask the children to predict what will happen to the drawings in the *rain*.
- Children explore evaporation with water color paint. The children wet their paper with clear water. Then they use water colors or dilute tempera paint to make a painting. Observe what happens to the paint on the wet paper. Set the paintings aside to dry. How do they change as the water *evaporates*?
- Children draw a line with a permanent marker down the center of their paper. They paint one half on the page with clear water, leaving the other half dry. Then they use water color to paint both the wet side and the dry side. How do the colors compare?

- Children draw on the sidewalk with chalk during the *rain*. Or they draw on dry sidewalk and wet with squirt bottles.
- Children use spray bottles with diluted water color to spray giant paper on the ground or hung up on a fence. Watch the *drops* run and the colors combine. Remind the children to point the spray bottles only at the paper.

SCIENCE/MATH

- Help the children set up drip *drop* races in the water table. Set out sheets of Plexiglas, metal cookie sheets, wooden boards, and short lengths of plastic *rain* gutters. Ask the children which material they think a drip will run down the fastest. After listening to their suggestions, count how long it takes a *drop* to run all the way down each material.
- Draw shapes (circle, square, triangle, hexagon) on paper towels using permanent markers. The children fill in the shapes with liquid water color *drops*. If they add *drops* slowly their color stays inside the shapes. Children can count the number of *drops* it takes to fill in a shape. Variations: Using a bull's eye set of rings, children can count how many *drops* it takes to fill the inner ring, and how many more to overflow the inner ring and fill the second, larger ring.
- Children estimate how many *drops* it will take to fill a small plastic bottle cap. Make it BIG by using turkey basters and measuring cups.
- Children make rainsticks by cutting berry baskets in half and inserting several pieces in a paper towel tube, empty tennis ball can, or a clear plastic cover for fluorescent light tubes. Add about ¼ cup birdseed to make the noise. Cover the ends with plastic lids or paper secured with masking tape or duct tape. Count how long it takes the bird seed to fall. Compare sounds with those in a longer gift wrap paper tube.

COOKING/MATH

- Help the children make lemonade to discover how water is an essential ingredient. First have the children squeeze a lemon. Does the juice taste like lemonade? What else do you need? The children can make individual portions to practice measuring:

  ½ teaspoon lemon juice
  ½ cup water
  ½ teaspoon sugar
  Mix in a paper cup and enjoy.

DRAMA/MUSIC

- Children sing and dance to "Singin' in the Rain." Charlotte Diamond has a recording on her CD, *Charlotte Diamond's World*.

BIG Outcomes

Group assessment: Review the graph of sunny, *rainy*, and cloudy days and photo boards about walking in the *rain,* testing to find out what is waterproof, and experimenting with water in the water table. Review the chart paper sheets from the beginning of the exploration of what the children know about *rain* and what they want to learn. On a third sheet of chart paper titled "What We Learned About Rain," record the children's comments about what they learned, including the name of the child who made the comment. Note answers to the children's original questions, or note if you still have more to learn and explore.

Individual assessment: Review your notes and quotes from individual observations during activities, such as the *waterproof experiments*, water table explorations, and evaporation and *rain gauge experiments*. Review the children's work and save in portfolios. Be sure to note areas in which the children need further practice and those in which they excel.

GOOD BOOKS FOR FACTS AND FUN

From sizzling sidewalks to sun-baked savannahs, rain refreshes the parched Earth and brings relief from heat. Stories of storms and puddles add drama and humor to your exploration of the science of the earth's water cycle. Visit your library if the children want more information about floods, weather forecasting, or waterfalls.

INFORMATION ABOUT RAIN

Down Comes the Rain by Franklyn M. Branley
Cheery drawings of an active, multi-cultural quartet of children and their dogs who
   explore and explain rain, the water cycle, storms, clouds, and hailstones. Ages 4–6

Let's Look at a Puddle by Angela Royston
An elementary introduction to water, as a liquid shown in puddles of different shapes
   and sizes, splashing and floating, and water as a solid, presented in a question-and-
   answer format. Ages 3–4

A Rainy Day by Sandra Markle
Watercolor illustrations accurately suggest the look of a rainy day experienced by a
   young girl out and about in her yellow slicker and boots. The information-filled text
   flows easily in a gentle story format. Ages 3–6

The Rainy Day by Anna Milbourne and Sarah Gill
A trio of cheerful young explorers enjoys an enthusiastic and realistic rainy day ramble
   in spite of some wet socks along the way. Their delightfully illustrated walk forms
   the backdrop for basic information about rain. Ages 3–5

Rainy Days by Jennifer S. Burke

This overview covers many aspects of rain—from *rain* gear to raindrops, from playing outside to staying inside. All are shown and described with color photos, simple sentences, and bold words. The book includes a glossary and an index. Ages 3–4

Rainy Weather Days by Pam Rosenberg

Combining a word hunt, vocabulary words in bold text, and bright color photos, this book highlights meteorologists, sleet, close-up pictures of drops, and drop sizes, as well as a glossary and index. Ages 4–6

The Water Cycle by Joy Richardson

Three brief, one- to two-sentence paragraphs offer explanations, including numbers and facts, relating to each full page. Simple images of salt water, solid, liquid, and gas states of water, of treatment plants, and of water taps help tell the story. Ages 3–6

What Do You See in a Cloud? by Allan Fowler

Color photos focus on shapes, cloud shadows, the water cycle, storms, and cloud types. Accurate details are ideal for sharing with older students. Ages 4–6

When a Storm Comes Up by Allan Fowler

In a positive tone, Fowler offers facts and clearly defines drizzle and downpour using examples of a familiar shower and pouring rain. He also covers the danger of lightning, rain, hail, and snowstorms, including some photos of serious destruction. Ages 4–6

Where Do Puddles Go? by Fay Robinson

Puddle evaporation provides a focus to introduce the water cycle. Simple, color photos, a photo-illustrated glossary, and a clear diagram of happy clouds and sun help to clear up the mystery. Ages 3–6

STORIES ABOUT RAIN

Come On, Rain! by Karen Hesse

Sweltering in the city heat, Tess senses the coming storm and gathers her friends to dance in the streets in their bathing suits. Their joy brings their mothers out to join them in a summer celebration illustrated in spare, graceful watercolors. Ages 4–6

I Love the Rain by Margaret Park Bridges

Sophie shares her poetic vision of freckle-faced puddles, streets that shine like patent-leather shoes, and race car raindrops with rain-hating Molly in this exuberant celebration of nature and friendship. Ages 4–6

It's Raining, It's Pouring by Andrea Spalding

Determined to end the rain, Little Girl bravely helps heal Old Man's head cold, taking the suffering giant in the sky a wheelbarrow full of lemon juice and honey. A well-drawn, imaginative twist on the old rhyme ends with sunshine returning. Ages 4–6

Like a Hundred Drums by Annette Griessman
Fluttering leaves, a change in the breeze; little by little the birds, animals, and people
realize that a booming and cracking thunderstorm is on its way. Realistic details
reveal the power of the storm but muted illustrations soften the threat. Ages 3–5

Listen to the Rain by Bill Martin Jr.
This rain classic is a poetic combination of sound words, lyrical rhythms, and elegant,
spare images. It's not so much a story but an invitation to hear and see a common
natural event in a new way. Ages 3–6

Monsoon by Uma Krishnaswami
Surrounded by the sounds, smells and heat of a sun-drenched town in Northern India,
a young girl waits and watches for signs that the monsoon is about to begin. An
explanatory note adds more information about this loved and feared season of rain.
Ages 4–6

The Puddle by David McPhail
Out to play in the rain, a little boy obeys his mother and stays out of the puddle, but the
frog, crocodile, pig, and elephant don't. The silliness of this afternoon adventure ends
with a soak in the tub for the boy and his bedraggled boat. Ages 3–5

Rain by Manya Stojic
Bold and exuberant art compliments the drama of an impending rainstorm on a hot
African plain. A drumbeat of simple sentences focuses on the animals' senses,
smell, sound, and touch before and after the rain crashes down. Ages 3–6

Storm Is coming! by Heather Tekavec
Herded into the barn by the clueless dog's storm warning, farm animals, after
proposing goofy ideas based on fears and misinterpreted facts, conclude that
"Storm" never came. Wry and suspenseful, this book ties in science observation.
Ages 3–6

This Is the Rain by Lola M. Schaefer
Jazzy, vibrant photo collages illustrate a cumulative-style rhyme that follows rain from
the vast blue ocean into water vapor, raindrops and rivers and back to the sea
again, watering parched canyons along the way. Ages 4–6

A Note to Families About Rain

Dear Families,

You know how much children love water! At school, your children are exploring how water falls as rain. We want to take a walk in the rain one day at school so your children can use their senses to experience the outdoor world when it is wet. Please send your child to school with rain gear if you have some. We know not everyone has rain gear, so if you have extra rain jackets, boots, or umbrellas could you lend them to us to share with other children? We will be careful to go for a walk only during a gentle rain, but children sometimes get wet anyway, so please send an extra set of clothes with your child.

At home, you can help children learn about water as they wash their hands and take a bath. They will enjoy using different plastic containers to fill and pour in the sink or in the bathtub. Empty water bottles or shampoo bottles are fun to squeeze. Just tell your child to aim the squeeze towards the water. You can set up a target practice with a plastic bowl or container.

We are also learning about the weather, specifically how rain comes from clouds, falls to the ground, and then goes back up into the air through evaporation. You can help your child learn about the weather by watching the weather forecast on television or checking the newspaper.

Here are some of the words we've been learning about rain:
- When puddles get warmed by the sun, the water evaporates and goes back into the air.
- Something that keeps out water is waterproof.
- A meteorologist is a person who studies the weather.

Have fun splashing in the puddles and watching clouds with your meteorologist!

5 THINKING BIG ABOUT LIGHT, COLORS, AND RAINBOWS

THE BIG PICTURE

Exploring rainbows lets children discover that what seems like magic—a band of colors appearing in the sky—really is science; amazing, delightful science.

All you need are two everyday ingredients—sun and water—to explore the beautiful physics of rainbows. It is truly awesome to make a rainbow appear by spraying a fine mist of water high into the sky on a sunny day. Children can see for themselves that the little drops of water bend and bounce the white light from the sun, making all the individual colors visible. Children can create the same rainbow band of colors when they hold a CD or prism in the sun or a flashlight beam. (Technically, this is not a rainbow because it is not light shining through water, but it is a great opportunity to consider "same" and "different" aspects of light.)

This unit also helps children experiment with color and color combinations. No matter how many times they mix red and blue, it is still wondrous to create purple.

TIMING TIP

It's fun to use the rainbow topic to begin the school year. Children love the beauty of rainbows and what seems like magic. Children also feel comfortable exploring color. It's wonderful to study rainbows after the children have seen one at school, or around St. Patrick's Day when you read folk tales about pots of gold at the end of the rainbow. Plan your rainbow study for warm, sunny weather to allow children to make their own rainbows outside. Rainbows also connect to the rain unit in this book (pages 95–122).

OBJECTIVES

- Learn about a natural phenomenon that fascinates children.
- Learn about the science and beauty of light, colors, and color combinations.
- Start to understand that while rainbows seem like magic, scientists have learned how rainbows form.

STANDARDS

National Science Education Content Standards

- Science as inquiry—ask questions; plan and conduct a simple investigation; use simple equipment and tools; communicate investigations and explanations
- Physical science—explore the properties of light
- Earth and space science—recognize changes in the Earth and sky

National Council of Teachers of Mathematics Standards

- Number and operations—count with understanding
- Algebra—sort, classify, and order objects
- Geometry—recognize, name, and draw two- and three-dimensional shapes
- Measurement—understand how to measure using nonstandard and standard tools
- Data analysis and probability—represent data using pictures and graphs
- Communication—organize, analyze, and evaluate mathematical thinking; use the language of mathematics

Standards for the English Language Arts

- Experience a wide range of print and non-print texts, including fiction and non-fiction, to build an understanding of the world and acquire new information
- Use spoken, written, and visual language to communicate and learn
- Generate ideas and questions and pose problems
- Build vocabulary

Introducing Rainbow Colors

FOCUS AREAS

Science: studying light and color

Math: counting, sequencing, learning about an arc as a shape

Language Arts: communicating and generating ideas and questions

MATERIALS

Photograph or book illustration of a rainbow (See Good Books for Facts and Fun on pages 142–143)

White poster board or chart paper mounted on an easel or wall to make a backdrop for rainbow colors

3 sheets of chart paper and markers

Construction paper in rainbow colors—red, orange, yellow, green, blue, indigo (dark blue), and violet

Scissors (adult-only)

2 trays

Several glue sticks or dispensers of transparent tape

Prism, crystal decoration, or CD you don't mind being handled

Flashlight

TEACHER-TO-TEACHER TIPS

- A classic way to remember the rainbow order (also called the color spectrum) is the name ROY G BIV: red, orange, yellow, green, blue, indigo, and violet. Young children may not understand how the letters stand for the colors, but it is handy information for you and will help you remember red is always on the top.
- You can create the rainbow colors by shining a flashlight on an old CD or through a prism or crystal decoration. This technically is not a rainbow because it is not shining through mist. A prism will show the colors in rainbow order more clearly than a CD but it is sometimes hard to see the colors in a bright room. A flashlight shining on a CD works every time.

PREPARATION

- Label one sheet of chart paper "What We Know About Rainbows" and another "What We Want to Learn About Rainbows."
- Draw a large rainbow on the third sheet of chart paper using 1" bands of color. Color in the bands with markers or paint.
- Cut the construction paper into 1" squares, one per child of each rainbow color.
- Place the squares on two trays in stacks by color so children will have a choice of squares to pick from.
- Practice making a spectrum of rainbow colors. Shine a bright flashlight through a prism or a crystal decoration and project it onto the white poster board. This can be hard to do but it does show the rainbow colors in order. The colors often show up better in a dark room so try closing the curtains and dimming the lights. Shining a flashlight on an old CD reliably shows a vivid display of colors that changes as you move the CD but the order of the colors isn't as clear.

WHAT TO DO

1. When the children gather for group time, show them a photo or illustration of a rainbow. Introduce the word *rainbow*. Say and clap **rain**-bow, with the emphasis on the "rain" syllable. Say *rainbow* as you make the ASL sign, four fingers on both hands spread apart, thumbs tucked in. The fingers of both hands touch on your left side, and then your right hand outlines a rainbow in front of you. Point out the shape, an arc, part of a circle.

2. Ask the children if they have ever seen a rainbow. Talk about when (night or day) they saw a rainbow, where

Rainbow

they saw it, and what the rainbow looked like. Ask what they think is needed to make a rainbow in the sky (sunlight, rain). Write down their responses, including each child's name, on the chart paper labeled "What We Know About Rainbows."

3. Ask the children what they want to find out about rainbows and record those responses on the second sheet of chart paper.

4. Hang up your rainbow drawing low enough so the children will later be able to add to it. Say, "We can make these rainbow colors with a flashlight. We are going to close the curtains and dim the lights so we can see the colors better." Ask a child to be your rainbow color assistant and to shine the flashlight on a prism or CD to make the rainbow colors. (Tell the children that this isn't a real rainbow because it is not shining through mist.) Ask the children what colors they see. Write down all the colors they name and say that in rainbows red is always at the top, then orange, yellow, and so on. Explain that *indigo* is often very hard to see but it's about the color of dark blue jeans. You can formally introduce the words *indigo* and *violet* here or wait until a later activity (see BIG Beginning II).

5. Invite the children to choose a construction paper square from the tray you pass to each child. The process will go faster if an adult assistant passes a second tray in the opposite direction. Say, "You can add your rainbow colors to my drawing. We will start with all the people who chose red." Help the children glue or tape their red squares to the red band in your drawing. Repeat this with the remaining colors.

6. Admire your rainbow by counting the colors and by reviewing the names and the order of the seven rainbow colors.

A Note from the Author: The activities in this chapter are designed to build on each other. However, please feel free to choose those that meet the interests and abilities of your class. If parts of an activity seem like too much to do on a particular day, save them for a later time. Every class is different, even from day to day, and the activities are adaptable to meet the needs of your class.

MORE IDEAS

● Put old CDs, plastic prisms, plastic mirrors and flashlights at a learning center table for children to explore later independently.

BIG BEGINNING II:
Mixing Rainbow Colors

FOCUS AREAS

Science: studying light and colors

Math: counting, sequencing

MATERIALS

Photograph (See Good Books for Facts and Fun on pages 142–143) or your rainbow drawing from Introducing Rainbow Colors

7 clear plastic bottles with caps, 1 quart or larger, with labels removed

Red, blue, and yellow food coloring

Funnel

Bowl of water to rinse the funnel

Low table

PREPARATION

- Fill three bottles to the top with water and leave four empty.
- Line up the plastic bottles on the low table, alternating filled and empty bottles. You will have two empty bottles on the end.

WHAT TO DO

1. When the children gather for group time show them a photo or the drawing you made of a rainbow. Review the colors in rainbow color order—red, orange, yellow, green, blue, indigo, violet. Count the colors.

2. Say, "Let's see if we can make the colors we see in rainbows." Show them the food coloring and ask if they know what it is and what will happen if you put some into the clear water.

3. Start by adding several drops of red food coloring into the first bottle. Ask the children to identify the color. Cap and shake the bottle and add more coloring if you do not have a deep true red.

4. Drip a couple drops of yellow food coloring into the third bottle. Go slowly, adding just enough to make yellow. (Too many drops will make the yellow appear orange.) Ask the children to name the color. Drip several drops of blue coloring into the fifth bottle to make a medium blue. Ask the name of the color.

5. Count the colors. Ask the children if these three colors are all the colors in rainbows. Ask, "Do you know how we can make the other colors?" After listening to the children's ideas, tell them that you are going to try mixing red, blue, and yellow to make the colors. Pour one quarter of the red into bottle number two, (using a funnel if necessary and rinsing the funnel between different colors) then pour in just enough yellow to make orange. Pour half of the remaining yellow into bottle number four and add a little blue to make green. Pour a third of the remaining blue into the last bottle and add about half as much red as the blue to make violet. Introduce the word *violet*, another word for purple. Say and clap **vi**-o-let, with the emphasis on the "vi" syllable. Say *violet* as you point to the bottle of violet water.

6. Count the colors. Ask, "What color are we missing?" Then say you are going to try to make the hardest color to see in a rainbow. Pour some of your blue water into the sixth bottle then add some more blue food coloring so it's really dark. Add a tiny bit of violet. Say, this is indigo. Say and clap **in**-di-go, with the emphasis on the "in" syllable. Say *indigo* as you point to your bottle of indigo water.

7. Count the colors. Ask the children to close their eyes while you mix up the order of the bottles. Invite the children to suggest how to put them back in rainbow order.

8. Save the bottles of colors to enjoy at the water table or to use in art projects.

TEACHER-TO-TEACHER TIP

If you make a mistake with the color mixing and add too much yellow so it looks orange, for example, use it as a teachable moment. Say, "I made a mistake and added too much yellow. Do you have any ideas how I can make this look more like yellow to fix my mistake?" (Pour out some of the yellow water and add more clear water.) It is actually a relief for children to know that even their teacher makes mistakes.

BIG QUESTIONS FOR GROWING MINDS

Use the following questions to engage the children in a discussion about rainbows during group time or with an individual child during activity time:

- What is surprising about rainbows?
- What do you like about rainbows?
- Have you seen rainbows of different sizes and shapes? What did they look like?

ANSWERING BIG QUESTIONS

What makes a rainbow? The exact science of rainbow formation involves angles and rays but the basic ideas can be explained simply. First, sunlight shines into a raindrop. Then the light reflects (bounces back) off the far side of the raindrop, bounces once more inside the drop and comes out separated into the rainbow colors. We see rainbows when the sun is behind us and the raindrops are in front of us because of these reflections in the drops.

WORDS FOR BIG THINKING

Look for these words highlighted in italics throughout the activities in this chapter. Write the words out in large letters and introduce them a few at a time with the "**S**ay, **C**lap, **A**ct out, **D**o again" (SCAD) system. Using the words during activities and discussions will reinforce their meaning.

- Indigo—deep blue-violet, the color of blue jeans
- Rainbow—an arc of colors formed in the sky when sunlight shines through rain
- Reflect—to bounce back
- Separate—to take apart
- Violet—another word for purple

PHOTO TIP

You can record children's explorations of rainbows by creating photo boards about making a giant *rainbow* outdoors, hunting for colors, and observing *rainbow* colors by using CDs, crystals, and prisms. Look for close-ups of individual children and groups of children interacting. Also include vocabulary words and quotes from children on the photo boards to document their learning.

Make a Giant Rainbow

TEACHER-TO-TEACHER TIPS

- If it's a hot day, you may want your young scientists to wear swimsuits when you make *rainbows* with the hose. They will love running through the *rainbow*. If it's chilly, make sure they stand out of the water spray.
- Children will enjoy having a turn to spray the nozzle but you must supervise this closely so children don't spray each other. Say, "You may take turns as long as you spray the water up into the air away from others."
- If you don't have access to water and a hose outdoors it may be possible to arrange a field trip to a fire station and have the firefighters spray one of their hoses in the air in addition to showing off their fire trucks. Or you might be able to arrange a field trip to a car wash, car rental agency, garden nursery, or any type of business that uses a hose, and ask if they would shoot water into the air for your class. It must be a sunny day.

FOCUS AREAS

Science: asking questions about events in the environment

Math: measuring—time

Language Arts: communicating and generating ideas and questions

MATERIALS

Garden hose
Hose spray nozzle
Spray bottles

PREPARATION

- Find an open area where you can spray a hose into the air. Practice making a *rainbow*, spraying fine mist in to the air, with your back to the sun. You may need an assistant to tell you if the *rainbow* is visible. Experiment to find out which background—light or dark—shows the best colors.

WHAT TO DO

1. On a sunny day, tell the class they are going to go outside and make *rainbows*.
2. Once you are outside, invite everyone to face the sun, but not stare directly at it. While standing off to one side, spray a fine mist of water from the garden hose nozzle up into the air across the children's field of view. Look for the *rainbow*. There won't be one because the children are looking toward the sun.
3. Now have everyone turn their backs to the sun. They should be able to see their shadows. While standing off to one side, spray a fine mist of water from the garden hose nozzle up into the air across the children's field of view. Look for the *rainbow*. Make sure there is plenty of room for children to move around to find the best spot to view the *rainbow*.
4. Vary the stream of water to change the size and intensity of the *rainbow*. Experiment to find which background—light or dark—gives the best colors.
5. Invite the children to count how long they can see the *rainbow*. (Often a breeze will come up or the size of the mist will change so the *rainbow* doesn't last forever.)
   Note: See the following activity—Make a Giant Rainbow, Part Two—for Discussion Starters and Skills Assessments.

Make a Giant Rainbow, Part Two

WHAT TO DO

1. After you have made a giant *rainbow* outdoors, come back as a group to talk about how *rainbows* are formed. Ask, "What did we use to make *rainbows*?" "What did the *rainbow* look like?" Record the children's comments, including each child's name.

2. Say, "It's hard to see how tiny raindrops and sun make *rainbows* but we'll do some BIG demonstrations to show what happens." Invite a child to bounce a ball on the floor. Ask the group, "Where does the ball go when it bounces?" (up, back to you).

3. Place a mirror on the floor. Invite a child to shine a flashlight on the mirror. Ask, "What happens to the light?" (It bounces off the mirror and shines on the ceiling.)

4. Introduce the word *reflect*, which means to bounce back. A mirror *reflects* light just like the ball bounces back. Say and clap re-**flect**, with the emphasis on the "flect" syllable. Say *reflect* as you make the ASL sign. The left palm faces out. The right flat hand touches the left palm and bounces so the right palm faces out.

5. Say, "When the sun shines on raindrops, each drop *reflects* the sunlight and bounces it back, separating the light into the colors we see. This is similar to the way the light *separates* into colors when it shines through a prism or on a CD."

6. Conclude by making the ASL sign for *rainbow*—four fingers on both hands touching each other, then the right hand moves in a giant arc above the head.

MORE IDEAS

- Introduce the word *separate*. Say and clap **sep**-a-rate, with the emphasis on the "sep" syllable. Say *separate* as you move your two hands apart. Sunlight *separates* into the *rainbow* colors when it bounces around the raindrops.

DISCUSSION STARTERS

Use these questions to spark children's thinking during and after the activity:

- What did you find out about making *rainbows*?
- What did the *rainbows* that we made with the hose look like?
- What did the *rainbows* that we made with the spray bottles look like?
- How were the *rainbows* the same? How were they different?

SKILLS ASSESSMENT

Use these questions to determine a child's abilities and understanding:

- Does the child have the fine motor skills to squeeze the hose sprayer or squirt bottle?
- Does the child see the connection between the sunlight and water and the *rainbow*?
- Is the child willing to experiment?
- Does the child use descriptive language when talking about the *rainbows*?

FOCUS AREAS

Science: asking questions about events in the environment

Language Arts: communicating and generating ideas and questions

MATERIALS

Chart paper
Marker
Small bouncy ball
Mirror
Flashlight

Reflect

Separate

Rainbow

Hunt for Rainbow Colors

FOCUS AREAS

Science: planning and conducting a simple investigation, communicating investigations and explanations

Math: counting, graphing

Language Arts: labeling, learning spoken language—words to song

MATERIALS

Recording sheets listing the rainbow colors in order, 2 per child (see PREPARATION)

Sheet of chart paper

Clipboards, 1 per child or small pieces of cardboard plus large paper clips or alligator clips to make clipboards

Pencils, 1 per child

PREPARATION

- Make recording sheets by drawing and coloring seven squares, one for each *rainbow* color, in *rainbow* order on the sheets or attach cut-paper squares in *rainbow* order. Make two sheets per child, one for an indoor hunt and one for an outdoor hunt, plus extras for you to demonstrate how to use. Attach one sheet to each clipboard or cardboard piece with two large paper clips or with alligator clips.

RAINBOW HUNT RECORDING SHEET						
red	**orange**	**yellow**	**green**	**blue**	**indigo**	**violet**

WHAT TO DO

1. Invite the children to go on a *rainbow* color hunt. You can do this either indoors or outside. It's fun to do two hunts on two different days and compare the results. On the first day, ask the children which colors they think they will see the most frequently outdoors. Write down their responses on the sheet of chart paper.
2. Make up verses to the classic song, "Here We Go 'Round the Mulberry Bush." For example: "Here we go on a color hunt...," or, "This is the way we look for red...."
3. Give each child a recording sheet. When the children observe a color they can make a mark on their recording sheet next to the corresponding color. Demonstrate how to make a tally mark.
4. An adult can make notes about the specific things the children notice such as the red bulletin board and blue chair.

5. Conclude the hunt shortly before the end of activity time or when the children begin to lose interest. Review the children's recording sheets. Help them count how many items of each color they found.
6. On another day, repeat the hunt outdoors. Ask the children whether they think they will get similar results.
7. The children create another tally on a second recording sheet.
8. Save the recording sheets in the children's portfolios.

MORE IDEAS
- With young children sing, "This is the way we look for red…" while everyone in the group looks for red at the same time. After everyone has found at least one red thing, move on to, "This is the way we look for orange…."
- For older children, create a class graph of how many items of each color were found. Compare the indoor graph and the outdoor graph. Use the instructions for the following activity "What's Your Favorite Rainbow Color?" to set up the graphs.

DISCUSSION STARTERS
Use these questions to spark children's thinking during and after the activity:
- What color did we find the most outside (inside)?
- What color did we find the least outside (inside)?
- Which colors were hard to find?
- What colors did we find that are not on the *rainbow* chart?
- Do some blue colors look different from other blue colors?

SKILLS ASSESSMENT
Use these questions to determine a child's abilities and understanding:
- Can the child name the *rainbow* colors?
- Can the child count accurately?
- Does the child notice and describe varieties of colors (light, dark, blue-green)?
- Is the child eager to hunt for colors?

TEACHER-TO-TEACHER TIP
Children love hunts. A search opens their eyes to everyday objects. They exclaim, "I see a red bookcase!" as if they had uncovered pirate treasure. For this reason, it can be more fun to do the hunt in small groups so you can comment and note all the children's discoveries. The hunts are not a competition. It is fine if many children notice the same green sign. Encourage them all to mark it on their recording sheets and point it out to the children who did not notice it right away.

What Is Your Favorite Rainbow Color?

FOCUS AREAS

Math: counting, graphing
Language Arts: learning vocabulary
Fine Motor: printing names

MATERIALS

Sheet of chart paper
3" squares of construction paper in the 7 rainbow colors
Markers
Glue sticks

PREPARATION

- Label the chart paper "Our Favorite Colors." Create the beginning of a graph by gluing one set of 3" color squares in *rainbow* order along the bottom. Label the colors. See page 301 in the Appendix for directions to create a graph.

WHAT TO DO

1. Work with a small group of children. Ask each child to name his favorite rainbow color.
2. Ask each child to choose his favorite *rainbow* color from the stack of construction paper squares.
   Note: Be flexible if a child wants to choose more than one color.
3. After the child writes his name on the construction paper square (or an adult writes it for him), the child glues the square in the correct column.
4. Review the graph. Use the discussion starters below to talk with the children about the graph.

DISCUSSION STARTERS

Use these questions to spark children's thinking during and after the activity:
- What color has the most squares?
- What color has the fewest squares?
- How many people chose the same color as you did?
- What do you like about your favorite color?
- If you like more than one color, how did you make your choice?
- Do you have a favorite color that is not part of the *rainbow*?

SKILLS ASSESSMENT

Use these questions to determine a child's abilities and understanding:
- Does the child know the names for colors?
- Can the child count using one-to-one correspondence?
- Does the child use size vocabulary—more, less, most, fewest?
- Can the child make observations about the graph?
- Is the child engaged in the activity?

BIG Rhythm: Rainbow Rap

WHAT TO DO

1. Read the poem to the children slowly, pointing to the different colors in your *rainbow*.

Rainbow Rhyme by Tim Dobbins
ROY G. BIV up in the sky
All my colors shine so high.
Rain and sun at the same time?
I know it's rare but hear my rhyme.
Find the sun and turn your back.
See my colorful curvy track!
Spell my name and you will say
Initials for my colors today:
R for red, simple enough.
O for orange, that's the stuff!
Y for yellow,
G for green,
B for blue. See what I mean?
I for indigo. It's hard to see.
V for violet. That's all of me.
Cherry, mango, banana, bean,
Berry, plum, and grape are seen.
Rainbow colors are everyplace,
Down on earth and up in space.
Please look fast, 'cause I won't last.
Quick, before the clouds have passed!

2. Recite the poem twice to the children as you point to each color and then ask them to name other fruits, vegetables, or other items for each color. Record their responses on the construction paper *rainbow* or on the strips of colored paper, listing each child's name next to his or her response. Count and record the tally for each color.

MORE IDEAS

- Discuss words in the poem that rhyme such as *see* and *me*, *green* and *bean*. See if children suggest words that rhyme.
- Create new verses to the poem using the children's suggestions.

DISCUSSION STARTERS

Use these questions to spark children's thinking during and after the activity:
- Is it hard to think of ideas for some colors?
- Which color names are easy to rhyme?
- Which color names are hard to rhyme?

SKILLS ASSESSMENT

Use these questions to determine a child's abilities and understanding:
- Is the child engaged in group time?
- Does the child contribute ideas?
- Does the child understand the concept of *rhyme*?
- Can the child produce a simple rhyme?

FOCUS AREAS

Math: counting, sequencing
Language Arts: rhyming, communicating ideas

MATERIALS

Large construction paper *rainbow* or colored strips of paper
Photos of the different fruit mentioned in the poem (optional)
Chart paper
Markers in the *rainbow* colors

PREPARATION

- Write the words to "Rainbow Rhyme" in large letters on chart paper. Write the color words with the appropriate color marker for greater visual appeal.
- On a large construction paper *rainbow* or on colored strips of paper write the initials ROY G BIV next to each color (R next to red, and so on).

Make a Living Rainbow

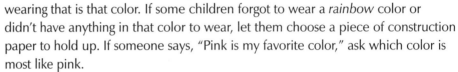

FOCUS AREAS

Science: observing

Math: counting, sorting, estimating, making patterns

MATERIALS

Photo or drawing of a *rainbow*

Construction paper in the *rainbow* colors in case children forget to wear their favorite *rainbow* color

PREPARATION

- At least a day before you plan to do the activity, tell the children and parents you want to create a *rainbow* with all the children in your class on a specific day. Ask everyone to wear their favorite *rainbow* color to school that day.

WHAT TO DO

1. When you gather for group time, tell the children that they are going to make a class *rainbow*. Invite each child to tell the group his or her favorite *rainbow* color and show what they are wearing that is that color. If some children forgot to wear a *rainbow* color or didn't have anything in that color to wear, let them choose a piece of construction paper to hold up. If someone says, "Pink is my favorite color," ask which color is most like pink.
2. Show the children the *rainbow* photo or drawing and review the sequence of colors—red, orange, yellow, green, blue, *indigo*, *violet*.
3. Invite the children to create an arc of *rainbow* colors beginning with the children wearing red (and pinks) on the left and ending with those wearing *violet* on the right.
4. Count how many people are wearing or holding each color.

TEACHER-TO-TEACHER TIP

You can wear your favorite color but do not name it until the end to see where you are needed. Sometimes the lone child wearing green needs back-up, so you can grab a sheet of green construction paper and join in as green.

DISCUSSION STARTERS

Use these questions to spark children's thinking during and after the activity:

- Which *rainbow* color has the most people?
- Which *rainbow* color has the fewest people?
- Why do you think people have different favorite colors?

SKILLS ASSESSMENT

Use these questions to determine a child's abilities and understanding:

- Can the child name a *rainbow* color and group similar colors together?
- Does the child recognize and name color variations?
- Does the child enjoy being part of the BIG *rainbow*?

Giant Rainbow Bubbles

PREPARATION

- Assemble several large bubble wands. For each wand, cut a drinking straw in half. Thread about 36" of absorbent string such as cotton twine through the two pieces of straw then tie the ends together, creating a BIG rectangle when stretched out. (Absorbent string holds more bubble mixture allowing you to create bigger bubbles than non-absorbent nylon string.) Use the BIG wands for a demonstration at the end of the activity. Older children will also enjoy using the BIG wands.
- Make the bubble mixture. Measure 1 gallon of water into a clean bucket. Add 1 cup of Dawn. Add ⅛ cup of glycerin. Stir gently so you don't create bubbles on the surface. If possible, make the solution the day before you want to use it.

WHAT TO DO

1. Help the children twist pipe cleaners into a circle with a short handle.
2. The children dip their wands into the bubble solution and blow gently. Remind them to blow up into the air (not into their friends' faces).
3. Help the children count how long their bubbles last. Record some of the counts so they can compare later. Encourage them to experiment with the effect of how hard they blow on how well the bubbles form. (If they blow slowly and steadily, they will have more success making bubbles.)
4. Observe the *rainbow* colors in the bubbles.
5. After the children have had plenty of time to make bubbles themselves, show them how you can make really BIG bubbles with the giant bubble wand you made from string and straws. Stretch out the wand and lay it on the surface of the bubble mixture. Hold the straws and gently lift the wand with both hands, making sure you have a film of bubble mixture. Blow gently on the wand or move it slowly through the air to make a bubble. Help the children count how long the really BIG bubbles last. Older children will enjoy trying to make really BIG bubbles themselves.

TEACHER-TO-TEACHER TIP
Although it seems like the outdoors would be the best place to experiment with bubbles, the indoors normally works well too. Bubbles burst quickly in a breeze and the sun makes the water evaporate quickly, causing the bubbles to pop. Wind-blown bubbles can get into children's eyes. If your floor is not carpeted, lay down newspaper or an old sheet to prevent slipping. Setting out several bubble mixture containers around the perimeter (edge) of the sheet helps prevent children from bumping into each other and breaking each other's bubbles. After the experimenting is done, the children can chase and pop bubbles in a safe place outdoors. Bubbles last the longest outdoors in a cool, shady place or on a cloudy day when there is a lot of humidity in the air. Provide berry baskets to make BIG bubble masses outdoors. Children need space to wave the baskets to make wind. See *The Unbelievable Bubble Book* by John Cassidy for information on making giant bubbles outdoors.

DISCUSSION STARTERS
Use these questions to spark children's thinking during and after the activity:
- What did you learn about making bubbles?
- What colors do you see in the bubbles?
- What did you have to do to make a really BIG bubble?
- What do you notice about different sizes of bubbles? Which last longer, small bubbles or BIG bubbles?

SKILLS ASSESSMENT
Use these questions to determine a child's abilities and understanding:
- Does the child have the patience to keep experimenting with blowing bubbles?
- Can the child blow gently?
- Does the child share access to the bubble mixture?

Experiment: Are Rainbow Colors Always in the Same Order?

WHAT TO DO

1. Review with a small group of children how to make the rainbow colors (the color spectrum) by shining flashlights, overhead lights, or sunlight on a variety of prisms and CDs. Give them lots of time and materials to experiment with. You may need to help hold the CD, prism or crystal while the children shine the flashlight. What happens when the CD moves or the flashlight moves? (The colors move and change shape.) Do the colors look the same with different CDs, prisms, and crystals?

2. Ask, "Which colors do you see?" "What color is at the top?" What color is at the bottom?" "Which colors are in the middle?" "Which band of color looks widest?"

3. Ask, "How do the colors you see compare to the *rainbow* photos?"

4. Invite the children to record the order of the colors they observe using crayons, markers, or colored pencils to make a drawing.

5. Save the drawings in each child's portfolio.

FOCUS AREAS

Science: planning and conducting a simple investigation, communicating investigations and explanations

Math: making patterns, sequencing

MATERIALS

Prisms, various sizes and shapes (available at scientific supply outlets), decorative crystals or old CDs

White paper

Flashlights

Plastic mirrors

Markers, crayons, or colored pencils in all the rainbow colors

Photos or illustrations of *rainbows*

TEACHER-TO-TEACHER TIP

Children love drawing *rainbows* so they may draw a stylized version of a *rainbow* rather than what they actually observe with the CDs or prisms. That is okay. The observations will inspire them nonetheless.

DISCUSSION STARTERS

Use these questions to spark children's thinking during and after the activity:

- How would you describe the colors you see?
- How many do you see?
- How can you change how the colors look? (moving the CD)
- Do the colors made with the prism or the CD look like a real outdoor *rainbow*? How are they different?

SKILLS ASSESSMENT

Use these questions to determine a child's abilities and understanding:

- Does the child observe the sequence of colors?
- Can the child name the different colors?
- Does the child independently experiment by moving the CDs and prisms?

Rainbow Color Toss Game

FOCUS AREAS

Math: counting, measuring—distance, estimating

Gross Motor: throwing

MATERIALS

Seven hula hoops or large cardboard boxes

Crepe paper or construction paper in rainbow colors

Glue or tape

Variety of different colors of balls, plastic lids, beanbags, balled up pairs of socks, or anything else that might be fun to toss

PREPARATION

- Decorate each of the seven hula hoops or large cardboard boxes with one color of crepe paper or construction paper OR simply lay a sheet of construction paper in each hula hoop.

WHAT TO DO

1. Work with a small group of children in a safe, open area. Help the children arrange the hula hoops or boxes on the ground in an arc with red on the left and *violet* on the right. The children stand and toss items into a hula hoop or box of their choosing.

2. Add interest and use direction vocabulary words by commenting, "Your beanbag went *over* the *rainbow*," "Your beanbag landed *under* the *rainbow*," or "Your beanbag landed *beside* yellow."

3. Invite the children to predict whether they will be able to reach a certain color. Model and encourage them to try underhand, overhand, and side-arm throwing. Ask the children which way of throwing gives them the most distance or control.

4. Have the children count how many tries it takes to get an item in a particular color.

5. This is a free-form game. If the children want to stand closer to the hoops or boxes so it's easier to make a basket, that's fine.

MORE IDEAS

- Arrange the hoops in a line with violet closest to the children and red the farthest away. The children throw to any color in the line, jump from hoop to hoop until they reach their beanbag, and throw again until they reach red.
- Include color guessing as part of the activity. For example, say, "Aim for the color that is the same color as the grass." "Aim for the color that is a combination of red and yellow."

DISCUSSION STARTERS

Use these questions to spark children's thinking during and after the activity:

- Which color was the easiest for you to reach?
- Why do you think some colors were harder to reach than others?

SKILLS ASSESSMENT

Use these questions to determine a child's abilities and understanding:

- Can the child aim for a target?
- Can the child throw with any accuracy?
- Does the child throw underhand, overhand, or side arm? Does the child try different throwing methods?
- How does the child respond to missing a target? Is the child willing to keep trying?
- Does the child know the names of colors?

Create a Giant Mural of Rainbow Colors

PREPARATION

- Cut the tissue paper and/or crepe paper into strips, about 1" x 4" and place by colors on small trays.
- Cover a table with newspaper or plastic. Place a BIG sheet of paper on the table.

WHAT TO DO

1. Work with a small group of children. Let them choose a strip of tissue paper, place it on the BIG paper, dip their paintbrush in water, and paint over the tissue paper.
2. Some children may want to make their own *rainbow* section. Others may experiment with piling different colors on top of each other.
3. The color from the tissue paper or crepe paper will bleed onto the white paper. Leave the tissue paper in place to dry for the most vivid color. When the BIG paper is full, you can move it to an out-of-the-way place while it dries and the children can make a second mural. Remove the tissue paper before mounting on the wall inside or outside your classroom.
4. Label your mural "BIG Picture of Rainbow Colors."

DISCUSSION STARTERS

Use these questions to spark children's thinking during and after the activity:

- What happens when you paint the tissue paper with water?
- What happens when two colors overlap?
- What do you like about different parts of the mural?
- What do you think will happen when the mural dries out?

SKILLS ASSESSMENT

Use these questions to determine a child's abilities and understanding:

- Can the child work in a group?
- Does the child work in a small concentrated area of the paper or "work large"?
- Can the child predict the results of mixing different colors?
- How long does the project hold the interest of the child?

FOCUS AREAS

Science: observing color mixing
Art: exploring design

MATERIALS

Sheets of giant white paper—bulletin board or table size, sturdy enough to absorb water without tearing easily
Newspaper or plastic to cover the table
Tissue paper and/or crepe paper, in a variety of rainbow colors (Most tissue paper and crepe paper will bleed when it comes in contact with water but those labeled "bleeding tissue paper" are particularly vibrant.)
Small trays
Smocks to protect children's clothing, optional
Paintbrushes
Containers of water

Rainbow Dance

FOCUS AREAS

Math: sequence of rainbow colors

Language Arts: learning vocabulary, communicating ideas

Gross Motor: learning about rhythm, dancing

MATERIALS

Felt board or bulletin board (optional)

Felt or construction paper squares in rainbow colors

Scarves or crepe paper streamers in rainbow colors

Instrumental music

WHAT TO DO

1. Hold up the red square. Ask the children what color it is and what objects are usually red: fire engine, stop light, and so on. Then ask, "How does the color red make you feel?"
2. Do this with each of the colors in *rainbow* order as you place the colors on the felt board.
3. After you've reviewed all the colors have each child choose a scarf or streamer and invite them to do a *rainbow* dance by moving how the color of the scarf or streamer they selected makes them feel. Maybe blue makes them feel calm, cool, and quiet like gentle waves so they make their streamer move like waves. Maybe yellow makes them think of bright summer sunshine and they feel happy, bouncy, and twirly.
4. Play instrumental music and let the children dance.
5. After they have danced with one color, invite the children to choose a different color. How does this one make them feel?

MORE IDEAS

- Read selections from the book *Hailstones and Halibut Bones* by Mary O'Neill or *A Rainbow All Around Me* by Sandra L. Pinkney for vivid color descriptions to help introduce the idea of feelings connected with colors.
- Have all the children dance with the same color, "Now we are all are going to dance yellow." If the children are in a circle, each child can have all seven colors of crepe paper in front of them. The children will enjoy changing at random moments or with "stop and start" music, such as some of Hap Palmer's instrumental music.

DISCUSSION STARTERS

Use these questions to spark children's thinking during and after the activity:

- What colors did you try?
- Which colors make you feel like dancing quietly?
- Which colors make you feel like dancing with fast movements?

SKILLS ASSESSMENT

Use these questions to determine a child's abilities and understanding:

- Did the child try a variety of colors?
- Did the child suggest color associations with objects or feelings?
- Did the child vary the dancing with the different colors?
- Was the child engaged in the activity?

BIG CONNECTIONS:
More Activities Across the Curriculum

LANGUAGE ARTS

- Children draw *rainbows* or draw with their favorite color and dictate stories for an adult to write on their drawings. Include vocabulary words and *rainbow* books at the table for inspiration. Possible topics for different days:
  - What is your favorite *rainbow* color? What do you think it would be like if the whole world were that color?
  - Where do you see your favorite color—in what types of things or places?
  - Have you ever seen a *rainbow*? If you could float inside a *rainbow* what do you think you would see?

  Mount the drawings and stories in a rainbow arc on the bulletin board or classroom wall. When you take down the display, keep the drawings and stories in each child's portfolio.

MATH/SCIENCE IN THE SENSORY/ WATER TABLE

- Fill the water table with bubble mixture (see the Giant Rainbow Bubble activity on page 135). Include a variety of materials to make bubbles, such as wands and berry baskets. Ask the children which containers make the biggest/smallest bubbles. Time how long the bubbles last. Are the *rainbow* colors easier to see in the sun or the shade?

ART/MATH

- Children make paper chains of *rainbow* colors. Suggest that the children attach the loops in *rainbow* color order to emphasize patterning. Have them count how many loops they have on their chains, and how many complete *rainbow* patterns—red, orange, yellow, green, blue, *indigo, violet*. The children can create a BIG paper chain *rainbow* arc by working together to make a long red chain first. Each color chain will need to be slightly shorter than the previous one to make an arc under the red band. Pin the chains to a bulletin board or tape to a wall for display.
- Children experiment with drawing *rainbows* by tracing part way around a variety of flat round items of different sizes, such as clean plastic lids, plastic plates, and pie plates. How do the different items compare in size?

ART/SCIENCE

- Color mixing—fill ice cube trays or clean Styrofoam egg cartons with water. Add red, yellow, and blue food coloring to three of the sections. With eyedroppers or pipettes, the children can make color combinations.

BIG Outcomes

Group assessment: Review the photo boards about making a giant *rainbow* outdoors, hunting for colors, and observing *rainbow* colors by using CDs, prisms, and crystals. Review the graphs from the color hunt and favorite colors. Review chart sheets from the beginning of the exploration of what the children know about *rainbows* and what they want to learn. On a third sheet of chart paper titled "What We Learned About Rainbows," record the children's comments about what they learned, including the name of the child who made the comment. Be sure to note answers to their original questions, or note if you still have more to learn and explore.

Individual assessment: Review your notes and quotes from individual observations during activities such as the color hunts, the *rainbow* mural, and the *rainbow* colors experiment. Review the children's work and save it in their portfolios. Note areas in which the children need further practice and those in which they excel.

GOOD BOOKS FOR FACTS AND FUN

Finding books that offer accurate scientific information about *rainbows* at the preschool and kindergarten level is challenging. Good rainbow stories, like those colorful arcs after a storm, are also few and far between.

INFORMATION ABOUT RAINBOWS

All the Colors of the Rainbow by Allan Fowler
A solid, basic background source for the concepts of light, color, and rainbows in an easy-to-read format, this book is illustrated with color photographs. Ages 4–6

I See Myself by Vicki Cobb
Veteran science writer Cobb explores light, mirrors, and reflection through questions and experiments supported by fresh, bright text variations. Ages 4–6

The Rainbow and You by E. C. Krupp
Follow the character, Roy G Biv, through accurate scientific explanations of rainbow formation and optics with added snippets of multicultural lore relating to the colorful arc of water and light—useful for background information and sharing. Ages 4–6

STORIES AND POETRY ABOUT COLORS

Color, Color, Where Are You Color? by Mary Koski
Each large, double-page spread presents a single color and examples from nature. The simple rhyming text encourages children to look for more colors in the world around them. Ages 3–6

Dog's Colorful Day: A Messy Story About Colors and Counting by Emma Dodd
Big and bold, this tale recounts the adventures of a pudgy black-and-white pup that
    comes home with new spots. Alert children may spy the out-of-order colors on the
    bone. Ages 3–4

Hailstones and Halibut Bones by Mary O'Neill
In print since 1961, O'Neill's lovely poems evoke emotions and the senses in her
    highly creative responses to the colors of our world. Single line quotations make
    expressive captions for bulletin boards, highlighting children's art and writing. Ages
    3–6

Little Blue and Little Yellow by Leo Lionni
Lionni's classic fable introduces color mixing while blending in themes of friendship,
    prejudice, and acceptance of those of other colors. Ages 3–6

Lunch by Denise Fleming
Follow a fearless, rowdy, and very hungry mouse through a fabulous feast of colorful
    food. Read it again to spot the clues and find all the colors. Ages 3–5

A Rainbow All Around Me by Sandra L. Pinkney
Crisp photographs of children from a variety of ethnicities and cultures present
    characteristics of "rainbow" colors. Purple appears as "wild, crazy" and "jammin'
    on a slice of bread." Ages 3–6

White Is the Moon by Valerie Greeley
Short, lyrical rhymes trace the arc of day to night, moving from woodlands to the sea
    while linking a color to each creature shown in beautifully painted illustrations.
    Ages 3–6

STORIES ABOUT RAINBOWS

A Rainbow of My Own by Don Freeman
Freeman's classic story captures a child's fascination, delight, and desire to possess the
    beautiful, fleeting phenomena for himself. Ages 3–6

That's What Leprechauns Do by Eve Bunting
Three wee mischievous men offer a humorous twist on the Irish pot of gold legend.
    Watercolor illustrations by Caldecott medalist, Emily Arnold McCully, add to the
    charm. Ages 3–6

A Note to Families About Rainbows

Dear Families,

Although rainbows seem like magic, your children have been learning what is really happening. We have been making our own rainbows by spraying water into the sky on a sunny day. The little drops of water bend and bounce the white light from the sun, making all the individual colors visible, just the way the sun shining through the mist creates a giant rainbow in the sky. You can see the same band of rainbow colors at home by shining a flashlight or sunlight on a CD. Ask your child to show you how to do this.

We have been learning all the colors of the rainbow in order. One way to remember the order is the name ROY G. BIV, which stands for red, orange, yellow, green, blue, indigo, and violet. Indigo is an unusual word that describes the color of dark blue jeans. Violet is another word for purple. Naming colors is a great way to increase vocabulary.

We are going to make a rainbow with everyone in our class. Have your child wear his or her favorite rainbow color to school on _____. We will arrange ourselves in rainbow order.

We will also make a giant graph of the children's favorite colors. You can ask your child which colors most children chose as their favorite.

Have fun with your rainbow scientist!

6

THINKING BIG ABOUT WIND: HUFFING AND PUFFING AND BLOWING

THE BIG Picture

We can't see air but we can feel it move when the wind blows. Powerful winds can be frightening to children. This unit enables children to start understanding wind and therefore feel a little more in control by experimenting with different ways to make air move—such as blowing out their breath, blowing with straws, and using cardboard fans and hair dryers. Children can also begin to understand wind power.

OBJECTIVES

▸ Learn about air, a natural substance that is essential for life, but something we rarely think about.
▸ Understand that wind is air in motion.
▸ Become more comfortable with powerful winds that can be scary

STANDARDS

National Science Education Content Standards

▸ Science as inquiry—ask questions; plan and conduct a simple investigation; use simple equipment and tools; communicate investigations and explanations
▸ Earth and space science—recognize changes in the Earth and sky

National Council of Teachers of Mathematics Standards

▸ Number and operations—count with understanding; make reasonable estimates
▸ Algebra—sort, classify, and order objects; recognize patterns
▸ Measurement—understand how to measure using nonstandard and standard tools
▸ Data analysis and probability—represent data using pictures and graphs
▸ Communication—organize, analyze, and evaluate mathematical thinking; use the language of mathematics

Standards for the English Language Arts

▸ Experience a wide range of print and non-print texts, including fiction and non-fiction, to build an understanding of the world and acquire new information
▸ Use spoken, written, and visual language to communicate and learn
▸ Generate ideas and questions and pose problems
▸ Build vocabulary

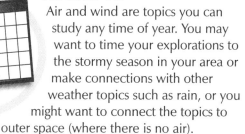

TIMING TIP

Air and wind are topics you can study any time of year. You may want to time your explorations to the stormy season in your area or make connections with other weather topics such as rain, or you might want to connect the topics to outer space (where there is no air).

BIG BEGINNING:
Introducing Air and Wind

FOCUS AREAS

Science: asking questions
Language Arts: learning
 vocabulary

MATERIALS

2 turkey basters or 2
 small pieces of
 cardboard, about 4"
 square
Strips of tissue paper,
 about 4" long,
 enough to make a
 line across your
 group area
2 sheets of chart paper
Marker

PREPARATION

● Label one sheet of
 chart paper "What We
 Know About Air and
 Wind," and the other
 "What We Want to
 Learn About Air and
 Wind."

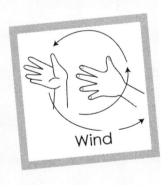

Wind

WHAT TO DO

1. Invite the children to take a
   breath, hold their hands in
   front of their mouths, and then
   gently let out their breath. Ask,
   "What do you feel?" Have the
   children take a deep breath
   and this time blow out their
   breath. Ask, "What does it
   feel like when you blow out
   your breath?"

2. Ask the children to shut their eyes while you and another
   adult go around the circle in opposite directions and either
   blow a puff of air on each child's cheek with a turkey
   baster or wave a piece of cardboard by each child's cheek
   to create a little breeze. Ask, "What do you feel?"

3. Introduce the word *air*, something that we cannot see, but
   we need to live. *Air* is all around us. Say and clap **air**, just
   one syllable. Say *air* as you hold your hands up, palms
   facing out and moving gently.

Air

4. Introduce the word *invisible*, which describes something
   you cannot see. Air is *invisible*. Say and clap in-**vis**-i-ble,
   with the emphasis on the "vis" syllable. Say *invisible* as you
   place your thumbs on the other four fingers and draw your
   two hands apart as if something were disappearing.

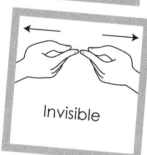

Invisible

5. Introduce the word *wind*. Wind is air that is moving. Say
   and clap **wind**, just one syllable. Say *wind* as you move
   your open hands in BIG circles in front of your body.

6. Arrange the children seated in two lines facing each other
   at least 3' apart. Place strips of tissue paper on the floor along the length of one line
   of children. Invite the line closest to the tissue paper to kneel down facing the
   tissue paper strips and become a BIG wind to blow the tissue paper strips to the
   other line of children. The second line of children remains seated until the tissue
   paper reaches them, then the first line sits down while the other children blow the
   tissue paper back to them. Collect the tissue paper. Tell the children they can do a
   blowing experiment during activity time.

7. Ask the children what they know about air and wind. Record their responses and
   names on the chart paper, labeled "What We Know About Air and Wind."

8. Ask the children what they want to find out about air and wind. Record those
   responses on the second sheet of poster paper, labeled "What We Want to Learn
   About Air and Wind."

BIG QUESTIONS FOR GROWING MINDS

Use the following questions to engage the children in a discussion about air and wind during group time or with an individual child during activity time:

- What does air feel like?
- What does wind feel like?
- What does wind do?
- What have you noticed blowing in the wind?

ANSWERING BIG QUESTIONS

Q&A

What makes the wind blow? The surface of the Earth is made up of a variety of land and water masses such as mountains, deserts, plains, and oceans. These areas absorb heat from the sun differently. As these surfaces heat up, the air above them also warms up. Some parts of the Earth and surrounding air get hotter than others. Hot air is less dense than cold air. Dense, cold air pushes the warmer air up, creating wind. (Source: *Air, Water, and Weather* by William C. Robertson)

A Note from the Author: The activities in this chapter are designed to build on each other. However, please feel free to choose those that meet the interests and abilities of your class. If parts of an activity seem like too much to do on a particular day, save them for a later time. Every class is different, even from day to day, and the activities are adaptable to meet the needs of your class.

WORDS FOR BIG THINKING

Look for these words highlighted in italics throughout the activities in this chapter. Write the words out in large letters and introduce them a few at a time with the "**S**ay, **C**lap, **A**ct out, **D**o again" (SCAD) system. Using the words during activities and discussions will reinforce their meaning.

- Air—something that we breathe to keep us alive
- Breeze—a gentle wind
- Experiment—a test to see what will happen
- Gust—a sudden strong rush of wind
- Hurricane—a BIG storm with powerful, fast winds
- Invisible—something that we can't see. Air and wind are invisible.
- Prediction—what you think might happen, a guess based on what you already know
- Scientist—a person who studies the natural world
- Tornado—air spinning violently in the shape of a funnel
- Wind—air that is moving

PHOTO TIP

You can record the children's explorations of wind by creating photo boards about *experimenting* with different types of *wind* power, playing *air* soccer, and performing "The Three Little Pigs." Look for close-ups of individual children and group shots of children interacting. Also include vocabulary words and quotes from children to document their learning.

Experiment: Wind Power

FOCUS AREAS

Science: planning and conducting a simple investigation, using simple equipment and tools, communicating investigations and explanations

Math: counting, measuring—distance

MATERIALS

Duplicated recording sheets, 1 per child (see Preparation)

4 rigid cardboard pieces, about 8" square

Drinking straws, 1 per child

2 hair dryers, each with low or cool settings

3 items of different weight, at least 4 of each item, such as packing noodles, paper cups, and wooden blocks. (Optional: straw or grass, sticks, and stones as a preview to acting out "The Three Little Pigs" at another time.)

Pencils or markers

Masking tape

Table

4 lengths of plastic rain gutter or large plastic trays

PREPARATION

- Choose three types of items the children will *experiment* with—one that will be easy to move, such as packing noodles, an item that will be harder to move, such as small paper cups, and one difficult to move, such as wooden blocks.
- Create a recording sheet by drawing pictures of each item and the different methods the children will use to blow. Make copies, 1 for each child
- Tape four lengths of plastic rain gutter to a table or set out large plastic trays.

WHAT TO DO

1. Tell a small group of children they are going to be *scientists* who study the *wind*. Say and clap out the syllables, **sci**-en-tist, with the emphasis on the "sci" syllable. Say *scientist* as you hold your closed hands in front of your body, thumbs sticking out. Move your hands in alternate circles, pointing the thumbs down as if they were test tubes being poured out. This is the sign for *science*. Then add the sign that indicates a person's occupation: flat palms face each other in front of the chest, then move the hands down to indicate the sides of the body.

2. Introduce more BIG vocabulary words. Say, "*Scientists* make *predictions*, what they think might happen, based on what they already

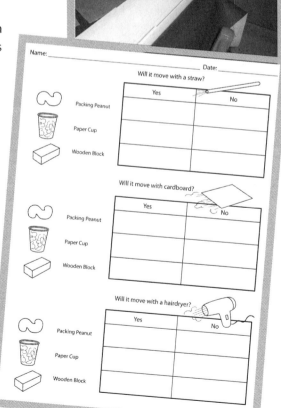

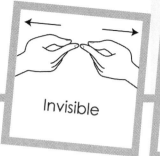

Invisible

Air

know. *Scientists* test their *predictions* by doing *experiments*, which are tests to see what will happen. **Note**: For more information about the vocabulary words of *prediction* and *experiment*, see pages 40–41.

3. Allow the children time to try blowing and fanning a variety of items down the rain gutter or tray. After the children have had time to explore, invite them to choose items to *experiment* with.

4. Ask the children, "When you blow through the straw, will you be able to move your item?" After they blow, ask, "Did your item move?" Have them record the result on their recording sheets. The children then predict and try moving the other items with straws and then cardboard.

5. To increase interest, use BIG vocabulary words by saying, "See if you can make *hurricane winds* with your cardboard." "You can make a little *breeze* with your straw."

6. After all the children have had a chance to *experiment* with the various items and different kinds of *wind* power, allow two children at a time to *experiment* by moving items with a hair dryer on the low or cool setting.
   Safety note: It is essential at all times to have an adult supervising the children's use of the hair dryer.

7. Save the children's recording sheets in their portfolio.

DISCUSSION STARTERS

Use these questions to spark children's thinking during and after the activity:

- What did you find out about how things move in the *wind*?
- What was the hardest to move?
- Why do you think some items move and others don't?
- Where does it work best to blow? (Children need time to figure out that they need to apply the *air* behind the item to make it move forward. They usually start off blowing and fanning from above.)
- What type of *wind* power did you like using the best—blowing with the straw, fanning with the cardboard, or the using the hair dryer?

SKILLS ASSESSMENT

Use these questions to determine a child's abilities and understanding:

- Can the child make a *prediction*?
- Do the child's *predictions* become more realistic with experience?
- Can the child mark the correct box on the recording sheet?
- Does the child enjoy *experimenting* with different materials and methods of *wind* power?
- Is the child curious about the results?
- How well does the child wait for a turn using the hair dryer?

How Does the Wind Blow?

FOCUS AREAS

Science: studying different types of *wind*

Language Arts: learning vocabulary, experiencing different types of text—poetry

Gross Motor: making arm movements

MATERIALS

Chart paper
Marker
Funnel (optional)
Tornado tube (optional)

PREPARATION

- Write the words to the poem "Wind" on chart paper.

Hurricane

Tornado

WHAT TO DO

1. Read the poem to the group, pointing to the *wind* words.

   Wind by Tim Dobbins
   The BREEZE starts as a whisper,
   Brushing against my face.
   Now it blows much faster,
   As if it's in a race.

   A GUST blows hard
   Across the yard;
   Then suddenly
   It stops.

   A HURRICANE is really strong,
   It can last all day and all night long.

   TORNADOES show us spinning air,
   Where will they touch down?
   Here or there?

   Again we feel our gentle BREEZE
   Blowing softly in the trees.

2. Introduce the various *wind* vocabulary words. A *breeze* is a gentle *wind*. Say and clap **breeze**, just one syllable. Say *breeze* as you hold your two hands in front of you, palms facing out, moving them slightly more than you do when you make the ASL sign for *air*.

3. Introduce the word *gust*, a sudden strong rush of *air* or *wind*. Say and clap **gust**. Say *gust* as you make the sign for *air*, but move your hands in one quick motion, like a *gust* of *air*.

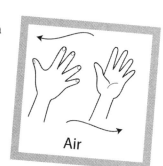

Air

4. Introduce the word *hurricane*, a BIG storm with powerful fast *winds*. Say and clap **hur**-ri-cane, with the emphasis on the "hur" syllable. Say *hurricane* as you make both claw hands face each other (left palm up and right palm down) and move sideways in a spiral.

5. Introduce the word *tornado*, violently spinning *air* in the shape of a funnel. Show the children a real funnel if you have one, or a *tornado* tube. Say and clap tor-**na**-do, with emphasis on the "na" syllable. Say *tornado* as you as you make the ASL sign for *tornado*, which is similar to the sign for hurricane but with middle fingers extended. The hands move sideways in circles to suggest the swirling wind of a tornado. Make the signs as you say the poem again with the children.

DISCUSSION STARTERS

Use these questions to spark children's thinking during and after the activity:
- How do different types of *wind* feel?
- What do you like to do when it's *windy*?

SKILLS ASSESSMENT

Use these questions to determine a child's abilities and understanding:
- Can the child make the different ASL signs?
- Is the child engaged in the group activity?

Air Soccer

WHAT TO DO

1. Work with a small group of children. Two children stand on opposite ends of the table, each holding an 8" x 8" cardboard piece. Invite them to fan their faces with the cardboard so they can feel the *air* move.

2. A third child places a packing noodle in the center of the table. The children with cardboard try to fan the packing noodle to the goal at the opposite end of the table. Tell them, "Use only *wind* power. No touching the noodle."

3. The children enjoy moving the packing noodle up and down the table. There is no need to keep score. If other children are waiting, set a timer to take turns.

4. Invite the children to observe where it works best to fan the packing noodle— behind it or above it. This is a good opportunity for you to reinforce directional vocabulary words, such as *above*, *behind*, and *in front of*.

SUPERSIZE IT!

The children can play *air* soccer indoors or outdoors with a light beach ball or partially inflated sturdy balloon on the ground. Remind the children not to kick the ball. Say, "In this game, only the *wind* can touch or move the ball." Several children may need to fan together to get a beach ball to move. **Safety note**: If a balloon pops, it is essential to pick up **all** the pieces.

DISCUSSION STARTERS

Use these questions to spark children's thinking during and after the activity:

- How can you make the packing noodle go where you want?
- Which type of fanning works best, light waves or strong waves?
- How is this game like any other games you have played?

SKILLS ASSESSMENT

Use these questions to determine a child's abilities and understanding:

- Can the child manipulate the cardboard?
- Does the child try different methods of fanning?
- Does the child enjoy the game?

FOCUS AREAS

Science: experimenting with air movement

Gross Motor: practicing eye-hand coordination

MATERIALS

Packing noodles
2 rigid cardboard pieces about 8" x 8"
Cardboard strips about 5" wide, enough to cover both long sides of a classroom table
Table
Masking tape
Sand timer (optional)

PREPARATION

- Create a "playing field" by taping strips of cardboard about 5" high to the sides of a table.
- Make goals at the ends of the table with masking tape. (See photo)
- Mark the centerline with masking tape.
- Cut cardboard into two pieces that are about 8" x 8".

BIG DRAMA:

"The Three Little Pigs"

FOCUS AREAS

Math: counting, sequencing

Language Arts: experiencing a wide range of texts, retelling the story

MATERIALS

Story of "The Three Little Pigs" to read (see Good Books for Facts and Fun on page 163)

Large sheets of cardboard or BIG boxes

Straw or grass

Sticks

Clear tape and glue

Yellow, brown, and red tempera paint (optional)

Sponges

Strips of corrugated cardboard about 6" x 3" to dip in paint (optional)

Foam or cardboard blocks (optional)

A real brick (optional)

Cooking pot or smaller cardboard box (optional)

Construction paper, brown and pink

Scissors (adult-only)

Markers

PREPARATION

- Gather large sheets of cardboard or boxes so you can construct three pig's houses with the children. Houses should be as tall as a child.
- Cut construction paper into strips about 2" wide and 8½" long to make headbands. Each child will need two strips per headband, pink for pigs, brown for wolves. Provide additional paper for the children to make ears. For younger children, precut the ears. Older children will enjoy drawing and cutting out the ears themselves.

WHAT TO DO

1. Read a story of "The Three Little Pigs." Review the storyline and the characters: the mother pig, the three pigs, and the wolf. It's also fun to add a farmer who grows the hay, a stick seller, a brick mason, and neighbors so more children can participate in each performance.

2. Ask the children what supplies they need to put on the play. You can make the straw, stick, and brick houses as simple or as elaborate as you want. For the straw house, the children can tape or glue grass or straw to a sheet of cardboard. Or they can paint straw by dipping the edge of cardboard strips into yellow paint and applying it to the BIG cardboard. When decorated, lean the cardboard against a tall chair. An adult can cut a window in the cardboard for the pig to peer through or the pig can just poke her head above or around the cardboard. In a similar fashion, the children can tape twigs to the stick house or draw sticks with markers or paint with cardboard edges dipped in brown tempera. For the brick house, the

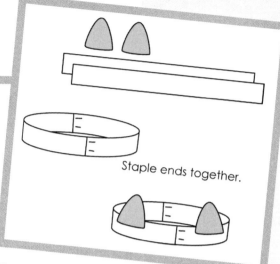

Staple ends together.

children can sponge paint bricks on a sheet of cardboard or build a brick house with cardboard or foam blocks. If you have a real brick, show the children how heavy and sturdy it is.

3. The children make construction paper headbands for themselves—pig ears or wolf ears.

4. Invite the children to act out the story. You will be the narrator and line prompter. Feel free to ad lib depending on your class: "The first little pig said, 'I'm going to make my house of straw. That will be easy and then I can play.'" The pigs get supplies from the farmer and salespeople. They like pretending to add materials to their already-constructed houses.

5. Help the children create the wolf character by asking questions: "Can you give us a scary howl?" The pigs talk to the wolf through the window or peek around the side of the house. After huffing and puffing, the wolf pulls down the house and the pig scampers over to the next house.

6. Perform the play multiple times and encourage the children to try different roles. Children look at the story differently when they portray different characters.

7. Invite the children to invent new endings to the story. Maybe the wolf decides to build his own house. (Ask the children what kind of house the wolf might build and help them gather materials.) Maybe the pigs think of another way to trick the wolf.

DISCUSSION STARTERS
Use these questions to spark children's thinking during and after the activity:
- Why do you think the wolf could blow down the straw and stick houses?
- Why couldn't the wolf blow down the brick house?
- What kind of house would you like to build if you were one of the pigs?
- How do you think the pigs felt when the wolf came to the house?
- How do you think the wolf felt?
- How did the pigs take care of each other?
- How can families take care of each other when they have problems?

SKILLS ASSESSMENT
Use these questions to determine a child's abilities and understanding:
- Does the child remember the sequence of the story?
- How does the child work in a group preparing for the performance?
- Does the child enjoy performing?
- Could the child recite any lines with prompting?

Hear the Wind Blow: Wind Chimes

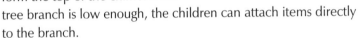

FOCUS AREAS

Science: observing
Math: counting, estimating, measuring—length
Fine Motor: using tape

MATERIALS

Long stick, dowel, length of PVC pipe, or heavy clothesline, about 3' long
Yarn or string cut into 18" lengths
Masking tape
Assortment of objects that will make noise when they bump into each other, such as aluminum pie tins, metal spoons and forks, lids to pots and pans
Pieces of rigid cardboard about 8" square
Manufactured wind chime (optional)

PREPARATION

- Choose an outdoor location to hang your *wind* chime. A low tree branch is ideal, but you can hang the *wind* chime from your climbing structure. Attach a long stick, dowel, length of PVC pipe or heavy clothes line to the branch or climbing structure to form the top of the chime. If the tree branch is low enough, the children can attach items directly to the branch.
- Gather the materials for the chime so you can bring them outside when you go with the children.

WHAT TO DO

1. At group time, talk to the children about what they hear when it's *windy*. Demonstrate a *wind* chime if you have one. Ask, "What could we use at school to make a giant *wind* chime?" Show them some of the materials you gathered and add their ideas if feasible. If, for example, someone suggests a tambourine, include it.
2. Go outside and invite the children to choose an item and tape it to a piece of yarn or string.
3. The children then wrap and tape the other end of their strings to the BIG stick. Ask the children how close their items need to be to the other items so they will bump into each other.
4. If it isn't *windy* outdoors, challenge the children to make *wind* with cardboard pieces. How many children does it take to make the items chime together?

DISCUSSION STARTERS

Use these questions to spark children's thinking during and after the activity:
- Which objects make the most noise when they bump into each other?
- Which objects are the quietest?
- Why do you think the items bump and bang?

SKILLS ASSESSMENT

Use these questions to determine a child's abilities and understanding:
- Can the child manipulate the tape?
- Does the child see the relationship between the strength of the *wind* and how vigorously the chimes bang?
- How well does the child work in a group?

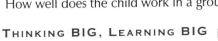

Hear the Wind Blow: Small Wind Chimes

WHAT TO DO

1. Work with a small group of children. Let them choose a pipe cleaner and twist the ends together to make a circle for the base.
2. Ask the children how many items they think they need to make a chime.
3. The children tape yarn to each item and then tape the yarn strings to the pipe cleaner (see illustration). They can add yarn to hang up the chime.
4. The children take turns fanning cardboard to make each other's chimes bump in the *wind* and make a BIG noise.

MORE IDEAS

- Older children estimate how long yarn strips need to be and then measure and cut yarn strips themselves. **Note**: Yarn should be about 6" long. Longer strips get tangled and then items don't bump into each other.

DISCUSSION STARTERS

Use these questions to spark children's thinking during and after the activity:

- What did you find out about making wind chimes?
- Where do you think you might hang your wind chime at home?

SKILLS ASSESSMENT

Use these questions to determine a child's abilities and understanding:

- Can the child manipulate the tape?
- Does the child enjoy fanning cardboard to make other children's chimes make noise?

FOCUS AREAS

Science: observing
Math: counting, estimating, measuring—length

MATERIALS

Yarn strips about 6" long, about 4 per child
Pipe cleaners
Masking tape
Assortment of small objects that will make noise when they bump into each other, such as old CDs, plastic ware, metal juice lids, about 3 items per chime
Manufactured wind chime (optional)

It's a Great BIG Flag

FOCUS AREAS

Science: observing
Math: making patterns
Art: exploring design

MATERIALS

Light, solid color fabric (part of an old sheet works well)
Fabric paint
Permanent markers
Sturdy stick
Flag samples, ideally a real flag, or photos of flags in books or magazines

WHAT TO DO

1. Show the children different flags. Talk about how some flags have pictures and some have patterns.
2. Invite the children to create a class flag. Ask what the flag might look like.
3. Depending on the age of your class and the children's ideas, you might create a formal pattern with stripes, or you may want to have something more informal, such as each child's handprint with their name underneath in a random design or in a handprint tree.
4. Use masking tape to block off a 3" border on the left side of the fabric so there is room to attach the fabric to the stick.
5. The children take turns putting their handprint on the flag or drawing part of the design. An adult prints the names on masking tape. When the handprints are dry the children can print their names in permanent markers or an adult can print the names on the fabric.
6. Attach the flag to the stick and hang it outdoors so the children can see the *wind* blow their flag.

DISCUSSION STARTERS

Use these questions to spark children's thinking during and after the activity:

- Where have you seen other flags? What did they look like?
- How does a flag look when the *wind* is blowing softly?
- What sounds do you hear when the flag blows?
- Where should we put our flag so it will blow in the *wind*?

SKILLS ASSESSMENT

Use these questions to determine a child's abilities and understanding:

- Does the child enjoy working on a group project?
- Does the child see the overall pattern?
- Does the child contribute ideas for the flag design?

Take Flight

WHAT TO DO

1. The children decorate two paper cups with markers and crepe paper streamers attached to the outside of the cup. Invite the children to create a pattern with their streamers, such as red, blue, red, blue; or any other pattern.

2. The children slide their hands into the cups and out through the bottom, then move their arms like wings. They will enjoy pretending they are a bird, raptor, airplane, or their own creation. Invite them to make noises and have people guess what they are.

3. The children use the "wings" outdoors where there is enough room to run safely. Ask them what they think will happen to the streamers when they run. If it is a *windy* day, have them compare running into the *wind* to running with the *wind*. How does the movement of the streamers change? How does running fast change the way the streamers move compared with walking or standing still?

DISCUSSION STARTERS

Use these questions to spark children's thinking during and after the activity:
- Which animals and machines fly?
- What kind of flying animal or machine would you like to be?
- Where would you like to fly?
- What could you see way up in the sky?
- How would it feel to fly?
- How could the *wind* help you fly?

SKILLS ASSESSMENT

Use these questions to determine a child's abilities and understanding:
- Did the child make a pattern with the streamers?
- Does the child enjoy running with her wings?
- Does the child use her imagination? "I'm flapping my wings really hard so I can get to the North Pole."

FOCUS AREAS

Science: making *predictions* and observations
Math: exploring patterns
Gross Motor: making upper body movements, running

MATERIALS

10-ounce paper cups, 2 per child
Crepe paper in multiple colors
Masking tape or transparent tape
Markers

PREPARATION

- Cut out the bottom of all the paper cups so a child's hand will fit through. It's not necessary to remove the bottom; you can just fold it into the cup (see illustration).

Run Like the Wind

FOCUS AREAS
Science: planning and conducting a simple investigation
Gross Motor: running

MATERIALS
Several large sheets of stiff corrugated cardboard, about the size of a large pizza box

WHAT TO DO
1. On a *windy* day choose a location outside where the children can run safely.
2. Invite a small group of children to run into the *wind*, and then run back.
3. Let each child take a turn holding a large sheet of cardboard in front of her body while walking and then running into the *wind*. Ask, "How does it feel running into the *wind* with the cardboard?"

   Safety note: Be sure the cardboard is not so BIG that the children could trip while running.
4. Then have each child try running the opposite direction, with the *wind*. Ask, "How does that feel?"

MORE IDEAS
- After all the children have tried running with the flat cardboard, bend some pieces in the middle to create wedges. Let the children try running with the wedge held horizontally and then vertically. How does that feel?

DISCUSSION STARTERS
Use these questions to spark children's thinking during and after the activity:
- What did you find out about running in the *wind*?
- Is it easier for you to run with or without the cardboard?
- Is it easier to run against the *wind* or with the *wind*? Why do you suppose that is?
- What do you think the cardboard does to the *air*?

SKILLS ASSESSMENT
Use these questions to determine a child's abilities and understanding:
- Does the child enjoy running?
- Can the child describe the different running experiences?
- Does the child use comparative vocabulary words, such as *easier, harder, faster,* and *slower*?

More Activities Across the Curriculum

LANGUAGE ARTS

- Children draw pictures and dictate stories for an adult to write on their drawings. Include *wind* books and vocabulary words at the table for inspiration. Topics for different days:
  - What was is your favorite way to make *wind*—waving cardboard, blowing through a straw, or using the hair dryer?
  - A BIG *wind* is blowing stuff around. What would it blow to you?
  - Where would you like to travel if you could fly or be blown by the *wind*?

  Mount the stories on giant blue paper in a swirl to represent the *windy* sky. When you take down the display save the drawings in each child's portfolio.

MATH/ART

- Children blow drops of watercolor paint with a straw. They can *experiment* with different types of paper: How far can they blow the drops on absorbent construction paper compared with shiny finger paint paper? After the paint dries, invite the children to measure with rulers or Unifix cubes how far they blew their drops of paint. Make this a BIG experience by using a turkey baster to place drops of watercolor on a long sheet of paper. The children lift and lower the paper in the *wind*, and measure the drop trails when they are dry. If the *wind* flips the paper, say it is helping you paint.

SCIENCE/ART

- Children blow bubbles into soapy water and make bubble prints using turkey basters to make BIG bubbles.
- Children make paper airplanes and fly them. Fold BIG paper airplanes from chart paper and measure their flights outside. Try launching them from different heights. Do BIG paper airplanes fly differently from smaller planes?
- Children make *wind* socks.

SCIENCE/MATH/DRAMATIC PLAY IN THE SENSORY/WATER TABLE

- Provide doll clothes for the children to scrub in the water table and then hang up to dry on a clothesline. Ask the children to estimate how long it will take the clothes to dry. Try this activity over several days and compare results. Do the clothes dry faster if it's *windy*? Use the BIG vocabulary word *evaporate* (see page 106 in the Rain Chapter).

DRAMATIC PLAY

- Provide hollow blocks or small chairs for the children to create an airplane. The children can pretend they are pilots and passengers.

GROSS MOTOR/MUSIC

- Children choose a crepe paper streamer or silk scarf and let it float in the *air* and twirl around to various types of music representing stormy *winds*, *gusts*, and mild *breezes*.

GROSS MOTOR

- Parachute play—use *air* to make a BIG parachute bounce, wave, and create a dome that everyone can sit under.

BIG Outcomes

Group assessment: During group time, review the photo boards about *experimenting* with different types of *wind* power, playing *air* soccer, and performing "The Three Little Pigs." Review the chart paper sheets from the beginning of your exploration of what the children know about *air* and *wind* and what they want to learn. On a third sheet of chart paper titled "What We Learned About Air and Wind," record the children's comments about what they learned. Note the child's name beside each comment. Be sure to note answers to their original questions, or note if you still have more to learn and explore.

Individual assessment: Review your notes and quotes from individual observations during activities, such as the *wind experiment*, story dictation, and the *wind* games. Review the children's work and save in portfolios. Note areas in which the children need further practice and those in which they excel.

GOOD BOOKS FOR FACTS AND FUN
Easy non-fiction books about wind are generally aimed at the older preschool and kindergarten audience. Select the information and pictures from these books that suits the interest level of younger children. Many stories and folktales about the wind are long but provide opportunities to extend the children's focus and attention. Most storm tales are best used with older children or shared individually so you may answer questions or allay any fears.

INFORMATION ABOUT THE WIND
Air Is All Around You by Franklyn M. Branley
New illustrations jazz up this solid introduction to air, from how fish breathe to how astronauts breathe using air tanks. Clear directions are included for experiments to prove invisible air is really there. Ages 4–6

Can You See the Wind? by Allan Fowler
This simple overview of wind basics written by a veteran science writer discusses how the wind moves and the uses for the wind. The book is illustrated with color photographs. Ages 3–5

Feel the Wind by Arthur Dorros
Offering more detail for older students, this entry in a reliable series explains Earth's heating and cooling, the movement of air, storms, Chinooks, and siroccos. Watercolor and line drawings illustrate the text and the weather vane project. Ages 5–6

I Face the Wind by Vicki Cobb

Explore the wind through questions and easy-to-do activities illustrated in appealing collages and descriptive type styles. Pick and choose experiments from this whirlwind of fun. Ages 3–6

Searching for Stormy Weather with a Scientist by Judith Williams

Meet a meteorologist and learn about forecasting severe weather events, all explained in simple sentences, clear diagrams, and color photos. A twister-in-a-bottle demonstration, a booklist, and websites are included. Ages 3–6

Windy Days by Jennifer S. Burke

Common wind experiences—flags, bubbles, paper plates, and hats blowing away—are captured in color photos alongside simple sentences. The wind word list includes definitions and pronunciation guides. Ages 3–5

Who Likes the Wind? by Etta Kaner

Questions, with answers revealed when the flap is lifted on each fold-out page, focus on unique positive aspects about the wind. Pleasant, child-friendly illustrations add to an attractive presentation of facts. This book is a bit fragile but fun. Ages 3–6

STORIES ABOUT WIND

Blow Away Soon by Betsy James

Sophie's Nana helps her face her fear of the "old lady wind" by building a "blow-away-soon" on a hill near their house in the desert Southwest. Dreamy, soft pastels underscore the love and trust Sophie and Nana share. Ages 4–6

Elmer Takes Off by David McKee

Elmer, the patchwork elephant, fools his friends by pretending to blow away in a big wind. Imagine everyone's surprise when he really does lift off and fly. Ages 4–6

Gilberto and the Wind by Marie Hall Ets

Little Gilberto plays outside alone with the wind. Drawings in brown, white, and gray on tan pages don't dazzle but perfectly echo this gentle, classic story, which captures a real child's exploration of the world around him. Ages 3–5

How the Ladies Stopped the Wind by Bruce McMillan

Clever and creative ladies join forces with chickens and cows to solve the problem of the disappearing trees on the very windy island of Iceland. Brightly colored folk-style illustrations add to the fun. Ages 3–5

Like a Windy Day by Frank Asch and Devin Asch

Breezy, brief poetic phrases filled with wind action verbs describe a little girl's enjoyment of the wind's many moods. Swirling colors and flowing lines suggest movements in the air. Read this book once and then go back for a closer look. Ages 3–6

The Match Between the Winds by Shirley Climo
On the island of Borneo, the fierce West Wind challenges the gentle East Wind to a
contest to blow Kodok, the little tree frog, out of his palm tree. This colorful
retelling of an entertaining folktale holds a surprise ending. Ages 4–6

The Wind Blew by Pat Hutchins
An old British favorite told in rhyme in which everyone chases newspapers, a hanky,
the judge's wig, the postman's letters, and more until they all tumble down in a
jumble when the wind blows out to sea. Lively details illustrate a merry chase.
Ages 3–4

The Windy Day by G. Brian Karas
A bit of a *breeze* picks up speed and blows chaos into a tidy town, upsetting everyone
except Bernard, who exults in his encounter with a wind that long-ago tickled the
chins of dinosaurs. Use this as a whimsical jumpstart for creative story writing,
"Where has your wind been blowing?" Ages 4–6

STORIES OF "THE THREE LITTLE PIGS"

The Three Little Pigs by James Marshall
This traditional text is embellished with the artist's sly, humorous asides in dialog
bubbles. Marshall's wolf is lean, mean, and comes to a bad end. Flat, cartoon-like
illustrations take the edge off the violence of the tale. Ages 3–6

The Three Little Pigs by Paul Galdone
Three sweet pink pigs face off with the big, bad wolf, who ends up as the last pig's
dinner in this classic English folktale. Retold clearly and illustrated simply, this story
of the smart pig who survives stays true to tradition. Ages 3–6

The Three Little Wolves and the Big Bad Pig by Eugene Trivizas
A complete swap of roles enlivens this reworked story, which ends peaceably.
Delightfully illustrated, filled with details to discover, this book inspires new ways to
approach an old, old tale. Ages 4–6

The True Story of the 3 Little Pigs by Jon Scieszka
In this wry, quirky version, we hear the story from Alexander T. Wolf's view as he
defends his innocent intentions and actions from his prison cell. Edgy, angular art
appeals to older children who have heard the traditional tale before. Ages 5 and up

A Note to Families About Air and Wind

Dear Families,

We can't see air but we can feel it move. At school we have been experimenting with different ways to make air move—by blowing out our breath, by blowing with straws, and by using cardboard fans. Of course, electric fans and hair dryers move the air really fast. We turned our explorations into games because children often learn best through playing. Ask your child to show you how to play air soccer with a cotton ball or packing noodle.

We can also hear the wind working when it makes things like leaves and wind chimes bump into each other. We made a giant wind chime at school with old forks, pie tins, and pot lids. What noise that created on a windy day! Can you find a place at home to hang up the small wind chime your child made?

Exploring wind at school may help your child feel more comfortable during storms when the wind is scary.

These are some of the big words your child is learning:
- Air is invisible. We can't see it. We can't see the wind either, but we can see it moving leaves and flags.
- A breeze is a gentle wind.
- A gust is a sudden rush of air or wind.

Have fun making air move with your child!

THINKING BIG ABOUT ICE: BRRR, IT'S COLD!

THE BIG PICTURE

Ice is a familiar substance. Even in areas where it rarely freezes outside, children know about ice cubes and ice cream. Studying ice helps children explore the scientific concepts of freezing and melting, and the states of matter: solid and liquid. This unit also introduces children to the concept of temperature and a useful scientific tool, the thermometer.

TIMING TIP

Ice is a good winter topic for extending weather explorations of wind and rain. If you live in an area with freezing weather, it makes sense to explore ice on cold days when there are frozen puddles, or you can freeze a bucket of water outdoors. Studying ice and cold is especially interesting during the Winter Olympics. It's also fun to study ice during hot weather.

OBJECTIVES

- Understand that ice is frozen water
- Explore temperature and methods of measuring temperature
- Start to learn about different states of matter
- Begin learning about freezing and melting

STANDARDS

National Science Education Standards

- Science as inquiry—ask questions; plan and conduct a simple investigation; use simple equipment and tools; communicate investigations and explanations
- Physical science—explore properties of objects and materials; understand that materials can exist in different states—solid, liquid and gas; learn that water can be changed from one state to another by heating or cooling; experiment with position and motion of objects
- Earth and space science—explore properties of Earth materials; observe changes in the Earth and sky

National Council of Teachers of Mathematics Standards

- Number and operations—count with understanding; make reasonable estimates
- Measurement—understand how to measure using nonstandard and standard tools
- Data analysis and probability—represent data using pictures and graphs
- Communication—organize, analyze, and evaluate mathematical thinking; use the language of mathematics

Standards for the English Language Arts

- Experience a wide range of print and non-print texts, including fiction and non-fiction, to build an understanding of the world and acquire new information
- Use spoken, written, and visual language to communicate and learn
- Generate ideas and questions and pose problems
- Build vocabulary

BIG BEGINNING:

Introducing Ice

FOCUS AREAS

Science: using simple equipment and tools— thermometers, eyedroppers, and tongs; studying states of matter—water can exist as a solid and a liquid

Math: measuring— temperature

Language Arts: learning vocabulary, using spoken language to communicate

MATERIALS

2 containers of water at room temperature

2 eyedroppers

2 containers of ice cubes in water

2 tongs

Sturdy child-safe thermometer (**Safety note:** Do not use thermometers that are made with mercury.)

Masking tape, red is ideal

2 sheets of chart paper

Marker

Hat and mittens for you to wear (optional)

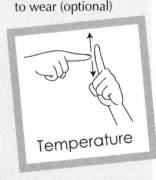

Temperature

PREPARATION

- Label one sheet of chart paper "What We Know About Ice and Cold" and the other "What We Want to Learn About Ice and Cold."

WHAT TO DO

1. Before group time, put on your hat and mittens. When children gather, ask if they have any ideas why you are wearing a hat and mittens. Say, "We are going to explore something that is cold."

2. Ask children to hold out a hand, palm up. Squirt a few drops of water in each child's palm with an eyedropper. (If you and an adult assistant go around the circle in opposite directions, you will cut the waiting time in half.) Ask, "How does this water feel?" Then, holding an ice cube with tongs, lightly touch each child's palm with the ice cube. Ask, "How does the ice feel?"

3. Ask, "How are the water and the ice different?" "How are they the same?" Record the children's comments, including the name of the child who made the comment, on the chart paper labeled, "What We Know About Ice and Cold."

4. Say, "We can measure the temperature of the water and ice." Introduce the word *temperature*, a measurement of how hot or cold something is. Say and clap the syllables, **tem**-per-a-ture, with the emphasis on the "tem" syllable. Say *temperature* as you make the ASL sign for temperature. The tip of your right index finger slides up and down the back of your left index finger as if your left index finger is the thermometer and the right is the mercury rising and falling.

5. Say, "We measure *temperature* using a *thermometer*." Say and clap the syllables, ther-**mom**-e-ter, with the emphasis on the "mom" syllable. "A thermometer is an instrument for measuring temperature." Say *thermometer* as you show the children a thermometer.

6. Place the thermometer into one container of room-temperature water. Mark the level with a strip of red masking tape, read the number, and show the thermometer to the children. Move the thermometer into the container of ice cubes and water. Wait for the temperature to stop falling and then go around to each child showing how the red line is now much lower than it was in the room-temperature water.

7. Tell the children they will be able to explore how a thermometer works and how different temperatures feel during activity time.

8. Ask the children what they want to find out about ice and cold. Record those comments on the chart paper labeled, "What We Want to Learn About Ice and Cold." Use their questions and interests to guide your activities. Some children may be especially interested in winter sports or ice cream.

A Note from the Author: The activities in this chapter are designed to build on each other. However, please feel free to choose those that meet the interests and abilities of your class. If parts of an activity seem like too much to do on a particular day, save them for a later time. Every class is different, even from day to day, and the activities are adaptable to meet the needs of your class.

BIG QUESTIONS FOR GROWING MINDS

Use the following questions to engage the children in a discussion about ice and cold during group time or with an individual child during activity time:
- Which cold foods do you like to eat?
- Do foods taste the same when they are cold as they do when they are warm?
- What happens to an ice cube if you leave it out of the freezer?
- What other foods melt like an ice cube left out of the freezer?

WORDS FOR BIG THINKING

Look for these words highlighted in italics throughout the activities in this chapter. Write the words out in large letters and introduce them a few at a time with the "**S**ay, **C**lap, **A**ct out, **D**o again" (SCAD) system. Using the words during activities and discussions will reinforce their meaning.
- Experiment—a test to see what will happen
- Freeze—to change from a liquid to a solid by cooling (losing heat)
- Liquid—has no shape of its own. A liquid flows, taking the shape of its container.
- Melt—to change from a solid to a liquid by warming (adding heat)
- Prediction—like a guess—what you think might happen based on what you already know
- Scientist—someone who studies the natural world
- Solid—has shape, a solid keeps its shape
- Temperature—a measurement of how hot or cold something is
- Thermometer—a tool to measure temperature

PHOTO TIP

You can record children's explorations of ice and temperature by creating photo boards about experimenting with thermometers and melting ice, racing ice cubes, and building ice castles. Look for close-up of individual children and group shots that show children interacting. Also include vocabulary words and quotes from children on the photo boards to document their learning.

Make Icees

FOCUS AREAS

Science: using simple equipment and tools; studying *liquids* and *solids*

Math: counting, measuring—volume, time and *temperature*

Language Arts: experiencing different types of text—recipe, poem

Fine Motor: pouring, measuring

MATERIALS

Liquid measuring cup

½ cup dry measuring cup

Sturdy child-safe thermometer (no mercury) washed and disinfected with bleach

Sturdy, sealable sandwich bags, 2 per batch

1 gallon freezer bags, 2 per batch

Apple or other juice, ¼ cup per batch, refrigerated

Pitcher of ice water

Crushed or cubed ice, (about 3 trays of cubes per batch)

Salt, regular or coarse. ½ cup per batch

Small towel per batch

Paper cups, 1 per child

Plastic spoons, 1 per child

1-minute sand timer (5 timers if you have them to mark 5 minutes)

3 sheets of chart paper

Marker

TEACHER-TO-TEACHER TIP

This activity works best if you use very cold ice cubes just out of the freezer. Adding salt to the ice cubes creates super-cold water (colder than regular ice water), which freezes the apple juice. Diluted apple juice freezes more quickly than full-strength juice.

PREPARATION

● Write the Icee recipe (on the next page) on chart paper. Include drawings of each step, if possible.

● Write the words to the Icee Chant (on the next page) on chart paper.

WHAT TO DO

1. Ask the children if they have ideas how they could turn apple juice from something *liquid* they can drink into something *solid* they can eat with a spoon. Record their responses on chart paper.

2. Have one child help fill the gallon freezer bag about half full with ice. Invite another child to measure and add ½ cup salt. Set the bag aside.

3. Measure the *temperature* of the refrigerated juice in the bottle with the clean *thermometer*. Note the temperature and mark it on the *thermometer* with a piece of masking tape. Ask one child to help you measure ¼ cup apple juice and pour it into the sandwich bag. Another child can help you measure ¼ cup ice water and add it to the sandwich bag.

4. Squeeze all the air out of this bag of apple juice to help keep it from popping open. Seal the bag tightly. Put it inside a second small plastic bag to prevent leaking, squeeze out the air, seal the bag well, and place it inside the freezer bag filled with ice and salt.

5. Place everything in a second gallon freezer bag, squeeze out the air, and seal tightly to help prevent leaking.

6. Tell the children they can now turn *liquid* apple juice into a frozen treat. The bag is **very** cold. After everyone touches the bag, wrap it in a towel for easier handling. Show the children the sand timer (or timers). It takes about five minutes to turn the juice into a fruit Icee. If you line up five one-minute timers, the children can take turns turning them over one at a time. Have one child flip the first timer while another shakes the bag for five shakes while everyone counts to five, then passes it to the next child. The children take turns flipping the timer at the end of each minute.

7. After the bag has gone around the circle once, recite the following "Icee Chant" instead of counting to five for each child's turn. They can pass the icy bag to the next child at the end of each line:

Icee Chant by Tim Dobbins
I'm going to make, make, make.
I'm going to shake, shake, shake.
How long will it take, take, take?
How long will it take?

Oh, please, please, please,
Won't you freeze, freeze, freeze?
I won't squeeze, squeeze, squeeze.
I will pass it on to you!

8. At the end of five minutes the juice should be *freezing.* If not, send it around the circle a few more times and keep chanting. When it *freezes,* place the *thermometer* in the outer bag of ice to check the *temperature.*

9. Ask, "What do you think made the juice *freeze?*" Explain that the ice and salt made the apple juice really cold so it changed from a *liquid* like water to a *solid* like ice. Say, "Everyone will get a chance to make and taste Icees during activity time."

MORE IDEAS

- Make ice cream with the same procedure. Add 1 tablespoon sugar and ½ teaspoon vanilla to ½ cup milk. Compare the starting *temperature* of the milk to the juice. Are the juice and the milk the same *temperature* after five minutes? Which one is harder, more solid? Compare the *freezing* time to the juice Icees.
- Compare types of juice. Do they take the same amount of time to become an Icee?
- Add small chunks of frozen fruit or berries to the Icee or ice cream mixture. Does this change the starting *temperature?* Does this change the time it takes to *freeze?*

DISCUSSION STARTERS

Use these questions to spark children's thinking during and after the activity:

- What did you find out about making Icees?
- What else could you measure with a *thermometer?*
- What tools did you use for measuring? (measuring cups, sand timers, and *thermometers)*
- What did you measure? (juice, salt, temperature, how long it took to freeze)

SKILLS ASSESSMENT

Use these questions to determine a child's abilities and understanding:

- Is the child engaged in the group activity?
- Does the child join in the shaking and chanting?

Icee Recipe

One batch of Icees yields enough for six children, each receiving about a spoonful.

Fill the gallon-size freezer bag half full of ice.

Add ½ cup of salt to the ice in the bag.

Mix the ice and salt in the bag and set it aside.

Pour ¼ cup cold apple juice into a sandwich bag.

Add ¼ cup ice water to the juice in the sandwich bag, squeeze out the air, and carefully seal well.

Place the bag of juice and water in a second sandwich bag, squeeze out the air and seal well.

Place the bag of juice in the freezer bag. Squeeze out the air and seal carefully.

Place everything in a second gallon bag, squeeze out the air, and seal.

Pass the bag around the circle so the children can feel how cold it is.

Wrap the bag in a small towel.

It will take about 5 minutes of shaking to freeze the Icees.

Scoop the Icees into small paper cups.

BIG Thermometer

FOCUS AREAS

Science: using a *thermometer;* studying weather

Math: measuring— temperature, com

Language Arts: learning vocabulary, experiencing different types of print and non-print texts

MATERIALS

Felt board

Felt snowman

Felt sun

Felt *thermometer* (directions below)

Chart paper

Marker

Props to indicate heat, such as sunglasses and a paper fan (optional)

Props to indicate cold, such as mittens and a scarf (optional)

PREPARATION

- Make a felt *thermometer.* Make a red circle, about 2″ in diameter for the bottom and tape or glue it to a white, black, or blue vertical strip about 1 ½″ wide and 18″ tall. Make two red strips about ½″ wide, one about 6″ tall to indicate a cold *temperature,* and one about 18″ tall to indicate a hot *temperature.*
- Make a felt snowman and sun.
- Fold a paper fan.
- Write the words to the poem (see below) on chart paper.

WHAT TO DO

1. At group time, show the children a real *thermometer* and place your felt *thermometer* on the felt board. Add the sun next to the top of the *thermometer* and the snowman to the bottom. Say the following poem with the children as you point to the felt board and add the different red strips.

   Thermometer by Tim Dobbins
   Rising sun, (point to sun)
   And falling snow, (point to snowman)
   Hot is high, (place long red strip on thermometer)
   And cold is low. (replace long strip with short red strip)
   Skinny red line tells us for sure
   Exactly what's the temperature.

2. Give each child a chance to choose the short or the long piece of felt to show either a hot *temperature* or cold *temperature.*
3. The children place the felt strip on the board and put on the appropriate prop. If they choose the short strip for cold, they put on the mittens and pretend they are shivering and the rest of the group shivers with them. If they choose the long strip, they put on the sunglasses and pretend they are hot by fanning themselves along with the rest of the class.

DISCUSSION STARTERS

Use these questions to spark children's thinking during and after the activity:
- What do you like to do when the weather is hot? What do you wear when it's hot?
- What do you like to do when the weather is cold? What do you wear when it's cold?

SKILLS ASSESSMENT

Use these questions to determine a child's abilities and understanding:
- Does the child contribute ideas to the group discussion?
- Does the child enjoy acting out whether it is hot or cold?

Learning About Temperature and Thermometers

PREPARATION

- Prepare three containers of different water temperatures: cold with ice floating in the water, cool (room *temperature*), and hot. **Safety note**: Make sure the hot water won't burn a child's hand. About 100° F will feel hot enough.

WHAT TO DO

1. Work with a small group of children. Give each child a *thermometer*. Invite each child to put one finger in one of the water containers and say if the water is hot, cold, or cool. Then place a *thermometer* in the container and note the height of the red line measuring the *temperature*. Older children may enjoy noticing the number.

2. Ask them to stick their finger in another container and say if it's hot, cold, or cool. Invite the children to predict whether the *thermometer* line will go up or down. They then place the *thermometer* in the water to see what happens.

3. The children move the *thermometer* between all the bowls noting if the water is hot, cool, or cold, and what happens to the *thermometer* line.

4. When you gather as a group, discuss what they discovered and say the poem from the BIG Thermometer activity again.

Thermometer by Tim Dobbins
Rising sun
And falling snow,
Hot is high,
And cold is low.
Skinny red line tells us for sure
Exactly what's the temperature.

MORE IDEAS

- The children place a *thermometer* in a small container of room-*temperature* water and then add ice or hot water from an insulated coffee pitcher and watch the *thermometer* reading change in their container.

DISCUSSION STARTERS

Use these questions to spark children's thinking during and after the activity:

- What did you learn about how a *thermometer* works?
- When does the red line on the *thermometer* go up?
- When does the red line on the *thermometer* go down?
- How can you make the water colder or hotter?
- What else could you measure with a *thermometer*?

SKILLS ASSESSMENT

Use these questions to determine a child's abilities and understanding:

- Can the child predict whether the *thermometer* level will go up or down depending on the *temperature* of the water?
- Does the child use the vocabulary words of *thermometer*, *temperature*, *cold*, and *hot*?
- Did the child enjoy varying the *temperature* by adding more ice or hot water?

What Is Your Cold Count?

WHAT TO DO

1. Work with a small group of children. Invite each child to write with a pencil on their recording sheets. (They will write again later with a pencil when their hand is cold and compare it to this writing.) Older children can usually print their name. Younger children can make some letters or a squiggle.

2. Demonstrate the activity. Say, "I wonder how long I can hold my hand in the ice water. I *predict* I'll be able to keep my hand in the water for a count of five." Have the children count with you. It's up to you whether you keep your hand in the water for more or less time. (See Teacher-to-Teacher Tips on estimating and *predicting*.)

3. Invite the children to place a *thermometer* in the ice water and notice how the "skinny red line" goes down.

4. Challenge the children to predict how long they can hold their

FOCUS AREAS

Science: planning and conducting a simple investigation, communicating investigations and explanations, exploring properties of objects and materials

Math: counting, estimating, communicating results

Fine Motor: writing with pencil

MATERIALS

Bowl of ice water large enough to fit a child's hand
Paper towels
Pencils, 1 per child
Sturdy child-safe *thermometers* (not mercury)
Recording sheets, 1 per child

PREPARATION

● Prepare recording sheets for children to *predict* how long they can keep their hands in a bowl of ice water—five or 10 seconds. Make one copy for each child.

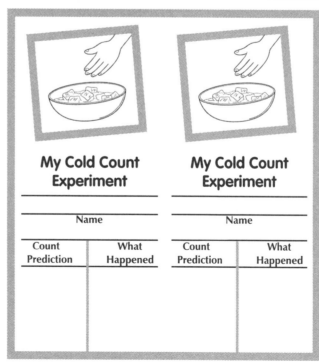

My Cold Count Experiment		**My Cold Count Experiment**	
Name		Name	
Count Prediction	What Happened	Count Prediction	What Happened

hands in the ice water. Help them circle the five or the 10. Older children may enjoy writing the number or choosing a different number.

5. The children put their hands in the ice water. They count to five or 10, or as long as they have their hands in the water.

6. The children write their names with their cold hand and circle their actual count or write the number. Is it longer or shorter than their prediction? Ask, "Is it easier or harder to write with an ice-cold hand?" (Our sense of touch doesn't work as well when we are cold.)

7. The children dry off their hands and rub them together to warm up.

8. Save the recording sheets in each child's portfolio.

MORE IDEAS

● After the children have done the first cold count, they coat an index finger in Vaseline. Ask them to feel the ice water with a bare finger and the Vaseline-coated finger. Do they feel a difference? The Vaseline is similar to blubber that Arctic animals have. Their blubber insulates them from the cold.

DISCUSSION STARTERS

Use these questions to spark children's thinking during and after the activity:

● How does your hand feel when it is in the water?

● How does it feel when you take it out?

● How does your hand look when it is cold? What changes can you see?

● How does your body feel when your hand is cold?

● How can you warm up your hands when they are cold?

SKILLS ASSESSMENT

Use these questions to determine a child's abilities and understanding:

● Is the child able to count to 10?

● Does the child know the concepts of *more than* and *less than?*

● What is the child's pencil grip?

TEACHER-TO-TEACHER TIPS

● *Predicting* and estimating are tough skills for children to master, especially because they want to be right. You can help children understand that it is okay not to always be right by *predicting* incorrectly yourself. Say, "I predicted that I could leave my hand in the ice water while I counted to five but the water was so cold I could only leave my hand in the bowl for three."

● Don't worry if the children are not counting at an even pace. It's natural for them to speed up or slow down to make their *prediction* accurate.

● Many children can keep their hands in the ice water much longer than a count of 10.

Ice Experiment: Where Will Ice Cubes Melt the Slowest and Fastest?

| Where Will Ice Cubes Melt the... | | |
Slowest?		Fastest?

Miriam	Closet	Windowsill in the sun
Derrick	Under the sink	By the heat vent
Carlos	By the door	Window in the sun
Kaitlin		
Tasha		
Michael		

WHAT TO DO

1. At group time, tell the children they are going to be *scientists,* people who study the natural world. Say, "*Scientists* make *predictions,* another word for guesses, what they think might happen, based on what they already know. Scientists test their predictions by doing *experiments,* which are tests to see what will happen."

2. Ask the children to make a *prediction* about what they think will happen if they put an ice cube on a sunny windowsill.

3. Introduce the word *solid,* something that has shape. Ice is *solid.* Say and clap the syllables, **sol**-id, with the emphasis on the "sol" syllable. Ask the children to show you some other *solids* in the classroom (blocks, books, virtually everything in the room). Introduce the word *melt.* When something melts, it changes from a *solid* to a *liquid.* When ice *melts,* it absorbs heat and becomes *liquid* water. Say and clap *melt,* just one syllable. Say *melt* as you make the ASL sign for *dissolve.* Begin with both hands palms up, thumbs touching little fingers.

FOCUS AREAS

Science: asking a question, conducting a simple investigation, exploring different states of matter—solid and liquid

Math: measuring—time, communicating results

Language Arts: learning vocabulary

MATERIALS

Ice cubes, 2 per child
Paper cups, 2 per child with their names on each
Chart paper
Blue and red dot stickers
Permanent markers

PREPARATION

- Write each child's name in permanent marker on two paper cups. Draw or place a red dot sticker on one of each child's cup and a blue dot on the child's other cup.
- Label the sheet of chart paper "Where Will Ice Cubes Melt?" Set up a chart to record the children's *predictions* for the slowest locations and fastest locations.

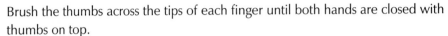

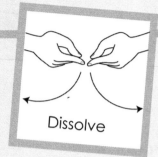

Dissolve

Brush the thumbs across the tips of each finger until both hands are closed with thumbs on top.

4. Say, "During activity time, you are going to do an *experiment* to see where ice cubes *melt* the fastest. You will get two paper cups. Your name is on each of your cups so you know they are yours. You can put an ice cube in each of your cups. Then you can decide where to put the cups. Choose one place where you think the ice cube will *melt* very fast. You will put your cup with the red dot in that place. Choose another place where you think it will *melt* more slowly. Put the cup with the blue dot there. We will write down for you what you *predict*. (See illustration on the previous page). Then you can set out your cups and see what happens. We want to see how long it takes for the ice cubes *melt,* so leave the ice and the water in the cup."

5. Note the time the children start their *experiment*. Set a timer to ring every 10–15 minutes during activity time so the children can check on their ice cubes. They tell an adult when the ice cube *melts* completely so the adult can record the time next to the location on the chart. How long did it take for the ice cubes to *melt*?

MORE IDEAS

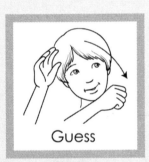

Guess

- Introduce the word *prediction*, which is like a guess, what the children think might happen. Say and clap out the syllables, pre-**dic**-tion, with the emphasis on the "dic" syllable. Say *prediction* as you make the ASL sign for *guess*—an open hand makes a grab as it quickly passes by your forehead.

- Introduce the word *experiment*, which is a way to test a *prediction,* to see what will happen. Say and clap out the syllables, ex-**per**-i-ment, with the emphasis on the "per" syllable. Say *experiment* as you make the sign for *science*, (hands moving in alternate circles) but using the E handshape, fingers curled, resting on the thumb.

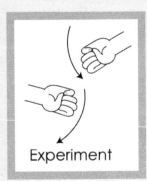

Experiment

- Introduce the word *liquid*. When something *solid melts* it becomes a *liquid*. *Liquid* means it doesn't have its own shape. It flows. It becomes the shape of the container. Say and clap the syllables, **liq**-uid, with the emphasis on the "liq" syllable. Ask the children to give examples of *liquids* (water, milk, juice).

DISCUSSION STARTERS

Use these questions to spark children's thinking during and after the activity:
- What did you discover about *melting* ice cubes?
- Where did your ice cube *melt* the slowest?
- Did your *prediction* match what happened?

SKILLS ASSESSMENT

Use these questions to determine a child's abilities and understanding:
- Does the child use the vocabulary words?
- Could the child make a *prediction*?
- Was the child curious about what would happen to the ice cubes in different locations?

BIG Building:
Make an Ice Castle

PREPARATION

- If you live in a cold climate, invite the children at school to set water outside in a variety of containers such as juice cartons (tops cut off) and yogurt containers to *freeze* overnight. They can add marbles or plastic beads as a kind of treasure which will be fun to recover when the ice melts. If you live in a warm climate, *freeze* numerous containers of water in a school *freezer* or ask families to *freeze* ice at home and bring into school.

TEACHER-TO-TEACHER TIP

Ordinarily, the blocks of ice don't adhere well to each other once they start warming up, making it hard to build something that looks like a castle. The children don't mind, however. They love stacking the blocks and squirting them with water and shaking salt on them. (**Note:** Salt will make cuts sting.) A great discovery we made is that children can use biodegradable packing noodles as a kind of mortar between the ice blocks. The noodles help stabilize the ice blocks, making them easier to stack. The noodles dissolve as the ice *melts*. If you have ready access to snow, children can pack snow around the ice blocks to build walls. If the children are working outside in cold weather, they will need mittens to handle the ice, which makes it harder to use eyedroppers; turkey basters will be easier to use.

FOCUS AREAS
Science: exploring solids and liquid
Math: measuring—time
Fine Motor: pinching and releasing eyedroppers

MATERIALS
Water table or rigid wading pool
Numerous containers of ice in different size shapes such as ½ gallon juice cartons and yogurt containers (all washed thoroughly)
Cooler for keeping the ice during the activity
Biodegradable packing noodles
Snow (optional)
Containers of *liquid* watercolor or food coloring in water
Eyedroppers or turkey basters (see Tip below)
Salt shakers
Coarse salt in a small container
Paper and marker to record *predictions*

WHAT TO DO

1. Set up the sand and water table or a rigid wading pool either in your classroom or outdoors. Tell a small group of children, "You will be able to use ice to build an ice castle. I will write down what time you begin. How long do you *predict* it will take for all the ice to *melt*? Do you think it will last for all of activity time?" Record their *predictions* with their names.

2. The children empty the ice from some containers to start building an ice castle. Keep some of the ice containers in the cooler for the children who start the activity later.

3. The children stack blocks of ice on top of each other to construct a castle. They also enjoy layering biodegradable packing noodles between the ice blocks to help them balance and stick. If the ice blocks slip, ask, "What could you do to make them balance better? If you have access to snow, the children can use it like mortar, filling gaps to make the castle sturdier.

4. Demonstrate eyedropper use—dip, squeeze, hold until you are ready to drop, and let go. Then invite the children to squirt *liquid* water color with eyedroppers on the ice. What happens? Admire the color mixing.

5. The children can sprinkle salt from a salt shaker and coarse salt on some of the blocks of ice. What happens? (The coarse salt dissolves slower so it is easier for the children to observe the hole it makes in the ice.) Admire the ice caves.

6. Note how long it takes the castle to *melt*. (Depending on the temperature and the size of the ice blocks, parts of the castle may last overnight. The children may notice that larger blocks take longer to *melt*.)

DISCUSSION STARTERS

Use these questions to spark children's thinking during and after the activity:

- What did you discover about building with ice?
- What is happening to the ice?
- What happened when you dropped on the colors?
- Which kinds of blocks *melted* the fastest?
- What happened when you put salt on the ice?
- How did the different kinds of salt change the ice?

SKILLS ASSESSMENT

Use these questions to determine a child's abilities and understanding:

- Does the child enjoy building with ice or does he get frustrated?
- How does the child work as part of a group?
- Does the child experiment with building techniques?
- Did the child make any *predictions* about the results of mixing colors?
- Did the child observe the differences between the two types of salt on the ice?
- Did the child use BIG vocabulary, such as *freezing*, *solid*, *melting*, and *liquid*?

Ice Races

TEACHER-TO-TEACHER TIPS

- Children might prefer to race the cubes down the giant rain gutter track, which is more exciting than the small water table races. But the water table helps occupy children while they are waiting their turn with the giant track. Start the cubes by holding them with the tongs at the top of the trays and releasing them after a countdown. This adds a challenge to the shorter slides.

- If you don't have a plastic rain gutter to build a giant track, you can do this activity on your outdoor slide. Children will not have the experience of designing and *experimenting* with the track but they love climbing to the top of the slide and sending the cubes down.

SFOCUS AREAS

Science: planning and conducting a simple investigation, using simple equipment and tools, exploring the position and motion of objects

Math: counting, measuring—time and height

Language Arts: learning vocabulary

Fine Motor: moving ice cubes with shovels, tongs, and spatulas

MATERIALS

Pictures of bobsled tracks or ski jumps
Water table or rigid plastic wading pool
Various metal cookie sheets and plastic trays to use as ramps
Plastic rain gutters or a playground slide
Ladders, tables, and chairs to prop up rain gutters
Plastic sand shovels, spatulas, various tongs
Plastic dish pans or containers to catch ice cubes at the end of the rain gutters
Ice cubes
Cooler to contain ice cubes
Paper towels to dry hands
Variety of timers

WHAT TO DO

1. Show a small group of children photos of bobsled tracks and ski jumps.

2. Suggest that the children set up an ice cube racing station in the water table or a rigid wading pool with several plastic trays and metal cookie sheets and a number of ice cubes.

3. The children slide ice cubes down the different trays to see which surfaces and which heights help the ice go faster. Encourage the children to vary the tilt of the trays to see how the height affects the speed. They can also see if the size of the ice affects speed. (As the children use the ice cubes, they will start to melt and get smaller.)

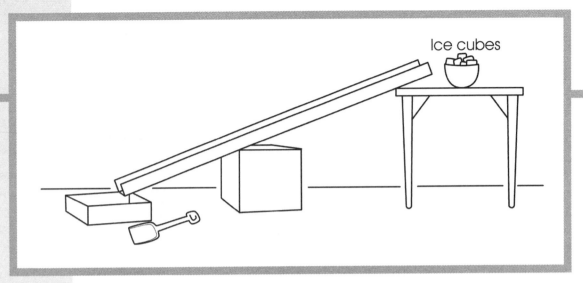

Ice cubes

4. Help the children set up a giant runway or two, depending how much space and rain gutter you have. Encourage the children to *experiment* with the height and length of the track.

5. The children can count, 1–2–3, or count down, 5–4–3–2–1, before they send the ice cubes down the track. They can compare and time how similar-sized cubes and different-sized cubes travel.

6. The children can vary the angle of the gutters to create faster and slower race courses. They can also *experiment* with the best way to catch the ice cubes and carry them back to the top of the gutter. A plastic bin at the bottom of the track will help catch the cubes. Carrying the cubes with small sand shovels helps keep their hands from getting too cold.

MORE IDEAS

- With two sets of tongs, a child can release ice cubes with his left and right hands at the same time. Compare the results. Did one ice cube start before the other? Try it again with two small sand shovels at the same time.

DISCUSSION STARTERS

Use these questions to spark children's thinking during and after the activity:

- How are the ice races different on the small race course and the BIG race course?
- How are they the same?
- Do the ice cubes move differently if the ramps are longer?
- Do the ice cubes move differently if the ramps are wet?

SKILLS ASSESSMENT

Use these questions to determine a child's abilities and understanding:

- Can the child count down 5–4–3–2–1?
- Can the child move and release ice cubes using the tongs?
- Does the child observe differences in the ice cube speeds?
- Is the child curious about how the ice travels on different ramps?
- Can the child communicate his observations?

Making Ice Crystals

WHAT TO DO

1. Work with a small group of children. Help them fill a can about ¼ full with salt. They take turns stirring the salt and adding crushed ice to fill the can to the top.

2. Leave the can in a cool place while you read the children a story about ice or snow. Droplets of water will form in a few minutes, but it may take 30 minutes or more for ice crystals to form. Invite the children to check back later.

3. The children use magnifying glasses to examine the outsides of their cans. Look for ice crystals with the children. Encourage the children to discuss the similarities and differences between the outsides of their cans.

4. Put a *thermometer* inside each can and measure the *temperature*. Are the *temperatures* the same in different cans?

TEACHER-TO-TEACHER TIP

It is natural that children will want to touch the outside of the can, which will instantly melt the ice crystals. To take advantage of their curiosity and encourage scientific thinking, ask them to *predict* what will happen if they touch the can. Allow each child to touch with one finger.

DISCUSSION STARTERS

Use these questions to spark children's thinking during and after the activity:

- What do you notice about the cans?
- What do you think is on the outside of the cans? (The cold cans cool the air around them so the air can't hold as much water. The tiny invisible water droplets in the air condense and *freeze* on the cold cans to make ice crystals, also called *frost*.)
- Where should we put the cans in the room to keep the ice cold?
- What do you think will happen if we put the can in a place where the sun shines on one side?

SKILLS ASSESSMENT

Use these questions to determine a child's abilities and understanding:

- Is the child curious about what is happening to the can?
- Does the child speculate about what might be causing the changes?
- Does the child make the connection between the cold can and the ice crystals?

FOCUS AREAS

Science: planning and conducting a simple investigation, using simple tools— *thermometers* and magnifying lenses

Math: measuring— temperature

MATERIALS

Book about ice or snow (see Good Books for Facts and Fun on pages 187–189)

Empty metal cans, such as soup cans, 1 per small group (tall cans are best; remove the labels from the cans and make sure the cans are clean, with no rough edges)

Salt to fill each can ¼ full (rock salt is cheaper but regular salt works.)

Crushed ice to fill each can to the top

Magnifying lenses

Sturdy, child-safe *thermometers* (not mercury)

Spoons

Ice Cube Hockey

FOCUS AREAS
Math: counting
Gross Motor: aiming, practicing eye-hand coordination

MATERIALS
Story about ice skating, such as *Polar Skater* by Sally Grindley (See Good Books for Facts and Fun on pages 187–189.)
Large tarp, preferably silver on one side
Colored masking tape
2 large cardboard boxes about the same size
Ice cubes or ice "pucks" (see PREPARATION)
2 small hockey sticks, plastic golf clubs, or child-size brooms
1 BIG push broom
Several small towels
Wooden clip clothespins
Whistle (optional)

PREPARATION
- Create a two-lane "hockey rink" by spreading out the tarp and placing masking tape down the middle. Mark the center line across each half with masking tape. Set one cardboard box as a goal on each half of the tarp.

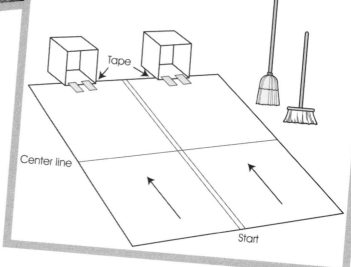

- *Freeze* 1" of water in small, clean yogurt containers to make "pucks" (optional step).
- Read a book to the children about ice skating.

TEACHER-TO-TEACHER TIP
This is a non-competitive game. Children enjoy simply trying to get the cube in the goal. It is important to tell the children that they need to keep their hockey sticks down, on the tarp, for safety.

WHAT TO DO

1. Four children can play at one time—two children trying to make a "goal" and two children dropping the ice cube or "puck." Caution the puck droppers that they need to move out of the way after they drop the puck.

2. A child or adult drops an ice-puck in front of each child at the end of the tarp opposite one of the goals. The two children dropping the puck move out of the way and the other two children "skate" with their cube up to the center line. Then they can try to make a goal. If they miss, they retrieve the ice cube and try again. If they make a goal, the ice dropper can take a turn. Other children can help retrieve the ice cube as goalies.
   Note: You can blow a whistle to signal when it is time to drop the pucks.

3. The children count how many strokes of the stick it takes to make a goal.

4. Wrap a towel around the brush of a BIG push broom and fasten it with clothespins to make a "Zamboni" machine for cleaning the ice. The children take turns "cleaning" the tarp to help clear water off.

MORE IDEAS

- Add elements of an obstacle course with orange cones or cardboard boxes to "skate" around.
- Children drop their own pucks and then skate.
- Invite the children to try shooting from the right and from the left. Which is easier?

DISCUSSION STARTERS

Use these questions to spark children's thinking during and after the activity:

- Have you ever walked on ice or tried skating? What does it feel like?
- Is this game like any other games you've played?
- What do you think would happen if you tried making a goal when you are farther away?

SKILLS ASSESSMENT

Use these questions to determine a child's abilities and understanding:

- Can the child aim accurately?
- Does the child keep trying to make a goal?
- How does the child interact with other children while playing?
- Does the child prefer to skate, drop the puck, or clean the ice?
- Does the child enjoy the experience of trying ice cube hockey?

BIG DRAMA:

"Goldilocks and The Three Bears"

FOCUS AREAS

Math: counting, sequencing

Language Arts: experiencing different types of text, retelling the story

Fine Motor: cutting, taping, curling paper

MATERIALS

Story of "Goldilocks and the Three Bears" to read (See Good Books for Facts and Fun on page 189)

Props to act out the story:

3 plastic bowls, in 3 sizes, if possible

3 spoons, in 3 sizes, if possible (wooden spoons with different handle lengths work well)

3 chairs, in 3 sizes, if possible

3 mats or blankets to suggest beds, folded or extended to make 3 sizes

Child-safe scissors

Staplers and tape

Brown and yellow construction paper

PREPARATION

● Cut construction paper into strips about 2" x 8½" to make headbands. Each child will need two strips per headband, brown for bears, yellow for Goldilocks. Provide additional paper for the children to make bear ears or Goldilocks curls. For younger children, precut the ears and curls. Older children will enjoy drawing and cutting the ears in different sizes and curls.

WHAT TO DO

1. Read a story of "Goldilocks and the Three Bears" and review what happens to the characters in the story: Papa Bear, Mama Bear, Baby Bear, and Goldilocks.
2. Ask the children how Goldilocks could test the *temperature* of the porridge without tasting it, if she were thinking like a scientist? (Use a *thermometer*. Feel the outside of the bowls. Look for steam on hot porridge.)
3. Ask the children what they do at home to find out if their food is a good *temperature* for eating.
4. Help the children make construction paper headbands using brown construction paper bear ears or yellow construction paper to make curling "corkscrew" paper strips stapled on for Goldilocks. Demonstrate how to make the curls by wrapping paper strips around a BIG crayon or short piece of PVC pipe.
5. Invite the children to act out the story. You will be the narrator and line prompter.
6. Perform the play multiple times and encourage the children to try different roles. The children look at the story differently when they are one of the bears or Goldilocks.
7. Encourage the children to try some of their ideas about how Goldilocks could be more of a *scientist*. Challenge the children to make up different endings to the story. What might happen if Goldilocks woke up and said, "Sorry" to the bears?

DISCUSSION STARTERS

Use these questions to spark children's thinking during and after the activity:

● What would you do if you were Goldilocks and you found the bears' door open?
● What else could Goldilocks have done when she saw the bears weren't home?
● What would have happened if the bears were home when Goldilocks knocked?
● How would feel if you were one of the bears?

SKILLS ASSESSMENT

Use these questions to determine a child's abilities and understanding:

● Can the child use scissors to cut out ears or curl strips?
● Does the child have patience to create a full set of curls? Can he curl the paper?
● Can the child remember the sequence of the story?
● Does the child understand how Goldilocks could test *temperatures* without tasting the porridge?

More Activities Across the Curriculum

LANGUAGE ARTS

- Children draw pictures and dictate stories to an adult who writes on the children's drawings. Include books about ice, *temperature,* and *thermometers* as well as vocabulary words at the table for inspiration. Topics for different days:
  - How would you like the "Goldilocks and the Three Bears" story to end?
  - What do you like to do when it's cold outside?
  - Tell about a snow or ice storm. What does snow feel like?

  In warm climates, vary the questions:
  - Have you ever been in the snow?
  - What would it be like to live in an ice castle?
  - What would you do if you could play in the snow?

  Mount the children's drawings in the shape of a snowflake or ice castle. When you take down the display, keep the drawings in each child's portfolio.

ART

- Make colored ice cubes with liquid watercolor or food coloring frozen with craft sticks. The children can "skate" the ice cubes around individual sheets of heavy paper or work together to create a painting on a BIG sheet of poster paper.

MATH/GROSS MOTOR

- Play "Pass the Ice Cube" with a BIG line of children. Count how long it takes for the cube to get from one end of the line to the other. Use mittens and gloves for variety.
  - Try passing the ice cube with tongs, salad servers, spatulas, BIG spoons, or ladles. Tools can be passed along the line just ahead of the cube, and retrieved just after it is passed by you and other helpers.
  - Give each child a small plastic or paper cup and pass the ice cube from cup to cup. Count how long it takes to pass along a line of five or six children.

GROSS MOTOR/MUSIC

- Play Freeze Dance. While the music plays, the children dance or move as they like. When the music stops, they *freeze* in position. They *"melt"* and move and flow again when the music starts up.

SCIENCE/COOKING

- *Freeze* juice in cups with craft sticks to make BIG popsicles.
- Make snow cones flavored with juice by using an ice shaving machine or grinding up ice in a blender. Observe how the texture changes and how fast the pieces *melt* when they are small.

SENSORY TABLE

- Fill the table with ice cubes and crushed ice. Provide ice cream scoops, tongs, measuring cups, small shovels, and a variety of containers to explore the ice. How many scoops does it take to fill various containers? Observe what happens to the ice over time.

BIG Outcomes

Group assessment: Review the photo boards about experimenting with *thermometers* and *melting* ice, racing ice cubes, and building ice castles. Review the chart papers from the beginning of your exploration of what the children know about ice and what they want to learn. On a third sheet of chart paper titled "What We Learned About Ice and Cold," record the children's comments about what they learned, including the name of the child who made each comment. Be sure to note answers to their original questions or note if the class still wants to learn and explore more.

Individual assessment: Review your notes and quotes from individual observations during activities, such as the icy water experiment, melting experiment, and *thermometer* activity. Review the children's work and save in portfolios. Note areas in which the children need further practice and those in which they excel.

GOOD BOOKS FOR FACTS AND FUN
Books for preschoolers that explain ice and icy weather can be hard to find. Expanding your search to include stories about winter, the arctic, bears, frosty days, and ice skating will help fill your story corner. Seek out the biography of "Snowflake Bentley" to inspire your scientists to explore the amazing variety of ice crystals that form snowflakes.

INFORMATION ABOUT ICE AND SNOWY WEATHER
Cold Days by Jennifer S. Burke
Simple sentences and photos present cold weather basics that are easy to understand, even for those who do not live in snowy areas. This book will help younger children recall their first experiences of winter. Ages 3–5

Snowflake Bentley by Jacqueline Briggs Martin
Born in 1865, Wilson Bentley spent his life capturing photographs of ice crystals. This lovely, poetic tribute celebrates this self-taught observer's fascination with the beautiful, unique patterns formed in the air from frozen water. Ages 4 and up

Snowy Weather Days by Katie Marsico
Snow words are defined throughout this easy reader text, which uses questions to stimulate observations. Color photos feature children enjoying and exploring winter weather. Ages 3–5

Water as a Solid by Helen Frost
Well-chosen color photos present close-ups of water in various solid forms of ice from ice cubes to icebergs. Simple sentences contrast the textures and sizes of snow, hail, and frost while presenting facts in an easy-to-read format. Ages 3–6

STORIES AND POETRY ABOUT ICE AND SNOW

Can't Catch Me by John and Ann Hassett
One hot day, an ice cube escapes and, in bad gingerbread boy-style, refuses to stop despite pleas along the way before coming to a quick end inside a whale. Older children will appreciate the new twist on the classic chase tale. Ages 3–6

Cold Little Duck, Duck, Duck by Lisa Westberg Peters
Returning too early to the pond, Little Duck gets frozen in the ice until her warm spring thoughts bring freedom. Just enough suspense, a happy ending, and sweet illustrations combine with sound words and repetition to make this a satisfying story. Ages 3–6

Frozen Noses by Jan Carr
A brisk outdoor winter play day described in catchy short rhymes and illustrated in cut-paper collages includes snowball throwing, snowman building, sledding, and skating before everyone ends up sharing cocoa before a cozy fire. Ages 3–5

In the Snow by Huy Voun Lee
A winter's walk becomes a guessing, learning game as Xiao Ming's mother writes Chinese characters in the snow. Each character specifically connects to the natural setting illustrated with cut-paper collages. Ages 4–6

Kumak's Fish: A Tall Tale from the Far North by Michael Bania
One day, Kumak, an Iñupiat father, sets out to fish through the ice. Watercolors accurately depict the Arctic spring light, while presenting the entire village's entertaining tug-of-war efforts to land the "biggest fish ever." Ages 3–6

Little Cliff and the Cold Place by Clifton L. Taulbert
Little Cliff wants to experience the Arctic after hearing about it in school in Mississippi. His Poppa works with a friend to put together a unique, creative solution to support Little Cliff's curiosity in this long but satisfying story. Ages 5 and up

Millions of Snowflakes by Mary McKenna Siddals
One small picture of a little snowflake starts off this brief, playful story of a young child's enthusiastic experience with falling snow. Counting from 1–5, the text pairs well with the expressive illustrations that subtly increase in size. Ages 3–4

No Bath for Boris by Diana White
Boris's polar bear mom fills the bathtub with cold water and ice cubes, but Boris will have nothing to do with it. Children will enjoy this humorous tweak of a common experience. The large format works well for sharing. Ages 3–6

Once Upon Ice and Other Frozen Poems selected by Jane Yolen

Seventeen poets created verse responses to Jason Stemple's dramatic photographs of ice. While some are best suited to older children, several, including "Cold Snap," "Ice Cubes," "Winter Wraps," "Hieroglyph," and "Ice Cycle," may inspire younger poets. Ages 3–6

Pearl's New Skates by Holly Keller

Pearl, an overconfident owner of new skates, disdains Uncle Jack's help and Thistle's offer to skate with her. She falls flat on the ice, embarrassed. Encouraged to try again and again by her uncle, Pearl succeeds and renews her friendship with Thistle. Ages 3–5

Polar Skater by Sally Grindley

Nervous and awkward on her first ice skates despite Dad's reassurance, a little girl quickly learns to glide smoothly on her own and expresses her joyful freedom and grace before an appreciative imaginary audience of Arctic animals. Ages 3–6

Straight to the Pole by Kevin O'Malley

Remember when a snowy walk to school turned into a challenging Arctic trek? Follow the imaginative, melodramatic struggle of a solitary student battling his way to "the pole" in this delightful, tongue-in-cheek winter tale. Ages 5 and up

Tacky and the Winter Games by Helen Lester

That odd bird, Tacky the Penguin, tries to keep up with his perfect penguin friends through winter training and the athletic events, only to cause one misadventure after another until he ultimately saves the day in his own inimitable style. Ages 3–6

GOLDILOCKS AND THE THREE BEARS STORIES

The Three Bears by Byron Barton

Pared down to the basic story, boldly and simply illustrated, this version works well to introduce the classic folktale to the youngest students or to provide a simple script for acting out Goldilock's adventure. Ages 3–4

The Three Bears by Paul Galdone

In print since 1979, this retelling remains popular with preschoolers and their families. Large illustrations and a traditional text contribute to a story for that works well for sharing. Ages 3–5

The Three Snow Bears by Jan Brett

Polar bears and Aloo-ki, a curious Inuit girl, transform the classic folktale into an Arctic adventure illustrated with lovely, well-drawn pictures, authentic patterns and detailed borders to enjoy over and over again. Ages 4 and up

BIG NEWS FROM SCHOOL:

A Note to Families About Ice

Dear Families,

Ice is a familiar substance that your children can explore to learn about the science of temperature and a common tool, the thermometer. Ice also introduces children to the concepts of freezing and melting—how water can change from liquid to solid and back again.

Your children became scientists by doing an experiment at school. They placed ice cubes in paper cups in two different locations around the classroom to see where ice cubes would melt quickly and where they would melt more slowly. Ask your child to tell you how the experiment turned out.

You can continue the learning at home by letting your child make ice cubes and then seeing how long they take to melt. Does the ice cube melt quickly near the heater?

Here are some of the words we've been learning:
- Temperature is a measurement of how hot or cold something is.
- An experiment is a test to see what will happen.

Have fun watching your scientist explore freezing and melting!

8 THINKING BIG ABOUT OUTER SPACE: ASTRONAUTS AND THE MOON

THE BIG PICTURE

Exploring the topic of outer space, with a specific focus on the moon, gives children a chance to imagine they are powerful pioneers making discoveries about the great beyond. Pretending to be astronauts helps children channel their passion for superhero play into this science, math, and language arts curriculum. Children exercise their imagination as they blast off in a spaceship and land on the moon where they can jump six times higher than on Earth due to the moon's weaker gravity. Imagining what the moon is like with just dust and rocks—no water, blue sky or plants—helps children notice the world around them. There is a wealth of information on all aspects of space exploration at the website for the National Aeronautics and Space Administration—www.nasa.gov.

OBJECTIVES

- Begin understanding the concept of outer space
- Use imagination to picture space travel and moon exploration
- Explore differences between the Earth and the moon
- Explore the concept of gravity

STANDARDS
National Science Education Content Standards

- Science as inquiry—ask questions; plan and conduct a simple investigation; communicate investigations and explanations
- Physical science—study properties of objects and materials; study the position and motion of objects
- Earth and space science— recognize that objects in the sky have properties, locations, and movements that can be observed and described
- Science and technology—explore abilities of technological design; develop an understanding about science and technology; distinguish between natural objects and objects made by humans

National Council of Teachers of Mathematics Standards

- Number and operations—count with understanding; make reasonable estimates
- Algebra—sort, classify, and order objects
- Measurement—understand how to measure using nonstandard and standard tools
- Data analysis and probability—sort and classify objects according to their attributes
- Communication—organize, analyze, and evaluate mathematical thinking; use the language of mathematics

Standards for the English Language Arts

- Experience a wide range of print and non-print texts, including fiction and non-fiction, to build an understanding of the world and acquire new information
- Use spoken, written, and visual language to communicate and learn
- Generate ideas and questions and pose problems
- Build vocabulary

TIMING TIP

Space exploration works anytime of year. It is fun to connect it to a time when a child notices the moon during the day.

BIG BEGINNING:

Introducing the Moon and Space Travel

SFOCUS AREAS

Science: studying objects in the sky; learning about space vehicles

Language Arts: learning vocabulary; experiencing fiction and non-fiction texts; using spoken language to communicate, generating ideas and questions

MATERIALS

Story about the moon such as *Mooncake* by Frank Asch (see Good Books for Facts and Fun on pages 222–224)

Ball, about soccer-ball size (White is ideal but you can cover any ball with white tissue paper or put any ball in a white garbage bag and tape it so the ball looks white.)

Flashlight (optional)

2 sheets of chart paper

Marker

PREPARATION

● Label one sheet of chart paper "What We Know About the Moon and Traveling in Space" and the other "What We Want to Learn About the Moon and Traveling in Space."

● Close the curtains or blinds and dim the lights.

WHAT TO DO

1. After the children are gathered, hold up the white ball. If possible, have an adult assistant stand some distance away, behind the group of children, and shine a flashlight on the ball to simulate a glowing moon.

2. Ask the children, "When it's dark at night, what do you sometimes see in the sky?" (stars and moon) Introduce the word *moon*, the BIG object in the sky that revolves around the Earth. Say and clay the one syllable, **moon**. Say *moon* as you make the ASL sign for moon. Your right hand makes a BIG C like a crescent moon, and taps the side of your forehead.

3. Turn up the lights a bit and say, "I'm going to read a story about traveling to the moon."

4. After the story, ask the children what they know about the moon and traveling in space. Record their answers, including the name of the child, on the chart paper labeled "What We Know About the Moon and Traveling in Space."

5. Introduce the word *astronaut*, a person who travels in outer space. Say and clap the syllables, **as**-tro-naut, with the emphasis on the "as" syllable. Say *astronaut* as you make the ASL signs for *rocket* and *person*. For *rocket* (or *spaceship*), the middle and index fingers of your right hand are extended and pressed together. The other fingers are curled into the palm. Move your hand above your head from one side to the other. Then add the sign that indicates a person's occupation: flat palms face each other in front of the chest, then move down to indicate the sides of the body.

6. Say, "We are going to pretend we are astronauts and learn about what it takes to travel in space and go to the moon, a really BIG trip. What do you want to find out about the moon and traveling in space?" Record those responses including names of the children on the second sheet of chart paper labeled "What We Want to Learn About the Moon and Traveling in Space." Use the children's interests to guide your activities.

A Note from the Author: The activities in this chapter are designed to build on each other. However, please feel free to choose those that meet the interests and abilities of your class. If parts of an activity seem like too much to do on a particular day, save them for a later time. Every class is different, even from day to day, and the activities are adaptable to meet the needs of your class.

Moon

Spaceship

Person Marker

BIG QUESTIONS FOR GROWING MINDS

Use the following questions to engage the children in a discussion about astronauts and the moon during group time or with an individual child during activity time:

- Do you ever see the moon during the day? Does it look different than it does at night?
- If you could get to the moon, what would you like to do there?

ANSWERING BIG QUESTIONS

Why does the moon seem to change shape? Understanding the phases of the moon can be challenging. Children will probably not grasp the concept for years to come. For your own understanding, the key information is that the moon is like a mirror. It reflects light from the sun. The moon moves around the Earth, and each night we see a different amount of the side that has sunlight on it. The moon looks like a thin crescent at times because we can only a bit of the side that is lit up. The rest of the moon is there, it's just dark because the Earth is blocking the sun's light.

WORDS FOR BIG THINKING

Look for these words highlighted in italic throughout the activities in this chapter. Write the words out in large letters and introduce them a few at a time with the "Say, Clap, Act out, Do again" (SCAD) system. Using the words during activities and discussions will reinforce them.

- Astronaut—a person who travels in outer space
- Crater—a bowl-shaped hole created when rock or metal traveling through space crashes into the moon or a planet. Craters can be as tiny as the size of your fingernail or as BIG as huge cities.
- Experiment—a test to see what will happen
- Gravity—a force that pulls objects together. The Earth's gravity pulls us and everything on the Earth down, towards its center. The Earth's gravity is six times stronger than the moon's gravity because the Earth is much bigger than the moon.
- Launch—to send off
- Lunar rover—a small car used to travel on the moon
- Moon—the BIG object in the sky that revolves around the Earth
- Prediction—like a guess—what you think might happen based on what you already know
- Spaceship—a vehicle that can travel into outer space

PHOTO TIP

You can document children's delight in imagining they are astronauts by creating photo boards of making jet packs and space helmets, building Mission Control and a giant space-ship, and turning the sandbox into the moon. Look for close-ups of individual children and group shots that show children interacting. Also note vocabulary words and quotes from children on the photo boards to document their learning.

What Do Astronauts Need to Breathe in Outer Space? Make Jet Packs

FOCUS AREAS

Science: learning about abilities of science and technology

Language Arts: learning vocabulary

Fine Motor: gluing, taping

MATERIALS

Books about astronauts, such as *If You Decide to Go to the Moon* by Faith McNulty, (see Good Books for Facts and Fun on pages 222–224) or photos of astronauts wearing their jet packs (Internet search term: astronaut images)

Cereal boxes, 1 per child

Sturdy string or yarn

Pointed scissors (adult-only)

Aluminum foil

Colored masking tape or white glue and plastic glue spreaders

Permanent markers

Stickers—American flags and stars (optional)

PREPARATION

- Poke four holes in the front of each cereal box so you'll be able to thread two pieces of sturdy string or yarn to make backpack straps.
- Cut the string or yarn into pieces about 30" long. Each child will need two pieces.
- For younger children, thread and tie the loops ahead of time and tape the top of the cereal box shut. They will focus on covering the box and decorating it.

WHAT TO DO

1. Read a book about *astronauts* to a small group of children or show them pictures of what *astronauts* wear in space when they are not in their *spaceship*.
2. Tell the children there is no air in outer space so *astronauts* need to bring air with them so they can breathe.
3. Have each child choose a cereal box.
4. Help older children poke the string through the holes and tie it securely to make the jet pack straps.
5. The children tape or glue pieces of aluminum foil to their boxes.
6. The children can decorate the foil with permanent markers and stickers.

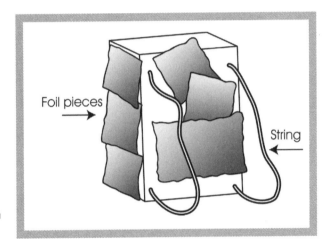

Foil pieces

String

DISCUSSION STARTERS

Use these questions to spark children's thinking during and after the activity:

- How does it feel to wear a jet pack?
- What would it be like to have to wear a jet pack all the time you were outside?
- Tell me about the decorations on your jet pack.

SKILLS ASSESSMENT

Use these questions to determine a child's abilities and understanding:

- Is the child able to do the fine motor activities such as cutting and attaching tape?
- Does the child use the vocabulary words of *astronaut* and *moon*?
- Does the child use imagination while making the jet pack? "I'm going to use this so I can walk in space."

Make a Space Helmet

PREPARATION

- If you are working with young children who have trouble cutting, pre-cut an 8" x 8" square out of a wide side of each paper grocery bag, at least 2" up from the bottom of the bag.
- If the children are able to cut their own squares, draw the 8" x 8" square at least 2" up from the bottom on each bag and cut a small hole to allow the children to insert their scissors along one edge of the square to start cutting.
- Cut about 3" out of the side of the bags so the bags will fit over the children's shoulders.

WHAT TO DO

1. Read a book about *astronauts* to a small group of children or show the children pictures of *astronauts* in their space suits. Notice the space helmets. Ask the children why they think *astronauts* need helmets (There is no air in outer space).

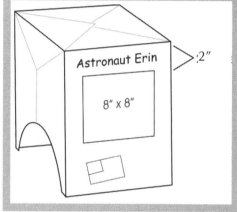

Astronaut Erin   2"

8" x 8"

2. If the children are cutting out the holes in their helmets, show them how to insert the scissors and cut along the lines. The children may need help.
3. The children decorate their space helmets with aluminum foil, markers, and stickers. Older children can write the word ASTRONAUT and their name on the helmet or on masking tape, which they can then attach to the helmet (see illustration).

DISCUSSION STARTERS

Use these questions to spark children's thinking during and after the activity:

- How would it feel to wear a space helmet all the time you were outside?
- How does wearing a helmet change how you can see?
- When you wear a helmet, how does it change the way you move?

SKILLS ASSESSMENT

Use these questions to determine a child's abilities and understanding:

- How well can the child use scissors?
- Can the child cut on the lines?
- How does the child grip markers?

FOCUS AREAS

Science: learning about abilities of science and technology

Language Arts: learning vocabulary

Fine Motor: cutting, taping, using markers

MATERIALS

Books about *astronauts,* such as *If You Decide to Go to the Moon* by Faith McNulty, (see Good Books for Facts and Fun on pages 222–224) or photos of astronauts (available on the Internet— search term: astronaut images)

Large paper grocery bags, 1 per child

Markers

Stickers, American flags and stars (optional)

Aluminum foil

Colored masking tape or white glue and plastic glue spreaders

Child-safe scissors

The word ASTRONAUT written out for older children to copy

Blasting Off to the Moon: Make a Giant Spaceship

FOCUS AREAS

Science: learning about abilities of science and technology

Math: counting, learning about geometry—shapes

Language Arts: learning vocabulary, labeling

Fine Motor: taping, gluing

MATERIALS

Books about *spaceships,* such as *Space Travel* by Patricia Whitehouse, (see Good Books for Facts and Fun on pages 222–224) or images downloaded from the Internet (search term: spaceship images)

Large cardboard boxes

Assortment of clean plastic bottle caps, lids, old CDs, paper plates

Color dot stickers

Aluminum foil

White glue

Plastic glue spreaders

Colored masking tape

Sharp knife to cut windows in cardboard (adult use only)

Tempera paint

Paintbrushes

Newspapers

Sheet of chart paper

Marker

Clipboards, paper, and markers for children to draw plans

WHAT TO DO

1. Read a book about *spaceships* to a small group of children or look at photos downloaded from the Internet.

2. Introduce the word *spaceship,* a vehicle that can travel into outer space. Say and clap out the syllables, **space**-ship, with the emphasis on the "space" syllable. Say *spaceship* as you make the ASL sign for *rocket.* For *rocket* (or *spaceship*), the middle and index fingers of your right hand are extended and pressed together. The other fingers are curled into the palm. Move your hand above your head from one side to the other.

Spaceship

3. Brainstorm with the children what they want to include in a giant *spaceship* and record their ideas, including the child's name. Ask how they can include all those ideas. Ask, "What do you want to do first?" to highlight sequencing.

4. Let the children start working. If you have multiple large boxes, the children can make multiple *spaceships,* or they can take turns working on one giant ship. If you have two boxes of the same size you can cut each box along one seam and join the boxes to make an octagon-shaped *spaceship* with room for more children inside.

5. The children indicate where they want windows cut by outlining the area with colored masking tape. An adult cuts the holes.

6. The children tape plastic bottle caps, lids, CDs, and paper plates inside the *spaceship* to represent the control panels. Invite the children to note what shape

the dials are and how many they install.

Note: Young children have a hard time cutting masking tape. It helps if an adult precuts the tape and rolls it into loops that the children can use to attach the lids, bottle caps, and CDs.

7. The children cover the outside of their spacecraft with aluminum foil. They spread white glue on the box, and then press on the foil. It takes a long time for the glue to dry so adding masking tape helps anchor it.
8. On another day, provide tempera paint so the children can cover the inside of the *spaceship*. Spread out newspapers to catch drips.
9. Help the children label the parts of their *spaceship*.

DISCUSSION STARTERS

Use these questions to spark children's thinking during and after the activity:
- Where would you like to go in the *spaceship*?
- How long will your space journey take?
- What supplies do you need to take?
- How do your dials work?

SKILLS ASSESSMENT

Use these questions to determine a child's abilities and understanding:
- How is the child interacting with other children?
- Is the child working as part of a team?
- Is the child demonstrating imaginative thought as she works? "I'm making a computer so we know where we're going."

Building Mission Control

FOCUS AREAS

Science: learning about the abilities of science and technology

Math: counting

Language Arts: learning vocabulary

MATERIALS

Downloaded photos from the Internet (search term—NASA Mission Control images)

Large cardboard box, additional boxes are desirable to make a bigger center

Table

Chairs

Optional old equipment that helps make Mission Control feel more "real": computer keyboards, telephones, cell phones, remote controls, headphones, radios

Clipboards and paper

Markers

Assortment of clean plastic bottle caps, lids, CDs, paper plates

Color dot stickers for indicator lights

Clear packing tape

Sheet of chart paper

Marker

TEACHER-TO-TEACHER TIPS

- Young children have a hard time cutting masking tape. It helps if an adult precuts the tape and rolls it into loops for the children to use.
- You can add further interest to Mission Control by adding a small *spaceship* children can *launch*. Make a *spaceship* out of a paper towel tube, attach it securely to string, and loop it over a tree branch or a door. One child can *launch* the *spaceship* by pulling on the string while other children are in Mission Control doing the count-down.

WHAT TO DO

1. Show a small group of children downloaded images of Mission Control.
2. Introduce the word *launch*, which means to send off. Say, "Scientists at Mission Control *launch spaceships*." Say and clap out the one syllable, **launch**. Say *launch* as you act out *launching* with your whole body. Crouch down and then jump straight up into the air, arms close by your sides. (**Note:** This is not ASL.)
3. Brainstorm with the children about what they want to include in their Mission Control center. Ask, "How can you talk to the *astronauts*?" "What machines will you need?" Record the children's ideas and their names on the chart paper.
4. Help the children carry out their ideas. Place a low table and chairs near your giant *spaceship*. An adult cuts a cardboard box and partially opens it up to form the back of the control panel. Anchor the box to a table with packing tape or masking tape.

5. The children tape plastic bottle caps, lids, dot stickers, CDs, and paper plates to the cardboard to simulate dials and controls.

6. Place old computer keyboards, telephones, and clipboards on the table and encourage the children to imagine they are *launching* and guiding the *astronauts* in the *spaceship*. Ask questions to extend their imaginations (see Discussion Starters).

7. Invite the children to do a countdown to *launch* a *spaceship*.

DISCUSSION STARTERS

Use these questions to spark children's thinking during and after the activity:

- What are you checking so you know the *spaceship* is ready to *launch*?
- How many seconds to *launch*?
- Will the *spaceship* change speeds? Why will it need to slow down?
- Where is the *spaceship* flying?
- How does it know where to go?

SKILLS ASSESSMENT

Use these questions to determine a child's abilities and understanding:

- How is the child interacting with other children?
- Is the child demonstrating imaginative thought? "I'm telling the *spaceship* to slow down because it's almost to the *moon*."
- Is the child enjoying creating the Mission Control center?
- Can the child do a countdown: 3–2–1 blastoff for young children, 10–9–8 and so on for older children?

Build Your Own Spaceship

FOCUS AREAS

Science: learning about the abilities of science and technology

Math: counting

Language Arts: learning vocabulary

Fine Motor: taping, cutting

MATERIALS

Books about *spaceships,* such as *Space Travel* by Patricia Whitehouse, (see Good Books for Facts and Fun on pages 222–224) or pictures downloaded from the Internet (search term: spaceship images)

Empty paper towel and wrapping paper rolls (cut in smaller lengths) or frozen juice cans, 1 per child

Assortment of milk jug lids

Aluminum foil

Rolls of colored masking tape

Stickers—American flags and stars

Wooden clothespins or Q-tips to make pretend astronauts

Corks to use as booster rockets (optional)

Construction paper

Yellow, red or orange crepe paper for pretend flames

Scissors (adult-only)

Markers

Hula hoops or rope to make targets for children to aim their spaceships

PREPARATION

- Cut wrapping paper rolls into lengths about 12" long
- Make nose cones to fit rolls and juice cans. First cut construction paper circles about 3" wide. Make a slit from the edge to the center of the circle. Overlap the edges of the cut paper until the cone fits the end of the roll. Tape the cone. Juice cans will need larger nose cones. Older children may enjoy cutting out the circles and making the cones themselves.

WHAT TO DO

1. Read a book about *spaceships* to a small group of children or show them photos downloaded from the Internet.
2. The children choose a paper towel or gift wrap roll (cut into smaller lengths) or frozen juice can as a base to construct their own *spaceship* (see illustration).
3. Older children can make and attach a construction paper cone for the top. See directions above in Preparation. Younger children will need help taping on a ready-made cone.
4. The children use tape to add tubes or corks for rockets, and then decorate the *spaceship* with foil, markers and stickers.
5. Older children decorate a clothespin or Q-tip "*astronaut*" and place it in the *spaceship.* Then they place strips of masking tape across the bottom of the

cutting line

Pattern for rocket top

spaceship to close it and hold the *"astronaut"* inside. For younger children, skip the *astronaut* and taping the bottom.

6. The children cut and tape crepe paper streamers to the bottom to show the flames coming out of the *spaceship*.

7. The children pretend the *spaceship* is *launching* and flying. Set out hula hoops or rope circles so the children have something to aim for. Label the circles *"moon"* and names of planets such as Venus, Mars, Saturn, and Jupiter. If possible, take the *spaceships* outdoors so the children can run with them and *launch* them from the playground climbing structure. Before *launching*, tell the children that the *spaceships* might need repairs after rough landings.

TEACHER-TO-TEACHER TIP
Children need lots of tape to make their *spaceships*, and they may need your help holding the parts. Cut pieces of tape ahead of time and line them up on the edge of the table for easy use or help the children cut multiple pieces of tape.

DISCUSSION STARTERS
Use these questions to spark children's thinking during and after the activity:
- How does your *spaceship* work?
- Where will your *spaceship* fly?
- How long will your space journey take?
- Can your *spaceship* fly all the way to Jupiter? What do you think it might find on Jupiter?

SKILLS ASSESSMENT
Use these questions to determine a child's abilities and understanding:
- How are the child's fine motor skills when cutting and using tape and stickers?
- Does the child enjoy imagining her *spaceship* can travel in outer space?

A Really BIG Idea: Gravity

FOCUS AREAS

Science: learning about position and motion of objects

Math: measuring—height, using standard and non-standard tools

Language Arts: learning vocabulary, generating ideas and questions, experiencing a wide range of texts

Gross Motor: jumping

MATERIALS

Assortment of objects to drop, such as a crayon, cotton ball, Lego block

Cotton swabs, such as Q-Tips

Yarn or string

Scissors (adult-only)

Chart paper and marker

PREPARATION

- Make a pretend *astronaut* for each child in your class. Cut yarn or string into 18" lengths. Tie each piece around a cotton swab.

WHAT TO DO

1. Pick up a crayon and ask the children, "What do you think will happen if I let go of this crayon?"
2. The children will probably say, "It will fall." Try it. Point out that you didn't throw the crayon down. You just let go of it. Repeat with other another object, such as a cotton ball.
3. Ask, "What will happen if instead of just dropping something, I throw it into the air? Will throwing it up high help keep it from falling down?" Throw the cotton ball straight up so it won't hit anyone.
4. Ask the children if they know the word that describes why objects fall to the ground. Introduce the word *gravity*. Say and clap **grav**-i-ty, with the emphasis on the "grav" syllable. Say *gravity* as you act it out by standing up with your right arm outstretched, then quickly crouching down and touching the floor. (**Note:** This is not an ASL sign.)
5. Tell the children that *gravity* is a force that pulls objects together. The Earth's *gravity* pulls us and everything on the surface down, towards its center.
6. Say, "The Earth's *gravity* is six times stronger than the *moon's gravity* because it is much bigger than the moon. Let's try jumping now." Estimate about how high the children jumped—maybe as high as three unit blocks stacked on top of each other. Say, "On the moon you could six times as high." Make a stack of 18 blocks to show the children how high six times higher would be.
7. Tell the children they will get a lot of chances to see how high and how far they can jump on Earth and then imagine how far they could jump on the *moon*.

DISCUSSION STARTERS

Use these questions to spark children's thinking during and after the activity:

- How high can your *astronaut* jump?
- Is it hard to make your *astronaut* jump just a little?

SKILLS ASSESSMENT

Use these questions to determine a child's abilities and understanding:

- Can the child control the height of the *astronaut* jumps?
- Does the child participate in the group activity?

THINKING BIG, LEARNING BIG

Astronauts Jump High

TEACHER-TO-TEACHER TIPS

- Children love pretending they are *astronauts* on the *moon* who can jump really high and far. The *moon* has much less *gravity* than the Earth because it is so much smaller, so you can jump six times as high on the *moon* as you can on Earth. It's fun to do the high jump on one day and long jump on another. You can include vocabulary and concepts by saying, "Look how high you can jump, but *gravity* always pulls you back down to Earth."
- This activity provides a good opportunity to practice estimating. Say, "Show me about how high you think you can jump here on Earth. Now show about how high you could jump on the *moon*."

WHAT TO DO

1. Set up a high jump stand with a small group of children. Place two unit blocks a yard apart with a yardstick set across the distance.

2. The children take turns jumping over this first height. If they knock the bar off that's okay; they just go to the end of the line for another turn.

3. When everyone has had a turn and it's the second round, the children can then decide if they want to raise the bar by adding a block to each side or if they want to keep it at the same height as before. If a child has knocked off the yardstick at the low level but wants to try a higher level, that's fine. The children can keep jumping and trying higher levels as long as they like.

4. They can measure with a ruler or a second yard stick to see how high they are jumping in inches. If appropriate, help them calculate how high six times higher that would be on the *moon*.

   Note: Unit blocks are 1¼" high. If the children can jump four blocks high on the Earth—about 5"—that would be 24 blocks, or 30" high, on the *moon*. They can also measure with lengths of yarn.

FOCUS AREAS

Science: using simple tools and equipment

Math: counting, measuring—height, using standard and non-standard tools, estimating

Language Arts: learning vocabulary

Gross Motor: jumping

MATERIALS

Unit blocks to make a high jump stand

Yardstick or bamboo stick about 1 yard long

Large sandbox or another soft surface for landing, such as tumbling mats

Rulers

Yarn

MORE IDEAS

- Tape a yardstick or measuring tape to a door or doorway at the floor. Highlight the 1′ and 2′ heights with colored tape. Ask the children, one at a time, to make their Q-tip *astronauts* hop 1′ high and then land back on the ground, then 2′ high, then 3′ high.

DISCUSSION STARTERS

Use these questions to spark children's thinking during and after the activity:

- How does it feel to jump high?
- Show me with your arm how high you think you could jump on the *moon*.

SKILLS ASSESSMENT

Use these questions to determine a child's abilities and understanding:

- Can the child jump over the yardstick?
- Can the child measure how high she jumped?
- Does the child use measurement vocabulary such as *higher* and *lower*?

Astronauts Jump Far

PREPARATION

- Create a starting line with masking tape or rope. Place the measuring tape on the ground perpendicular to the starting line.

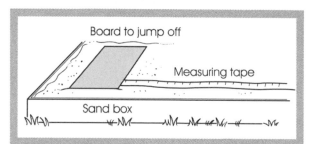

Board to jump off

Measuring tape

Sand box

WHAT TO DO

1. Demonstrate for a small group of children how to do a long jump—becoming "springs" so they can jump long by coiling up and letting loose. Have them bend their knees and swing their arms back and forth a few times, then lean forward, throw out their arms in front, and jump.

2. If the children are jumping in the sandbox, they will see their footprints. If they are jumping on carpet or a tumbling mat, another child can mark where the children land with a piece of tape or unit block.

   Note: It's possible to do the standing long jump in a small area. A sandbox works well because the landing is soft and the children's feet make an impression in the sand. It also gives other children the opportunity to be the raker or brusher who erases the footprints with a rake or broom to make the sand smooth for the next jumper.

3. Help the children see how far they could jump on the *moon* by measuring a distance six times farther using a measuring tape or non-standard unit such as carpet squares.

DISCUSSION STARTERS

Use these questions to spark children's thinking during and after the activity:
- How do you think swinging your arms helps you jump farther?
- Have you ever jumped this far before?

SKILLS ASSESSMENT

Use these questions to determine a child's abilities and understanding:
- Does the child enjoy jumping?
- Can the child measure how far she jumped?
- Does the child use distance vocabulary such as *farther, closer, shorter,* and *longer*?

FOCUS AREAS

Science: using simple equipment and tools
Math: counting, measuring—length, using standard and nonstandard tools
Language Arts: learning vocabulary
Gross Motor: jumping

MATERIALS

Cloth tape measure or yard stick
Soft surface for landing, such as tumbling mats or a sandbox
Masking tape or rope
Nonstandard measuring units, such as carpet squares or mats

Make Pretend Moon Dust

FOCUS AREAS

Science: learning about the surface of the *moon*

Math: counting, measuring—volume, following a recipe

Language Arts: learning vocabulary

Sensory: feel of ingredients

MATERIALS

Chart paper
Marker
Assortment of 1 cup and ½ cup measuring cups
Spoons
Sturdy bowl or tub
Sensory table or other large flat container
Small rocks and pebbles (optional)
Toy *astronauts* and space vehicles (optional)
Variety of gloves, such as dishwashing gloves, so the children can pretend they are astronauts feeling "*moon* dust" **Note:** The gloves are an optional astronaut prop. "*Moon* dust" is safe for the children to handle without gloves.
Magnifying lenses

PREPARATION

- Ahead of time, ask a coffee shop to save used coffee grounds for you, the more the better. Dry out the grounds by spreading them out on cookie sheets in the sun or a 250° oven.
- Write the recipe on chart paper. Add illustrations of the ingredients or steps (optional).

WHAT TO DO

1. Invite a small group of children to take turns measuring the ingredients into a bowl or plastic tub. The measurements do not have to be exact. Use a variety of sizes of measuring cups to compare amounts: "How many of these smaller ½-cup measures will it take to fill this BIG 1-cup measure?"

2. The children take turns stirring with spoons and mixing with their hands. When mixed, add the "*moon* dust" to the sensory table.

3. Make as many batches as you need for your sensory table. Consider making additional batches for the following *crater experiment*. The mixture looks remarkably like the gray dust of the *moon*. The mixture compacts well and makes a nice squeaking sound when squeezed. The children enjoy adding "*moon* rocks" and *astronauts*.

4. Encourage the children to use magnifying lenses to examine the *moon* dust and *moon* rocks.

Moon Dust Recipe

For each batch you will need:

- 4 cups dried coffee grounds (Used grounds are free from some coffee shops)
- 4 cups cornstarch
- 2 cups sand
- Measure ingredients and stir with spoons and hands.

DISCUSSION STARTERS

Use these questions to spark children's thinking during and after the activity:

- How does the "dust" feel?
- How does the "dust" sound when you squeeze it?
- What do you think it would feel like to walk in dust like this on the *moon*?

SKILLS ASSESSMENT

Use these questions to determine a child's abilities and understanding:

- Does the child note the difference between different size measuring cups?
- Does the child use the measurement vocabulary of *more than, less than, larger,* and *smaller*?
- Does the child use the sensory vocabulary of *soft, smooth,* or *powder*?

Crater Experiment: How Do Craters Form?

FOCUS AREAS

Science: planning and conducting a simple investigation; using simple equipment and tools to gather data; learning about the position and motion of objects

Math: measuring—size, estimating

Language Arts: learning vocabulary

MATERIALS

Books with photo illustrations of the *moon* surface, (see Good Books for Facts and Fun on pages 222–224) or downloaded images from the Internet

Prepared "*moon* dust" from the sensory table

Assortment of marbles, golf balls, small stones, baseballs, and other balls

Metal baking pans or plastic tubs, the larger the better

Tongue depressors, craft sticks, or combs to smooth the "moon dust" surface

Standard and nonstandard tools to measure, such as rulers and Unifix cubes

Assortment of round plastic or metal lids in different sizes, such as lids from milk jugs and yogurt and deli containers, washed thoroughly

TEACHER-TO-TEACHER TIPS

- It's possible to do the *crater experiment* in the sensory table but children may approach the activity more scientifically if they work in metal baking pans or shallow plastic tubs.
- Children often hesitate to make *predictions* because they don't want to be wrong. You can encourage *predictions* by making one yourself that is not likely to happen, such as saying, "I think this tiny marble will make a huge *crater*, much bigger than the one the golf ball made. Let's see if that's what happens."

WHAT TO DO

1. Show a small group of children photos of the *moon's* surface.
2. Introduce the word *crater*. A *crater* is a bowl-shaped hole created when a chunk of rock from space crashes into a *moon* or planet. *Craters* can be as tiny as the size of your fingernail or as BIG as huge cities. Say and clap out the syllables, **cra**-ter. Say *crater* as you act it out with your whole body, standing up, then crouching down, and standing back up while moving your outstretched arm in a giant arc from shoulder height down to the floor and back up. (**Note**: This is not an ASL sign.)
3. Tell the children they are going to do an *experiment* to explore how *craters* are formed on the *moon*. Remind the children that an *experiment* is a test to see what will happen. When scientists do an *experiment*, they predict what they think will happen. This is called a *prediction*. (See pages 40–41 for signs for *experiment* and *prediction*). Say, "When we do the *experiments*, you can make *predictions* about what will happen when we make *craters* like the ones on the *moon*."
4. The children choose a marble, pebble, or ball. Ask, "What do you think will happen when you drop it in the *moon* dust? Will the dust fly out? What's your *prediction*? Try it."
5. How wide across is the *crater* that formed? The children measure the *crater* with a ruler or Unifix cubes. Invite them to compare the *crater* with an assortment of round plastic lids. Is the *crater* bigger than the milk cap? Smaller than the jar lid?
6. The children then smooth out the dust with a tongue depressor or craft stick and choose a different size "space rock." Ask the children to *predict* whether that object will make the same size *crater* or a larger or smaller *crater*. Then they drop their object. What happens? (For younger children, have them drop two different items and compare the *craters* before smoothing out the dust.)
7. What happens if they drop the pebble from a much higher distance? What about a closer distance?
8. What happens if the children make a deep pile of dust and then drop a rock into the pile?

MORE IDEAS

- Try dropping objects that are different shapes such as a key, a stick, and a crayon. What shape *craters* do they make?
- To be more scientific, use large cardboard blocks to keep the drop height consistent. The children rest their wrist on the top of a block and then drop the pebble. Stack two blocks for higher drops.

DISCUSSION STARTERS

Use these questions to spark children's thinking during and after the activity:

- What would it be like to climb in a BIG *crater* on the *moon*?
- What would it feel like to walk in *moon* dust?

SKILLS ASSESSMENT

Use these questions to determine a child's abilities and understanding:

- Is the child able to make a *prediction*?
- Does the child see a connection between the size of the object dropped and the size of the *crater*?
- Is the child able to compare the *crater* size with a lid?
- Does the child enjoy repeating the process of making *predictions* and testing them?

Turn the Sandbox into the Moon

FOCUS AREAS

Science: studying objects in the sky—the *moon* surface

Language Arts: experiencing a wide range of texts, learning vocabulary

Large Motor: digging, scooping

MATERIALS

A book about the *moon* and *moon* landings, such as *What the Moon Is Like* by Franklyn M. Branley and *One Giant Leap: The Story of Neil Armstrong* by Don Brown (See Good Books for Facts and Fun on pages 222–224)

Sandbox

American flag on a stick

Rocks

Sand buckets to collect rock samples

Cardboard and aluminum foil

Paper towel tubes

Old mixing bowls

Sand shovels or homemade scoopers (see page 302 in the Appendix)

Sand trucks, which can be lunar rovers

Q-tip "astronauts" from the gravity activity

Space helmets and jet packs children have made earlier

Gloves or mittens (optional)

PLANNING TIP

It is fun to turn your sandbox into the *moon* during this entire unit. Children will enjoy recreating the surface and making changes every day. Introduce new elements over time: Neil Armstrong's *moon* landing, telescopes, solar panels, and *lunar rovers*. If you do not have ready access to a large sandbox, see More Ideas on the next page for a way to create the *moon* surface indoors.

PREPARATION

- If necessary, reinforce a cloth flag with a pipe cleaner or plastic straw so it sticks out straight, like the flags in photos from *moon* explorations.

WHAT TO DO

1. Read a book about the *moon* or *moon* landings. Ask the children how they could turn the sandbox into the *moon*.
2. In the sandbox, ask the children how they can use old mixing bowls to make *craters*. (Two possibilities: Scoop out sand with the bowl or shovels. Swivel the bowl in the hole to make it round and firm. Pile sand around the edge of the *crater*. Or, first pile up sand and then place a bowl on top and swivel it.)
3. The children can add "*moon* rocks" to the sandbox but be sure to allow for time to remove all the rocks later. They can use sifters to remove the rocks.

4. After they have created the *moon*, perhaps on another day, invite the children to become *astronauts* and act out Neil Armstrong's landing on the *moon*. They can put on gloves and the helmets and jet packs they made earlier and can take turns planting the flag, making footprints, and saying, "One small step for man; one giant leap for mankind."
5. The children can gather rocks in sand buckets and use paper towel tube telescopes to look back at the Earth.
6. Invite the children to make solar panels to generate energy by covering cardboard with aluminum foil.
7. The children use the Q-tip *astronauts* to hop *craters* and mountains in the sandbox.

MORE IDEAS

- Create the surface of the *moon* indoors. Children can use blocks to create hills and *craters*. They can also include bowls from the dramatic play area, chairs, tables, and anything else to create a *moon* landscape. Drape the landscape with an old sheet and use the Q-tip *astronauts* to jump around the *moon*.
- Use the "*moon* dust" in the sensory table to recreate a lunar landscape of mountains and *craters* where the Q-tip *astronauts* can go exploring.

DISCUSSION STARTERS

Use these questions to spark children's thinking during and after the activity:
- How would it feel to be the first person to go to the *moon*?
- What would you say when you landed?
- What parts of the *moon* would you like to explore?
- What do you think it would be like to live on the *moon*?

SKILLS ASSESSMENT

Use these questions to determine a child's abilities and understanding:
- Can the child work as part of a team?
- Is the child participating in imaginative play: "I landed on the *moon*. I can jump so high."
- What aspects of recreating the *moon* landing appealed to the child—making the lunar landscape, re-enacting the landing, exploring the surface with a Q-tip *astronaut*?

Make a Giant Lunar Rover

FOCUS AREAS

Science: learning about the abilities of science and technology

Math: counting, learning about geometry—shapes

Language Arts: learning vocabulary, labeling

MATERIALS

Books about lunar vehicles or images downloaded from the Internet (search term: lunar rover images)

Wagon

Large cardboard box

Smaller boxes such as cereal boxes

Paper towel and gift wrap cardboard rolls

Assortment of old CDs, plastic caps, paper plates, pie tins

Aluminum foil

Masking tape

White glue and glue spreaders

WHAT TO DO

1. Invite a small group of children to look at photos of the *lunar rovers*.

2. Introduce the vocabulary words *lunar rover*, a scientific way of saying "*moon* car." Say and clap out the syllables, **lu**-nar **rov**-er, with the emphasis on the "lu" and "rov" syllables. Say *lunar rover* as you make the ASL signs for *moon* and *car*. *Moon* is the right hand making a BIG C like a crescent *moon* and tapping the side of your forehead. The sign for *car* is closed hands moving a steering wheel.

3. Show the children a large cardboard box and ask what it would take to turn it into a *lunar rover*.

4. Cut down along both corners of one side of a large cardboard box (adult-only) fold the side into the bottom. Place the open box in the bed of a wagon to form the sides and back of the rover.

5. The children tape or glue aluminum foil to the outside surface and then add equipment to the rover. They use long cardboard tubes to mount the antenna and steering wheel (pie plates) solar panels (cereal boxes) TV camera (small box with cardboard tube "lens").

6. The children cover the equipment with foil to give it the true "outer space" look and attach CDs and plastic caps to the *lunar rover* for headlights and controls.

7. Help the children label the parts of their rover.

8. The children take turns sitting in the rover one at a time while the other *astronauts* take turns pulling. Encourage the *astronauts* to report what they see on the *moon*.

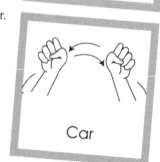

Moon

Car

MORE IDEAS

- Children can use biodegradable packing noodles to create their own *lunar rovers* to take home. You can save the packing noodles from packages or buy them from office or school suppliers. The noodles easily stick to themselves with just a touch of water. Provide a damp sponge. The children start with a small piece of cardboard about 8" x 8". They stick packing noodles to the base by dampening the noodles on a sponge. They then add more noodles in whatever design they want. The *"lunar rovers"* can be totally their imagination, or they can use photos for inspiration.

DISCUSSION STARTERS

Use these questions to spark children's thinking during and after the activity:

- What happens when you drive your rover into deep *craters*?
- What would it be like to drive in *moon* dust?
- If you were on the *moon,* how might you communicate back to your spaceship?

SKILLS ASSESSMENT

Use these questions to determine a child's abilities and understanding:

- How does the child work as part of a group?
- Is the child engaged in imaginative play?

Gravity Painting

FOCUS AREAS

Science: exploring gravity

Language Arts: learning vocabulary

Art: mixing colors, learning about design

MATERIALS

6 old stockings or socks
Sand
Long sheets of butcher paper
Easel paper
Tempera paint
Starch
Liquid soap
Small trays
Newspaper to cover the floor
Paint smocks
Sturdy chairs (optional)

PREPARATION

● Fill the old stockings or socks with sand and tie off each one.
● Mix tempera paint with starch and liquid soap. (The soap and starch extend the paint and make it easier to wash out of clothes.) Place this mixture in small trays.
● Cover the area with newspaper and set out a BIG sheet of butcher paper for a group painting.

TEACHER-TO-TEACHER TIPS

● This is a messy activity. Paint splatters everywhere. Do it outside if possible. Alert family members the day before, if possible, so the children wear old clothes. If it's warm they can do it barefoot.
● Children often want to whack the paper with the sock. Emphasize that in this activity *gravity* is going to do the work. Have the children just let go of the sock and see what happens.

WHAT TO DO

1. Tell a small group of children they are going to paint using "space rocks" and *gravity*. The stockings or socks are the "rocks." The children dip the stocking or sock in the tempera paint, lift it above the paper, and let go. Splat!

2. They drop "space rocks" as many times as they want, watching what happens as they use different colors.

3. The children also *experiment* by standing on a chair and dropping their "space rock" from a higher distance. Are the splats different if the rock falls from higher up?

4. If you have enough socks, the children can drop two socks at the same time (one from each hand). What happens? Do they land at the same time?

5. Hang the giant painting on a classroom wall or outdoors.

DISCUSSION STARTERS

Use these questions to spark children's thinking during and after the activity:

● Are the splats different if the "space rock" starts close to the paper or higher up?
● What happens when different color splats overlap?
● How do these look the same or different compared to our "*moon* dust" *craters* and sandbox *craters*?

SKILLS ASSESSMENT

Use these questions to determine a child's abilities and understanding:

● Does the child see the relationship between the size of the splat and the distance dropped?
● Can the child *predict* what will happen when two different colors mix?
● Did the child want to *experiment* with different colors and dropping heights?

Astronaut Drawing

PREPARATION
- Make masking tape loops for young children to use. For older children, demonstrate how they can make loops themselves.

WHAT TO DO
1. Read a book about living and working in space to a small group of children.
2. Ask the children, "How would it feel to float in the classroom instead of sitting on the floor or on a chair?" Ask, "How would it feel to have to wear space suits and gloves to make repairs outside the space craft?"
3. Invite the children to pretend they are *astronauts* and draw pictures while they are lying on their backs on the floor.
4. Help the children stick loops of masking tape to the paper, and then press the paper to the underside of classroom tables. The children draw on the paper while lying on their backs.
5. For an extra challenge, encourage the children to try drawing while wearing mittens or gloves.

DISCUSSION STARTERS
Use these questions to spark children's thinking during and after the activity:
- How does it feel to draw while lying on your back?
- How does it feel drawing with gloves on?
- What is happening in your picture?
- Is it easier to draw with crayons, markers, or colored pencils?

SKILLS ASSESSMENT
Use these questions to determine a child's abilities and understanding:
- Does the child enjoy the challenge of drawing on her back?
- Is the child open to new experiences?
- What grip does the child use when drawing?

FOCUS AREAS
Science: imagining working without gravity
Language Arts: experiencing a wide range of texts
Art: drawing
Fine Motor: using crayons, markers or colored pencils

MATERIALS
Book about working in space, such as *Floating in Space* by Franklyn M. Branley or *Living in Space* by Patricia Whitehouse (see Good Books for Facts and Fun on pages 222–224)
Paper
Masking tape loops, at least three per child
Assortment of crayons, markers, or colored pencils
Mittens or gloves (optional)

Astronaut Food

FOCUS AREAS

Language arts: experiencing a wide range of print and non-print texts, learning vocabulary

Math: measuring—volume

Fine Motor: sealing plastic bags

MATERIALS

Book about *astronauts* eating in space, such as *Living in Space* by Patricia Whitehouse or *Floating in Space* by Franklyn M. Branley (see Good Books for Facts and Fun on pages 222–224) or information downloaded from the NASA website

Container of Tang powdered orange drink

Large jar of applesauce

Sealable small plastic bags, 1 per child

Straws, 1 per child

Measuring spoons

Plastic liquid measuring cup

Large spoon to dish up applesauce

Child-safe scissors

TEACHER-TO-TEACHER TIP

This activity can be as simple or as elaborate as you like. A simple snack (described here) includes Tang to drink and applesauce. Children could prepare a whole meal including granola bars, tortillas, and freeze-dried food. See the NASA website for ideas: www.spaceflight.nasa.gov/living/spacefood/index.html.

WHAT TO DO

1. Work with a small group of children. Read a book to them or show them information downloaded from the Internet about *astronauts* eating in space. Tell the children the story of Tang and applesauce (see curriculum tip)

2. The children wash their hands. Then give each child a small sealable plastic bag. The children measure 1 teaspoon of Tang into their bags.

3. The children measure ½ cup of water and add it to their bags. An adult will need to hold the bag open as each child pours water into her bag.

4. Continue holding the bag while the child gently squeezes it to mix the Tang and water. Help the child seal the bag shut except for a tiny space at the end. The child inserts a straw into this tiny space and drinks.

5. Tell the children that *astronauts* try to create as little garbage as possible so now the children will reuse their bag to eat applesauce. (If the children don't like the Tang they can pour it down the sink and then rinse and reuse the bag.)

6. The children open up the plastic bag, take out the straw and then spoon in two large spoonfuls of applesauce. With adult help, the children seal the bags shut.

7. The children snip off one of the bottom corners of the bag and suck out the applesauce.

DISCUSSION STARTERS

Use these questions to spark children's thinking during and after the activity:

- What makes it hard to eat like *astronauts*?
- Does the food and drink taste different when you eat and drink out of plastic bags?
- What are your favorite foods? Would they be easy or hard to eat in space?

SKILLS ASSESSMENT

Use these questions to determine a child's abilities and understanding:

- Does the child enjoy the new experience of eating applesauce out of a plastic bag?
- Does the child imagine what it would be like to be an *astronaut*?

Moon Bounce Adventure Game

FOCUS AREAS

Math: counting, learning one-to-one correspondence

Gross Motor: jumping, hopping

MATERIALS

Yarn
Scissors (adult-only)
Chalk
Hula hoops
Laminated game cards (see illustration to copy)
Photo or drawing of a lunar *spaceship* (optional)

TEACHER-TO-TEACHER TIP

This is a non-competitive game. Children just enjoy picking cards and hopping. They can play for as long as they like.

PREPARATION

- Copy and laminate two sets of game cards (see sample below).

Meteor Shower Jump Back 4 • • • •	**Fall in a Crater** Stay Where You Are	**Plant the Flag** Jump Ahead 1 •	**Ride in Moon Rover** Jump Ahead 4 • • • •
Rover Breaks Down Stay Where You Are	**Lost in Dust Storm** Jump Back 2 • •	**Gather Rocks** Jump Ahead 3 • • •	**Take Pictures** Jump Ahead 2 • •
Jumping Contest Jump Ahead 4 • • • •	**Out of Radio Range** Jump Back 3 • • •	**Lose Map** Stay Where You Are	**Climb Mountain** Jump Ahead 1 •

- If playing indoors, cut yarn into 4′ lengths and help the children use these to make about 12 circles ("*craters*") on the floor of the classroom. The circles should be close enough to each other that the children can easily hop from one to the next in a circle or oval. Anchor the yarn *craters* with a few masking tape strips. If you have a photo of a *spaceship* you can place that in one of the circles to show the starting and ending place.
- If playing outdoors, help the children use chalk to trace the hula hoops to make circles ("*craters*") in an open area.

WHAT TO DO

1. Help a small group of children play this game. Each child begins at the starting circle. The first child chooses a picture card and follows the directions. An adult can help the child interpret the picture and move the correct number of spaces.
   For example, the child may choose a picture of *moon* rocks with the numeral 2 and 2 dots. The *astronaut* is collecting *moon* rocks to study so the child would hop two craters forward.

2. The children take turns choosing a card and following the directions. Some cards are bad news; for example, when the *astronaut* gets lost in a dust storm and the child jumps backward.

3. Any number of the children can play. It's okay if two children land on the same "*crater*." When a child makes it around the *moon* and returns to the lunar *spaceship,* she can immediately start another *moon* adventure.

MORE IDEAS

- Give the children a choice of picking a card or rolling a giant die (see directions for how to make in the Appendix on page 300) and jumping the number shown on the die.
- Place a bucket of "*moon* rocks" near one of the *craters*. The children pick up a rock when they land in the *crater* or pass by it.
- Challenge the children to change the types of jumps, "three giant leaps, four little hops so you barely move the *moon* dust." (Model using descriptive vocabulary: "I see you are making gigantic jumps in those huge *craters*. Are you getting all dusty?")
- Change the movement: hop on one foot, take giant steps.

DISCUSSION STARTERS

Use these questions to spark children's thinking during and after the activity:

- What kind of adventures did you have on the *moon?*
- What other kinds of adventures do you think *astronauts* might have?

SKILLS ASSESSMENT

Use these questions to determine a child's abilities and understanding:

- Can the child count correctly the number of dots on the card?
- Can the child move the correct number of *craters?*
- Does the child understand one-to-one correspondence?
- How long does the child stay with the activity?
- How does the child respond to taking turns or choosing a card that is bad news?

BIG CONNECTIONS:

More Activities Across the Curriculum

LANGUAGE ARTS

- Children draw pictures of *spaceships* and the *moon* and dictate stories. Include space books and vocabulary words at the table for inspiration. Topics for different days:
  - Where would you like to travel in space?
  - What do you think it would be like to live on the *moon*?
  - What would you see on the trip to the *moon* and back?

  For added interest, give the children the choice of drawing on circles or crescents of white or pale yellow paper. Mount the stories on a black background on a classroom wall. Or use the *gravity* painting mural as a background and mount stories on it. When you take down the display keep the drawings in each child's portfolio.

SCIENCE/MATH/GROSS MOTOR

- Count down for *launching*. Write the numbers 10–1 on sturdy paper or cardboard. Arrange the children standing in order holding their number 10, 9, 8…. The children count down by saying their number and then crouching down. After the last child says "1" all the children jump up and say BLASTOFF!! Scramble the numbers and count how long it takes for the children to rearrange themselves in countdown order.

ART

- Children make finger painting prints that resemble the Earth from space. You may be able to get large circles of linoleum from a countertop supplier, or use large round plastic or metal trays. Place the trays upside down on a table covered with newspaper or a plastic tablecloth. The children squirt blue and yellow tempera paint directly on the underside of the tray and mix with their fingers. They finger paint as long as they like. When they are ready to make a print, the children wash their hands. An adult helps them place a sheet of easel paper over the tray. The children press down over the entire circle to create a print. (The advantage of finger painting on linoleum or plastic circles instead of paper is that the children can work as long as they like without the paper getting soggy and tearing. The prints often look remarkably like the famous photos of the Earth with blue, green and white swirls.)
  Variations to finger paintings to try on additional days:
  - Children use white and yellow paint on the back of a large plastic plate or pie pans and print on black paper to make *moon* pictures.
  - Children use yellow and orange paint to finger paint sun pictures.
  - Children use whatever color they want to finger paint a variety of planets.
  - Children cut around their prints and mount them on BIG sheets of black paper to create a dramatic backdrop.
- Children create the night sky by splatter painting white paint with old toothbrushes on black paper. Mount pictures together to create a giant mural.

- Children make orbiting *moon* paintings. Put black construction paper in shallow boxes. Children dunk marbles in small containers of white paint and then place the marble in the box and tilt it so the "*moon*" orbits around the box. After the paintings are dry, children can add the *moon* that they cut themselves or a precut *moon* shape. If you use pie tins or cake pans, the orbits will look more realistic.

DRAMA/ MUSIC

- Children act out Greg and Steve's narrative, "An Adventure in Space" on their CD *On the Move*.

DRAMATIC PLAY/BLOCKS

- Children build a *spaceship* with unit blocks or hollow blocks and pretend they are *launching* it into space. Add Lego space sets or small plastic *spaceships* and other manipulatives to the block area if available.

SENSORY/PLAYDOUGH

- Make white playdough. Add clear or silver glitter to simulate the shining *moon* in outer space. Provide BIG jar lids and smooth pebbles so the children can create their own *moon* surface with *craters*.

BIG Outcomes

Group assessment: Review the photo boards about making jet packs and space helmets, building Mission Control and a giant *spaceship*, and turning the sandbox into the *moon*. Review chart paper sheets from the beginning of the exploration of what the children knew about the *moon* and what they want to learn. On a third sheet of chart paper titled "What We Learned About the *Moon* and Space Travel" record the children's comments about what they learned. Be sure to note answers to their original questions, or note if you still have more to learn and explore.

Individual assessment: Review your notes and quotes from individual observations during activities such as the *crater experiments*, high jump, and *astronaut* food. Review the children's work and save in portfolios. Note areas in which the children need further practice and those in which they excel.

GOOD BOOKS FOR FACTS AND FUN

Searching for preschool books about spaceships, the moon, and astronauts may seem like "rocket science" until a new space mission spurs more publishing on these topics. Visit your library before you start this unit for help in collecting a selection from the list below. Other useful sources include library book sales, flea markets, garage sales, and online sites that sell used books in good condition.

INFORMATION ABOUT GRAVITY

Floating in Space by Franklyn M. Branley
Branley, an astronomer, describes sensations and challenges of the "zero gravity"
   aboard the space shuttle. Details of how astronauts eat, sleep, exercise, and work in
   and outside the shuttle will appeal to future astronauts. Ages 4–6

Gravity Is a Mystery by Franklyn M. Branley
Colorful artwork brightens this science classic, which describes the effects of gravity
   through imagination-provoking examples, such as digging through the center of the
   Earth, and compares weight differences on the planets, the sun, and the moon. Ages
   5 and up

I Fall Down by Vicki Cobb
An experiment-based exploration of gravity suggests a step-by-step approach to
   understanding this basic force. Expressive illustrations follow a young boy through
   the questions and answers as he drips, drops, and discovers. Ages 4–6

What Is Gravity? by Lisa Trumbauer
This brief book introduces the concepts of weight and gravity to young preschoolers
   through questions and observations of common examples and clear color
   photographs often featuring children in everyday situations. Ages 3–6

Zero Gravity by Gloria Skurzynski

Excellent as a teacher resource or for sharing with highly curious students, this award-winning explanation of zero-g contains accurate information, clear examples of children's active experience with gravity, and large color photos of astronauts in weightlessness during shuttle flights. Ages 5 and up

INFORMATION ABOUT THE MOON

The Moon by Patricia Whitehouse

Color photos and clear diagrams present an easy-to-understand, fact-filled introduction to our natural satellite and partner in space. Orbit, size, surface features, temperature, phases, and effects on tides are all covered here. Ages 4–6

Tell Me Why the Moon Changes Shape by Shirley Willis

Simple, cheerful drawings of children of many cultures actively performing experiments add charm and interest to the question-and-answer format which describes the moon's properties. Ages 3–6

What the Moon Is Like by Franklyn M. Branley

True Kelley's simple drawings form colorful and sometimes dramatic new backgrounds for Branley's straightforward and accurate text in this updated version first written in 1963. A large moon map shows the astronaut landing areas. Ages 3–6

INFORMATION ABOUT THE MOON AND SPACE EXPLORATION

Exploring Space with an Astronaut by Patricia J. Murphy

Eileen Collins, the first woman space shuttle pilot, and her crew's mission to take an X-ray telescope into space anchor this short introduction to space missions, which offers inspiration for potential astronauts. Ages 3–6

If You Decide to Go to the Moon by Faith McNulty

For aspiring astronauts, this attractive, large format guide offers many details and realistic descriptions of what you need to take, what you will experience and see on a trip to the moon, and what your return to our beautiful planet Earth will be like. Ages 3–6

The International Space Station by Franklyn M. Branley

Mercury astronaut Scott Carpenter introduces this excellent overview of space station history, size, international components, daily life, and experiments. Clearly labeled, colorful drawings highlight details for avid future space explorers. Ages 4 and up

Living in Space by Patricia Whitehouse

All the basics, from what to wear to taking out the garbage, are explained and illustrated with color photos of the crew of men and women from different countries living aboard the international space station. Fun facts are included. Ages 3–6

Man on the Moon by Anastasia Suen

This simplified account of the 1969 Apollo 11 moon mission omits scientific details but retains the suspense and drama in its vivid language and varied perspectives in the watercolor and colored pencil illustrations. Ages 3–6

One Giant Leap: The Story of Neil Armstrong by Don Brown

Young Neil's hard work and dreams of flying propel him through pilot training into outer space where he sets the first human foot on the moon. Simple facts and watercolor pictures describe a modest hero's amazing achievement. Ages 4–6

Space Travel by Patricia Whitehouse

Historical photos in black and white and color add perspective to this brief overview of our journey into space from Sputnik to the space station to speculation about future. The book features the success stories and omits the disasters. Ages 4–6

STORIES ABOUT THE MOON

Bringing Down the Moon by Jonathan Emmett

A charming version of the old folklore theme of a character who desires the moon, finds, and loses it in a reflection. Mole won't listen to others. He has to learn through his own efforts that the moon is not as close as it looks. Ages 3–6

I Want to Be an Astronaut by Byron Barton

One of the best stories for young preschoolers featuring the space shuttle, one line of simple text per page and bold, clear paintings outlined in black show a multi-ethnic, multi-gender crew working together as astronauts. Ages 3–5

Mooncake by Frank Asch

Bear wants a taste of the moon. Preschoolers will understand the gentle joke when Bear falls asleep and hibernates in his home-built spaceship. Waking in winter, he mistakes a taste of snow for a bite of the moon, reporting that it is delicious. Ages 3–5

Richie's Rocket by Joan Anderson

Inventive Richie Rodriguez blasts off from his apartment roof in his imaginary rocket, constructed out of odds and ends and cardboard. Clever photography supports Richie's enthusiastic response to his dream journey. Ages 3–6

Zoom! Zoom! Zoom! I'm Off to the Moon by Dan Yaccarino

Whoosh and away, this short, zippy trip to the moon begins on the run and accelerates to the successful splashdown, celebration, and homecoming. Brief rhyming couplets and bold, complimentary colors of oranges and blues add to the energy. Ages 3–5

BIG NEWS FROM SCHOOL:
A Note to Families About Astronauts and the Moon

Dear Families,

Although we can't touch the moon or travel there right now, your children are fascinated by our nearest neighbor in space, shining so brightly in the night sky. Learning about the moon and space travel encourages children's imaginations about the future and gives focus to their desire to be strong and adventurous. Who knows, maybe they will one day blast off in a spaceship to the moon or beyond!

At school, your children pretended they were astronauts. They sampled astronaut food like the first astronaut to eat in space, John Glenn, who sucked applesauce out of a tube. The children learned that on the moon they could jump six times higher than they could here on Earth because the moon's gravity is weaker than Earth's gravity. They turned the sandbox into the moon and pretended they were planting the flag like astronaut Neil Armstrong. They gathered "moon rocks" and drove lunar rovers. Thank you for sending in cereal boxes that your children used to make pretend jet packs.

At home, you can help your child notice the moon at night and during the day. You can also observe with your child how the moon seems to change shape.

Here are some of the words we've been learning about astronauts and the moon:
- Gravity is a force that pulls objects together. The Earth's gravity is strong because the Earth is so big.
- A spaceship is a vehicle that can travel into outer space.
- Craters are bowl-shaped holes created when rocks hit a moon or a planet. The moon has many craters.

Have fun looking at the moon with your astronaut!

THINKING **BIG**, LEARNING **BIG**

THINKING BIG ABOUT BUILDING: HOW BIG CAN WE BUILD?

THE BIG PICTURE

Block building is common in early childhood programs, but is rarely a focus of study. It's easy to think children are "just playing" when they build towers or a house for their stuffed animals, but they are also learning scientific concepts such as stability. (Towers tip over if they aren't stable.)

You can observe children's development through their building. First, children simply hold blocks and carry them around. Next, children try stacking blocks and lining them up on the floor. The next stage often involves making bridges. Then children make enclosures—zoos for animals or rooms in a house. Next, they make patterns and finally, they make structures for dramatic play, such as a doctor's office (Dodge, Colker, & Heroman 2002).

Building is a fun way to learn many math concepts such as size, shape, and pattern. Children learn to notice details in buildings that they can use in their own construction and drawing. They learn to solve problems and experiment with different designs, such as putting bigger blocks on the bottom of their building to keep a tower from falling down.

It is our experience that construction appeals to both boys and girls, particularly when you include props for imaginative play.

The block area will be a focal point while exploring this topic. *Building Structures with Young Children* by Ingrid Chalufour and Karen Worth contains a wealth of ideas for the block area.

TIMING TIP
Building and construction are topics you can do any time of year. Connecting classroom building to a project near your school adds to the excitement of creating new structures. Construction links easily with studying roads, ramps, bridges, and tunnels.

OBJECTIVES
▶ Enrich and expand familiar block building
▶ Explore stability, size, and measurement
▶ Explore how buildings are constructed in sequence
▶ Experiment with different construction materials
▶ Gain experience with tools and carpentry

STANDARDS
National Science Education Content Standards
▶ Science as inquiry—ask questions; plan and conduct a simple investigation: use simple equipment and tools to gather data and extend the senses; communicate investigations and explanations
▶ Physical science—study properties of objects and materials; observe position and motion of objects
▶ Science and technology—explore abilities of technological design; develop understanding about science and technology; develop abilities to distinguish between natural objects and objects made by humans

National Council of Teachers of Mathematics Standards
▶ Number and operations—count with understanding; make reasonable estimates
▶ Algebra—sort, classify, and order objects; recognize, describe, and extend patterns
▶ Geometry—recognize, name, build, draw, compare and sort two- and three-dimensional shapes
▶ Measurement—understand how to measure using nonstandard and standard tools
▶ Communication—organize, analyze, and evaluate mathematical thinking; use the language of mathematics

Standards for the English Language Arts
▶ Experience a wide range of print and non-print texts, including fiction and non-fiction, to build an understanding of the world and acquire new information
▶ Use spoken, written, and visual language to communicate and learn
▶ Generate ideas and questions and pose problems
▶ Build vocabulary

Introducing Construction

FOCUS AREAS

Science: exploring the abilities of technological design

Language Arts: learning vocabulary; using spoken and written language to communicate; generating ideas and questions

MATERIALS

Orange traffic or soccer cones and yellow caution tape or orange construction paper and yellow crepe paper

Hand-made or purchased sign that says HARD HAT AREA

Photos of about four different types of buildings—skyscrapers, stores, houses, castles

Two bins of unit blocks, enough so each child can choose one

Hard hat, goggles, and tool belt (optional, for you to wear)

2 sheets of chart paper

Marker

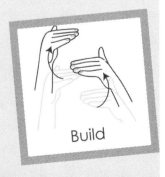

Build

PREPARATION

- Label one sheet of chart paper "What We Know About Construction" and the other "What We Want to Learn About Construction."
- If you don't have soccer cones and caution tape, make construction paper cones, and use yellow crepe paper as the tape.
- Turn your group area into a "construction site" by outlining it with soccer cones and caution tape. Post the HARD HAT AREA sign on a traffic cone. Put on the hard hat, goggles, and tool belt.

WHAT TO DO

1. As the children arrive at the group area, welcome them as construction workers coming to the building site, "Welcome, Builder Keisha. We need all our builders on site today."

2. When all the children have entered the group area, tell them they are going to learn about building BIG buildings. Show the children the photos one at a time and ask what they are. Start with buildings that are most familiar to the children. Ask the children what kinds of buildings they have seen being built.

3. Introduce the word *construction*. Say and clap the syllables, con-**struc**-tion, with the emphasis on the "struc" syllable. Say *construction* as you make the ASL signs for *build*. Your right and left hands face each other, bent at the knuckles with fingers straight, and then climb over each other moving upward as if you were building a tower.

4. Say, "We are going to be construction workers today." Offer a bin of unit blocks to each child and invite them to choose a block. (Two people passing out blocks in opposite directions cuts down the waiting time.) Invite the children, one at a time, to start building a tower in the center of the circle. If the blocks tip over, make an observation in a neutral tone such as, "Block towers often fall down. Let's keep building."

5. Invite comments about the building they created and what the children know about construction. Record their responses, including each child's name, on a sheet of chart paper labeled "What We Know About Construction."

6. Ask what the children would like to find out about construction. Record those responses on a second sheet of paper labeled "What We Want to Learn About Construction." Use the children's questions and interests to guide your explorations. Some children may be particularly interested in skyscrapers, others in houses, others in tools or BIG earth movers.

BIG QUESTIONS FOR GROWING MINDS

Use the following questions to engage the children in a discussion about construction during group time or with an individual child during activity time:

- Why does a block tower fall down if you push on it, but our school building doesn't fall down if you push on it?
- How are buildings made of blocks different from buildings you live in?
- How are block buildings the same as buildings you live in?

WORDS FOR BIG THINKING

Look for these words highlighted in italic throughout the activities in this chapter. Write the words out in large letters and introduce them a few at a time with the "**S**ay, **C**lap, **A**ct out, **D**o again" (SCAD) system. Using the words during activities and discussions will reinforce their meaning.

- Architect—person who designs and draws plans for buildings and bridges
- Construction—another word for building
- Exterior—outside
- Foundation—the base that supports a building
- Interior—inside
- Skyscraper—a tall building, so tall it looks like it scrapes the sky
- Stable—steady, balanced, not likely to fall down

A Note from the Author: The activities in this chapter are designed to build on each other. However, please feel free to choose those that meet the interests and abilities of your class. If parts of an activity seem like too much to do on a particular day, save them for a later time. Every class is different, even from day to day, and the activities are adaptable to meet the needs of your class.

TEACHER-TO-TEACHER TIP

Ask families to start saving Styrofoam egg cartons in the beginning of the school year. They make wonderful lightweight building blocks. Several weeks before you plan to explore buildings, ask families to save BIG boxes and smaller boxes such as cereal boxes.

PHOTO TIP

You can capture children's interest in building by creating photo boards of the building hunt, building projects, and egg carton *skyscrapers*. Look for close-up shots of individual children and group shots that show children interacting. Also note vocabulary words and quotes from children on the photo boards to document the learning.

Go on a Building Hunt

FOCUS AREAS

Science: exploring the abilities of technological design

Math: counting, communicating results

MATERIALS

Duplicated recording sheets (see Preparation)

Pencil or marker for each child

Cardboard to use as clipboards (optional)

Clothespins or paper clips to use on cardboard clipboards (optional)

Sheet of chart paper

Marker

Camera

PREPARATION

- If you don't already have permission for the children to take a walk from school, send permission slips home. Ask for additional adult volunteers to accompany the class on the walk.
- Before taking the children on a walk, go on a building hunt yourself to decide the best route for a 15- to 30-minute walk that will take you by a variety of buildings.
- Recording sheets: Photograph, draw, or use computer clip art of about six distinctive features you noticed on your walk to create a small chart of items the children can search for, such as stairs leading to a front door, a handicapped access ramp, a large picture window, a chimney, a large office building, or a storefront. Duplicate the chart for each child.

WHAT TO DO

1. During activity time, tell the children you are taking them on a building hunt. Ask them what kinds of buildings they think they will see. Ask, "What do you think the buildings might be made of?" Record their responses with their names on chart paper.
2. Tell the children you found special things for them to find on the walk. Pass out the duplicated

Name: Steven		
I'm going on a building hunt.		
△	ramp	
▭	window	
▯	door	
⌐	rain gutter	X
⊞	shutters	X
◹	stairs	

sheets, pencils, and pieces of cardboard to use as clipboards. Ask them to identify the features. Demonstrate how they can make a mark when they see one.

3. Sing "Here We Go on a Building Hunt" to the tune of "Here We Go 'Round the Mulberry Bush." Make up verses using the children's ideas, such as, "This is the way we look for stairs…."

4. Go for a walk, helping the children note when they see a feature on their recording sheet. This is not a contest. Encourage the children to help each other. Invite the children to tell you about other special features they observe so you can note them and take photos to create a photo board of the walk.

5. When you return to the classroom, compare the children's observations with what they thought they might see. Note special items the children observed. Save the children's recording sheets in their portfolios for assessment.

TEACHER-TO-TEACHER TIP
Children may be more excited about a dog or pebbles or a garbage can than the buildings. That is okay. One of the purposes of the walk is to heighten their observation skills, which you can feel confident they were using.

DISCUSSION STARTERS
Use these questions to spark children's thinking during and after the activity:
- What kind of building did you see the most?
- Which building was the biggest, the tallest, the smallest?
- Were there more homes or other kinds of buildings?
- How are houses and other buildings different? How are they the same?
- What are some of the most unusual things you saw?

SKILLS ASSESSMENT
Use these questions to determine a child's abilities and understanding:
- What kind of pencil grip does the child use (fist, three-point)?
- Can the child make a mark in the correct box?
- Does the child understand that the drawings on the recording sheet represent the real item?

Architects Draw Building Plans

FOCUS AREAS

Science: exploring the abilities of technological design

Math: counting, drawing, comparing two-dimensional and three-dimensional shapes, measuring—length

Language Arts: dictating a description, labeling

MATERIALS

Photographs or drawings of the interiors and exteriors of buildings, such as homes, office buildings, and schools

Sheets of white paper or graph paper, at least one per child

Colored pencils, crayons, or markers

Rulers

Stencils of squares and rectangles

Sample blueprints (optional, available from architectural firms) or images downloaded from the Internet (search term: blueprint images)

WHAT TO DO

1. Tell a small group of children, "Today you are going to be *architects*. An *architect* is a person who designs and draws plans for buildings." Say and clap the syllables, **ar**-chi-tect. Say *architect* as you make the ASL signs for *draw* and *building*. For *draw*, your right pinkie finger slides down the palm of your left hand with a wavy motion. The sign for *building* is the same as build, hands bent at the knuckles, fingers straight, climbing over each other, then the hands move down to show the sides of the building.

2. Show the children real blueprints, if possible, or an illustration. Focus on the *exterior* view (technically called an elevation). Ask, "What shape is the roof?" "What shape is the door?"

3. Introduce the BIG word *exterior*, which means outside. Say and clap the syllables, ex-**te**-ri-or, with the emphasis on the "te" syllable. Say *exterior* as you make the ASL sign—right hand comes out from a hole made by the left hand. Show a picture of the *exterior* of a building.

4. Introduce the word *architects* use for the inside of a building, the *interior*. Say and clap the syllables, in-**te**-ri-or, with the emphasis on the "te" syllable. Say *interior* as you make the ASL sign for *inside*. Hold your left hand horizontally, bent at the knuckles while your right hand repeatedly moves inside from above. Show a picture of the inside of a room, or a blueprint of an *interior*.

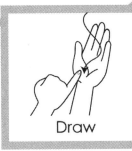
Draw

Build

Exterior

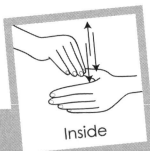
Inside

VOCABULARY TIP

The word *blueprint* came from a time when the original plans were white lines on a blue background. Today, the plans are typically black and white.

5. Invite the children to draw the *exterior* or *interior* of their home or a building. Ask which shapes they might draw. Talk about how many windows and doors they want to include. Challenge your older *architects* to draw a floor plan, the top down, bird's eye view of a room (see the Teacher-to-Teacher Tip).

6. Show older children how to draw straight lines with a ruler and trace rectangular and square stencils.

7. Help the children label their drawings. Have them dictate a description of their building.

MORE IDEAS

- Prepare numerous small boxes of the same height (cut small milk cartons and juice boxes about 2" tall). The children can construct models of rooms in a building by taping the boxes together. They then paint the top edge of their model and press a piece of paper on the top edge to create a "blueprint." This helps the children connect the three-dimensional model to the two-dimensional print.

TEACHER-TO-TEACHER TIP

It is difficult for children to grasp the concept of an *interior* floor plan that shows the building layout from the top down. Stretch their imaginations by having them lie down and look up at the ceiling shape. Explain that a floor plan shows how a room looks if you could lie on the ceiling and look down.

DISCUSSION STARTERS

Use these questions to spark children's thinking during and after the activity:

- What did you learn about drawing buildings?
- What kind of shapes did you use to draw your building?

SKILLS ASSESSMENT

Use these questions to determine a child's abilities and understanding:

- What kind of pencil grip does the child use (fist, three-point)?
- Can the child hold and trace around a stencil shape?
- How much detail did the child include in his drawing?
- Can the child count correctly the number of windows he drew?
- Can the child describe the building using vocabulary such as *windows* or *doors*?

BIG Building

FOCUS AREAS

Science: exploring the abilities of technological design

Math: sequencing, recognizing, drawing and building two-dimensional and three-dimensional shapes, measuring

Language Arts: learning vocabulary, labeling

MATERIALS

Sheet of chart paper

Clipboards, paper, and markers

Large cardboard boxes, BIG enough for children to sit inside (available from appliance stores), at least one for each small group of 3–4 children

Smaller boxes of all types and sizes for decoration and to make smaller buildings

Colored masking tape

Sharp knife to cut windows and doors (adult use only)

Construction paper

Tempera paint and sponges

Measuring tapes

T-square (optional)

Props for dramatic play, such as hard hats, tool belts, plastic tools

Yellow caution tape (optional) or yellow crepe paper

Orange traffic or soccer cones (optional)

WHAT TO DO

1. Set out the boxes and tape. Invite a small group of children to plan a BIG building project, or even a whole "street" if you have enough boxes. Ask the children what they would like to build. Ask if there are any features they noticed on the building hunt that they would like to include in their buildings. Record each group's ideas on a sheet of paper.

2. Ask how they might build what they want. There will likely be a huge range of ideas. You don't need to decide on one plan; multiple plans can go forward. Say, "I see lots of different ideas here. How can we include all of them?" Ask, "What should we do first?" to highlight sequencing.

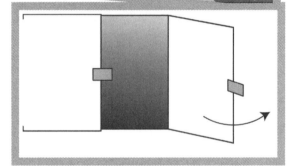

3. Provide paper, clipboards, and markers at the building site and encourage the children to draw their plan.

4. Invite the children to start building. Help them outline windows and doors with masking tape so an adult can make the cuts. You can make some of the windows open and close by cutting only three sides, creasing the cardboard on the last side and making a tab with duct tape for the children to pull open and shut, or make two shutters that open from the middle (see illustration). The children could create skylights by covering cut-out windows in the roof with waxed paper.

5. Use BIG vocabulary words. Say, "You are being an *architect* when you design where these windows should go." "What shape is your door?" "What do you need to decorate the *interior* of your building?"

MORE IDEAS

- Invite the children to add elements to the *exteriors* of their buildings such as roofs, chimneys, planter boxes, and parking garages.
- Suggest that the children measure their buildings. How wide is the window? How tall is the door?

- Suggest that the children use *construction* paper to make signs for the buildings, such as a store sign and street address.
- On another day, set out the painting supplies so the children can paint the *exterior* and *interior*. Invite older children to use sponges to create rows of bricks for a *foundation* layer or on the chimney.

TEACHER-TO-TEACHER TIPS

- It is fun to do this activity outside so the children have lots of room to work and can create multiple buildings. A covered walkway would be ideal to protect it from the weather, or you could cover the buildings with a tarp. You can set up indoors if you have enough room.
- The children may be more interested in playing inside their buildings than they are in constructing them. Spark their imaginations by asking them what they need to live or work in their building. Encourage them to make or find props to extend their play.
- At the end of the unit, involve the children in taking down the buildings and recycling the materials they used to make the buildings.

DISCUSSION STARTERS

Use these questions to spark children's thinking during and after the activity:
- What are you learning about building BIG buildings?
- How is your building different from another group's building?
- Who do you think might like to live or work in your building?
- What other kids of buildings would you like to make?

SKILLS ASSESSMENT

Use these questions to determine a child's abilities and understanding:
- Does the child work with other children or focus on his own project?
- How does the child react when things don't go as expected?
- Does the child use building vocabulary words such as *architect*, *interior* and *exterior*?

How High Can We Build Egg Carton Skyscrapers?

FOCUS AREAS

Science: exploring the abilities of technological design

Math: counting, learning numerals, estimating, sequencing, comparing, creating three-dimensional shapes, measuring—height

Language Arts: learning vocabulary, experiencing a wide range of texts, labeling

MATERIALS

Books about *skyscraper construction* (see Good Books for Facts and Fun on page 246)

Sheet of chart paper

Marker

BIG cardboard box for foundation, wide enough to fit at least 3 egg cartons side by side

Styrofoam egg cartons, about 50, if possible (Ask families to donate egg cartons. **Safety note:** Wash cartons thoroughly to remove any egg residue.)

Boxes, such as cereal boxes

Masking tape or duct tape

Chair, stepstool, or ladder

Paper and markers

Measuring tape and nonstandard measuring tools, such as yarn

TEACHER-TO-TEACHER TIPS

- Decide where to build the *skyscraper*. It could be in the corner of your classroom, or outdoors near the climbing structure or a tree or under an overhang. If the *skyscraper* is near the climbing structure, the children can add to the tower from above. As the building grows taller, allow the children to climb on a stepstool or ladder to add cartons, but only one at a time with close adult supervision. The children can pass cartons to an adult on a ladder to complete the top.
- The *skyscraper* will tip over easily. When it falls, ask for the children's ideas about how to reinforce the building to make it sturdier. Try taping the cartons or boxes to each other. Introduce the idea of diagonal braces. A lightweight, inexpensive brace is newspaper rolled tightly on a broom handle, then slipped off and taped at the ends.

WHAT TO DO

1. Read a book about *skyscraper construction* to the builders in your class.

2. Introduce the word *skyscraper*, a tall building, so tall it looks like it scrapes the sky. Say and clap the syllables, **sky-scrap**-er, with the emphasis on the "sky" and "scrap" syllables. Say *skyscraper* as you make the ASL sign for *building*—your right and left hands climb over each other as if you were building a tower. Keep going up over your head, then move your hands down to outline the sides of the building.

3. Show the children your BIG collection of egg cartons and BIG cardboard box. Ask how they think they could make a *skyscraper* from the cartons and box. Introduce the word *foundation*, the base that supports a building. Say and clap foun-**da**-tion, with the emphasis on the "da" syllable. Say *foundation* as you make the ASL signs for *building* and

Build

support. For *building*, your right and left hands climb over each other as if you were building a tower, then move your hands down to outline the sides of the building. *Support* is both hands in the S shape (fingers closed, thumb lies across fingers.) Your right hand moves up and supports left hand. Show the children the BIG cardboard box that you will use for the *foundation*.

Support

4. Ask what the children can do so the *skyscraper* they build won't fall down. Introduce the word *stable*. When something is *stable*; it is balanced, it doesn't tip over or fall down. Say and clap **sta**-ble, with the emphasis on the "sta" syllable. Say *stable* as you make the ASL sign for *balance*, holding your two hands open, palms down and move them up and down as if trying to balance, then hold them steady.

5. Ask, "How can we make our *skyscraper stable*?" Have each child take a turn placing an egg carton (intact and closed) or a cereal box on the BIG cardboard box to start making a *skyscraper*. Use three egg cartons for the first level of a sturdy building that you can then build taller.

Balance

6. Ask how many cartons the children think it will take to reach the ceiling if working indoors, or to reach the top of a ladder, if outside. Record their answers on the chart paper.

7. Begin building one level at a time. Help the children measure the height as they build with measuring tapes and non-standard measuring tools such as yarn. Encourage comparisons: Is it taller than the children, the teacher, the doorway? Supervise carefully as you allow the children to use a sturdy ladder to add levels.

8. Encourage the children to draw pictures of the building as it gets taller.

MORE IDEAS

- When the children are finished building the *skyscraper*, guide them to do all sorts of counting: How many stories (levels of egg cartons or cereal boxes) tall is the building? How many cartons or boxes did you use altogether? How many cartons are left? How many cartons or boxes are on the top floor? Record all these numbers on chart paper. Compare the actual numbers with the estimates.
- The children can write a street address and make a sign for the building.
- When complete, help the children wrap the building with newspaper to improve its stability. Use a section with dense text like the classified ads to make the building look urban.

DISCUSSION STARTERS

Use these questions to spark children's thinking during and after the activity:
- How do you think people could use this building—for a store or for apartments?
- How could people get from the bottom to the top of the building?
- How could you make your building fancier?

SKILLS ASSESSMENT

Use these questions to determine a child's abilities and understanding:
- Can the child count the number of floors in the building?
- Can the child problem solve when the cartons fall?
- Can the child work as part of a group?

Sandbox Construction: Sandcastles to Skyscrapers

FOCUS AREAS

Science: exploring the abilities of technological design

Math: counting, estimating, creating three-dimensional shapes

Language Arts: labeling

MATERIALS

Large assortment of containers to use as molds, such as sand pails, yogurt containers, plastic cups (**Safety note:** Thoroughly wash all recycled containers.)

Sand shovels or homemade scoopers from detergent containers (see page 302 in Appendix for directions)

Garden hose or buckets of water

Dramatic play props, such as hard hats

Paper and markers

WHAT TO DO

1. Brainstorm with a small group of children to figure out how to turn your sandbox into a giant *construction* site. One possibility is posting a sign saying "Hard Hat Zone."
2. Provide water with a garden hose or in buckets to make sand structures.
3. Invite the children to create a whole city or castle in the sandbox.
4. Encourage the children to make signs for their buildings.

DISCUSSION STARTERS

Use these questions to spark children's thinking during and after the activity:

- Can you think of another way to make your building?
- Which containers work the best to make sand shapes?
- What are some of the differences between building with blocks and building with egg cartons?

SKILLS ASSESSMENT

Use these questions to determine a child's abilities and understanding:

- How does the child respond when sand towers fall?
- Does the child solve problems while building?
- Can the child work as part of a team?

We've Been Building Up a Building

PREPARATION
● Write the words to the song on chart paper.

WHAT TO DO
1. Review the words of the following song with the children.
2. Sing the song to the tune of "I've Been Working on the Railroad."

We've Been Building Up a Building *by Tim Dobbins*

We've been building up a building,
All the morning long.
We've been building up a building,
And we've made it tall and strong.
Can't you see the towers gleaming,
Rising so high up in the air?
Can't you hear the workers shouting,
"We hope it stays right there"?

Building don't you fall,
Building don't you fall,
Building don't you fall oh nooooo.
Building don't you fall,
Building don't you fall,
Building don't you fall oh nooooo.

Something knocked over our building.
Something knocked it over I know.
Something knocked over our building,
But we can build it back. Let's go.

We're building, tap, tap, tappity, tap,
tap,
Tappity, tap, tap, tap, tap, tap, tap, tap,
Tap, tap, tappity, tap, tap.
We can build it back. Let's go!

3. After singing the song several times, invite the children to take turns building up a building out of blocks and then knocking it down while the rest of the children sing the song. *Construction* workers can wear hard hats.

DISCUSSION STARTERS
Use these questions to spark children's thinking during and after the activity:
● Did you ever build a building that fell down? What did it look like?
● What did you do when it fell?

SKILLS ASSESSMENT
Use these questions to determine a child's abilities and understanding:
● Did the child join in singing?
● Did the child participate in the group discussion?

FOCUS AREAS
Math: sequencing
Language Arts: learning vocabulary, experiencing a wide range of texts

MATERIALS
Dramatic play hard hats
Egg cartons or cardboard or foam blocks
Chart paper and markers

Tool Time: What Tool Is This?

FOCUS AREAS

Science: exploring the abilities of technological design, distinguishing between natural objects and objects made by humans

Math: counting

Language Arts: learning vocabulary

MATERIALS

A variety of real tools, including hammers (preferably small and lightweight), wrenches, pliers, screwdrivers, and C clamps (**Note:** Ask families if they can lend tools for a day. If real tools aren't available, use plastic tools.)

Names of the tools written in large letters

Pieces of Styrofoam from boxed appliances that hold together well (available from appliance or furniture stores)

Wooden golf tees

Large screws

Safety goggles

Paper

Markers

PREPARATION

- Set out a variety of tools. Depending on the size of your group and the number of adults available to supervise the children as they use the tools, set up one or more stations for the children to try the tools. **Safety note:** Close adult supervision is essential when the children are exploring and using tools.

WHAT TO DO

1. Put on safety goggles. Start by asking the children to choose a tool and then say what it is and what it is used for. Add humor by asking, "Could I use these pliers to pull a splinter out of my finger?" "Could I use a hammer to crack open an egg to make a cake?" Show the name of the tool and sound it out with the children, "Hammer." Demonstrate how you use a hammer (see Teacher-to-Teacher Tips).
2. After the children have explored the tools, invite the class to try them out at a nearby station. Have the children wear safety goggles so they get in that habit while doing carpentry. It's easiest to begin with a small hammer and wooden golf tees. Show the children how to gently insert the tip of the tee into a piece of Styrofoam and then hammer it in. Have them count how many taps it takes to get the tee all the way in. Ask the children to estimate how many taps the next tee will take.
3. The children can create various shapes or letters with the tees, or use the tees to join together "boards" of thinner, flat sheets of Styrofoam.
4. When they are finished they can take out the tees with pliers.

MORE IDEAS

- The children can insert the tip of a large screw into the Styrofoam and then screw it in and unscrew it.
- The children can use real nails with wide heads in Styrofoam or soft wood. Start the nail by putting it into a pre-tapped hole. After a couple taps, have the children try to remove the nail with their fingers. Demonstrate how to use the "claw" of the hammer to pull the nail. Let the children try pounding another nail and then pulling it out under close supervision.
- The children can use pliers to pull out nails.
- The children can use C-clamps to attach pieces of Styrofoam or wood.

DISCUSSION STARTERS

Use these questions to spark children's thinking during and after the activity:

- Which tool do you think is the easiest to use?
- Which tool do you think is the hardest to use?
- Show the children two tools, such as a hammer and a screwdriver. How are these tools alike? How are they different?

SKILLS ASSESSMENT

Use these questions to determine a child's abilities and understanding:

- Can the child count the number of "nails" and hammer hits?
- Does the child know the tool vocabulary?
- How does the child grip the tools?
- Can the child observe and express the differences and similarities between screws and nails? Use comparative vocabulary?

Create a BIG City

FOCUS AREAS

Science: exploring the abilities of technological design

Math: counting, creating three-dimensional shapes, measuring—height

Language Arts: labeling, dictating information

MATERIALS

Biodegradable packing noodles (Save them from mail-order packages or purchase them from school and office suppliers.)

Wet sponges on small trays

Cardboard for a base, about 8½" x 11", at least one piece per child

Markers

Paper

Child-safe scissors

Rulers and non-standard measuring tools, such as Unifix cubes

TEACHER-TO-TEACHER TIP

Biodegradable packing noodles are fun and amazingly simple for children of all ages to use to create all types of structures. The noodles stick together after being dampened just slightly. It works best to moisten the noodles lightly by touching them to a damp sponge. Dipping them in a container of water can make them dissolve.

WHAT TO DO

1. Invite a small group of children to create a building or many buildings on their cardboard.

2. Ask them to tell you about their creations and record their responses on the cardboard base.

3. The children color their creations with markers. They can also use paper, child-safe scissors, and markers to make signs.

4. Invite them to count how many noodles they used.

5. Have them measure how tall their buildings are with the Unifix cubes and rulers.

6. Reinforce shape vocabulary by commenting, "The *foundation* of your building looks like a square."

7. When the children are finished, have them set their building on a table or a quiet area of the floor so you can build a whole street or city.

DISCUSSION STARTERS

Use these questions to spark children's thinking during and after the activity:

- Who could live in your building?
- What would happen if it rained on your building?
- What would it be like to live in a building made out of packing noodles?
- What other materials make strong, warm places to live?

SKILLS ASSESSMENT

Use these questions to determine a child's abilities and understanding:

- Can the child count the number of packing noodles used?
- How high can the child count accurately?
- Can the child measure the height of the building?

Knock Down the Building Game

TEACHER-TO-TEACHER TIP
It is fun to play this game outdoors where children have plenty of room to throw a ball without knocking over something else. If you play indoors, set up in a safe area and use beanbags with small blocks.

FOCUS AREAS
Science: studying stability and force, exploring the abilities of technological design
Math: counting, learning one-to-one correspondence, representing numbers
Gross Motor: throwing

MATERIALS
Large cardboard or foam blocks or shoeboxes taped closed
Beanbags or a soccer ball

WHAT TO DO
1. Work with a small group of children. One child throws a giant die (see page 300 in the Appendix for directions), notes the number, and then collects the same number of blocks as the number on the die and then builds the blocks in any design.
2. The child rolls the die a second time if he wants a bigger building.
3. When the child's tower is as BIG as he wants it to be, he throws a beanbag or ball at the tower and tries to knock it down.
   Note: This is a non-competitive game. The children can keep throwing until they knock the blocks down. The children can choose how difficult a challenge they want. They can build a tall tower that will be easy to hit or a shorter, more *stable* one. They can stand close to the tower or farther away.

MORE IDEAS
- Older children can compare a structure built with Duplos to a structure built with wooden blocks to see which is easier to knock down.
- Create a "wrecking ball" instead of using beanbags or a ball to knock down blocks. Attach a soccer ball to a string with duct tape, or by twisting a screw eye into the ball's inflation valve and tying a string to the head of the screw. Attach a second string to the ball so the children can pull the "wrecking ball" and aim it at the "building." Attach the wrecking ball to a small support (see illustration).

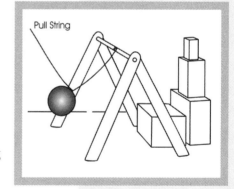

Pull String

DISCUSSION STARTERS
Use these questions to spark children's thinking during and after the activity:
- What did you learn about knocking down buildings?
- What shape tower do you think is the most *stable*, the hardest to knock down?
- Is it harder for you to knock down a tall or a short building?

SKILLS ASSESSMENT
Use these questions to determine a child's abilities and understanding:
- Can the child count correctly the number of dots on the die?
- Does the child gather the correct number of boxes for building?
- Does the child use vocabulary words such as *stable*?
- How is the child's aim when throwing?

BIG CONNECTIONS:
More Activities Across the Curriculum

LANGUAGE ARTS
- The children draw buildings and dictate stories about the buildings in their drawings. Include *construction* books and vocabulary words at the table for inspiration. Topics for different days:
  - What kind of building would you like to create?
  - What tools would you put in a tool belt for building? How would you use them?
  - Would you like to live in a house built of straw, glass, pancakes?
  Mount the stories in the shape of several *skyscrapers*. When you take down the display, keep the drawings in each child's portfolio.

ART/MATH
- The children glue wood scraps to a cardboard base to create towers and note the geometric shapes.

CONSTRUCTION/MATH
- The children work with unit blocks and small colored wooden blocks on a table top and then measure buildings with tape measures and non-traditional measures, such as yarn and Unifix cubes. Invite them to count how many blocks they can stack before the tower falls. Compare the smaller buildings to the BIG buildings and note the differences.
- Add a variety of building materials to the block area such as berry baskets, egg cartons, paper cups, laundry detergent caps, and cereal boxes to enhance the children's *construction* projects. The children measure the structures they build.

COOKING/MATH
- The children make *skyscraper* towers with cucumber rounds and cherry tomatoes on short bamboo skewers. Caution the children to be careful with the sharp ends of the skewers. Encourage the children to create a pattern. See if they can make their tower stand up. Eat the towers for lunch or snack.

DRAMA
- Children act out the story of "The Three Little Pigs" (see pages 152–153 in the wind chapter).
- Create a variation of This Is the House that Jack Built: This Is the *Skyscraper* that Jasmine Built.

SENSORY TABLE
- Gather scraps of wood (splinters removed) and different types of sandpaper so the children can sand the edges and feel the variety of textures.

BIG Outcomes

Group assessment: Review the photo boards from the building hunt, building projects, and egg carton *skyscrapers*. Review the chart paper sheets from the beginning of your exploration of what the children know about *construction* and what they want to learn. On a third sheet of chart paper titled "What We Learned About Construction," record the children's comments about what they learned, including the name of the child who made the comment. Be sure to note answers to their original questions, or note if you still have more to learn and explore.

Individual assessment: Review your notes and quotes from individual observations during activities such as the "knock down the building" game, the packing noodle creations, and drawing building plans. Review the children's work and save it in their portfolios. Note whether the children use new vocabulary words in conversation. Note areas in which the children need further practice and those in which they excel.

GOOD BOOKS FOR FACTS AND FUN

Construction sites fascinate young children. The books listed below are just a starting place. Vehicle-centered construction titles are more common than those that offer accurate technical building details in simple formats.

INFORMATION ABOUT CONSTRUCTION

At a Construction Site by Don Kilby
Descriptive language accurately represents actions and sounds of the various vehicles, from a wrecking ball crane to a tree spade, on site at a new community center. Colorful paintings on rough canvas include realistic details. Ages 3–6

How It Happens at the Building Site by Jenna Anderson
Surveying, *foundation* laying, framing—step-by-step, with clearly defined construction terms and color photographs, a new suburban house takes shape. The glossary focuses on names of tools and materials. Ages 3–6

If You Were a Construction Worker by Virginia Schomp
Broad coverage of construction and wrecking projects, emphasizing basic building elements and the teamwork required for creating skyscrapers, houses, roads, bridges, and tunnels and knocking down old ones. Good photos, but the longer text works best for sharing with older students. Ages 5–6

Tool Book by Gail Gibbons
Gibbons names common building tools and illustrates their functions in her trademark plain style. Objects are thinly outlined in black, filled in, and set against solid, flat colors. This book is an easy introduction to basic construction vocabulary for young builders. Ages 3–6

Tools by Ann Morris

A guide to tools used around the world. Short sentences identify tool categories. A map and an index add details, naming each country, the tool, and the task shown in expressive color photographs. Ages 3–6

INFORMATION ABOUT SKYSCRAPERS

Skyscrapers by Seymour Simon

Excellent photos, history, definitions, and facts about the super-tall buildings presented in an early-reader format that works for sharing with younger children. Ages 4–6

Skyscrapers! Super Structures to Design & Build by Carol A. Johmann & Michael P. Kline

This compendium of skyscraper history, facts, and activities provides teachers with a solid, easy-to-read overview of big buildings. Grades 3–6

STORIES ABOUT CONSTRUCTION

Alphabet Under Construction by Denise Fleming

Fleming's wild mouse puts the alphabet together, letter by letter, using a wide range of construction techniques expressed in varied vocabulary, vivid verbs such as airbrushes, kinks and prunes, and flamboyantly colored illustrations. Ages 3–5

Building a House by Byron Barton

Brief phrases present the basic outline of a house-building project while the illustrations in bright primary colors show many details that can be described to avid young listeners as this classic is read again and again. Ages 3–4

Building with Dad by Carol Nevius

The realistic paintings and unusual perspectives will capture your construction crew's attention from the start to finish of this school building project, shared by a son and father in rhyming couplets. Ages 3–6

The House in the Meadow by Shutta Crum

This "Over in the Meadow"-based countdown rhyme features a varied group of talented men and women who build their friends, the new bride and groom, a new house. Cheerful collages add fun to this community effort. Ages 3–6

The Lot at the End of My Block by Kevin Lewis

A simple, clearly illustrated, cumulative construction tale based on "This Is the House That Jack Built" that results in a new apartment building and a new friend for the boy who observes the progress of the project. Ages 3–6

Mike Mulligan and His Steam Shovel by Virginia Lee Burton

Mike and his beloved steam shovel, Mary Anne, obsolete after years of building big projects, find a final home in Popperville's new town hall. Their story lives on in this classic tale of change, creativity, and teamwork. Ages 3–6

A Note to Families About Construction

Dear Families,

It is easy to think that children are "just playing" when they build block towers or homes for their stuffed animals, but they are learning many scientific concepts, such as stability. (Towers tip over if they are not stable.) They learn to solve problems and experiment with different designs, such as putting bigger blocks on the bottom of their building.

Children's block building often progresses in stages. First, children simply hold blocks and carry them around. Next, children try stacking blocks and lining them up on the floor. The next stage often involves making bridges. Then children make enclosures— zoos for animals or rooms in a house. Finally they make structures for dramatic play, such as a doctor's office.

At school, we are learning about building in a big way. We are making skyscrapers with egg cartons and buildings with big appliance boxes. We are also learning about real buildings in our community.

You can help your children develop building skills by giving them lots of opportunities to explore. You do not need special materials. Children can build with individually wrapped rolls of toilet paper and empty juice cartons. When you are out doing errands with your child, you can notice parts of buildings, such as windows and doors and roofs.

Here are some of the words we've been learning about building:
- Architects draw plans for buildings.
- A foundation is the base that supports a building.
- Skyscrapers are really tall buildings.

Have fun watching your architect design and build structures!

THINKING BIG ABOUT TRAVELING: ROADS, RAMPS, BRIDGES, AND TUNNELS

THE BIG PICTURE

Many early childhood programs include vehicles and transportation as part of their curriculum. This unit adds a scientific component to these popular subjects as children learn how ramps and different road surfaces impact how fast and how far toy cars will travel. These activities in physical science provide opportunities for children try out their ideas and see immediately how they work. "What will happen if I raise the ramp on one more block?" "What will happen if I roll the car over a bumpy road made of bubble wrap?" Children can test their hypotheses (their guesses) over and over and make changes based on their experiences, just like scientists do.

Road building also provides many opportunities to practice problem solving: "How can my toy car get over this river?" "How can I get around this hill?" When children practice solving problems like these in the block area they are better able to figure out how to solve other challenges, such as "How can I fit my jacket in my backpack?"

TIMING TIP

Roads, ramps, bridges, and tunnels are topics you can investigate any time of year. It's particularly interesting when road repair is happening near school. These topics also connect to construction units and traffic safety.

OBJECTIVES

▶ Enrich and expand familiar classroom vehicle and transportation activities
▶ Experience scientific inquiry through experiments with ramps and road surfaces
▶ Introduce the concept of gravity
▶ Practice problem solving

STANDARDS

National Science Education Content Standards

▶ Science as inquiry—ask questions; plan and conduct a simple investigation; use simple equipment and tools to gather data and extend the senses; use data to construct a reasonable explanation; communicate investigations and explanations
▶ Physical science—study properties of objects and materials; observe position and motion of objects
▶ Science and technology—observe abilities of technological design; develop understanding about science and technology; develop abilities to distinguish between natural objects and objects made by humans

National Council of Teachers of Mathematics Standards

▶ Number and operations—count with understanding; make reasonable estimates
▶ Measurement—understand how to measure using nonstandard and standard tools
▶ Data analysis and probability—represent data using concrete objects, pictures, and graphs
▶ Communication—organize, analyze, and evaluate mathematical thinking; use the language of mathematics

Standards for the English Language Arts

▶ Experience a wide range of print and non-print texts, including fiction and non-fiction, to build an understanding of the world and acquire new information
▶ Use spoken, written, and visual language to communicate and learn
▶ Generate ideas and questions and pose problems
▶ Build vocabulary

BIG Beginning: Introducing Roads

FOCUS AREAS

Science: observing the position and motion of objects

Language Arts: generating ideas and questions

MATERIALS

Red and green construction paper
Craft stick
Glue or tape
Pictures of three different kinds of roads—a city street, a highway, and a country road
Two sheets of chart paper
Marker

PREPARATION

- Label one sheet of chart paper "What We Know About Roads" and the other "What We Want to Learn About Roads."
- Make a traffic signal by attaching a large red construction paper circle to one side of a craft stick and a large green construction paper circle to the other side.

WHAT TO DO

1. Invite the children to pretend they are driving a car to the group area. To help the children "drive" into the group area one at a time, an adult shows the red or green traffic light and says, "Green light" or "Red light." The children then take their place in the circle.

2. When all children have entered the group area, tell them they are going to learn about roads. Show the children the pictures of different types of roads one at a time, starting with the kind most familiar to them.

3. Ask who has traveled on each kind of road and in what type of vehicle—car, bus, truck, and so on. Record comments, including each child's name, on the chart paper labeled "What We Know About Roads." Repeat with each road example.

4. Ask the children if they've seen a road being built or repaired. What did they notice about the road work? Record their comments on the chart paper labeled "What We Know About Roads."

5. Ask the children what they want to find out about roads. Record those comments on the chart paper labeled, "What We Want to Learn About Roads." Use their questions and interests to guide your activities. Some children may be especially interested in road signs; others may be interested in bridges.

BIG QUESTIONS FOR GROWING MINDS

Use the following questions to engage the children in a discussion about roads during group time or with an individual child during activity time:

- Why do we have roads?
- Where do roads go?
- How do people share roads?
- Why do people need rules for sharing roads?
- Which type of transportation vehicles need roads? Which don't?

WORDS FOR BIG THINKING

Look for these words highlighted in italics throughout the activities in this chapter. Write the words out in large letters and introduce them with the "**S**ay, **C**lap, **A**ct out, **D**o again (SCAD) system. Using the words during activities and discussions will reinforce them.

- Bridge—a structure carrying a path or road over an obstacle
- Bumpy—rough or uneven
- Curve—a smooth change in direction
- Gravity—a force that all objects exert on each other. The Earth is the biggest object near us and Earth's gravity pulls us and everything on the Earth down, towards its center.
- Intersection—a place where two roads cross
- Obstacle—something that blocks a pathway
- Ramp—a slope leading from one level to another
- Smooth—even, not bumpy
- Straight—having the same direction
- Tunnel—a path through the ground

A Note from the Author: The activities in this chapter are designed to build on each other. However, please feel free to choose those that meet the interests and abilities of your class. If parts of an activity seem like too much to do on a particular day, save them for a later time. Every class is different, even from day to day, and the activities are adaptable to meet the needs of your class.

PHOTO TIP

You can document children's explorations of roads by creating photo boards about studying the road near your school, building roads in the sandbox, and experimenting with ramps and road surfaces. Look for close-ups of individual children and group shots that show children interacting. Also note vocabulary words and quotes from children on the photo boards to document their learning.

Studying Our Road

Name: Kasey		
Our Road		
⬡	stop sign	
⌣	curb	
🚦	traffic light	X
===	lines in road	
Elm St. 🪧	street sign	X

FOCUS AREAS

Science: learning about the abilities of technological design

Math: counting, communicating results

MATERIALS

Duplicated recording sheets (see below)
Pencil or marker for each child
Chart paper
Marker
Camera

PREPARATION

- Label the sheet of chart paper "Our Road."
- Recording sheets: Find a place outside your school where it is safe for the children to stand and observe the road. Note about six features the children can see right from their safe observation spot such as the curb, traffic signal, cross walk, street sign, and lines painted on the road. Create a small recording sheet of these items by sketching or using clip art from the computer.

WHAT TO DO

1. During activity time tell the children that they are going to look at the road close to the school. Ask them what they think they will see. Record their responses on a chart sheet labeled "Our Road."
2. Tell the children you noticed special things for them to find. Pass out the duplicated sheets and pencils. Demonstrate how they can make a mark when the see each thing.
3. Walk to the safe spot you selected. Help the children note when they see an item. This is not a contest. Encourage the children to help each other. Invite the children to tell you about other special features they observe so you can take photos to create a photo board of "their" road. Also, write down comments the children make while walking, including the child's name.

   Note: Although looking at a road may not sound very interesting, children usually enjoy noticing familiar features.
4. When you return to the classroom, compare the children's observations with what they thought they might see. Note special things the children observed. Save the children's recording sheets in their portfolios.

SUPERSIZE IT!

Go for a walk and spend more time observing more street features. Make sure you have permission slips and ask for extra adults to accompany you on the walk.

DISCUSSION STARTERS

Use these questions to spark children's thinking during and after the activity:
- Did you see anything that surprised you?
- What kinds of vehicles travel on the road in front of our school?

SKILLS ASSESSMENT

Use these questions to determine a child's abilities and understanding:
- What kind of pencil grip does the child use (fist, three-point)?
- Can the child make a mark in the correct box?

Over, Under, Across, Around, and Through: Ramps, Curves, Bridges, and Tunnels

WHAT TO DO

1. At group time, create a road out of long unit blocks and place a large block at the end of the road. Introduce the word *obstacle*, something that blocks a path. Say and clap the syllables for **ob**-sta-cle. Say *obstacle* as you make the ASL sign for *prevent* and *obstruct* by holding your two hands in an X so the pinkie finger of the right hand touches the index finger of the left hand, and moving both hands forward together as if you were blocking something. Ask the children, "How can my road get past this *BIG* hill?" Demonstrate a car driving right up to the large block. Drive the car *straight* up the side of the block. Ask the children,"What is the car doing? Can a real car drive like that? What would happen if it did?"

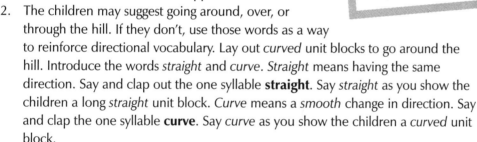

Prevent

2. The children may suggest going around, over, or through the hill. If they don't, use those words as a way to reinforce directional vocabulary. Lay out *curved* unit blocks to go around the hill. Introduce the words *straight* and *curve*. *Straight* means having the same direction. Say and clap out the one syllable **straight**. Say *straight* as you show the children a long *straight* unit block. *Curve* means a *smooth* change in direction. Say and clap the one syllable **curve**. Say *curve* as you show the children a *curved* unit block.

3. Invite the children to create a giant road system throughout your whole classroom with blocks and *obstacles* that will require problem solving.

4. Set out sand timers so the children can time how long it takes them to run a car from one end of the road to the other.

5. The children can use tape measures and yarn pieces to measure their road system.

MORE IDEAS

- Set up a *ramp* to go over the hill. Introduce the word *ramp*, a slope leading from one level to another. Say and clap the one syllable **ramp**. Say *ramp* as you hold a long unit block at an angle.

- Ask what a path through the ground is called. Introduce the word *tunnel*. Say and clap the syllables, **tun**-nel, with the emphasis on the "tun" syllable. Say *tunnel* as you show your cardboard tube and cover it with a towel or mat to represent the dirt.

- Ask the children what other *obstacles* there might be for a road. If a child mentions a river you can represent the river with a piece of blue paper and ask for ideas how the road can go across the river. The children may suggest a *bridge*. Show pictures of different kinds of *bridges* and introduce the word *bridge*, a structure that helps a path or road get across an *obstacle*. Say and clap the one syllable **bridge**. Say *bridge* as you show a photo of a *bridge* or make one with unit blocks.

FOCUS AREAS

Science: observing the position and motion of objects, learning the abilities of technological design

Math: estimating, sequencing, measuring—length and time

Language Arts: learning vocabulary, labeling

MATERIALS

Unit blocks, *curved* and *straight*

Toy cars

Large block

Several sheets of blue construction paper

Large cardboard tube (available from BIG rolls of bulletin board paper or from carpet and linoleum suppliers)

Pictures of *ramps, bridges, curves, tunnels* (see Good Books for Facts and Fun on page 267–268)

Sand timers

Tape measures and other nonstandard measuring units, such as yarn

- Introduce the word *intersection*, a place where two roads cross. Say and clap the syllables in-ter-**sec**-tion, with the emphasis on the "sec" syllable. Say *intersection* as you build an *intersection* with the unit blocks.

SUPERSIZE IT!

- Help the children build a road with *obstacles* that they can travel themselves. They can make hills with pillows and add wooden *ramps* to go over the hills, create *tunnels* with sheets covering chairs, and make *bridges* they can walk across using wooden boards or a balance beam. Use the vocabulary words as you talk with the children about their creations.
- Help the children build a giant road and *ramp* system outdoors using plastic rain gutters held up by your climbing structure, saw horses, and chairs.

TEACHER-TO-TEACHER TIP

Allow extended periods of time for the children to experiment with developing huge road systems and building different kinds of *bridges*, *ramps*, and *tunnels*. If you have a large classroom, it's ideal to leave at least part of the road system in place for days (perhaps under a table) so the children can add and change it. The children may enjoy adding buildings to the road system. If your classroom is small, take photos and make prints quickly so the children can see what they did the previous day in case they want to rebuild it.

DISCUSSION STARTERS

Use these questions to spark children's thinking during and after the activity:

- How did you solve the problem of making a *bridge*?
- How did you make a *tunnel*?
- How long does it take a car to go from one end of the road to the other?
- How would it feel to drive up this *BIG* hill?

SKILLS ASSESSMENT

Use these questions to determine a child's abilities and understanding:

- Is the child using a variety of blocks?
- Is the child using the vocabulary words in conversation?
- Can the child brainstorm solutions to challenges?
- Is the child working cooperatively on the road building project?

Steep or Level?
Gravity at Work

WHAT TO DO

1. Place toy vehicles and balls along with a variety of materials to make *ramps* in the block area or outdoors. Invite the children to experiment with the *ramps* in open-ended exploration over a period of days or weeks. Observe the children's explorations and ask questions as appropriate: "What happens when you make the *ramp* higher at one end?" "Do cars roll farther down a taller *ramp* or a shorter *ramp*?"

2. Show the children how they can mark how far a car travels with a block or piece of colored masking tape. After the children have multiple opportunities to experiment with *ramps*, spend group time discussing what they have discovered. Start by placing a long block flat on the floor. Put a car on the block and move your hands away without pushing the car. The car doesn't move. Ask, "Why isn't the car moving? How can I get the car to move?"

3. Prop the long block up on another block to make a *ramp*. Hold the car at the top of the *ramp*. Ask the children what will happen if you let go. Let go of the car. Say, "I didn't push the car, but it rolled down the *ramp*. What made that happen?" Introduce the word *gravity*, a force that all objects exert on each other. The Earth is the biggest object near us and the Earth's *gravity* pulls us and everything on the surface down, towards its center. Say and clap the syllables, **grav**-i-ty. Say *gravity* as you act it out by standing up with your right arm outstretched, then quickly crouching down and touching the floor. Say, "*Gravity* is pulling the car down the *ramp*." (**Note:** This is not ASL.)

4. Stack up a few blocks. Say, "*Ramps* help cars go down hills smoothly so they don't crash." Demonstrate a car falling off the end of the stack. Set up a *ramp* and let the car roll down.

5. Tell the children they can be scientists and do experiments to see how the height of a *ramp* affects how fast and how far the car travels. If appropriate, introduce the words *scientist, prediction,* and *experiment* (see information about these words on pages 40–41).

6. During activity time, provide materials for children to set up multiple *ramps*. Invite the children to recreate the experiment you did during group time using one block under the *ramp*. Then invite them to make a second *ramp* with two unit blocks. Ask them to predict what will happen when they let a car go from the top. Say, "Now try it."

FOCUS AREAS

Science: exploring the position and motion of objects, learning the abilities of technological design

Math: measuring—distance using standard and nonstandard tools, communicating results

Language Arts: learning vocabulary

MATERIALS

Plastic rain gutters, wooden planks, or stiff cardboard, about 3' long

Unit blocks

Toy cars or trucks of the same size and type, the more the better

Small balls, such as tennis balls or plastic golf balls

Colored masking tape (optional)

Standard and nonstandard measuring tools such as measuring tape and yarn

7. Invite the children to experiment making *ramps* with multiple blocks. Suggest that the children mark how far they think the cars will travel with a block or a piece of colored tape. Let one child launch two cars at the same time on the different *ramps*. What happens? Were their predictions close?

8. The children can measure the distance traveled with a measuring tape or piece of yarn. Invite every child in the group to take a turn. Does the same thing happen every time?

MORE IDEAS

- Suggest that the children keep changing the height of the *ramps*. Encourage them to vary the experiment. What happens if they use bigger cars, smaller cars, or balls?
- Place empty water bottles at the end of the *ramps*. Can the cars knock down the bottles? Which level of steepness works best?

TEACHER-TO-TEACHER TIPS

- It's hard to do exact scientific observations with toy cars because there is often a *BIG* variation in how smoothly and quickly they roll. However, children enjoy experimenting with the cars so much we have found it's still very satisfying to use them. Children also enjoy testing how different cars travel down the *ramps* to see if they can find several that respond in a similar way. If they can find pairs of similar cars, their experiments will be more scientific.
- Researchers at the Regents' Center for Early Developmental Education at the University of Northern Iowa have found that using marbles and cove molding (available at home building stores) is effective for allowing children to do more scientific experiments with *ramps* and pathways.

DISCUSSION STARTERS

Use these questions to spark children's thinking during and after the activity:
- What happens when you add blocks to raise the *ramp*?
- What happens when you take blocks away?
- Do you think a car will go farther if the ramp is longer?

SKILLS ASSESSMENT

Use these questions to determine a child's abilities and understanding:
- Can the child predict how the *ramp* height will affect how far the car travels?
- Can the child release two cars at the same time when given a starting count?
- Can the child recount the results of the *ramp* comparison experiment?

Bumpy or Smooth? Road Surface Testing

PREPARATION

- Prepare two mystery touch boxes of different colors. Cover one top with blue construction paper and one top with yellow paper. Cut a hole just large enough for a child's hand in one end of each shoebox. Place a small sample of a material with a *smooth* texture, such as poster board in the yellow box and a sample of a *bumpy* texture, such as corrugated cardboard or bubble wrap, in the blue box. Tape the covers on or secure them with a rubber band.

WHAT TO DO

1. At group time, you and an adult assistant go around the circle in opposite directions so each child gets a turn to reach into both the yellow and blue boxes and feel the *smooth* and *bumpy* textures. The children should feel the items without looking at them. Ask them to think in their heads about what they are feeling but keep it a secret. What do the materials feel like? What could they be?

2. Open the yellow box and show the *smooth* sample. Ask, "Did you guess what was in the box?" Do the same with the blue box.

3. Introduce the vocabulary words of *smooth* and *bumpy*. Ask the children if they know what *smooth* means. Show the poster board and say, "This is *smooth*. It doesn't have anything that sticks up. Say and clap the one syllable **smooth**. Say *smooth* as you make the ASL sign by making the fingers of your right flat hand slide smoothly over the back of your left flat hand, palms down. Then ask the children if they know what *bumpy* means. Show the bubble wrap and say, "This is *bumpy*. It has lots of up and down." Say and clap the syllables, **bump**-y, with the emphasis on the "bump" syllable. Say *bumpy* as you make the ASL sign by making your flat hand go up and then bend down and go back up as if outlining the highs and lows of the road.

4. Say, "We are going to be scientists today and do some experiments with pretend roads that are *bumpy* and *smooth*. Review the vocabulary of *scientist*, *prediction*, and *experiment* (see pages 40–41 for more information). Ask the children to make

Smooth

Bumpy

FOCUS AREAS

Science: learning the properties of objects and materials, exploring the position and motion of objects

Math: measuring— distance

Language Arts: learning vocabulary

MATERIALS

2 shoeboxes

Blue and yellow construction paper

Scissors (adult-only)

Tape or rubber band

Plastic rain gutters, wooden boards, or strips of sturdy cardboard, about 3' long

Toy cars and trucks of the same size and type

Variety of materials with a bumpy texture, such as bubble wrap (small bubbles), corrugated cardboard, carpet, toothpicks glued crosswise on a strip of cardboard, about 2' long

Variety of materials of smooth texture, such as poster board, laminated paper, and linoleum, about 2' long

Unit blocks to prop up one end of the *ramps*

a prediction about whether they think toy cars can travel farther on a road that is *smooth* or *bumpy*. Say, "You'll get a chance during activity time to try several different surfaces to see what happens."

5. During activity time help the children set up several *ramps*. The children take turns experimenting. A child places a *smooth* texture at the end of one *ramp* and predicts how far the car will roll, marking the prediction with a unit block or piece of colored masking tape. (See tip about making predictions.) The child sends the car down the *ramp*. Was the prediction close? Repeat with different materials. What happens?

MORE IDEAS
- Children vary the experiments as they like, for example, sending two cars down the *ramps* at the same time to see which travels farther on the same or different surfaces. They can also vary the height of the *ramps* and try rolling different objects down the *ramps*.
- Cut different pieces of *bumpy* and *smooth* surfaces to fit on the *ramps*.
- Children sort the materials into two stacks—*bumpy* and *smooth*.

SUPERSIZE IT!
Prepare large pieces of *bumpy* surfaces, such as bubble wrap or carpet scraps, that will fit on the playground slide. The children send toy cars down the *smooth* slide and note how fast and how far they travel. Then they place *bumpy* surfaces on the slide and observe what happens when they send down the cars.

TEACHER-TO-TEACHER TIPS
- Children are often reluctant to make predictions because they don't want to be wrong. You can encourage them by making incorrect predictions yourself. Say, "I think the car going over the toothpicks is going to go much farther than the car going over the poster board." Of course your prediction won't happen. Then say, "Hmm. That wasn't right. Let's try again. What do you think?"
- Make a *bumpy* road or just a few speed bumps by gluing toothpicks across the width of a strip of poster board. You could also wrap rubber bands around strips of poster board.

DISCUSSION STARTERS
Use these questions to spark children's thinking during and after the activity:
- How would it feel to ride over rough roads like these?
- How can road builders make roads *smooth* for cars?

SKILLS ASSESSMENT
Use these questions to determine a child's abilities and understanding:
- Does the child use the vocabulary words *bumpy* and *smooth*?
- Can the child identify and sort *bumpy* and *smooth* textures?
- Can the child predict if a car traveling over a *smooth* surface will travel farther than one traveling over a *bumpy* surface?

Where Do These Roads Go?
BIG 3-D Maps

WHAT TO DO

1. Show a small group of children a map of your area. Identify a landmark, such as the street where your school is located. Point out that it is hard to see the roads on a map because they are so small but the children will be able to build a map with bigger roads.

2. Invite the children to use the packing noodles to create a road on their cardboard bases. They can also build *ramps* and *tunnels* and *bridges*. They dampen the noodles on the wet sponge and then press the noodles to the cardboard and to other noodles. The noodles stick almost instantly.

3. The children describe their road map to an adult who records their responses on the cardboard base. Help the children to make signs for their roads.

4. Challenge the children to count how many noodles they use. Suggest that the children measure how long their roads are with the Unifix cubes and rulers.

5. Develop and reinforce the children's BIG vocabulary by commenting, "Your *ramp* is really *steep*." "Your road is *straight* except when it *curves* around the mountain."

6. The children can color the noodles with markers and also draw on the cardboard. When the children are finished, have them set their roads on a table or a quiet area of the floor to build a giant map. Challenge them to make their road line up with other children's drawings.

MORE IDEAS

- Children can draw a map or a single road first and then stick on the packing noodles.
- Children can draw their home and a map to a favorite destination, such as school or a park. Then they stick on the packing noodles.
- Children can make a fantasy road system to a princess kingdom or a superhero hideout. Ask questions to spur their imagination: "Is there a *bridge* to the castle?" "How will the good guys get across the mountains to hide?" "Is the highway to the hideout *straight* or curvy?"

DISCUSSION STARTERS

Use these questions to spark children's thinking during and after the activity:

- Where does your road go?
- How long do you think it would take to travel the whole distance of your road?

SKILLS ASSESSMENT

Use these questions to determine a child's abilities and understanding:

- Does the child use the vocabulary words of *intersection*, *straight*, *curve*, and *bridge*?
- Can the child count the number of noodles used in part of the road?

FOCUS AREAS

Science: learning the abilities of technological design

Math: counting, studying three-dimensional shapes, measuring—length

Language Arts: labeling, dictating information

MATERIALS

Map of your area

Biodegradable packing noodles (Available free as packing materials from some mail-order companies or buy from office and school supply stores. Or ask families to save them for you.)

Wet sponges on small trays

Cardboard for a base, about 8½" x 11", one piece per child

Markers

Paper

Scissors (adult-only)

Rulers and nonstandard measuring tools, such as Unifix cubes

Roads, Ramps, Bridges, and Tunnels in the Sandbox

FOCUS AREAS

Science: exploring the position and motion of objects, learning the abilities of technological design

Math: counting, sequencing, measuring—distance

Language Arts: learning vocabulary, experiencing a wide range of texts, making signs

MATERIALS

A book on road construction, such as *Road Builders* by B.G. Hennessy (see Good Books for Facts and Fun on page 267)

Sandbox

Sand trucks, shovels, and pails

Styrofoam egg cartons (thoroughly washed), cardboard boxes, and sticks or branches to create obstacles

2 milk cartons

Sturdy string or rope

Hose with water (optional)

Wooden boards or rain gutters

Cars and trucks to travel on the roads

Sheet of chart paper

Marker

Paper and markers

Standard and nonstandard measuring tools, such as tape measure and string

Traffic or soccer cones, caution tape (optional)

Dramatic play hard hats

TEACHER-TO-TEACHER TIPS

- If your class is particularly interested in road construction, you can focus attention on planning the road—thinking where the road should go, what it will connect, what *obstacles* there will be, and how the road is designed with *curves* and *straight* stretches. But many children, particularly younger ones, will be eager to begin building right away. The road system will evolve as they work and will change as different children start constructing their ideas. Emphasize problem solving as the children work. "How can your road go over Mira's river?"

- If you have access to water and can hook up a hose, the children will LOVE creating rivers, lakes, and *bridges*. Water also makes the sand much easier to shape. If you don't have a hose, buckets of water will help wet the sand. Children can use a plastic tub or dishpan to make a lake that their road will have to cross. Or you can use blue construction paper for pretend rivers and lakes. **Safety note:** It is essential to have constant adult supervision when using containers of water. Empty them immediately when the activity is over.

PREPARATION

- Use orange construction paper to make paper cones and yellow crepe paper to make caution tape (optional).

WHAT TO DO

1. Read a book about road building to a small group of children. Review the stages of building a road with the children.

2. Ask the children which jobs they should do first to build a road in the sandbox, emphasizing sequence. Record their ideas on the chart paper. Depending on the number of children, "crews" can be formed to work on different road-building tasks. Some will want to start moving sand with trucks. Others may enjoy arranging traffic cones and putting up caution tape or drawing road maps and making signs. Depending on their age, they can draw or dictate signs, such as "Hard Hat Area," "Danger," "STOP," and the names of the roads.

3. Supply *obstacles* for the children to set up in the sandbox before they start building the road. Possibilities include egg cartons for boulders, cardboard boxes for old buildings, sticks or branches of bushes to represent trees. Later on, these can be incorporated into the road building—egg cartons can become a hill that needs a *ramp* to pass over or bridge foundations on each side of the river.

4. Create grading machines with the children by filling a milk carton with sand and taping the top closed. Then punch a hole (adult only) in the top of the carton and tie a string through it long enough to allow a child to drag it along the ground. The

children can drag these grading machines to *smooth* the road (see illustration).

5. When the road is finished, the children can run sand toys on it. Of course, the sand toys will mess up the grading job, giving the graders lots of continued work.

6. The children measure their roads and *bridges* with measuring tapes or lengths of string.

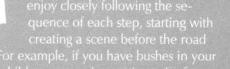

TEACHER-TO-TEACHER TIP

This activity is easily adaptable to the age of your class and the size of the group. With young children, focus on just a few steps, such as pushing the sand and digging trenches. Older children may enjoy closely following the sequence of each step, starting with creating a scene before the road goes in. For example, if you have bushes in your schoolyard that can tolerate trimming, the children may enjoy cutting twigs from the bushes (with adult permission and help) and sticking them in the sand. Then the children can clear the road with the trucks.

DISCUSSION STARTERS

Use these questions to spark children's thinking during and after the activity:

- What are you discovering about building roads?
- Where is your road going?
- Who do you think would like to drive on your road? What kind of vehicle would they drive?

SKILLS ASSESSMENT

Use these questions to determine a child's abilities and understanding:

- How does the child work as part of a team?
- Can the child solve problems when things don't go as expected?
- Does the child use vocabulary words such as *smooth*, *obstacle*, and *ramp*?

The Road Builders' Song

FOCUS AREAS
Math: sequencing
Language Arts: experiencing a wide range of print and non-print texts, learning vocabulary

MATERIALS
Dramatic play hard hats
Chart paper
Markers

PREPARATION
● Write the words to the song on chart paper.

WHAT TO DO
1. Review the words of the following song with the children.
2. Use hand motions to act out the song as you sing it with the children to the tune of "Row, Row, Row Your Boat."

Road Building by Tim Dobbins
Clear, clear, clear a path, (act out digging)
Make it straight and true.
We'll build a road from here to there,
So we can drive right through.

Tamp, tamp, tamp the dirt, (act out pushing down the dirt)
Make it hard and smooth.
We'll build a road from here to there
To help the traffic move.

Crunch, crunch, crunch some rock, (act out pounding rock with your fist)
Gravel nice and thick.
We'll build a road from here to there,
So we can get there quick.

Mix, mix, mix cement, (act out mixing with two curved hands)
We've got to pour it fast!
We'll build a road from here to there,
We're going to make it last.

Paint, paint, paint some lines, (act out painting lines on the ground)
Make them shiny white.
We've built a road from here to there,
We've made our road just right.

Drive, drive, drive it now, (act out driving by moving a steering wheel)
For now the road is done.
We've built a road from here to there,
Let's build another one!

DISCUSSION STARTERS
Use these questions to spark children's thinking during and after the activity:
● Have you ever seen a road being built? What did you see?
● Which jobs would like to do to build a road?

SKILLS ASSESSMENT
Use these questions to determine a child's abilities and understanding:
● Does the child participate in signing?
● Does the child act out the song?

BIG DRAMA:

The Three Billy Goats Gruff

PREPARATION

- Cut construction paper into strips about 2" x 8½" to make headbands. Each child will need two strips per headband. For younger children, pre-cut floppy billy goat ears and pointy troll ears. Older children will enjoy drawing and cutting the ears.

WHAT TO DO

1. Read a book that tells the story of "The Three Billy Goats Gruff."
2. Review the characters: the troll and the small, medium, and BIG billy goats.
3. Review what happens in the story.
4. Help the children make billy goat and troll headbands. The children staple two paper strips together, then an adult fits the headband around their head and helps them staple it closed. The children add ears and draw on the headbands as they like.
5. Have the children act out the story. You are the narrator and line prompter.
6. Perform the play multiple times and encourage the children to try different roles. The children look at the story differently when they are the troll instead of a billy goat.

Staple ends together.

DISCUSSION STARTERS

Use these questions to spark children's thinking during and after the activity:

- Do you think it would be scary to cross the *bridge*?
- Why do you think the troll acted the way he did?
- Is there something else the troll could have done?

SKILLS ASSESSMENT

Use these questions to determine a child's abilities and understanding:

- Can the child retell the story?
- Does the child know the sequence of events?
- Does the child enjoy performing?

FOCUS AREAS

Math: counting, sequencing

Language Arts: experiencing a wide range of texts, retelling the story

MATERIALS

Story of "The Three Billy Goats Gruff" to read (see Good Books for Facts and Fun on page 269)

Pretend *bridge* (could be carpet squares or mats)

Construction paper

Scissors (adult-only)

Staplers

Markers

Red Light/Green Light BIG Style

FOCUS AREAS

Language Arts: learning vocabulary

Gross Motor: jumping, hopping, balancing

MATERIALS

Red and green construction paper (optional)

Craft sticks (optional)

Glue or tape (optional)

PREPARATION

- (Optional) Make two sets of red and green traffic signals by attaching a red construction paper circle to one side of the craft sticks and a green construction paper circle to the other side of the sticks.

TEACHER-TO-TEACHER TIP

Traditional Red Light/Green Light has two BIG challenges: First, how do you keep children focused while they are standing far away? Second, some children bend the rules and push ahead while those who follow the rules are left behind. This variation solves those two problems and makes the game more interesting and fun for all the children. There is no incentive to keep moving after the Red Light call because that will only put children farther behind when they change directions. If you want, you can make traffic signals, but the game is fun without them. Just call out "Red Light" and "Green Light."

WHAT TO DO

1. In a large open space, invite the children to play Red Light/Green Light.
2. Decide on two callers, you and an adult assistant or a child. The callers stand at opposite ends of the open area. You will alternate calling Red Light/Green Light while holding up the appropriate signal if you have made them.
3. Before saying "Green Light" announce and demonstrate each new method of travel: taking giant steps, taking baby steps, walking heel to toe, hopping on one foot or both feet, rolling on the ground, tiptoeing, walking like a crab or an elephant, and any other motion you want to try.
4. The first caller announces a crab walk in her direction and then says "Green Light." The children walk toward her until she says, "Red Light." The first caller tells the children to stay right where they are, but turn around.
5. The children then face the second caller. She announces "Giant Steps" and says "Green Light." The children move in giant steps toward her until she says "Red Light." The children have to listen carefully and not go "too far."
6. Keep changing movements and directions as long as the children are interested.
7. After the children are familiar with the game invite them to take turns being the caller and choosing the movement.

DISCUSSION STARTERS

Use these questions to spark children's thinking during and after the activity:

- Which types of movements are hard to do?
- What movement was the most fun for you? Why?

SKILLS ASSESSMENT

Use these questions to determine a child's abilities and understanding:

- Can the child do the different types of movements?
- Does the child follow the directions?
- Does the child enjoy trying new movements?

More Activities Across the Curriculum

LANGUAGE ARTS

- Cut sheets of 11" x 14" paper lengthwise to create long "roads" for the children to draw roads and vehicles. The children dictate stories for an adult to write on their drawings. Include books about road building, *ramps*, *bridges*, and *tunnels* as well as vocabulary words at the table for inspiration. Topics for different days:
  - Where would you like to build a road? Where would it go?
  - What do you see when you walk or ride along your favorite street or road? Where do you like to travel?

  Mount the stories in the shape of a road map. When you take down the display keep the drawings in each child's portfolio.
- Review traffic signs and traffic safety with the children.

ART/MATH

- Children roll cars and trucks through trays of tempera paint and then roll the vehicles on long strips of paper. Invite the children to measure how wide the different tracks are. Do bigger cars make wider tracks?

- Supersize the activity by lining your outdoor slide with paper and invite the children to dip cars and trucks in paint and send the vehicles down the slide. Place a cardboard box at the end to catch the cars. Mount the giant paper on a wall or from the ceiling or use it as the background for the children's drawings and stories about roads.
- Children make *bumpy* roads by gluing toothpicks on poster board, cardboard, or sentence strips. Or make really BIG bumps by gluing pieces of straws to the cardboard. Invite the children to count how many toothpicks or straws they use.
- Children use brayers and black paint to create roads on sheets of BIG paper. They make both individual road systems to take home and create group road systems on long sheets of butcher paper. After the paintings are dry, the children glue white or yellow yarn or paper strips to create the center lines and bike lanes, and double lines for no passing.
- Children draw roads on paper strips, taping together numerous pieces of paper to make long roads. They measure how long their roads are. Create a giant mural on a classroom or outside wall with all the children's drawings. These can be mounted three-dimensionally to make hills and *bridges* as they go over and under each other.
- Make black playdough with the children using black tempera paint to simulate asphalt. Add rolling pins to the playdough table so the children can make *smooth* roads. Include tongue depressors and craft sticks to make *ramps* and *bridges*.

GAMES

- Children develop their visual discrimination skills by playing a matching or memory game made with stickers of traffic signs and vehicles placed on index cards or inside large colorful jar lids or round plastic can covers.

MATH

- Children sort and count vehicles by size, type, and color.
- Create a color spinner with round color stickers matching the colors of cars. The children spin for a color then line up the cars, arranging them in descending or ascending size order. Measure the length of the lines of cars.
- Create grids for parked vehicles of different sizes to match different vehicles. Have the children "park" vehicles in the parking spot that matches their size vehicle. Or have the children trace and cut rectangle shapes out of construction paper (use colors that match the car colors) and glue them to paper to create their own parking lot.

SCIENCE/MATH

- Create marble *tunnels* with paper towel tubes, gift wrap tubes, and any other tubes. Cut some of the tubes lengthwise to create *ramps* and allow the children to tape the tubes to wooden blocks for support or use purchased marble *tunnels*. The children make their own path designs and count and time how long it takes marbles to travel different paths.

SENSORY TABLE/MATH

- Create a different type of dirt (the recipe for Clean Dirt is on the left) with the children and place it in the sensory table with a variety of trucks so they can make roads in the dirt. (The aroma will make you crave coffee!)

GROSS MOTOR

- Set up a "Driver Training Obstacle Course" in your play yard. Place traffic cones and caution tape in your bike riding area that the children steer around with trikes or scooters to practice "driving" safely. The children use red light/green light traffic signals to stop and start traffic. Add a yellow caution signal and practice slowing down, getting ready to stop.
- Children stand up and make a *tunnel* with their legs and take turns crawling through it.

Clean Dirt

Depending on the size of your sensory table you will probably want to make at least two batches of clean dirt.

For one batch you will need:

6 cups used coffee grounds (available free from some coffee shops)

3 cups sand

Ahead of time, ask a coffee shop to save used coffee grounds for you, the more the better. Dry out the used coffee grounds (spread them out on cookie sheets in a 250° oven or leave in the sun). With the children, measure the coffee grounds and the sand directly into the sensory table. The children will enjoy using the trucks to mix the "dirt." When one batch is mixed, add more coffee and sand. You can keep adding material until the sensory table has enough. You don't need to measure exactly.

BIG Outcomes

Group assessment: At group time, review the photo boards you created about studying the road near your school, building roads in the sandbox, and experimenting with *ramps* and road surfaces. Review the chart paper sheets from the beginning of your exploration of what the children know about roads and what they want to learn. On a third sheet of chart paper titled "What We Learned About Roads," record the children's comments about what they learned, including the name of the child who made the comment. Be sure to note answers to their original questions, or note if you still have more to learn and explore.

Individual assessment: Review your notes and quotes from individual observations during activities such as the *ramp* experiments and three-dimensional maps. Review the children's work and save it in their portfolios. Note whether the children use new vocabulary words in conversation. Note areas in which the children need further practice and those in which they excel.

GOOD BOOKS FOR FACTS AND FUN

Unlike cars and trucks, which are popular topics with preschoolers and publishers, the topics of streets, roads, and road building get less attention. While the vehicles are fast and flashy or big and powerful, the lanes they travel are often ignored, as in real life. Seek help from your librarian to find well-worn, out-of-print favorites and rare, new road titles in addition to these suggestions.

INFORMATION ABOUT BRIDGES, RAMPS, ROADS, AND TUNNELS

Bridges Are to Cross by Philemon Sturges
Cut paper collages on painted backgrounds create realistic pictures of global bridges. Choose from three text options—a simple sentence, the name, date and type of bridge, or further details of the setting— to match the information with interest level. Ages 3–6

Ramps and Wedges by Chris Oxlade
Wedges and ramps—what they are, what they do, and how they work—are presented in clear photos and text with new vocabulary words highlighted in bold and defined in the glossary. Ages 4–6

Road Builders by B. G. Hennessy
A road building project with a focus on the big vehicles driven by an international, mostly male crew illustrated in bright drawings. Short on text, with lots of action up close, this one is a hit with the "things that go" crowd. Ages 3–5

Roll, Slope, and Slide: a Book About Ramps by Michael Dahl
Skateboarders on the cover will attract attention to this colorful explanation of ramps used for slides, handicapped access, and moving traffic. Bright pictures compliment slippery slopes, inclined planes, and ramps of different steepness. Ages 3–6

Straight and Curving by Sue Barraclough
Using same and different comparisons, this easy concept book shows obvious examples, side-by-side, in a question-and-answer format. Color photographs include pictures of slides, roads, and a bridge. Ages 3–4

Tunnels by Gail Gibbons
A basic introduction to tunnels illustrated with clear cross-section drawings. Gibbons moves in easy steps from ant, worm, and animal burrowings to tunnels made by people in the ground, and under water. Ages 3–6

Tunnels Go Underground by Lee Sullivan Hill
Snow tunnels, erosion tunnels, cut and covered, machine-bored, drilled and blasted tunnels and more are explained in short sentences covering the purpose, building processes, and prospectors. The index of color photos adds identification and details for more than 20 tunnels from around the world. Ages 3–6

STORIES ABOUT ROADS
Mrs. Armitage, Queen of the Road by Quentin Blake
Mrs. A. and her loyal dog Breakspear hit the road again, this time in Uncle Cosmo's old car, which falls apart piece by piece en route. Her uncle and his new biker pals approve of the pared down, sleek machine at the end of this comic treat. Ages 3–6

The Bridge Is Up! by Babs Bell
The line of waiting vehicles and their animal drivers and passengers grows and grows while everyone has to wait until the bridge comes down. Bright child-like drawings of sometimes frowning occupants perfectly compliment this brief tale. Ages 3–4

Make Way for Ducklings by Robert McCloskey
A burly, tender-hearted policeman stops traffic to protect the Mallard family, including eight new baby ducklings, as they make their way home through the streets of Boston in this classic tale. Ages 3–6

There's a Cow in the Road by Reeve Lindbergh
Imagine the chaos on a school morning when the road fills up with noisy animals, all refusing to move. Detailed watercolor illustrations add to the amusement. This clever, rhyming text is a storytime favorite. Ages 3–5

On the Road by Susan Stegall

Large torn and cut-paper collages illustrate brief prepositional phrases, tracing the
progress of a mom and two children in a red-and-white car along busy streets,
roads, and highways as they travel from their house through the city to the sea.
Ages 3–4

We All Go Traveling By by Sheena Roberts

This musical "I spy" game uses colors and sound effects to list the various vehicles that
are all traveling by on the way to school. Fred Penner performs the song on the CD,
and cheerful, stitched fabric pictures illustrate the story. Ages 3–5

THE THREE BILLY GOATS GRUFF STORIES

Three Billy Goats Gruff by Paul Galdone

Galdone's humorous watercolors and a traditional retelling of Asbjørnsen's Norwegian
folktale combine to create this classic. The large scale format facilitates sharing in a
circle time setting. Ages 4–6

The Three Billy Goats Gruff by Stephen Carpenter

Straightforward and simple, this presentation of the three goats and the troll, with
repetitive refrains and cheerful, pleasant illustrations, is not too scary—a good
introduction to the story for younger children. Ages 3–4

The Three Cabritos by Eric A. Kimmel

A Mexican border setting, musical goats facing a not-too-scary blue Chupacabra and a
magic accordion vary the original story in Kimmel's bilingual version with hand-
drawn, computer-colored pictures. Ages 4–6

A Note to Families About Roads

Dear Families,

Children love making roads and ramps for their toy cars and trucks to travel on. Running toy cars down ramps is a fun way to do lots of experimenting. Children can quickly test their ideas and make changes. "What happens if I make my ramp steeper? Do my cars travel faster and farther?"

Road building provides many opportunities for solving problems. This is an important skill that is necessary for all parts of life. "How can my car get over this river?" "How can I get around this hill?" You can help your child learn to solve problems by giving him or her lots of opportunities to experiment. You don't need special materials. Your child can make a bridge out of old cereal boxes and soup cans.

You can also help your child notice street signs while driving or riding public transportation. STOP is a fun word to learn to read.

Here are some of the words we've been learning about roads:
- An obstacle is something that blocks a path.
- An intersection is a place where two roads cross.

Have fun watching your road builder solve problems!

THINKING ABOUT BIG IDEAS: INVENTIONS

THE BIG PICTURE

Anyone can be an inventor. As Thomas Edison said, "To invent, you need a good imagination and a pile of junk." This unit introduces children to the power of imagination and brainstorming as well putting "junk" to good use. It also introduces the stories behind some familiar inventions such as Band-Aids.

Children learn that people have always had problems and have invented tools and techniques to solve those problems. Learning problem-solving skills is a key desired outcome of the science and technology standard. Children have an opportunity to take apart discarded appliances to see what's inside and how the machine might work. They then use their "pile of junk" to create new inventions. They learn how inventors make prototypes, models of their ideas, and how they keep experimenting to help their inventions work better. Children also practice teamwork as they brainstorm together and perform tasks side-by-side on an assembly line.

Experiencing the invention process from imagination and ideas, to experimentation and model-building encourages children to think of BIG possibilities.

TIMING TIP

Inventions can be explored at any time because children are always curious about familiar items, such as Velcro. The topic works especially well as a grand finale to the school year.

OBJECTIVES

⬧ Use imagination to explore what is possible
⬧ Begin to discover multiple ways to solve problem
⬧ Experiment using old parts in new ways
⬧ Explore familiar inventions

STANDARDS

National Science Education Content Standards

⬧ Science as inquiry—ask questions; use simple equipment and tools to gather data and extend the senses; use data to construct a reasonable explanation
⬧ Physical science—recognize properties of objects and materials
⬧ Science and technology—observe abilities of technological design; develop understanding about science and technology; develop abilities to distinguish between natural objects and objects made by humans
⬧ History and nature of science—recognize science as a human endeavor

National Council of Teachers of Mathematics Standards

⬧ Number and operations—count with understanding; make reasonable estimates
⬧ Algebra—sort, classify, and order objects: recognize, describe, and extend patterns
⬧ Geometry—analyze characteristics and properties of two- and three-dimensional geometric shapes
⬧ Measurement—understand how to measure using nonstandard and standard tools
⬧ Data analysis and probability—sort and classify objects according to their attributes; represent data using concrete objects, pictures, and graphs
⬧ Communication—organize, analyze, and evaluate mathematical thinking; use the language of mathematics

Standards for the English Language Arts

⬧ Experience a wide range of print and non-print texts, including fiction and non-fiction, to build an understanding of the world and acquire new information
⬧ Use spoken, written, and visual language to communicate and learn
⬧ Generate ideas and questions and pose problems
⬧ Build vocabulary

BIG BEGINNING:
Introducing Inventions

FOCUS AREAS

Science: learning about the abilities of technological design, designing inventions to solve problems

Language Arts: learning vocabulary, using spoken language to communicate and learn; generating ideas and questions

MATERIALS

An assortment of gadgets and tools, such as a stapler, child-safe scissors, tweezers, hammer, and camera
Piece of construction paper
Large Band-Aid
Square of gauze
First aid tape
2 sheets of chart paper
Marker

PREPARATION

- Lay out your assortment of gadgets and tools.
- Label one sheet of chart paper "What We Know About Inventions" and the other sheet "What We Want to Learn About Inventions."

WHAT TO DO

1. When the children gather for circle time say, "I want to cut this piece of construction paper into four pieces. I wonder what I can use." Pick up the hammer. Say, "I wonder if this will help me cut the paper?" Of course the children will say, "Noooo. Use the scissors." Pick up the stapler and say, "I know. This will help me cut the paper." Have as much fun as you like until you finally pick up and use the scissors. (Children enjoy thinking they know more than you do and like the silliness of goofy associations.)

2. Introduce other tasks:
   - What could I use if I want to take a picture?
   - What could I use if I have a splinter in my finger?

3. Then ask, "What could I use if I have a cut on my finger?" When the children say "Band-Aid," say, "Band-Aids are a useful invention that solves a problem. People didn't always have Band-Aids to use. A person named Earle Dickson invented Band-Aids."

This is the story of the invention of the Band-Aid. Almost 100 years ago there was a man named Earle Dickson who worked for Johnson & Johnson, the company that still makes tape like this, (show an example of first aid tape). His wife, Josephine, didn't know much about cooking when they first got married, and she sometimes hurt herself when she used a knife or touched something hot on the stove. Mr. Dickson made a lot of bandages for Mrs. Dickson using gauze like this (show gauze) and some of the tape his company made. He wanted to figure out a way to make bandages ahead of time so Mrs. Dickson could wrap up her cuts and burns by herself, right away.

He started experimenting with the special tape and gauze. He cut a piece of tape and laid it out on a table, sticky side up. Then he took a strip of gauze, folded it into a pad and put it in the middle of the tape.

But there was a problem. When he left the tape sitting out on the table, the sticky surface dried out. He tried covering the tape with different kinds of cloth. Some cloth stuck to the tape and then he couldn't get it off. Then he tried a fabric called crinoline that was very smooth. That worked. The next time Mrs. Dickson cut her finger she peeled off the smooth cloth and bandaged her cut all by herself using Mr. Dickson's new invention.

Mr. Dickson showed his invention to his bosses at work. They liked his idea. They decided to make his special bandages in the company factory. Another worker at the company thought of a name for the invention— "bandaid" "band" for the tape strip and "aid" for first aid. As you know, Band-Aids are still being made today. (Source: www.band-aid.com)

4. Introduce the word *invention*, something new and different that solves a problem. Say and clap the syllables, in-**ven**-tion, with the emphasis on the "ven" syllable. Say

Invent

invention as you make the ASL sign for invent by holding your right hand at the side of your head with your thumb tucked in, spreading your fingers wide and moving your hand outward from your head.

5. To demonstrate another common invention, ask if anyone has Velcro on a shoe. Ask the children what Velcro helps us do. Ask the children what other things they can think of that are inventions. Record their answers with the child's name on the sheet of chart paper labeled "What We Know About Inventions."

6. Ask the children what they want to find out about inventions. Record their responses on a second sheet of chart paper labeled, "What We Want to Learn About Inventions." Use the children's questions and interests to guide your activities.

7. Invite the children to bring in inventions from home to show the class another day.

BIG QUESTIONS FOR GROWING MINDS

Use the following questions to engage the children in a discussion about inventions during group time or with an individual child during activity time:

● What inventions do you like to use?

● Can you think of something that is hard for you to do? What could you invent to help you do it?

● Are there any problems you'd like to fix?

WORDS FOR BIG THINKING

These words are highlighted in italic throughout the activities in this chapter. Write the words out in large letters and introduce them with the "**S**ay, **C**lap, **A**ct out, **D**o again (SCAD) system. Using them during activities and discussions with the children will help reinforce their meaning.

● Brainstorm—thinking up lots of ideas

● Idea—a thought or plan

● Imagination—thinking up something that you cannot see right now. When you imagine you make a picture in your mind of what you are thinking about.

● Invention—a new and different creation that solves a problem

● Prototype—the first thing of its kind, a model

A Note from the Author:
The activities in this chapter are designed to build on each other. However, please feel free to choose those that meet the interests and abilities of your class. If parts of an activity seem like too much to do on a particular day, save them for a later time. Every class is different, even from day to day, and the activities are adaptable to meet the needs of your class.

TEACHER-TO-TEACHER TIP
Ask families to save small broken or discarded appliances such as alarm clocks, coffee makers, and vacuum cleaners, all year long. Also look for discarded appliances on trash day and at garage sales. Children will take them apart under close supervision in this unit. Tell families it is not safe for children to take apart computers, computer monitors, televisions, cell phones, items with glass parts, or smoke detectors.

PHOTO TIP
You can record children's explorations of the inventing process by creating photo boards about taking apart appliances, building new "inventions," running the shaker assembly line, and building the giant robot. Look for close-ups of individual children and group shots that show children interacting. Also include vocabulary words and quotes from children on the photo boards to document the learning.

Let's Make Band-Aids

FOCUS AREAS

Science: learning about the abilities of technological design, understanding science and technology

Math: sequencing

MATERIALS

Variety of Band-Aids of different sizes and shapes (plain Band-Aids will help children focus on the parts of the bandages, rather than the decorations)

Rolls of first-aid tape in a variety of sizes

Rolls of masking tape and transparent tape in a variety of sizes

Gauze squares

Cotton balls

Paper towels

Waxed paper, cellophane, fabric

Child-safe scissors

Markers

PREPARATION

- Cut the waxed paper, cellophane, and fabric into strips about 4" long by 1¼" wide for the children to use as backing to the bandages they make.
- Cut the gauze and paper towels into small squares, about 1" x 1".

WHAT TO DO

1. Show the children an assortment of Band-Aids. Ask, "What are all the parts of the Band-Aid?" "How are these Band-Aids the same?" "How are they different?"
2. Say, "Earle Dickson experimented with lots of different ways to make bandages before he found a model that worked. What do you think would make a good Band-Aid? You can try your *ideas* now."
3. Help the children cut strips of the tape of their choice—first-aid tape, masking tape, or transparent tape. The children choose which soft material they want to place on the tape—a pre-cut piece of gauze, paper towel, or cotton ball. The children place a pre-cut strip of waxed paper, cellophane, or fabric over the tape and soft material. Finally, the children decorate the back of their Band-Aid with markers.
4. After the children have made one Band-Aid, encourage them to experiment with the other materials and make several different Band-Aids. Ask, "Which tape sticks well but is not too sticky?" "Which type of soft material fits the best?" "Which cover stays on and comes off easily?" The children can use the Band-Aids on themselves or on classroom dolls or take their Band-Aids home. The bandages obviously are not sterile, so tell the children to use a Band-Aid they bought at the store for a real cut.

   Note: This is not a BIG activity in the sense of scale but is HUGE to the children because Band-Aids are so important to them. Children find it empowering to learn how Band-Aids are made and to be able to make Band-Aids for themselves. Band-Aids are an *invention* children understand and care about.

DISCUSSION STARTERS

Use these questions to spark children's thinking during and after the activity:

- What did you learn about making Band-Aids?
- Do you have *ideas* about what else would work well to make a Band-Aid?
- How do Band-Aids help when you have a cut?
- Why do you think Band-Aids come in different sizes and shapes?

SKILLS ASSESSMENT

Use these questions to determine a child's abilities and understanding:

- Can the child describe the sequence of steps he used to make the Band-Aids?
- Does the child use the BIG vocabulary word *invention*?
- Does the child enjoy trying different materials?

Look What's Inside: Taking Apart Machines

FOCUS AREAS
Science: learning about the abilities of technological design
Math: counting, sequencing, sorting

MATERIALS
Numerous small appliances to take apart
Numerous small screwdrivers, both Phillips head and flat head, tiny screwdrivers used for computer maintenance are especially useful (ask families to lend you some for a few days)
Safety goggles (child-size preferable)
Small containers to hold the assorted screws, bolts, washers, nuts, and wires
Large bins or boxes to hold the BIG parts of the appliances

SAFETY NOTES

- When asking families to send in broken appliances tell them it is not safe for children to take apart computers, computer monitors, televisions, cell phones, or smoke detectors.
- Cut off plugs from broken appliances with wire cutters before the children start taking them apart so no one can plug in a machine. Cover the ends of cut wires with tape if they are sharp.
- Remove all glass from appliances, such as a clock face or blender container.
- Discard any sharp parts of appliances that would be unsafe for children to handle.
- Pre-loosen the screws to reduce the children's frustration when they take apart appliances.
- The children must wear safety goggles to protect their eyes. Small, child-size goggles are the most comfortable. You could use swim goggles.
- Tell the children it is okay to take apart these machines because they are broken and they are not plugged in. At home, they must never try to take something apart without first asking an adult.

WHAT TO DO

1. Set up a "Take-Apart Shop" at a table in your classroom. Place an assortment of discarded appliances and tools on this table and invite a small group of children to choose something to take apart. See Safety Notes. The children put on safety goggles.
2. Advise the children that taking things apart is a BIG job that goes slowly. Applaud each small step.
3. While they are working, talk to the children about their discoveries. Ask, "How many screws do you see on the back of this machine. Let's count."
4. Save the screws, nuts, bolts, and wires in containers. The children will sort the hardware during another activity. (See What Did We Find Inside? on page 277.)
5. Save the BIG parts of the machines in large bins to use in future projects. Tell the children they are going to be able to use these pieces to create their own *inventions*.

TEACHER-TO-TEACHER TIP

Children love this activity. It works best if there are extra adult helpers to help loosen screws and talk the children through the process: "Do you see any more screws you can take out before this cover will come off?" Ahead of time, ask parents if anyone can come to school during activity time to help in the "Take-Apart Shop." As the children are working, it is helpful for the adult to ask questions such as, "What do you suppose this part does? Why do think this machine broke?" Adults don't need to be mechanically inclined or know the answers to help out.

DISCUSSION STARTERS

Use these questions to spark children's thinking during and after the activity:

- Why do you suppose this machine stopped working?
- What parts move in the machine? What do they do? What are they made of?
- What kind of machines do you have at your home?

SKILLS ASSESSMENT

Use these questions to determine a child's abilities and understanding:

- Can the child describe the sequence of taking things apart?
- Does the child speculate on the function of different parts and how the machine worked?

What Did We Find Inside? Sorting, Counting, and Graphing

Science: exploring properties of objects and materials

Math: counting, learning one-to-one correspondence, sorting, classifying, ordering by size, identifying two- and three-dimensional shapes, graphing, communicating results

Language Arts: learning vocabulary, experiencing a wide range of print and non-print texts

MATERIALS
Several containers of assorted hardware—screws, nuts, bolts, washers, springs, wires (saved from appliances you have taken apart or purchased at a hardware store)

Small plastic containers

Small die

Sheet of chart paper

Marker

PREPARATION
- Label empty containers with words and pictures for sorting hardware.
- Label chart paper "What We Found in Our Machines."

WHAT TO DO
1. Set out the containers of mixed hardware pieces from the dismantled appliances.
2. Invite a small group of children to roll a die. The children choose the number of items from the jumbled hardware that matches the number they rolled and sort the pieces into the correct labeled containers. If they roll a three,

What We Found in Our Machines					
screw	nut	washer	spring	wire	bolt

ask the children to find three items that are the same or three items that are different.

3. At the end of the activity count the different items in the sorting containers. Create a graph with pictures of the different hardware items across the bottom.

MORE IDEAS
- Use the different types of hardware to order objects by size. Which is the tiniest screw? Which screw is a little bigger? Which is the biggest?

TEACHER-TO-TEACHER TIP
Rolling the die to choose the number of items to sort makes the activity feel more like a game. Rather than a competition among children, make this a competition among the different types of hardware. Which container is winning? Is it the screws? Use comparative or numeric words to build vocabulary, such as *few, fewest, least,* and *most.*

DISCUSSION STARTERS
Use these questions to spark children's thinking during and after the activity:
- Which container has the most items?
- What container has the fewest?
- How many screws, nuts, or bolts can you count?
- How are the items the same? How are they different?

ASSESSMENT
- Does the child understand that four dots on a die correspond to the numeral 4?
- Can the child count to six?
- Does the child use one-to-one correspondence when choosing the items?
- Does the child understand the concepts of *same* and *different*?
- Can the child compare objects and identify similar and different aspects of the objects, such as *color, shape,* and *size*?
- Can the child use comparatives (*few, fewer, fewest*) appropriately?

Invention Workshop

PREPARATION

- Label the chart paper "Brainstorming Ideas for Our Box Inventions."
- Place the cardboard boxes and other materials on a table in the classroom that you will call the Invention Workshop.

WHAT TO DO

1. Tell a story about an *invention,* such as eyeglasses, or read a story book, such as *Sydney's Star*. Then tell the children that they are going to be able to make *inventions* today.

2. Introduce the word *brainstorm*, which means to think up lots of different *ideas*. Say and clap the syllables, **brain-storm**, which have equal emphasis. Say *brainstorm* as you make the ASL sign for *discuss in a group*. Your right index finger taps repeatedly your left palm as if you were emphasizing a point in a discussion. Move your left hand in a circle to show that there are many people discussing or *brainstorming*. Explain to the children that the sign is describing how people are discussing in a group.

3. Say, "These *inventions* are going to be powered by our *imaginations*. We'll use our *imaginations* to think of what we wish they can do. When you are imagining, anything is possible." Introduce the word *imagination*. Say, "When you use your *imagination* you are thinking up something that you cannot see right now. When you *imagine* you make a picture in your mind of what you are thinking about." Say and clap the syllables, i-mag-i-**na**-tion, with the emphasis on the "a" syllable. Say *imagination* as you make the ASL sign by having both hands closed except for the pinkie fingers sticking straight up. Move your hands outward from both sides of your forehead to represent thoughts coming out.

4. Say, "Let's see what we can *invent* with a box." Show the children a cardboard box and ask them to think of all the different things they could *invent* with a box. Record their *ideas* on the chart paper labeled, "Brainstorming Ideas for Our Box Inventions." Say, "Now that you have practiced *brainstorming*, you can go to the Invention Workshop and create whatever you want. We have extra boxes so you can make more inventions with a box. Remember that inventors usually try lots of different *ideas* before they find something that works. Don't worry if your *ideas* don't work the first time. You can keep experimenting."

Brainstorm

Imagination

FOCUS AREAS

Science: exploring properties of objects and materials, learning about the abilities of technological design, identifying a simple problem, proposing a solution

Math: counting

Language Arts: learning vocabulary, communicating through dictation

Art: exploring three-dimensional design

MATERIALS

A story about a real *invention* or a story book such as *Sydney's Star* by Peter H. Reynolds (see Good Books for Facts and Fun on pages 291–293)

Small cardboard boxes

Parts from appliances children have taken apart

Several rolls of colored masking tape

Duct tape

Additional items that could be used to make an *"invention,"* such as pipe cleaners, container lids, old CDs, paper cups, small cardboard boxes, and Styrofoam egg cartons

Sheet of chart paper

Marker

5. Help the children hold and tape pieces together as they build their *inventions*. These projects need **lots** of tape.

6. Help the children *brainstorm* solutions to problems as they arise. Items often won't stick together or won't stay balanced. Ask the children what they could do differently to solve the problem.

MORE IDEAS

- Children can make a sign saying, Invention Workshop.
- Children can draw pictures of their *inventions* and dictate to an adult what the *inventions* do and give directions for how to use them. Save the drawings and dictation for portfolios.
- Invite the children to take turns showing and describing their *inventions* to the children at group time.
- Introduce the BIG word *prototype*, which means "the first thing of its kind, a model for an *invention*." Say and clap the syllables, **pro**-to-type. Point to the items the children have been working on and say, "You are working on *prototypes* for new *inventions*."

DISCUSSION STARTERS

Use these questions to spark children's thinking during and after the activity:

- Tell me about your *invention*. What does your *invention* do? What is it called?
- What parts did you use? What did you add first?
- How does your *invention* help someone?
- What problems did you have trying to build your *invention*?

SKILLS ASSESSMENT

Use these questions to determine a child's abilities and understanding:

- Can the child problem solve?
- Can the child describe the sequence of steps he used to make the *invention*?
- Can the child describe the *invention*?

TEACHER-TO-TEACHER TIPS

- It's fun to connect the children's box *invention brainstorming* with stories about other children's *ideas*. At story time you might read *A Box Can Be Many Things* or another book about inventing things (see Good Books for Facts and Fun on pages 291–293).
- Children often start building first and decide afterwards what the *invention* is, rather than starting out saying, "I'm going to make a submarine that can eat monsters." That is fine. Many *inventions* begin as technology that needs a use. Post-it Notes evolved from an unsuccessful experiment. A scientist was trying to make a new type of strong glue but instead made glue that stuck lightly. He didn't know what to do with the weak glue. One of the people he worked with decided this super-weak glue would be handy to spread on paper that he could use to mark his place in his church choir book. Eventually the weak glue became the backing on Post-it Notes. (Source: www.3m.com, www.ideafinder.com)
- It is fun to save the *inventions* and the children's drawings and stories about the *inventions* for a family event. Children will enjoy showing off their *inventions* to their family and the rest of the class. Describing their *invention* is good public speaking practice.

Making an Assembly Line: BIG Productions

PREPARATION

- Read the story of Henry Ford and the assembly line (see What To Do on the next page).
- Cut construction paper into pieces that will encircle the water bottles covering the label.
- Cut colored masking tape into pieces about 5" long, one for each bottle top. Place the strips of tape on the edges of two long unit blocks so the children can quickly grab a piece.
- Set up an assembly line using both sides of two long tables so the stations mirror each other, Station 1 across

from the table from the other Station 1 (see illustration). If you have 16 the children in your class you need 8 stations. If you have more children, add tasks, such as rubber stamping the label or stacking the shakers at the end. If you have fewer children combine jobs. Do a practice run and make adjustments. Define and label the stations with masking tape so the children will know where to stand. These are the suggested stations:

1. Passer. Bin of plastic water bottles with caps removed
2. Filler. 2 containers of birdseed or beads for each side of the table, with 1 measuring cup and 1 funnel
3. Capper. 2 containers of bottle caps
4. Wrapper. Construction paper squares
5. Bander. Rubber bands
6. Taper. Precut strips of masking tape (half on each side of the table attached to a long unit block)
7. Sticker. Easy-to peel stickers from a roll or sheet
8. Tester

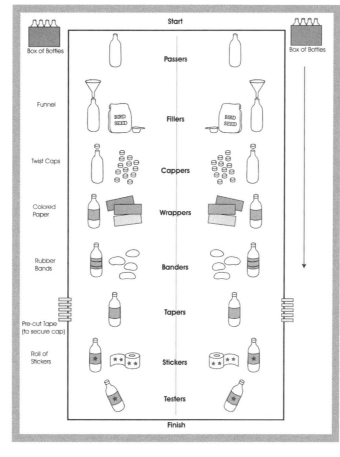

FOCUS AREAS

Science: learning about the abilities of technological design

Math: measuring—time

MATERIALS

Plastic water bottles with caps, 1 per child, thoroughly dry inside

Bin for bottles

2 containers for bottle caps

2 containers of birdseed or beads

2 trays

2 funnels

2 measuring cups, ¼ cup

Construction paper cut to cover water bottle labels

Rubber bands, one per bottle plus extras

Colored masking tape

Easy-to-peel stickers, 1 per bottle

Sand timer or watch for timing

Bell to announce when to begin work on the assembly line

2 long classroom tables

WHAT TO DO

1. At group time, tell the children the following story of Henry Ford and his assembly line for cars.

When cars were first built it took about 12 ½ hours to make one; that is about as long as the time from when you get up in the morning until the time when you go to bed, a whole day. Henry Ford had some ideas how people could make cars much faster by having each person work on just one small job, and having the cars roll by the workers. He called this an assembly line. Under his system, people could build a car in about 1 ½ hours, about as long from the time you arrive at school until snack time (or whatever example you want to use). For example, on the assembly line, one person might put in the front seat in cars all day long while another person bolts on the wheels all day long.
(Sources: www.ford.com, www.wikipedia.com, www.about.com)

2. Tell the children, "Today we are going work together to make (assemble) shakers in an assembly line so that everyone will get to take a shaker home. We can time how long it will take us to make all the shakers."

3. Bring the children to the assembly line. Have them each stand in front of a station. You and another adult will help the children on each side of the table do the steps one at a time. Time how long it takes to make one shaker.

    1. The passer picks up a water bottle and passes it to the next child, the filler, and helps hold the bottle.
    2. The filler measures and pours in ¼ cup of birdseed and passes it on.
    3. The capper screws on a cap and passes it to the wrapper.
    4. The wrapper wraps the construction paper around the bottle with help from the fifth child, the bander.
    5. The bander then puts on the rubber band with help from the wrapper (and perhaps an adult helper) and then passes it to the taper.
    6. The taper puts masking tape around the lid to seal it shut and then passes it to the sticker.
    7. The sticker puts a sticker on the top or side and passes it to the tester.
    8. The tester gives it a shake to make sure it works.

4. Now say, "We are ready to begin our assembly line." Note the time on the classroom clock and ring a bell to start the assembly line. Help the children learn their job. They will get better with practice.

5. When the last shaker is finished note the time. How long did it take to make all the shakers?

6. At the end, the children each choose a shaker to take home and write their name on it.

MORE IDEAS

- When the assembly line for shakers is complete, have the children work together to put everything away.

TEACHER-TO-TEACHER TIP

Children who are four to six years old love this activity, particularly at the end of the school year. For younger children, use fewer steps (skip wrapping the shaker) and provide plenty of adult help. Children are amazed to find they can make 20 shakers in about five minutes using an assembly line and are disappointed when the supply of water bottles is gone. The assembly line really highlights the value of teamwork and co-operation as well as demonstrating how some jobs are much harder than others. One child commented, "I could do this all day," while another said, "No way. I want a different job next time." The preparation and setup necessary for this activity are worth the effort. If possible, invite extra adult helpers for all ages. You can extend the children's interest in the assembly line with the following activity, Be a Cleaning Machine.

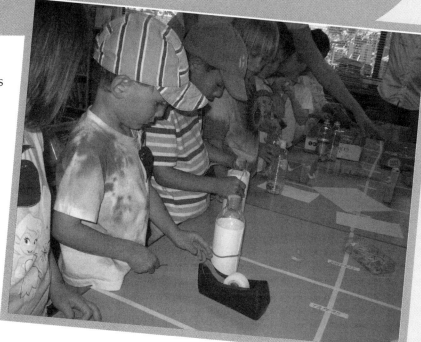

DISCUSSION STARTERS

Use these questions to spark children's thinking during and after the activity:

- What was the hardest part of your job?
- Which other jobs would you like to do?
- How did your job feel after you did it a few times?
- How would it feel to do this job all day long?

SKILLS ASSESSMENT

Use these questions to determine a child's abilities and understanding:

- Can the child describe the sequence of the activity—first someone has to fill the bottle, then someone else puts on the cap?
- Does the child have the fine motor skills to do his job?
- Does the child enjoy being part of the team?

Be a Cleaning Machine

FOCUS AREAS

Math: recognizing and extending movement and sound patterns, measuring—time

Language Arts: learning vocabulary, experiencing a wide range of print and non-print texts

Gross Motor: stretching, bending, twisting

MATERIALS

Blocks and manipulatives
Chart paper
Marker
Sand timer or clock to time the clean-up activity

PREPARATION

- Label a sheet of chart paper "Our BIG Cleaning Machines."

WHAT TO DO

1. At group time, tell the children that you would like to make an *invention* that will turn the children in the class into machines that will help clean up the classroom. Ask what needs to be done at clean-up time such as blocks picked up and returned to the shelves. Ask for their *ideas* of how a cleaning machine could work. Record *ideas* on the chart paper.
2. Ask what noises the clean-up machines might make. Record those *ideas*.
3. Sing "Cleaning Machine" to the tune of "I'm a Little Teapot."

   Cleaning Machine by Marie Faust Evitt and Tim Dobbins
   I'm a new invention. I do the job. (make the ASL sign for *invention* by holding your right hand at the side of your head with your thumb tucked in, spreading your fingers wide and moving your hand outward from your head)
   Flip the switch and turn the knob. (pretend to flip a switch and turn a knob)
   When I get all warmed up, I work fast. (pump your arms as if you were running)
   My classroom's really clean at last. (spread out your arms)

4. At clean-up time, gather the children and sing "Cleaning Machine." Say, "Ready, set, go. Flip your switch and turn your knob so you can become a cleaning machine. How will you move? What kind of noise will you make? Now let's see how fast we can clean up."
5. Set the sand timer or note the time on a clock.
6. When the job is complete note how long it took to do cleanup.

MORE IDEAS

- Challenge the children to become a giant cleaning machine by working together. Ask, "Do you think we could make a cleaning machine assembly line?" (One person could pick up the blocks, one person could pass them, and another could stack them.) Ask, "What noises would a BIG machine make? How would it move?"

DISCUSSION STARTERS

Use these questions to spark children's thinking during and after the activity:
- Do you think our clean-up machines helped the work go faster?
- How could we change the machines next time to help them work better?

SKILLS ASSESSMENT

Use these questions to determine a child's abilities and understanding:
- Did the child participate in the group discussion?
- Did the child become a cleaning machine using movements and noises?
- How did the child work as part of a team?

Make a GIANT Robot

PREPARATION
- Label a sheet of chart paper "Ideas for Inventing a Robot."
- Before the children arrive, use a knife to cut a BIG door in the back of the box—the robot—so the children or an adult can fit inside. Also cut a narrow horizontal flap in the box so the children can later slide in "circuit boards." This slit should be about the height of four Unifix cubes or the width of a unit block and about 12"–15" wide.

WHAT TO DO
1. Read a story about robots or show photos downloaded from the Internet. Ask the children what they know about robots. Record their responses along with the name of each child.
2. Tell the children they will be able to build a robot using their *imagination* during activity time. Introduce the word *idea*, a thought or plan. Say and clap the syllables, i-**de**-a, with the emphasis on the "de" syllable. Say *idea* as you make the ASL sign for *idea*. Your right hand is closed except for the pinkie finger which comes out from the side of your forehead.
3. Ask the children what they would like their robot to do. Say, "I will write your *ideas* on this paper labeled "Ideas for Inventing a Robot." Include the children's names with their *ideas*.
4. The children design the robot (the cardboard box). Help them *brainstorm* how to carry out their *ideas*, asking, "What should you do first?" to highlight sequence. For example, if a child says the robot should be able to make cookies, ask how he could make that happen. Does the robot need a mixer or an oven? If a child says the robot should have sharp teeth to scare away monsters, help the child figure out how to make sharp teeth.
5. The children tape various lids to the box to simulate buttons and dials and an on/off switch. After the dials are on, ask what the buttons control. Suggest that the children count how many buttons the robot has.
6. Save the robot for the children to play with and add features.

DISCUSSION STARTERS
Use these questions to spark children's thinking during and after the activity:
- What can this robot do?
- If you had your own real robot, what would you like it to do?

SKILLS ASSESSMENT
Use these questions to determine a child's abilities and understanding:
- Did the children participate in the group discussion?
- Can the child work as part of a team?

FOCUS AREAS
Science: learning about the abilities of technological des
Math: estimating,
Language Arts: learning vocabulary, experiencing a wide range of fiction and non-fiction, using spoken and written language to communicate and learn, generating ideas and questions, labeling

MATERIALS
Book about robots, such as *It Could Still Be a Robot* by Allan Fowler (see Good Books for Facts and Fun on pages 291–293. This book may be currently out of print, but you may be able to find at the library or as a used book.) or information downloaded from the Internet (search term: robot images)
Refrigerator-size cardboard box or two smaller boxes taped together
Duct tape and clear packing tape
Knife or box cutter (adult use only)
Assorted lids, old CDs, and paper
Chart paper
Marker

Circuit Boards

FOCUS AREAS

Science: learning about the abilities of technological design

Math: estimating, learning about three-dimensional shapes, measuring—length and height

Language Arts: using spoken and written language to communicate, generating ideas

Art: exploring three-dimensional design

MATERIALS

Sheets of rigid cardboard about 8½" x 11", 1 per child

Assortment of hardware (small pieces of appliances you took apart or purchased hardware such as screws, washers, and bolts)

Assorted wire, bottle caps, and other flat items

Masking tape or transparent tape

Unifix cubes or unit blocks for measuring

Real circuit board (optional, available from a computer repair shop) or an illustration of a circuit board online (search term: circuit board images)

WHAT TO DO

1. Show a small group of children a picture of a circuit board, or a real circuit board if you have one. Say, "Real circuit boards tell some machines, like computers, what to do. We are going to make pretend circuit boards using our *imaginations* and parts left over from machines that we took apart. Our circuit boards won't really work but we are going to pretend that they will give our robot special powers."

2. Invite the children to make a circuit board. Tell them that the boards need to be flat enough to fit into the slit that you cut into the front of the robot. With the children, measure the slit (about four Unifix cubes tall or the width of one unit block).

3. The children tape items to their cardboard. Have them measure how tall their board is with the Unifix cubes or block to make sure it will fit in the slot, then actually slide it through to check their measurement.

4. Ask the children what their circuit board will help the robot do. Write their descriptions on their boards.
   Note: Save the circuit boards for later use with the robot.

DISCUSSION STARTERS

Use these questions to spark children's thinking during and after the activity:

● What instructions will your circuit board give the robot?

● Do you have other *ideas* what a robot could do?

● How can you tell if your circuit board will fit in the slot?

SKILLS ASSESSMENT

Use these questions to determine a child's abilities and understanding:

● Can the child estimate height?

● Is the child able to use cubes or blocks to measure height?

TEACHER-TO-TEACHER TIP

If you are knowledgeable about electrical circuits, it is fun to explore how real circuits work with a small light bulb, wires, and a battery. If you do not have this expertise, one of the parents in your class might be able to help.

BIG DRAMA:
The Power of Imagination Brings the Robot to Life

PREPARATION

- Prepare a cardboard tray to fit through the slot for the circuit boards if you don't have a ready-made tray or metal baking pan that will fit through the slot.

TEACHER-TO-TEACHER TIP

You can help the children control the robot and make it come to life, or you and an adult assistant can surprise the children with a demonstration. It is fun to invite families or another class to attend the performance.

FOCUS AREAS

Science: learning about the abilities of technological design

Language Arts: using spoken and visual language to communicate

MATERIALS

The robot created by the children

Circuit boards made by the children

Tray to hold circuit boards as children feed them into the robot

Empty large plastic container (a 2- or 5-gallon water cooler bottle is ideal) or cardboard box

2 old CDs or 2 large jar lids

Pipe cleaners

Clear packing tape

Broom handle

Noisemakers, such as a bell, tambourine, kazoo, wooden blocks, and rhythm sticks

WHAT TO DO

1. Help the children make a robot "head." Use old CDs or jar lids (to make eyes) and pipe cleaners (to make a smile) to create a face for the robot on a large plastic container or cardboard box and mount it on a broom handle so it can be raised above the robot body the children made.

2. Set up the robot in a corner of your classroom, with the back against the wall so the children can take turns being inside the robot with an adult assistant, hidden from view. Lay out the various noisemakers so the child can make noise as each child inserts a circuit board. Have the robot head available, hidden from view.

3. At group time or the family event, quietly ask one child to stand inside the robot with an adult assistant.

4. Gather the children and audience and say, "It's now time to see if the power of our *imagination* can bring our robot to life. Let's see if our pretend circuit boards will help it work." Choose a child's circuit board, call the child to the front of the group, read the note the child dictated about what the circuit board will help the robot do, ("Jessie says this circuit board will help the robot make pizza") and then ask the child to put the board on a tray that the adult slides out through the slot.

5. Help slide the tray with the circuit board back into the robot. Then the child stationed inside the robot with the adult assistant takes the board and uses one of the noisemakers to make a sound. This is a BIG crowd-pleaser.

6. Continue with the whole class, with the children taking turns being in the robot and making a noise when a different child hands in a circuit board. When the children have all had a turn, the adult assistant stays inside the robot, hidden from view.

7. Say, "I wonder if our robot needs anything else to start up." The children may suggest plugging it in or saying magic words. You can pretend to plug it in or ask for suggestions for magic words. Say the words together, "Abracadabra, please, and thank you." The adult assistant who is inside the robot raises the robot head and "talks" to the children. For example, "I'm very excited to be here. I'm so glad to have all these circuit boards so I can do so many things." If the children wanted the robot to play basketball, the assistant can throw a small ball in the air from behind the box and say, "I can play ball now." If the children wanted the robot to sweep the floor, the assistant can wave a broom in the air and say, "I can clean."

8. After the performance, the children continue taking turns inserting circuit boards and making noises.

TEACHER-TO-TEACHER TIPS

- The children may get excited during the performance. It is helpful to have an extra adult assistant or parent to help the children take turns making the robot noises. Or, you may decide to have just the adult assistant make the noises the first time through and then invite the children to take turns making the noises, after the performance.
- Children love pretending and seeing the power of *imagination*. When they play with the robot they can enjoy that power themselves. Many inventors say they learned to invent through play and *imagination*.

DISCUSSION STARTERS

Use these questions to spark children's thinking during and after the activity:

- Does this robot seem real to you?
- Did anything surprise you about our robot?
- Do you have more *ideas* about what our robot could do?

SKILLS ASSESSMENT

Use these questions to determine a child's abilities and understanding:

- Could the child wait for a turn putting in a circuit board?
- Can the child work as part of a group?
- Did the child enjoy being inside the robot?

More Activities Across the Curriculum

LANGUAGE ARTS

- Invite children to draw pictures and dictate stories about their favorite inventions. Include vocabulary words and books about *inventions* at the table for inspiration. Topics for different days:
  - What *inventions* do you like to use?
  - What would you like to invent?

  Mount the stories on butcher paper in the shape of a light bulb. Label the display "Inventors at Work." When you take down the display keep the drawings in each child's portfolio.
- Children invent a new word or a new name for an *invention*. Encourage the children to think creatively by writing out names of items and adding them together to make up something new.

MATH

- Children practice estimating with screws. Prepare several containers with a variety of screws in each—for older children prepare containers that have about 8, 15, and 25 screws. Use fewer for younger children. The children take turns estimating how many are in each jar and then counting the screws. *Variation*: The children prepare jars with different amounts of screws and have another child or adult do the estimating and counting.
- Children compare shapes of washers, nuts, and other hardware. Encourage the children to make patterns: washer, washer, nut; washer, washer, nut; and so on.

ART

- Children experiment with a variety of gadgets to create art. Talk about how creativity and experimentation often means using familiar objects in new ways. Ask the children for their *ideas* of wild and crazy art. Once you get going there's no end to *ideas*. Who knows what they will invent:

  - Gadget printing. Children dip gadgets, such as potato mashers, whisks, dog toys, flyswatters, or toilet plungers (designated solely for art use, not used in a toilet), in trays of tempera paint and make prints on construction paper. Supersize the activity by using BIG paper to make an *invention* print mural.
  - *Eggbeater bubble prints*. Add liquid dishwashing detergent to a container of water. Children whip up bubbles, add liquid water colors or powdered tempera paint on top of the bubbles, and make prints of the bubbles.
  - *Salad spinner art*. Make your own spin art machine by cutting paper to fit inside an old salad spinner. The children place tempera paint on the paper in the bottom, put on the cover, and pump. Note how colors mix.

- *Feet art*. Children make pictures using their feet as "paintbrushes."
- *Record player art*. Children use an old record player to make pictures on paper plates. Punch a whole in the paper plates and place the plate on the turntable. While the plate turns, the children use markers to create circular patterns.

COOKING/MATH/LANGUAGE ARTS
- Children make lemonade with and without cooking gadgets. First try squeezing lemons by hand. Then use a hand juicer. Then use an electric juicer. Do the tools make lemon-squeezing easier?
- Experiment with cooking. All new recipes are a type of *invention*. Experimenting with different ingredients and different amounts will create new tastes. Invent new kinds of granola by setting out a variety of ingredients such as corn flakes, raisins, oats, and sunflower seeds. Let the children choose the ingredients and measure amounts to invent their own granola. Provide paper and markers to help them write their new recipe.
- Children invent new kinds of smoothies with a variety of ingredients. Provide paper and markers to write down the recipes.
- Invite everyone in the class to bring an ingredient for a BIG fruit salad, vegetable salad, or soup. The children prepare the food and see what they created.

GROSS MOTOR/MUSIC
- Listen and perform the song "Dancin' Machine," on Greg & Steve's *We All Live Together Volume 3*. The machines included: washing machine, eggbeater, oil well, railroad train, robot, and airplane.

SENSORY TABLE
- Children make Gak or Oobleck, truly amazing *inventions*. There are numerous recipes. (Search terms: Gak recipes, Oobleck recipes)

BIG Outcomes

Group assessment: Review the poster boards you created about taking apart the appliances, building new *"inventions,"* running the shaker assembly line, and building the giant robot. Review chart paper sheets from the beginning of your exploration of what the children know about *inventions* and what they want to find out. On a third sheet of chart paper labeled "What We Learned About Inventions," record the children's comments about what they learned, including the name of the child who made the comment. Be sure to note answers to their original questions or determine if the class still has more to learn and explore.

Individual assessment: Review your notes and quotes from individual observations during activities such as sorting machine parts, making *inventions* and circuit boards, and cooking projects. Save for the children's portfolios items such as photos of *inventions* and the children's dictation about their *inventions*, recipes, and sample artwork of gadget printings. Note whether the children use new vocabulary words in conversation. Note areas in which the children need further practice and those in which they excel.

GOOD BOOKS FOR FACTS AND FUN
Imagination + problem solving can = a BIG invention. While there are few non-fiction books about inventing suited to the pre-school level, inspiring stories and examples of brainstorming by young inventors can be found in these fun, creative, sometimes quirky stories.

INFORMATION ABOUT INVENTIONS
Girls Think of Everything: Stories of Ingenious Inventions by Women by Catherine Thimmesh
Twelve inventions by girls and women, from Liquid Paper to windshield wipers, are each explained in two to three pages. A list of 129 female inventors from 3000 B.C. to 1995 provides interesting facts for teachers to share with the children. Ages 9 and up

Imaginative Inventions: The Who, What, Where, When, and Why of Roller Skates, Potato Chips, Marbles, and Pie and More! by Charise Mericle Harper
This crazy quilt collection relates the history of random inventions in four-line rhyming stanzas illustrated with cartoon characters in hot colors. Some of the "histories" veer from known facts into story-like explanations, but it is fun nevertheless. Ages 5–6

It Could Still Be a Robot by Allan Fowler
Color photographs and a simple text introduce a variety of intelligent machines that may not resemble humans but are designed to help with difficult, dangerous, or just plain boring jobs. Look for this classic by the well-known science writer at your local library. Ages 4–6

The Kids' Invention Book by Arlene Erlbach
A baker's dozen of prize-winning inventions by real kids, each explained in two pages and illustrated with color photos. This book also covers the patent process, invention contests, clubs, and societies. A perfect book for teachers that provides background information for this unit. Ages 6 and up

Small Inventions That Make a Big Difference edited by Donald J. Crump
Three sections focus on inventors, the history and uses of plastics, and an A–Z list of inventions. Color photographs and line drawings add appeal. This collection offers invention facts for teachers to share with their avid inventors. Ages 6 and up

Steven Caney's Invention Book by Steven Caney
From problem solving to patents, all the practical nuts-and-bolts information for inventing is here. Stories of inventors and inventions, including Band-Aids, Kleenex, the basketball, and more, give teachers useful background for inspiring young thinkers. Ages 9 and up

STORIES ABOUT IMAGINATION, INVENTIONS, AND PROBLEM SOLVING

If I Built a Car by Chris Van Dusen
In Seuss-like rhyme, Jack, the backseat inventor, describes how his car would improve upon the family station wagon. Good-smelling, submergible, complete with a pool, Jack goes feature by feature, each shown in bold illustrations. Ages 3–6

Mrs. Armitage on Wheels and *Mrs. Armitage and the Big Wave* by Quentin Blake
Leave it to Mrs. A., an intrepid inventor, to solve her bicycle or surfing problems in her own eccentric style. These open-ended stories and others in the series offer creative writing or discussion opportunities for young inventors. Ages 4–6

No Problem by Eileen Browne
Rat's mysterious package of multiple mechanical parts delights and baffles Mouse, Badger, and Otter until Shrew reads the directions and correctly assembles the vehicle needed to transport everyone to the party in this long, but wonderful, story. Ages 4–6

Rattletrap Car by Phyllis Root
Inventive use of the beach gear saves the day when the family rattletrap car breaks down repeatedly on the way to the lake. Sound words, silliness, and detailed watercolor illustrations of the creative fixes add up to an entertaining tale. Ages 3–6

The Story of Chopsticks by Ying Chang Compestine
Hungry Kùai, youngest son, wants to reach hot tidbits without burning his fingers. He
    invents chopsticks, "Kùai zi" in Mandarin Chinese. Children adopt these "quick
    ones," creating an opportunity to learn good table manners from their elders.
    Brightly-colored cut paper illustrations. Ages 4–6

Sydney's Star by Peter H. Reynolds
Sydney the mouse works hard inventing her mechanical star. She gets upset when her
    invention malfunctions before saving the day. A brief, upbeat tale, this one may
    spark discussion about unexpected consequences, losing, and winning. Ages 4–6

Young MacDonald by David Milgrim
Silliness spreads Ee-i-ee-i-o around the farm when Young MacDonald uses his newly
    constructed machine to combine a horse with a pig creating a "hig." Ages 4–6

STORIES ABOUT BOXES
The Big, Beautiful Brown Box by Larry Dane Brimner
Three friends model communication and problem solving after they disagree about
    what they should do with the large, beautiful, brown box. This short, small-sized
    story can jump-start a discussion about making decisions together. Ages 3–6

A Box Can Be Many Things by Dana Meachen Rau
A big box, junk in Mom's opinion, but rescued by a big sister and a little brother, turns
    into a cave, a car, a house, and a cage before ending up in pieces. Not quite junk
    yet, even then the kids come up with more imaginative uses. Ages 3–5

My Book Box by Will Hillenbrand
An inventive young elephant brainstorms options for his brown box before creating a
    book box. No ordinary book box, this one doubles as a treasure chest, a table, a
    race car, a rocket, and more, all shown in colorful, clear illustrations. Ages 3–6

Not a Box by Antoinette Portis
What is the bunny doing with that box? Each question, shown in simple black outlines
    on white pages, is answered by turning the page. Bunny's ideas for the box are
    superimposed in red lines as each of his imagined uses come to life. Ages 3–6

A Special Kind of Love by Stephen Michael King
A creative, quiet father, who has trouble expressing his love for his son in words, shows
    he cares by sharing his own love for inventing with boxes. Use this gentle story one-
    on-one or in small groups and allow time for discussion. Ages 4–6

This Is Our House by Michael Rosen
In a small park between high-rises, neighborhood children try to gain access to the big
box "house" that George won't share. They settle their dispute after realistic upsets, a
tantrum, and tears, although the box falls apart at the end. Ages 4–6

A Note to Families About Inventions

Dear Families,

What would we do without Band-Aids or scissors or Velcro? These are inventions that children know and enjoy using. We are exploring all kinds of inventions—real and pretend—to spark children's imagination of what's possible. After all, it was a 15-year-old boy named Chester Greenwood who invented earmuffs because his ears kept getting cold when he was ice skating. We told your children the story of how Band-Aids were invented by a man who wanted to help his wife after she kept hurting herself when cooking.

Anyone can be an inventor. All you need is ideas. Some ideas are for something brand new, like the first telephone. Other ideas make existing inventions a little bit better. Wouldn't it be wonderful to have an invention that would keep markers from drying out when you leave the cap off? Maybe your child will figure out how to solve that problem some day.

You can help your child be an inventor by encouraging his or her problem solving. Perhaps you are making chocolate chip cookies and realize you don't have enough chocolate chips. Ask your child what you could use instead. (Make a small batch so you don't waste food if you don't like it.) Maybe you'll invent a wonderful new recipe, or maybe your experiment won't taste good and you'll decide you'll have to try something else next time.

Here are some of the words we've been learning about inventions:
- Brainstorm is thinking up lots of different ideas.
- When we use our imaginations we are thinking up something that we cannot see right now. When we imagine, we make pictures in our minds of what we are thinking about.

Have fun watching your inventor brainstorm new ideas!

APPENDIX

We're Going BIG: Letter to Families

Gathering BIG Stuff

Adding a Librarian to Your BIG Team: How to Get the Most Out of Your Public Library

BIG Materials
Giant Die
Giant Graph
Huge Funnel/Super Scoop

We're Going BIG: Letter to Families

Dear Families,

We are excited about trying new science, math, literacy, and language activities this year to capture children's love of BIG-scale projects. Children become totally engaged in learning when they can use their whole bodies, rather than sitting at a table just using their hands. We need some extra supplies for these activities and would really appreciate it if you can donate any items. Put them in a bag with your name on it and leave the bag in the basket by our classroom door. When we have all we need, we'll cross that item off the list. If you have other items that you think we might be able to use, ask us. We are great recyclers.

Also, please let us know if you can help with construction projects.

Here are our top priorities and how we'll use them:

Items you may have on hand
- Old CDs: Rainbow-color makers, wind chimes
- Plastic bottle caps thoroughly rinsed: Space ship instrument dials and robot features
- Styrofoam egg cartons: Light and rigid building blocks or sorting trays
- BIG cardboard boxes: Anything from a rocket ship to a house for the Three Little Pigs.
- Boards: 1'-wide and ¾"-thick in different lengths or pieces of rigid cardboard: ramps

Items you could donate used or could buy for the school
- Rain gutters: Pre-formed plastic gutters make wonderful ramps for toy cars and tracks for wind experiments. These are among our favorite BIG things.
- Ladder and step stools: To prop up ramps
- Magnifiers: Sturdy lenses help make little things look bigger.
- Portable insect magnifiers: These small plastic containers have magnifying glass built in so you can see critters close up without touching them.
- Clear packing tape: Sturdy wide tape for building projects
- Garden hose: To bring water to the sandbox or when empty an all-the-way-across-the-playground telephone
- Box cutter: For a teacher to cut windows and doors in BIG boxes
- Large plastic tarp: 6' x 10' or 9' x 12' with plenty of grommets makes a space station or a hockey rink. It's ideal to have one side blue and the other silver.

Other useful items
- Rope: A variety of lengths and thicknesses (⅜" clothesline rope is easy to use and gentle on little hands)
- Duct tape: Holds virtually anything to something else for as long as you want.
- Goo Gone or Goof Off: Dissolves the glue residue from surfaces after removing duct tape.
- Pulleys: An assortment of different sizes, from the 3" clothesline type to the ¾" awning type, to help make machines
- Plastic wading pool (rigid plastic is best): Great for a moon crater in the sandbox and an ice castle base
- Five-gallon plastic water bottles: For "rocket fuel" tanks or the heads of giant robots

Thanks so much for helping us go BIG!

Gathering BIG Stuff

BIG activities require a few supplies in addition to your basic stash of paper, yarn, and glue. You don't need to gather all of these items at one time; you can build up your collection slowly as you do different activities. Ask families and local stores for donations. Involving families and the community in small and BIG ways expands your team and builds enthusiasm. Once you have some things from the list, you'll find they come in handy every day.

Use the sample letter to ask for donations. You can add and subtract items to suit your program. Also, make a copy to post near your classroom door. When you don't need any more of an item you can cross it off the list.

Storing BIG Stuff
We know storage is often a problem. Can you find space and money for a storage shed outdoors? We keep our BIG stuff outside. You can put light materials such as egg cartons, cardboard tubes, and pipe insulation in plastic bags (we like the see-through kind) and hang them from the shed ceiling. Or, you can ask families to send in egg cartons and paper towel rolls shortly before you plan to use them. Keep a paper bag or laundry basket by the door for donations.

You may be able to store wooden or cardboard ramps in your block area. Try stashing other items under book cases.

You may find other nooks and crannies in your classroom. Can you keep items under your classroom desk? Can you shoehorn in a few extra tubs with your art supplies?

Some materials, like gutters, are weatherproof and can be stored outside, along the side of your classroom building or shed. It doesn't matter if they get dirty. A quick swipe will get rid of grit and spider webs.

Of course, you could stash the BIG stuff at home. Don't worry! You will be using it in no time.

Adding a Librarian to Your BIG Team: How to Get the Most Out of Your Public Library

"I've got to be at school in ten minutes," I tell the librarian, Bobbi. "My class is learning about ice. I want to find that funny story about the polar bear taking a bath but I don't remember the title."

Librarian to the rescue: "That's No Bath for Boris and there's a copy on the shelf," Bobbi says.

Librarians regularly help teachers save time, money, and classroom space. Using your public library means you don't have to buy and store a BIG book collection in your classroom, but you will still have plenty of books to share with the children.

When you establish a personal connection with a children's librarian, you add a strong partner to your education team. Take time one day to introduce yourself. Tell the librarian where you teach, what age level, how many children are in your class, and what your own interests are. Bring a list of books you are looking for, or just come with a topic and ask the librarian for suggestions. If possible, come at a quieter time of day. Library business often peaks after school during homework rush hours and after special programs.

Here are a few tips for finding what you need quickly:
- **Online catalogs**—Most libraries have online catalogs listing their materials, databases, booklists, and connections to other libraries. These catalogs may look different from library to library but most are quite easy to use. Library software evolves rapidly; there are often new features to explore even if you are a frequent library user. Ask for help at any time.
- **Check availability**—Many libraries let you access the catalog from home or school so you can check a book's availability before you stop by. Some libraries will even let you call ahead and ask a librarian to gather the books you need. Ask how many can be searched and held at a single time. When a book you want is already checked out, ask about placing a request for the next copy that comes in. Many libraries use phone and e-mail to speed up the notification process.
- **Inter-library loan**—What if the titles from the "Good Books for Facts and Fun" lists in each chapter of this book are all checked out or not owned by your library? You may be able to borrow them from another library. Most libraries cooperate through inter-library loan systems. In the San Francisco Bay Area, librarians call other city libraries daily to reserve items for quick pick-ups or arrange requests online from across the state for free.
- **Keyword search**—If you want to find more books on topics covered in Thinking BIG, Learning BIG try using a "keyword" search rather than a "subject" search. If you get too many results from your keyword search, most catalogs offer the option to limit results by material type (like books or CDs). Some even allow you to limit searches to just children's picture books. Ask your librarian to show you how to do this.

Children's librarians can do more than assisting with catalog searching and locating books. They can help you energize your familiar themes and explore new topics by suggesting new books you might not know. They can introduce you to the best stories and poetry, old and new, and provide you with books of facts at the right level for your class. Many librarians can also offer ideas for fingerplays, flannel board stories, music, and crafts. Some libraries will arrange a tour and a story session for your class that suits your current theme.

The one downside to checking out so many great books at the library is the potential for BIG fines if you don't return them on time. Try these tips to avoid fines:
● Ask if your library can give you a printed receipt to help you track the due dates.
● Ask if there is an after-hour book drop location.
● Ask if you can renew books online or by phone to extend the loan period.
● Ask if your library can send you e-mail reminders close to the due date.
● Put a long paper bookmark in all books to act as a date due reminder. Save your checkout receipt in the bookmark box. Consider color coding the due date strips.
● Use your classroom calendar to note "Library Books Due" and how many. Ask the children to help by counting all the books and reminding you to return them on time.
● Check out and return books on the same day of the week.

The children in your class may be new to using library books, so you are an important model for good book care in your classroom. Create a special location, shelf, or box for library books. If a book has an "accident," use this teachable moment to discuss careful book handling and tell the children that libraries have special ways and materials to mend books. When you return that book, let the librarians know about the damage. With quick attention, many books can be repaired. Remind the children to avoid keeping books close to drawing and water activities.

Become a library regular. Tell your class how you use the library and encourage parents and children to visit the library and get a library card.

Adding a librarian and a library to your learning team really makes it BIGGER.

GIANT DIE

A giant die helps children to play BIG games indoors and out. The die doesn't get lost and it's easier to count the dots.

MATERIALS

2 milk or juice cartons, ½ gallon-size, box-type not plastic
Kitchen shears or utility knife (used by adults only)
Ruler
Paper
Clear packing tape
Permanent marker or ¾" round "dot" stickers
Small die for sample

WHAT TO DO

1. Measure 3¾" from the bottoms of both containers. Mark a line across each of the four sides on both containers.
2. Cut both containers in half along the line.
3. Push the open end of one container into the other to create a closed cube 3¾" on all sides. It will be a very tight fit.
4. Cover the cube with paper. Tack the edges with small pieces of tape, being careful not to put tape where you will want to draw the dots.
5. Label each side with the correct number of dots, using the ready-made die as a model.
6. Cover all the edges of the cube with packing tape to reinforce them.

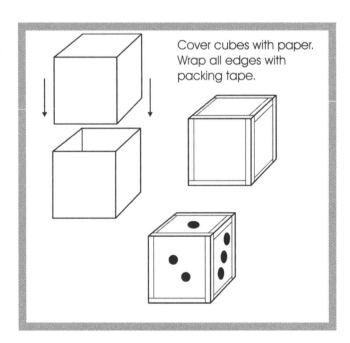

Cover cubes with paper. Wrap all edges with packing tape.

GIANT GRAPH

Note from the author: I never really looked at how graphs are put together until I created them for class. For the first one, "My Favorite Kind of Apple," I placed red, green, and yellow construction paper apples across the top. As the children tasted the different apples and decided on their favorite, they placed a little apple under corresponding color. At the end of activity time, they counted the apples and put the totals underneath each column. I noticed, however, that the children didn't really care that there were eight apples in the red column. What they really wanted to know was which apple was theirs.

Later, I noticed my apple graph didn't look like graphs in magazines and newspapers. Those graphs all recorded amounts from the bottom up. It was an "aha" moment. Building graphs from the bottom makes sense, especially for children. Graphs are like block towers. A taller tower means more blocks. And when I construct the graphs with apples BIG enough for the children to print their names, they know which apple is theirs.

MATERIALS
Chart paper
Markers
Construction paper shapes
Ruler

WHAT TO DO
1. Label the graph.
2. Create categories of what you are measuring along the bottom with words and pictures.
3. Cut strips or shapes large enough for children or an adult to print their names (about 3" wide).
4. Create a grid so items will line up across columns and children will be able to tell by looking which column has the most.

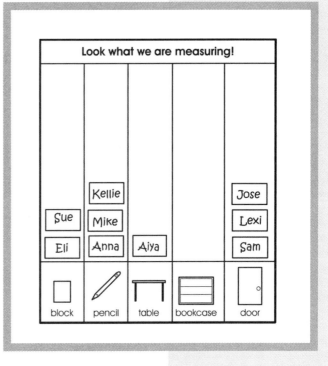

HUGE FUNNEL/SUPER SCOOP

Liquid laundry detergent containers make BIG heavy-duty tools for the sandbox or water table. Leave the cap on for use as a super-duper sand scooper, or unscrew the cap so sand and water will pour out of the giant funnel.

MATERIALS

Large liquid laundry detergent container with cap
Small towel or non-slip bath mat
Sharp paring knife or awl
Heavy-duty scissors or kitchen shears (adult-only))
Sandpaper

WHAT TO DO

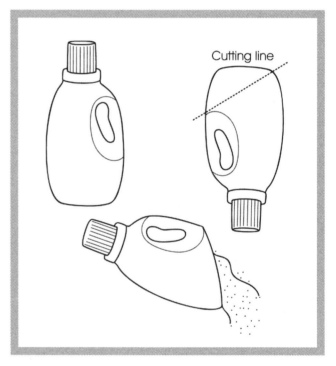

Cutting line

1. Rinse out the container well.
2. Set the container on the towel or mat with the handle side up. Holding the handle, carefully poke a small hole on the top edge of the container near the flat bottom end.
3. Insert the scissor or shears blade in the hole and cut the bottom out of the container.
4. Starting near the bottom on the right side of the container, cut diagonally upwards toward the top middle of the handle side to create an angled scoop.
5. Repeat on the left side.
6. Even out the edges and check for sharp spots. Smooth any rough places with sandpaper.

INDEXES

INDEX OF CHILDREN'S BOOKS

A

Aaaarrgghh! Spider! by Lydia Monks, 69
Air Is All Around You by Franklyn M. Branley, 161
Air, Water, and Weather by William C. Robertson, 147
All the Colors of the Rainbow by Allan Fowler, 142
Alphabet Under Construction by Denise Fleming, 246
Anansi and the Moss-Covered Rock by Eric A. Kimmel, 68
Anansi the Spider: A Tale from the Ashanti by Gerald McDermott, 55, 59, 68
At a Construction Site by Don Kilby, 245

B

Be Nice to Spiders by Margaret Bloy Graham, 55, 60, 65, 68
The Big, Beautiful Brown Box by Larry Dane Brimner, 293
Blow Away Soon by Betsy James, 162
A Box Can Be Many Things by Dana Meachen Rau, 280, 293
The Bridge Is Up! by Babs Bell, 268
Bridges Are to Cross by Philemon Sturges, 267
Bringing Down the Moon by Jonathan Emmett, 224
Building a House by Byron Barton, 246
Building Structures with Young Children by Ingrid Chalufour & Karen Worth, 227
Building with Dad by Carol Nevius, 246

C

Can You See the Wind? by Allan Fowler, 161
Can't Catch Me by John & Ann Hassett, 188
The Carrot Seed by Ruth Krauss, 92
Cold Days by Jennifer S. Burke, 187
Cold Little Duck, Duck, Duck by Lisa Westberg Peters, 188
Color, Color, Where Are You Color? by Mary Koski, 142
Come On, Rain! by Karen Hesse, 120

D

Dandelion Adventures by Patricia Kite, 92
Diary of a Spider by Doreen Cronin, 69
Diary of a Worm by Doreen Cronin, 28, 48
Dog's Colorful Day: A Messy Story About Colors and Counting by Emma Dodd, 143
Down Comes the Rain by Franklyn M. Branley, 119

E

An Earthworm's Life by John Himmelman, 47
Eensy-Weensy Spider by Mary Ann Hoberman, 69
Elmer Takes Off by David McKee, 162
The Empty Pot by Demi, 92
Exploring Space with an Astronaut by Patricia J. Murphy, 223
Exploring Water with Young Children by Ingrid Chalufour & Karen Worth, 102

F

Feel the Wind by Arthur Dorros, 161
Floating in Space by Franklyn M. Branley, 215–216, 222
From Acorn to Oak Tree by Jan Kottke, 91
From Bean to Bean Plant by Anita Ganeri, 76, 91
From Seed to Apple by Anita Ganeri, 91
From Seed to Dandelion by Jan Kottke, 91
From Seed to Pumpkin by Jan Kottke, 91
From Seed to Sunflower by Anita Ganeri, 91
Frozen Noses by Jan Carr, 188

G

Garden Wigglers: Earthworms in Your Backyard by Nancy Loewen, 47
The Giant Carrot by Jan Peck, 92
Gilberto and the Wind by Marie Hall Ets, 162
Girls Think of Everything: Stories of Ingenious Invention by Women by Catherine Thimmesh, 291
Goldilocks and the Three Bears by various authors, 184
Grandma Lena's Big Ol' Turnip by Denia Hester, 92
Gravity Is a Mystery by Franklyn M. Branley, 222

H

Hailstones and Halibut Bones by Mary O'Neill, 140, 143
The House in the Meadow by Shutta Crum, 246
How It Happens at the Building Site by Jenna Anderson, 245
How the Ladies Stopped the Wind by Bruce McMillan, 162

I

I Face the Wind by Vicki Cobb, 162
I Fall Down by Vicki Cobb, 222
I Love the Rain by Margaret Park Bridges, 120
I See Myself by Vicki Cobb, 142
I Want to Be an Astronaut by Byron Barton, 224
If I Built a Car by Chris Van Dusen, 292
If You Decide to Go to the Moon by Faith McNulty, 194–195, 223
If You Were a Construction Worker by Virginia Schomp, 245
Imaginative Inventions: The Who, What, Where, When, and Why of Roller Skates, Potato Chips, Marbles, and Pie and More! By Charise Mericle Harper, 291
In the Snow by Huy Voun Lee, 188
Inch by Inch by Leo Lionno, 48
The International Space Station by Franklyn M. Branley, 223
It Could Still Be a Robot by Allan Fowler, 285, 292
It's Raining, It's Pouring by Andrea Spalding, 120
Itsy Bitsy, the Smart Spider by Charise Mericle Harper, 69

K

The Kids' Invention Book by Arlene Erlbach, 292
Kumak's Fish: A Tall Tale from the Far North by Michael Bania, 188

L

The Lady and the Spider by Faith McNulty, 68
Let's Look at a Puddle by Angela Royston, 119
Life Cycle of a Spider by Jill Bailey, 67
Like a Hundred Drums by Annette Griessman, 121
Like a Windy Day by Frank & Devin Asch, 162
Listen to the Rain by Bill Martin Jr., 113, 121
Little Blue and Little Yellow by Leo Lionni, 143
Little Cliff and the Cold Place by Clifton L. Taulbert, 188
The Little Red Hen by Jerry Pinkney, 93
The Little Red Hen by Paul Galdone, 93
The Little Red Hen by various authors, 73, 83–84, 88, 91
Living in Space by Patricia Whitehouse, 215, 216, 223
The Lot at the End of My Block by Kevin Lewis, 246
Lowdown on Worms by Norma Dixon, 47
Lunch by Denise Fleming, 143

M

Make Way for Ducklings by Robert McCloskey, 268
Man on the Moon by Anastasia Suen, 224
The Match Between the Winds by Shirley Climo, 163
Mike Mulligan and His Steam Shovel by Virginia Lee Burton, 246
Millions of Snowflakes by Mary McKenna Siddals, 188
Monsoon by Uma Krishnaswami, 121
The Moon by Patricia Whitehouse, 223
Mooncake by Frank Asch, 192, 224
Mrs. Armitage and the Big Wave by Quentin Blake, 292
Mrs. Armitage on Wheels by Quentin Blake, 292
Mrs. Armitage, Queen of the Road by Quentin Blake, 268
My Book Box by Will Hillenbrand, 293

N

No Bath for Boris by Diana White, 188, 298
No Problem by Eileen Browne, 292
Not a Box by Antoinette Portis, 293

O

On the Road by Susan Stegall, 269
Once Upon Ice and Other Frozen Poems by Jane Yolen, 189
One Giant Leap: The Story of Neil Armstrong by Don Brown, 210, 224
One Little Seed by Elaine Greenstein, 92
Out of the Egg by Tina Matthews, 93

P

Pearl's New Skates by Holly Keller, 189
Plant Packages: A Book About Seeds by Susan Blackaby, 91
Polar Skater by Sally Grindley, 182, 189
A Promise Is a Promise by Eve Tharlet, 92
The Puddle by David McPahil, 121
Pumpkin Town! or, Nothing Is Better and Worse Than Pumpkins by Katie McKy, 93

R

Rain by Manya Stojic, 121
A Rainbow All Around Me by Sandra L. Pinkney, 140, 143
The Rainbow and You by E. C. Krupp, 142
A Rainbow of My Own by Don Freeman, 143
A Rainy Day by Sandra Markle, 119
The Rainy Day by Anna Milbourne & Sarah Gill, 119
Rainy Days by Jennifer S. Burke, 120
Rainy Weather Days by Pam Rosenberg, 120
Ramps and Wedges by Chris Oxlade, 267
Rattletrap Car by Phyllis Root, 292
Richie's Rocket by Joan Anderson, 224
Road Builders by B.G. Hennessy, 260, 267
Roll, Slope, and Slide: A Book About Ramps by Michal Dahl, 268
Rolli by Koji Takihara, 93

S

Searching for Stormy Weather with a Scientist by Judith Williams, 162
A Seed Is Sleepy by Dianna Hutts Aston, 93
Seeds by Vijaya Khirsty Bodach, 92
Seeds, Seeds, Seeds by Nancy Elizabeth Wallace, 93
Skyscrapers by Seymour Simon, 246
Skyscrapers! Super Structures to Design & Build by Carol A. Johmann & Michael P. Kline, 246
Small Inventions That Make a Big Difference by Donald J. Crump, 292
Snowflake Bentley by Jacqueline Briggs Martin, 187
Snowy Weather Days by Katie Marsico, 187
Space Travel by Patricia Whitehouse, 196, 200, 224
A Special Kind of Love by Stephen Michael King, 293
Spider by Karen Hartley, 67
A Spider's Web by Christine Back & Barrie Watts, 60, 65, 68
A Spiderling Grows Up by Pam Zollman, 67
Spiders by Gail Gibbons, 67
Spinning Spiders by Melvin Berger, 68
Steven Caney's Invention Book by Steven Caney, 292
Storm Is Coming! by Heather Tekavec, 121
The Story of Chopsticks by Ying Chang Compestine, 293
Straight and Curving by Sue Barraclough, 268
Straight to the Pole by Kevin O'Malley, 189
Sunflower House by Eve Bunting, 93
Sydney's Star by Peter H. Reynolds, 279, 293

T

Tacky and the Winter Games by Helen Lester, 189
Tell Me Why the Moon Changes Shape by Shirley Willis, 223
That's What Leprechauns Do by Eve Bunting, 143
There's a Cow in the Road by Reeve Lindberg, 268
This Is Our House by Michael Rosen, 293
This Is the Rain by Lola M. Schaefer, 121
The Three Bears by Byron Barton, 189
The Three Bears by Paul Galdone, 189
Three Billy Goats Gruff by Paul Galdone, 269
The Three Billy Goats Gruff by Stephen Carpenter, 269
The Three Billy Goats Gruff by various authors, 263
The Three Cabritos by Eric A. Kimmel, 269
The Three Little Pigs by James Marshall, 163
The Three Little Pigs by Paul Galdone, 163
The The Three Little Pigs by various authors, 147–148, 152–153, 161, 244
The Three Little Wolves and the Big Bad Pig by Eugene Trivizas, 163
The Three Snow Bears by Jan Brett, 189
The Tiny Seed by Eric Carle, 72, 93
Tool Book by Gail Gibbons, 245
Tools by Ann Morris, 246
The True Story of the 3 Little Pigs by Jon Scieszka, 163
Tunneling Earthworms by Suzanne Paul Dell'Oro, 48
Tunnels by Gail Gibbons, 268
Tunnels Go Underground by Lee Sullivan Ill, 268

U

The Unbelievable Bubble Book by John Cassidy, 136

V

The Very Busy Spider by Eric Carle, 60, 65, 68

W

Wake Up, It's Spring by Lisa Campbell Ernst, 48
Water as a Solid by Helen Frost, 187
The Water Cycle by Joy Richardson, 120
We All Go Traveling by Sheena Roberts, 269
What Do You See in a Cloud? by Allan Fowler, 120
What Is Gravity? by Lisa Trumbauer, 222
What the Moon Is Like by Franklyn M. Branley, 210, 223
When a Storm Comes Up by Allan Fowler, 120
Where Do Puddles Go? by Fay Robinson, 120
White Is the Moon by Valerie Greeley, 1433

Who Likes the Wind? by Etta Kaner, 162
Wiggling Worms at Work by Wendy Pfeffer, 48
The Wind Blew by Pat Hutchins, 163
The Windy Day by G. Brian Karas, 163
Windy Days by Jennifer S. Burke, 162

Y

Young MacDonald by David Milgrim, 293

Z

Zero Gravity by Gloria Skurzynski, 223
Zoom! Zoom! Zoom! I'm Off to the Moon by Dan Yaccarino, 224

INDEX

A

Addition, 80
Algebra, 27, 51, 71, 95, 123, 145, 191, 227, 271
Alike/different, 51, 63, 80, 241, 278
Aluminum foil, 113, 194–196, 200, 210, 212, 241
American Sign Language, 17–18, 35, 38, 40–42, 54–55, 59–60, 62–63, 74, 76–78, 96, 98–99, 105, 109–110, 111, 124, 129, 146, 148–150, 166, 176, 192, 196, 212, 228, 232, 236–237, 253, 257, 273, 279, 284–285
Appliances, 273, 275, 279
Armstrong, Neil, 210–211, 225
Art activities, 18, 24, 45–46, 89, 117–118, 139, 141, 156, 159, 185, 214–215, 220–221, 244, 265, 279, 286, 289–290
Ashbrook, Peggy, 23
Assembly lines, 281–283
Assessment, 19, 24, 30, 47, 67, 91, 119, 142, 161, 187, 222, 245, 267, 291
Astronauts, 194–196, 202–203, 205, 210–211, 215–217
    toy, 206

B

Bags
    freezer, 168–169
    garbage, 58, 192
    grocery, 58, 85, 195
    lunch, 38
    paper, 297
    plastic, 62, 98–99, 168–169, 297
    zippered, 168–169, 216
Balance beams, 254
Balance scales, 88
Balls, 129, 138, 192
    baseballs, 208
    beach, 151
    cotton, 202, 274
    golf, 208, 255
    soccer, 243
    tennis, 255
Band-Aids, 271–272, 274, 294
Beads, 281
    plastic, 177
Bean seeds, 72, 74, 78, 86
Beanbags, 138, 243
Bells, 281, 287
Berry baskets, 118, 135, 143, 244
Big arm drawing, 75
Biodegradable packing noodles, 177, 213, 242, 259
Birdseed, 89, 118, 281
Blocks, 211, 221, 227–247, 284
    cardboard, 152, 209, 239, 243
    Duplo, 243
    foam, 152, 239, 243
    hollow, 160, 221
    large, 253
    Lego, 202, 221
    Unifix cubes, 36, 159, 208, 242, 244, 259, 286
    unit, 109, 203, 221, 228, 244, 253–255, 257, 286
    wooden, 148, 242–244, 266, 287
Blueprints, 232
Bodrova, E., 19, 21
Bolts, 275, 277, 286
Books, 16 (*See also* Index of Children's Books)
    about construction, 244
    about ice and snow, 181
    about ice, 185
    about lunar vehicles, 212
    about rain, 117
    about rainbows, 124, 126
    about seeds, 72, 74, 76, 86, 88

about skyscrapers, 236
about space, 220
about spiders, 58, 66
about the moon, 208
about worms, 38, 42
Boote, C., 17, 20
Bottle caps, 88, 196, 198, 281, 286
Bottles
　dish detergent, 107
　laundry detergent, 108, 238, 302
　plastic, 102, 126
　spray, 36, 74, 78, 84, 107, 118
　squirt, 102, 118
　water cooler, 287, 296
　water, 107, 256, 281
Bowls, 83–84, 89, 126, 173, 206
　plastic, 64, 184
Bowman, B. T., 13, 16, 19–20
Boxes, 28, 44, 138, 260, 265, 287
　cereal, 193–194, 212, 229, 236, 244
　large, 28, 152, 182, 183, 193, 196, 198, 212, 229, 234, 236,
　　275, 285, 296
　shallow, 81, 85, 221, 241
　shoeboxes, 40, 243, 257
　small, 152, 212, 229, 233–234, 236, 279
Brainstorming, 60, 254, 271, 273, 279–280, 294
Branches, 260
Bredekamp, S., 13, 16, 19–21
Bricks, 85, 152
Bridges, 250–251, 253–254, 259–261, 263, 265
Bubble mixture, 135, 141, 159
Buckets, 106, 108, 135, 210, 219, 238
Building activities, 227–247
Bulletin board paper, 139
Bulletin boards, 19, 45, 140–141
Burns, M. S., 13, 16, 19–20
Butcher paper, 45–46, 117, 214, 265, 289

C
Cameras, 19, 230, 252, 272
Cans
　juice, 193, 200
　soup, 181
　tennis ball, 255
　tin, 181
Cardboard, 36, 56, 66, 130, 146, 148, 151–152, 154, 210, 213, 230,
　242, 244, 255, 257, 259, 265, 286
　corrugated, 152, 158, 257
Cardboard blocks, 152, 209, 239, 243
Cardboard tubes, 36, 297
　gift wrap, 36, 88, 118, 193, 200, 212, 266
　large, 253
　paper towel, 39, 118, 193, 200, 210, 212, 266, 297
　toilet paper, 247
Carpenter, Scott, 217
Carpet squares, 86, 205, 257, 263
Cars, 253, 255, 257, 260, 265–266
Cartons
　juice, 177, 233, 247, 300
　milk, 233, 260, 300
Caution tape, 228, 234, 260, 266
CDs, 124–125, 127, 137, 155, 196, 198, 212, 279, 285, 287, 296
Celery, 89
　leaves, 34
Cell phones, 198, 273, 275
Cereal, 290
　boxes, 193–194, 212, 229, 236, 244
Chairs, 28, 30, 44, 64, 160, 179, 184, 198, 211, 214, 236, 254
　plastic, 99

Chalk, 65, 86, 106, 115, 218
　sidewalk, 118
Chalufour, Ingrid, 102
Chart paper, 19, 28, 31–32, 47, 52, 54, 56, 60, 67, 72, 75, 80, 84, 96,
　100, 109, 112–113, 119, 124, 129–130, 132–133, 142, 146,
　150, 166, 168, 170, 175, 192, 196, 198, 202, 206, 228, 230,
　234, 236, 239, 250, 252, 260, 262, 267, 272, 277, 279, 284–
　285, 291, 301
Circle time, 23, 267
Circuit boards, 286–287
Classifying, 27, 51, 71, 95, 123, 145, 191, 227, 271, 277
Clean dirt recipe, 266
Climbing structures, 44, 254
Clipboards, 30, 130, 196, 198
Clocks, 36, 284
　alarm, 273
　watches, 281
Clothesline, 45, 107, 154, 160
Clothespins, 46, 182, 200, 230
Coffee grounds, 206–207, 266
Color squares, 132
Colored pencils, 137, 215, 232
Colors, 45, 103, 118, 123–144, 214, 266, 289
Communication skills, 31–32, 36, 40, 51, 56, 71, 76, 80, 95, 96,
　123–124, 128–130, 133, 137, 140, 145, 148, 165–166, 173,
　175, 191, 227–228, 230, 249, 252, 255, 271–272, 277, 285–
　287
Comparing, 30–31, 45, 56, 59, 112, 209, 232, 236, 237, 244, 256,
　278
Compost materials, 34
Composting bins, 33
Construction paper, 31, 38, 40, 46, 56, 58, 60, 80, 83, 86, 89, 98,
　109, 124, 133–134, 138, 140, 152, 159, 184, 200, 221, 228,
　234–235, 250, 257, 260, 263–264, 266, 272, 281, 289, 301
Contact paper, 36, 66, 111
Containers, 39, 45, 66, 72, 80, 88, 96, 98, 102, 108, 109, 166, 171,
　177, 186, 193, 238, 275, 277, 281, 289
　clear, 28, 56
　deli, 111
　large, 32, 206
　lids, 279
　plastic, 85, 111, 179, 277, 287
　yogurt, 177, 238
Cookie sheets, 74, 79, 118, 179, 206, 266
Cooking activities, 24, 89, 118, 168–169, 186, 244, 290
Coolers, 177, 179
Cooperation, 45, 59, 61, 108, 139, 153–154, 156, 178, 197, 199,
　211, 213, 237, 238, 254, 261, 271, 281–283, 284–285, 288
Copley, J. V., 20
Copple, C., 13, 16, 19–21
Corks, 102, 200
Cotton balls, 202, 274
Cotton swabs, 200, 202, 210
Counting, 27, 30–32, 38–39, 42, 44–46, 51, 56–58, 62–63, 65–66,
　71, 76–77, 80–81, 83–89, 100, 103, 106, 108–109, 111, 113,
　115–116, 118, 123–126, 128, 130–135, 138, 145, 148, 152,
　154–155, 165, 168, 173–174, 179–180, 182, 184–185, 191,
　196, 198, 200, 203, 212, 218–219, 227, 230, 232–233, 236–
　238, 240–244, 249, 252, 259–260, 263, 265, 271, 275,
　277–279, 289
　backwards, 199, 220
Cox, Gwen E., 18
Craft sticks, 32, 102, 111, 185–186, 208, 250, 264, 265
Crayons, 31–32, 34, 137, 184, 202, 209, 215, 232
Crepe paper, 138–140, 157, 160, 200, 228, 234
Crystals, 124, 127, 137
　making, 181

Cups
    measuring, 89, 102, 118, 118, 135, 168–169, 186, 206–207, 216, 266, 281
    paper, 81, 89, 118, 148, 157, 168–169, 175, 185–186, 244, 279
    plastic, 74, 78, 84, 102, 108, 185, 212, 238
Curriculum Focal Points, 15–16

D

Dancing activities, 39, 140, 186
Daniels, Marilyn, 18, 20
Data analysis, 27, 31–32, 40, 51, 56, 71, 95, 123, 145, 165, 191, 249, 271
DeBruin-Parecki, A., 20
Deli containers, 111
    lids, 208
Dickson, Earle, 272, 274
Die, 88
    giant, 65, 115, 219, 243, 300
    small, 277
Dirt, 32, 46, 75
Dishpans, 102, 135, 179, 260
Dishwashing liquid, 135, 289
Doll clothes, 107, 160
Donations, 296–297
Donovan, M. S., 13, 16, 19–20
Dramatic play, 18, 24, 83, 88, 102, 118, 147–148, 152–153, 160–161, 170, 184, 191, 195–196, 198–199, 203, 210–213, 215, 221, 227, 234–235, 238, 244, 262–263, 284, 286–288
Drinking straws, 135, 148, 159, 216, 265
Duct tape, 66, 118, 236, 243, 279, 285, 296

E

Earth/space science, 95–225
Edison, Thomas, 271
Egg cartons, 239, 244, 297
    Styrofoam, 103, 141, 229, 236, 260, 279, 296
English Language Arts Standards, 27, 51, 71, 95, 123, 145, 165, 191, 227, 249, 271
Epstein, A. S., 20
Estimating, 36, 45, 60, 66, 71, 81, 84, 108, 112, 118, 134, 138, 145, 154–155, 160, 165, 173–174, 191, 203, 208, 227, 236–238, 249, 253, 259, 271, 285, 286, 289
Evaporation, 103–107, 117, 119, 122, 160
Experiments, 14, 29, 71, 78, 81, 91, 95, 98, 106, 117, 119, 123, 128–130, 13, 145, 148–149, 158, 165, 167, 171, 173, 175–176, 179, 181, 191, 208, 214, 227, 249, 255–258, 271
Eyedroppers, 96, 98–99, 102–103, 141, 166, 177
Eye-hand coordination, 138, 151, 182–183, 200–201, 240, 243

F

Fabric, 99, 156, 274
    absorbent, 98
    cotton, 107
    felt, 42–44, 45, 62, 66, 140, 170
    gauze, 272, 274
Felt board, 140, 170
Fine motor skills, 18, 24, 45, 58, 60, 62, 66, 74, 83–84, 98, 102, 103, 129, 132, 141, 154–155, 159, 168, 173, 177, 179–180, 184–185, 194–196, 200, 215–216, 220, 232, 244, 281–283
Fingerplays
    "Five Little Earthworms" by Marie Faust Evitt & Bobbi Weesen-Baer, 42–43
First aid tape, 272, 274
Flags, 156, 210
Flannel boards, 42, 45, 62
Flashlights, 41, 124–125, 129, 137, 192
Flour, 85
    whole wheat, 85
Foam blocks, 152, 239, 243

Food coloring, 102–103, 126, 141, 177, 185
Ford, Henry, 281–282
Fruits, 33, 169, 290
    apples, 33–34
    berries, 169
    cherry tomatoes, 244
    lemons, 118, 290
    raisins, 290
Funnels, 102, 126, 150, 281
    making, 302

G

Gadgets, 272, 289
Gak, 290
Gallaudet University, 18
Game cards, 115, 218
Games
    air soccer, 151
    freeze dance, 186
    ice cube hockey, 182
    knock down the building, 243
    matching, 266
    memory, 266
    moon bounce adventure, 218–219
    pass the ice cube, 185
    puddle, 115
    rainbow color toss, 138
    red light/green light, 264
    sticky web, 65
    traveling seeds, 86, 91
Garbage bags, 58, 192
Garden hoses, 108, 128, 238, 260, 296
Gardening activities, 71–94
Gauze squares, 272, 274
Geometry, 123, 196, 212, 227, 244, 271
Giant die, 65, 115, 219, 243, 300
    making, 300
Gift wrap tubes, 36, 88, 118, 193, 200, 212, 266
Glenn, John, 217
Gloves, 185, 206, 210, 215
    plastic, 33
Glue, 46, 75, 132, 138, 152, 194–196, 212, 244, 250, 257, 264–266, 280
    sticks, 31, 56, 80, 124
Glue spreaders, 194–196, 212
Golf balls, 208, 255
Goodman, Laura Ristrom, 23
Granola, 89, 290
    bars, 216–217
Graphing activities, 15–16, 30–32, 40, 51, 56, 71, 80, 95, 109, 119, 123, 130–132, 145, 165, 249, 271, 277
Grass, 148, 152
Gravity, 191–193, 202–203, 205, 214–215, 220, 225, 249, 255–256
Grayson, Gabriel, 18, 21
Greenwood, Chester, 294
Grocery bags, 58, 85, 195
Grollman, S., 21
Gross motor skills, 18–19, 24, 28, 44, 65, 85–86, 115, 138, 140, 150–151, 157–158, 160, 182, 185–186, 202–203, 205, 210, 218, 220, 264, 266, 284, 290
Group time. See Circle time
Gutierrez, Keith, 18

H

Habitats, 27, 34–35, 51–52, 56, 60, 65
Hammers, 85, 240, 272
Hard hats, 228, 234, 238–239, 260, 262
Hardware, 286, 289
Hart, B., 18, 21

Hats, 64, 166
Helmets, 195, 210
Hollow blocks, 160, 221
Hot pads, 83, 104
Hula hoops, 138, 200, 218
Hypotheses, 14, 249

I

Ice, 104, 165–190
    crushed, 168–169, 181, 186
    cubes, 166, 168, 171, 173, 175, 179, 182, 185–186
Ice cube trays, 102–103, 141, 185
Index cards, 266
Ink pads, 28
Inquiry-based curriculum, 13–14
Insect magnifying containers, 56, 296
Inter-library loan, 298
International Reading Association, 16, 21
Inventions, 15, 271–294

J

Jackets, 96, 98–99
Jars, 73
    baby food, 89
    lids, 88, 221, 266, 287
    plastic, 56, 104, 107
Jet packs, 194, 210
Journals, 75
Juice, 168–169, 186
    cans, 193, 200
    cartons, 177, 233, 247, 300

L

Lab coats, 40
Labeling, 23, 32, 38, 40, 56, 60, 78, 80, 86, 130, 196, 212, 232, 234, 236, 238, 242, 253, 259, 285
Ladders, 179, 236, 296
Laminate, 115, 218, 257
Language arts, 13, 30, 32, 34, 38, 40, 42, 44, 45, 54, 56, 60, 62, 64, 66, 72, 74, 76, 78, 80, 83–86, 88–89, 96, 98, 100, 102–104, 106, 109, 111, 113, 115, 117, 128–129, 130, 132–133, 140–141, 146, 150, 152, 159, 166, 168, 170, 175, 179, 184–185, 192, 194–196, 198, 200, 202–203, 205–206, 208, 210, 212, 214, 216, 220, 228, 232, 234, 236, 238–240, 242, 244, 250, 253, 255, 257, 259–260, 262–265, 272, 277, 279, 284–287, 289–290
    benefits, 17
    big, 17–18
Laundry baskets, 297
Laundry detergent bottles, 108, 238, 302
    caps, 102, 244, 302
Leaves, 32, 34, 42, 99
Lego blocks, 202
    space sets, 221
Lemonade, 290
    recipe, 118
Leon, D. J., 19, 21
Libraries, 298–299
Lids, 285
    bottle caps, 88, 196, 198, 281, 286
    deli container, 208
    jar, 88, 221, 266, 287
    laundry detergent bottles, 102, 244, 302
    metal, 154–155, 208
    milk jug caps, 59, 200, 208
    plastic bottle caps, 118, 296
    plastic can cover, 266
    plastic, 102, 118, 138, 141, 196, 198, 208
    yogurt container, 208

Life cycles, 71–94
Life sciences, 27–70
Light, 123–144
    bulbs, 286
    flashlights, 41, 124–125, 129, 137, 192
Liquid watercolors, 102–103, 118, 177, 185, 289
Literacy skills, 13
    benefits, 16
    big, 16

M

Magnifying lenses, 32, 34, 74, 88, 98, 103, 181, 206, 296
Manipulatives, 221, 284
Maps, 259
Marbles, 102, 177, 208, 221, 256, 266
Markers, 28, 30, 32, 34, 36, 38, 40, 52, 54, 56, 58, 60, 72, 74, 76, 78, 80–81, 84, 96, 100, 109, 113, 124, 129, 133, 137, 146, 148, 150, 152, 157, 166, 168, 170, 177, 192, 195–196, 198, 202, 206, 215, 228, 230, 232, 236, 238–240, 242, 250, 252, 259–260, 262–263, 272, 274, 277, 279, 284–285, 290, 301
    permanent, 74, 78, 84, 103, 107, 111, 117–118, 156, 175, 194, 300
    washable, 117
Masking tape, 66, 86, 111, 118, 148, 151, 154, 157, 166, 205, 212, 236, 274, 286
    colored, 182, 194–196, 200, 234, 255, 258, 279, 281
Math activities, 30–32, 36, 38, 40, 42, 44–46, 54, 56, 58, 60, 62, 64–66, 74, 76, 78, 80–81, 83–86, 88, 100, 102–103, 106, 108–109, 111, 113, 115, 118, 124, 126, 128, 130, 132–135, 137–138, 140–141, 148, 152, 154–157, 159–160, 166, 168, 170–171, 173, 175, 177, 179, 181–182, 184–185, 196, 198, 200, 202–203, 205–206, 208, 212, 216, 218, 220, 227, 230, 232, 234, 236, 238–240, 242–244, 252–253, 255, 257, 259–260, 262–263, 265–266, 274–275, 277, 279, 281, 284–286, 289–290
    benefits of, 15
    big, 15–16
Mathematical concepts, 13
Mathematical language, 27, 51, 71, 95, 123, 145, 165, 191, 227, 249, 271
Mathematical thinking, 51, 71, 95, 123, 145, 165, 191, 227, 249, 271
Mats, 184, 205, 253, 263
    bath, 302
    napping, 44
    tumbling, 205
McAfee, O., 19, 21
Measuring cups, 89, 102, 118, 118, 135, 168–169, 186, 206–207, 216, 266, 281
Measuring spoons, 89, 118, 169, 216
Measuring tapes, 205, 234, 236, 244, 253, 255, 260
Measuring, 27, 51, 95, 123, 145, 165, 191, 227, 249, 271
    distance, 36, 44, 81, 138, 148, 159, 255, 257, 260
    height, 179, 202–203, 236, 242, 244, 286
    length, 45, 60, 111, 154–155, 205, 232, 253, 259, 265–266, 286
    size, 54, 100, 208, 227, 266
    temperature, 166, 168, 170–171, 181
    time, 36, 44, 74, 76, 81, 84–85, 106–107, 128, 135, 168, 175, 177, 179, 253, 281, 284
    volume, 78, 102, 168, 206, 216
    weight, 88
    width, 265
Metal lids, 154–155, 208
Michigan State University, 21
    ASL browser, 18
Milk, 169
    cartons, 233, 260, 300
    jug caps, 59, 200, 208
Mirrors, 125, 129, 137, 166, 170
Mittens, 185, 210, 215

Models, 38–39, 58–59, 66
Moon, 191–192, 196, 206–211, 218–219
    dust, 206–211, 213–214
    facts, 193
Motion, 179, 202, 208, 227, 249–250, 253, 255, 257, 260
Murals, 45–46, 66, 88–89, 139, 220, 265, 289
Music activities, 18, 54, 89, 113, 118, 160, 186, 221, 290

N

Napping mats, 44
National Academies Press, 14
National Academy of Sciences, 13
National Aeronautics and Space Administration, 191, 216
National Association for the Education of Young Children, 19
National Council of Teachers of English, 16
National Council of Teachers of Mathematics, 15–16, 21
    Standards, 27, 51, 71, 95, 123, 145, 165, 191, 227, 249, 271
National Education Content Standards, 13
National Research Council, 21
National Science Education Content Standards, 14, 27, 51, 71, 95,
    123, 145, 165, 191, 227, 249, 271
National Science Teachers Association, 33
Neuman, S. B., 16, 21
Newspaper, 33, 38, 58, 98, 136, 139, 196, 214, 220, 237
Number cards, 45, 66
Number lines, 76, 91
Numbers, 27, 51, 71, 76, 86, 95, 123, 145, 165, 191, 227, 236, 243,
    249, 271
Nuts, 275, 277, 289

O

Observation skills, 14, 134–135, 154–157, 231, 256, 266
One-to-one correspondence, 57, 65, 80, 86–87, 115–116, 132, 218–
    219, 243, 277–278
Oobleck, 290
Operations, 27, 51, 71, 95, 123, 145, 165, 191, 227, 249, 271
Ordering, 27, 51, 71, 88, 95, 123, 145, 191, 227, 271, 277
Outdoor activities, 32–33, 44, 51, 60–61, 65, 71, 85–86, 99–100,
    106–108, 115–118, 123, 127–128, 130, 151, 157–158, 160,
    177, 179, 182, 200–201, 203–205, 210–211, 214, 218, 230,
    235, 238, 243, 252, 254, 260, 265, 266

P

Packing noodles
    biodegradable, 177, 213, 242, 259
    Styrofoam, 102, 148, 151
Packing tape, 38, 58, 66, 111, 198, 285, 287, 296, 300
Paint, 46, 233, 235, 265
    fabric, 156
    tempera, 45–46, 117, 152, 196, 214, 220, 234, 289
    watercolors, 102–103, 117–118, 159, 177, 185, 289
Paintbrushes, 106, 139, 196
    large, 106
Pans, 40, 208, 221, 287
    bread, 83
    cookie sheets, 75, 79, 118, 179, 206, 266
    dishpans, 102, 135, 179, 260
    pie, 104, 141, 154, 212, 220–221
Paper, 30, 34, 36, 38, 40, 45–46, 56, 66, 74–76, 78, 81, 89, 99, 117–
    118, 137, 139, 141, 159, 177, 185, 196, 198, 215, 220, 222,
    232, 236, 238, 240, 242, 253, 257, 259–260, 265–266, 285,
    290, 300
    absorbent, 98, 40, 74, 78, 96, 98, 103, 118, 171, 173, 179, 274
    bulletin board, 19, 45, 140–141
    butcher, 45–46, 117, 214, 265, 289
    chart, 19, 28, 31–32, 47, 52, 54, 56, 60, 67, 72, 75, 80, 84, 96,
        100, 109, 112–113, 119, 124, 129–130, 132–133, 142,
        146, 150, 166, 168, 170, 175, 192, 196, 198, 202, 206,
        228, 230, 234, 236, 239, 250, 252, 260, 262, 267, 272,
        277, 279, 284–285, 291, 301

    construction, 31, 38, 40, 46, 56, 58, 60, 80, 83, 86, 89, 98, 109,
        124, 133–134, 138, 140, 152, 159, 184, 200, 221, 228,
        234–235, 250, 257, 260, 263–264, 266, 272, 281, 289,
        301
    contact, 36, 66, 111
    crepe, 138–140, 157, 160, 200, 228, 234
    easel, 214
    finger paint, 159
    graph, 232
    newspaper, 33, 38, 58, 98, 136, 139, 196, 214, 220, 237
    poster, 19, 185
    tissue, 46, 139, 146, 192
    waxed, 103, 274
Paper cups, 81, 89, 118, 148, 157, 168–169, 175, 185–186, 244, 279
Paper plates, 34, 196, 198, 212, 290
Paper towels, 40, 74, 78, 96, 98, 103, 118, 171, 173, 179, 274
    tubes, 39, 118, 193, 200, 210, 212, 266, 297
Paper clips, 130, 230
Parachutes, 160
Parts of speech, 44
Patience, 136, 149, 184
Patterns, 54, 79, 88–89, 134, 137, 145, 156–157, 227, 244, 271,
    284, 289
Pebbles, 102, 206, 209
Pencil grips, 74–75, 99, 231, 233, 252
Pencils, 36, 74, 83, 130, 148, 173, 230, 252
    colored, 137, 215, 232
Permanent markers, 74, 78, 84, 103, 107, 111, 117–118, 156, 175,
    194, 300
Photo boards, 19, 29, 47, 53, 67, 73, 91, 97, 119, 127, 142, 147,
    161, 167, 187, 193, 222, 229, 245, 251, 267, 273
Photocopiers, 76, 111, 148, 218, 230, 252
Physical science, 95–144, 165–294
Piaget, Jean, 19
Picture cards, 86
Pictures
    astronauts, 194–195
    bobsled tracks, 179
    bridges, 253
    buildings, 228, 232
    circuit boards, 286
    curves, 253
    flags, 156
    fruits, 133
    lunar rovers, 212
    moon, 208
    NASA Mission Control, 198
    plants, 86
    rain, 109
    rainbows, 124, 126, 134, 137
    ramps, 253
    roads, 250
    seed germination, 76
    ski jumps, 179
    spaceships, 196, 200, 218
    spider webs, 66
    spiders, 58, 62, 66
    tarantulas, 54
    tunnels, 253
Pie pans, 104, 141, 154, 212, 220–221
Pillows, 44, 254
Pipe cleaners, 58, 135, 155, 279, 287
Pipettes, 96, 98, 141
Pitchers, 78, 168
Plant misters, 74, 78, 84
Plastic, 139
    bags, 62, 98–99, 168–169, 216, 297
    beads, 177
    bins, 281
    bottle caps, 118, 296

bottles, 102, 126
bowls, 64, 184
can covers, 266
containers, 85, 111, 179, 277, 287
cups, 74, 78, 84, 102, 108, 185, 212, 238
gloves, 33
golf balls, 255
golf clubs, 182
gutters, 36, 88, 108, 118, 148, 179, 254, 255, 257, 260, 296
insects, 45, 62, 66
jars, 56, 104, 107
lids, 102, 118, 138, 141, 196, 198, 208
plates, 141, 220
prisms, 125
spider rings, 64
spiders, 45, 52, 62, 66
spoons, 98, 168
tablecloths, 99, 220
tools, 234, 240
trays, 34, 148, 179
tubing, 102
tubs, 84–85, 102, 206, 208, 260
ware, 155
worms, 45–46
wrap, 36, 38, 74, 79
Plates, 104
    paper, 34, 196, 198, 212, 290
    plastic, 141, 220
Playdough, 45, 221, 265
Plexiglas sheets, 118
Popsicle sticks. *See* Craft sticks
Portfolios, 20, 45, 67, 75, 88–89, 91, 117, 119, 141–142, 159, 161,
    174, 187, 220, 222, 244–245, 252, 265, 267, 291
Positional words, 138, 151, 179, 202, 208, 250, 253, 255, 257, 260
Poster board, 19, 124, 257–258, 265
Poster paper, 19, 185
Post-it notes, 36, 56, 280
Pots, 89, 152
Potting soil, 46, 84
Predictions, 14, 29, 36–37, 76–79, 81–82, 84, 99, 102–104, 107,
    110, 112, 117–118, 139, 148–149, 157, 167, 173–178, 208–
    209, 255–258
Print awareness, 16, 27, 51, 71, 95, 123, 145, 165, 170, 191, 216,
    227, 236, 239, 249, 260, 262, 271, 277, 284–285
Prisms, 124, 127, 137
Probability, 27, 51, 71, 95, 123, 145, 165, 191, 249, 271
Problem solving, 38, 108, 227, 237–238, 249, 254, 260–261, 271–
    273, 279–280
Pulleys, 59, 296
Pumpkin seeds, 80, 89
Puppets, 44, 52, 62, 64
PVC pipes, 154, 184

Q
Q-tips. *See* Cotton swabs
Question formulation, 40, 51, 71, 95–96, 123–124, 128–129, 145–
    146, 165, 171, 175, 191–192, 202, 227–228, 249–250,
    271–272, 285

R
Rain, 95–122
    facts, 97
Rain gauges, 111
Rain gear, 96–100
Rainbows, 123–144
    facts, 127
Rainsticks, 113
    homemade, 118
Ramps, 179–180, 250–262, 265, 296–297

Recipes
    bubble solution, 135
    clean dirt, 266
    granola, 290
    ice cream, 169
    icees, 168–169
    lemonade, 118
    moon dust, 207
    three-bean salad, 89
Recorded music, 160, 186
    by Hap Palmer, 140
    Charlotte Diamond's World by Charlotte Diamond, 118
    instrumental, 140
    On the Move by Greg & Steve, 221
    Singable Songs for the Very Young by Raffi, 52–53
    Walter the Waltzing Worm by Hap Palmer, 39
    We All Live Together, Vol. 3 by Greg & Steve, 290
Recording sheets, 98, 130, 148, 173, 230, 252
Rhyme, 16, 42, 54, 64, 133, 150, 168
Rhymes
    "Icee Chant" by Tim Dobbins, 168–169
    "Little Miss Muffet," 59, 64
    "Rain, Rain, Go Away," 117
    "Rainbow Rhyme" by Tim Dobbins, 133
    "Rainstorm" by Tim Dobbins, 113
    "Thermometer" by Tim Dobbins, 170–171
    "This Is the Skyscraper," 244
    "Wind" by Tim Dobbins, 150
Rhythm, 54, 140
Rhythm sticks, 287
Risley, T. R., 18, 21
Roads, 249–270
Robin, K. B., 20
Rocks, 206, 210, 219
Rope, 45, 205, 260, 296
Rubber bands, 257, 258, 281
Rulers, 30, 36, 45, 112, 159, 208, 232, 242, 259, 300–301

S
Safety goggles, 85, 228, 240, 275
Safety notes, 32–33, 81, 85, 102–104, 111, 149, 151, 158, 166, 171,
    236, 238, 240, 260, 275
Salt, 89, 168–169, 177, 181
    rock, 181
    shakers, 177
Sand, 207, 214, 266
Sand pails, 106, 108, 210, 238, 260
Sand timers, 36, 81, 151, 168, 253, 281, 284
Sand/water table. *See* Sensory table activities
Sandbox activities, 108, 205, 210–211, 238, 260
Sandpaper, 244, 302
Saw horses, 44, 108, 254
SCAD system, 17, 24, 29, 35, 38, 40–42, 53–55, 59–60, 63, 72–74,
    76–78, 96–99, 104, 106, 109–111, 124, 126–127, 129, 146–
    150, 166–167, 175–176, 192–193, 196, 198, 202, 208, 212,
    228–229, 232, 236–237, 251, 253–255, 257, 272–273, 279–
    280, 285
Scarves, 107, 140, 160, 170
School-home connections, 25, 49, 70, 94, 100, 122, 144, 164, 190,
    193, 225, 229, 240, 247, 270, 294, 296
Schweinhart, L. J., 20
Science activities, 14–15, 28, 32, 34, 36, 38, 40, 42, 45–46, 52, 56,
    58, 60, 62, 65–66, 72, 74, 76, 78, 80–81, 84–86, 88, 96, 98,
    100, 102–104, 106, 108–109, 111, 113, 117–118, 123–124,
    126, 128–130, 134–135, 137, 139, 141, 146, 148, 150–151,
    154–160, 166, 168, 170–171, 173, 175, 177, 179, 181, 186,
    192, 194–196, 198, 200, 202–203, 205–206, 208, 210, 212,
    214–215, 220, 228, 230, 232, 234, 236, 238, 240, 242–243,
    250, 252–253, 255, 257, 259–260, 266, 272, 274–275, 277,
    279, 281, 285–287

Scientific inquiry, 13, 51, 71, 95, 123, 145, 165, 181, 191, 227, 249, 271

Scientific method, 27, 40–41

Scissors, 30–31, 46, 58, 60, 83, 124, 152, 184, 194, 200, 202, 216, 218, 242, 257, 259, 263, 272, 274, 302

Scoops, 108, 210, 238
 ice cream, 186
 making, 302

Screw eyes, 59, 243

Screwdrivers, 240, 275

Screws, 240, 275, 277, 286, 289

Seeds, 71–94
 avocado, 73
 bean, 72, 74, 78, 86
 bean, 72, 74, 78, 86
 birdseed, 89, 118, 281
 Blue Lake beans, 74
 dandelion, 73
 lima beans, 72, 74
 pea, 78
 popcorn, 81
 poppy, 89
 pumpkin, 80, 89
 sesame, 89
 sunflower, 80, 89, 290
 wheat, 84–85

Sensory experiences, 18, 206, 221, 244, 257

Sensory table activities, 24, 46, 66, 102, 118, 141, 160, 177, 179, 186, 206, 208, 211, 244, 266, 290, 302

Sentence strips, 265

Sequencing, 38, 42, 58, 60, 64, 79, 83, 124, 126, 133, 137, 140, 152–153, 184, 234, 236, 239, 253, 260, 262–263, 274–276, 280, 283

Seriation, 54

Sesame seeds, 89

Shapes, 118, 124, 196, 212, 234, 244, 289
 three-dimensional, 38, 45, 58, 108, 123, 227, 232–234, 236, 238, 242, 259, 265, 271, 277, 279, 286

Sharing, 136

Sheets, 28, 44, 107, 254, 136, 156, 211

Shoeboxes, 40, 243, 257

Shovels, 32, 46, 83, 108, 179, 186, 238, 260

Sign2Me® Educational Network, 18

Slides, 179, 265

Small-scale projects, 24

Smoke detectors, 273, 275

Snacks
 astronaut food, 216
 bread, 89
 fruit salad, 290
 granola, 89, 290
 ice cream, 169
 icees, 168–169
 lemonade, 118, 290
 popcorn, 81
 popsicles, 186
 pumpkin seeds, 80
 salad, 290
 skyscrapers, 244
 smoothies, 290
 snow cones, 186
 soup, 290
 sunflower seeds, 80
 three-bean salad, 89

Soccer cones, 228, 234, 260

Socks, 138, 214

Songs
 "Cleaning Machine" by Marie Faust Evitt & Tim Dobbins, 284
 "Dancin' Machine" by Greg & Steve, 290
 "Eensy Weensy Spider," 54

"Here We Go on a Building Hunt," 231
"Here We Go on a Color Hunt," 130–131
"Here We Go to Find Some Worms," 32
"The Hokey Pokey", 28
"Itsy Bitsy Spider," 54, 59, 70
"Rain Falls Down" by Tim Dobbins, 105
"Road Building" by Tim Dobbins, 262
"Singin' in the Rain," 118
"Spider on the Floor" by Raffi, 52–53
"This Is the Way We Search for Spiders," 57
"Walter the Waltzing Worm" by Hap Palmer, 39
"We've Been Building Up a Building" by Tim Dobbins, 239

Sorting, 27, 51, 62, 71, 88, 95, 123, 134, 145, 191, 227, 258, 266, 271, 275, 277

Sorting trays, 62

Space, 191–225

Space vehicles, 206, 210, 212–213

Spaceships, 196–201, 218, 221

Spiders, 51–70
 benefits of, 51, 55
 plastic, 45, 52, 62, 66
 rings, 64

Splatter painting, 220

Sponges, 152, 213, 234, 235, 242, 259

Spoons, 64, 84, 154, 181, 185, 206, 216
 measuring, 89, 118, 169, 216
 plastic, 98, 168
 wooden, 83, 184

Spray bottles, 36, 74, 78, 84, 107, 118

Spring, 71, 95, 123

Squirt bottles, 102, 118

Stability, 227, 236–238, 243

Staplers, 75, 83, 184, 263, 272

States of matter, 103–107, 117, 119, 122, 160, 165–190

Stepstools, 44, 64, 108, 236, 296

Stickers, 175, 194–196, 198, 200, 266, 281, 300

Sticks, 148, 152, 154, 156, 209, 210, 260

Stones, 83, 85, 208

Stopwatches, 36, 44

Storage, 297

Storms, 113–114, 150

Storytelling, 42, 45, 64, 66, 83, 88, 91, 112–113, 117, 141, 147–148, 152–153, 184, 263, 289

Straw, 148, 152

String, 44–46, 58–60, 115, 135, 154, 194, 202, 243, 260

Styrofoam
 egg cartons, 103, 141, 229, 236, 260, 279, 296
 packing noodles, 102, 148, 151
 pieces, 240–241

Subtraction, 80

Sugar, 89, 118, 169

Sunflower seeds, 80, 89, 290

Superheroes, 55, 191

T

Tablecloths, 99, 220

Tables, 126, 148, 151, 179, 28, 44, 198, 211, 215, 281

Taking turns, 64, 87, 149, 155, 211, 219, 256, 288

Tallies, 31

Tang, 216–217

Tape, 39, 46, 60, 76, 115, 124, 138, 141, 152, 157, 184, 192, 215, 233, 243, 250, 257, 264–266, 274, 285–286
 colored, 182, 194–196, 200, 204, 234, 255, 258, 279, 281
 double-sided, 66
 duct, 66, 118, 236, 243, 279, 285, 296
 first aid, 272, 274
 masking, 66, 86, 111, 118, 148, 151, 154, 157, 166, 205, 212, 236, 274, 286
 packing, 38, 58, 66, 111, 198, 285, 287, 296, 300

Tarps, 44, 182, 235
Technological design, 227–247, 252–253, 255, 259–260, 272–274, 275, 279, 281, 285–287
Technology/tools, 95–122, 123, 145, 148, 165–166, 168, 179, 181, 191, 194–196, 198, 200, 203, 205, 208, 212, 227–228, 240, 249–272, 274
Telephones, 198
    cell, 198, 273, 275
Tempera paint, 45–46, 117, 152, 196, 214, 220, 234, 289
    powdered, 289
Tennis balls, 255
    cans, 118
Thermometers, 165–166, 168, 170–173, 181, 184
Three-dimensional shapes, 38, 45, 58, 108, 123, 227, 232–234, 236, 238, 242, 259, 265, 271, 277, 279, 286
Timers, 179
    sand, 36, 81, 151, 168, 253, 281, 284
    stopwatches, 36, 44
    watches, 281
Tissue paper, 46, 139, 146, 192
Tongs, 45, 62, 166, 179, 185, 186
Tongue depressors. See Craft sticks
Tool belts, 228, 234
Tools. See Technology/tools
Toothpicks, 73, 257, 265
Towels, 168, 182, 253, 302
    paper, 40, 74, 78, 96, 98, 103, 118, 171, 173, 179, 274
Traffic cones, 228, 234, 260, 266
Traffic safety, 264–266
Transportation, 249–270
Trays, 40, 46, 62, 72, 74, 81, 98, 103, 109, 124, 139, 214, 220, 241–242, 259, 281, 287, 289
    plastic, 34, 148, 179
    sorting, 62
Trucks, 210, 255, 257, 260, 265–266
T-squares, 234
Tumbling mats, 205
Tunnels, 253–254, 259–261, 265
Turkey basters, 102, 118, 146, 159, 177
Tweezers, 45, 62, 272

U
Umbrellas, 98–99
Unifix cubes, 36, 159, 208, 242, 244, 259, 286
Unit blocks, 109, 203, 221, 228, 244, 253–255, 257, 286
University of Northern Iowa, 256

V
Valli, C., 21
Vegetables, 33, 290
    carrots, 33–34
    celery, 89
    cucumbers, 244
    green beans, 89
    lettuce, 33
    parsley, 89
    waxed beans, 89
Velcro, 271, 273, 294
Visual discrimination skills, 266
Vocabulary skills, 13, 17–18, 20, 24–25, 27, 29, 34, 40–42, 44–45, 51, 53–54, 60, 62, 63–64, 66, 71–72, 74–77, 79, 84–86, 95–104, 106–107, 109, 111, 115–117, 123, 127, 132, 138, 140–141, 145–147, 150, 158–160, 165–166, 170, 172, 175–176, 178–179, 185, 191–196, 198, 200, 202–208, 210, 212, 214, 216, 219–220, 227–229, 232–236, 239–241, 243–244, 249, 251, 253–255, 257–262, 264–265, 267, 271–274, 277, 279, 284–285, 289, 291
Vygotsky, Lev, 19

W
Wading pools, 177, 179, 296
Washers, 275, 277, 286, 289
Water, 36, 73–74, 78, 95–122, 126, 135, 139, 141, 159–160, 165–190, 238, 242, 260, 289
Water bottles, 107, 256, 281
Water cooler bottles, 287, 296
Watercolors, 117, 159
    liquid, 102–103, 118, 177, 185, 289
Waxed paper, 103, 274
Weather, 95–122, 145–164, 170
Weesen-Baer, Bobbi, 16, 24
Wheat
    seeds, 84–85
    stalks, 84
Wind chimes, 154–155, 296
Winter, 95, 165–190
Wires, 275, 277, 286
Wooden blocks, 148, 243–244, 266, 287
Wooden boards, 118, 254–255, 257, 260, 296
Wooden spoons, 83, 184
Worms, 27–49
    benefits of, 27
    habitats, 34
    plastic, 45–46
Worth, Karen, 21, 102
Writing activities, 16, 24, 107, 132, 195, 290

Y
Yard sticks, 205, 203–204
Yarn, 30–31, 39, 42, 44, 45, 60, 111, 115, 154–155, 194, 202, 218, 236, 244, 253, 255, 265
Yogurt containers, 177, 238
    lids, 208

Z
Zippered plastic bags, 168–169, 216